Cognitive Psychology
· and Its Implications ·

A Series of Books in Psychology

Editors:
Richard C. Atkinson
Gardner Lindzey
Richard F. Thompson

Cognitive Psychology
· and Its Implications ·

Third Edition

John R. Anderson

CARNEGIE-MELLON UNIVERSITY

W. H. Freeman and Company
New York

Library of Congress Cataloging-in-Publication Data

Anderson, John R. (John Robert), 1947–
    Cognitive psychology and its implications / John R. Anderson. — 3d ed.
      p.   cm. — (A Series of books in psychology)
    Includes bibliographical references.
    ISBN 0-7167-2085-X
    1. Cognition.   2. Cognitive psychology.   I. Title.   II. Series.
BF311.A5895   1990
153 — dc20   89-28409
                                                          CIP

Printed in the United States of America

6 7 8 9 0 VB 9 9 8 7 6 5 4

This book is dedicated to

Gordon H. Bower

who taught me much about cognitive
psychology when I was his student

Contents

Chapter 7 • HUMAN MEMORY: ELABORATIONS AND DISTINCTIONS   178

Chapter 12 • LANGUAGE USE: COMPREHENSION 358

Chapter 13 • COGNITIVE DEVELOPMENT 399

Preface

Cognitive psychology has been an active area of research for just four decades. In the 1950s, a number of true pioneers broke with the behaviorist tradition and laid the foundations for the field. The 1960s saw a lot of hard work by psychologists who established experimental paradigms and theoretical models for the new discipline. When I entered the field at the beginning of the 1970s, I was able to take full advantage of the previous two decades of effort. The 1970s saw an amazing blossoming of research in a field that had become fully established. By the end of the decade it became apparent to me that there was a coherent structure to the field that could be communicated in a textbook. This led to the first edition of this book in 1980.

Reflecting the brief history of the field, the research described in that book was quite recent. Of all papers I cited in the 1980 text, 58 percent had been published in the previous ten years. A number of students asked me about this and why the field seemed to have such a short history. The answer I gave them is in part recounted in Chapter 1.

It was a bit difficult to accurately perceive where the field was going in 1980. In retrospect I think I did a pretty good job in the first edition, but I made some shifts of emphasis in 1985 and I have made others now in 1990. The 1980s have been as productive as the 1970s and have seen the field become much more mature in its research agenda. The literature cited in this edition reflects the longer history of the field: 40 percent of the citations are to the research of the last decade.

The actual interpretation of some phenomena has changed from the first edition, but the major changes consist of a streamlining of many discussions and the inclusion of a great deal of additional material. Besides updating topics in the original edition, I have included four new topics — the neural basis of cognition, the nature of expertise, cognitive development, and human intelligence. There has been a lot of recent research in each of these areas and it has become apparent to me how they fit into the larger context of cognitive psychology.

Numerous people have commented on this third edition and it is much better for their efforts: Irv Biederman, Pat Carpenter, Micki Chi, Bill Clancey, Chuck Clifton, Gus Craik, Bob Crowder, Martha Farah, Ronald Finke, Rochel Gelman, Kathy Hirsh-Pasek, Buz Hunt, Walter Kintsch, Dave Klahr, Steve Kosslyn, Maryellen MacDonald, Jay McClelland, Brian McWhinney, Peter Polson, Mike Posner, Roger Ratcliff, Steve Reed, Lance Rips, Roddy Roediger, Terry Sejnowski, Bob Siegler, Bob Sternberg, and Maria Zaragoza. In addition I would like to thank the people who read the first and second editions; much of their influence remains: Jim Anderson, Liz Bjork, Lyle Bourne, John Bransford, Bill Chase, Chuck Clifton, Lynne Cooper, Bob Crowder, Susan Fiske, Michael Gazzaniga, Ellen Gagne, Lynn Hasher, Geoff Hinton, Lynn Hyah, Marcel Just, Stephen Keele, Dave Klahr, Steve Kosslyn, Al Lesgold, Clayton Lewis, Beth Loftus, Brian MacWhinney, Al Newell, Don Norman, Gary Olson, Allan Paivio, Jane Perlmutter, Peter Polson, Jim Pomerantz, Lynne Reder, Steve Reed, Russ Revlin, Lance Rips, Miriam Schustack, Bob Siegler, Ed Smith, Kathy Spoehr, Charles Tatum, Dave Tieman, Tom Trabasso, and Henry Wall.

I have used this book every year in a course I teach at Carnegie-Mellon University. By now nearly a thousand of my students have read it and I would guess that a quarter of them have volunteered praise, criticisms, comments, and a great many suggestions. Their input has been truly valuable. Finally I would like to thank Helen Borek, who has worked heroically on the manuscript preparation.

John R. Anderson

Cognitive Psychology
· and Its Implications ·

The Science of Cognition

Summary

1. Cognitive psychology attempts to understand the nature of human intelligence and how people think.

2. The study of cognitive psychology is motivated by scientific curiosity, by the desire for practical applications, and by the need to provide a foundation for other fields of social science.

3. People have written about human cognition for more than 2000 years. Only in the last 100 years, however, has cognition been studied scientifically. In the last 35 years, knowledge about human cognition has greatly increased.

4. Cognitive psychology is dominated by the *information-processing approach,* which analyzes cognitive processes into a sequence of ordered *stages.* Each stage reflects an important step in the processing of cognitive information.

Our species is referred to as homo sapiens, or "man, the intelligent." This term reflects the general belief that intelligence is what distinguishes us from other animals. The goal of cognitive psychology is to understand the nature of human intelligence and how it works. Subsequent chapters in this book discuss what cognitive psychologists have discovered about various aspects of human intelligence. This chapter attempts to answer the following preliminary questions:

Why do people study cognitive psychology?

Where and when did cognitive psychology originate?

What are the methods of cognitive psychology as a science?

Motivations

Intellectual Curiosity

One reason for studying cognitive psychology motivates any scientific inquiry — the desire to know. In this respect, the cognitive psychologist is like the tinkerer who wants to know how a clock works. The human mind is a particularly interesting device that displays remarkable adaptiveness and intelligence. We are often unaware of the extraordinary aspects of human cognition. Just as we can easily overlook the enormous accumulation of technology that permits a sports event on television to be broadcast live from Europe, so we can forget how sophisticated our mental processes must be to enable us to understand and enjoy that sportscast. One would like to understand the mechanisms that make such intellectual sophistication possible.

The inner workings of the human mind are far more intricate than the most complicated systems of modern technology. Researchers in the field of artificial intelligence (AI) are attempting to develop programs that will enable computers to display intelligent behavior. Although this field has been an active one for more than 30 years and has had some notable successes, AI researchers still do not know how to create a program that matches human intelligence. No existing programs can recall facts, solve problems, reason, learn, and process language with human facility. This lack of success has occurred not because computers are inferior to human brains but rather because we do not yet know in sufficient detail how intelligence is organized in the brain.

It does not appear that there is anything magical about human intelligence or anything that is incapable of being modeled on a computer. For instance, consider scientific discovery. Herbert Simon, who won the 1978 Nobel Prize for Economics, has spent the last 30 years studying cognitive psychology and has more recently focused on the intellectual accomplishments involved in doing science. He and his colleagues (Langley, Simon, Bradshaw, & Zytkow, 1987) have built computer programs that simulate the problem-solving activities involved in such scientific feats as Keppler's discovery of the laws of planetary motion, Ohm's law for electric circuits, and the laws of chemical reactions. These programs are among the most impressive accomplishments of artificial intelligence. Simon has also examined the processes involved in his own, now-famous scientific discoveries (Simon, 1989). In all cases he finds that the processes of scientific discovery can be explained in terms of the basic cognitive processes that are being studied in cognitive psychology. He writes that much of the activities involved are just well-understood problem-solving processes (we will study these in Chapters 8 and 9). He adds:

> Moreover, the insight that is supposed to be required for such work as discovery turns out to be synonymous with the familiar process of recognition; and other terms commonly used in the discussion of creative work—such terms as "judgment," "creativity," or even "genius"—appear to be wholly dispensable or to be definable, as insight is, in terms of mundane and well-understood concepts. (p. 376)

Thus, Simon's basic argument is that when we look in detail at human genius we find that it involves basic cognitive processes operating together in complex ways to produce the brilliant results.[1] Most of this book will be devoted to describing what we know about those basic processes.

Practical Applications

The desire to understand is an important motivation for the study of cognitive psychology, as it is in any science, but the practical implications of the field constitute an important secondary motivation. If we really understand how people acquire knowledge and intellectual skills and

---

[1]Weisberg (1986) in *Creativity: Genius and other myths* comes to a similar conclusion.

how they perform feats of intelligence, then we will be able to improve their intellectual training and performance accordingly.

It seems inevitable that cognitive psychology will prove beneficial to both individuals and society. Many of our problems derive from an inability to deal with the cognitive demands made on us. These problems are being exacerbated by the "information explosion" and the technological revolution we are presently experiencing. Cognitive psychology is just beginning to make headway on these issues, but some clear and positive insights with direct application to everyday life have already emerged. There have been applications of cognitive psychology to law (e.g., Loftus, 1979, on the reliability of eyewitness testimony), to the design of computer systems (e.g., Card, Moran, & Newell, 1983, on using word processors), and to instruction (Gagne, 1985, on classroom practice).

At many points in this book, research in cognitive psychology will be shown to have implications for study skills. Students who read this text and learn the lessons it has to offer will improve the capacity of their intellects, at least modestly. In our own laboratory (Anderson, Boyle, Corbett, & Lewis, in press, we have merged the knowledge of cognitive psychology and the techniques of artificial intelligence to create "intelligent" computer tutors that have substantially enhanced human intellectual performance. So one reason for studying cognitive psychology and for encouraging its development as a field is to enable people to be more effective in their intellectual pursuits.

Implications for Other Fields

Students and researchers interested in other areas of psychology or social science have another reason for following developments in cognitive psychology. Cognitive psychology attempts to understand the basic mechanisms governing human thought, and these basic mechanisms are important in understanding the types of behavior studied by other social science fields. For example, understanding how humans think is important to understanding why certain thought malfunctions occur (clinical psychology), how people behave with other individuals or in groups (social psychology), how persuasion works (political science), how economic decisions are made (economics), why certain ways of organizing groups are more effective and stable than others (sociology), or why natural languages have certain constraints (linguistics). Cognitive psychology studies the foundation on which all other social sciences stand.

It is certainly true, nonetheless, that much social science has developed without a grounding in cognitive psychology. Two facts account for this situation. First, cognitive psychology is not that advanced. Second, researchers in other areas of social science have managed to find higher-order principles unrelated to cognitive mechanisms to explain the phenomena in which they are interested. However, much is unknown or poorly understood in these other fields. If we knew how these higher-order principles were explained in terms of cognitive mechanisms and how to apply cognitive mechanisms directly to higher-order phenomena, we might have a firmer grasp on the phenomena in question. Thus, throughout this text, the implications of cognitive psychology for other areas of social science are cited.

The History of Cognitive Psychology
Early History

In Western civilization, interest in human cognition can be traced to the ancient Greeks. Plato and Aristotle, in their discussions of the nature and origin of knowledge, speculated on memory and thought. These early discussions, which were essentially philosophical in nature, eventually developed into a centuries-long debate. The antagonists were the empiricists, who believed that all knowledge comes from experience, and the nativists, or rationalists, who argued that children come into the world with a great deal of innate knowledge. The debate intensified in the seventeenth, eighteenth, and nineteenth centuries, with such British philosophers as Locke, Hume, and Mill arguing for the empiricist view and such Continental philosophers as Descartes and Kant propounding the nativist view. Though these arguments were at their core philosophical, they frequently slipped into psychological speculations about human cognition.

During this long period of philosophical debate, such sciences as astronomy, physics, chemistry, and biology developed markedly. Curiously, no concomitant attempt was made to apply the scientific method to the understanding of human cognition; this undertaking did not take place until the end of the nineteenth century. Certainly, no technical or conceptual barriers existed to studying cognitive psychology earlier. In fact, many of the experiments performed in cognitive psychology could have been performed and understood in the time of the Greeks. But cognitive psychology, like many other sciences, suffered because of our egocentric, mystical, and confused attitude about ourselves and our own nature. It had seemed inconceivable before the nineteenth century that the workings of the human mind could be susceptible to scientific analysis. As a consequence, cognitive psychology as a science is only a little more than 100 years old and lags far behind many other sciences in sophistication. We have spent much of the first 100 years freeing ourselves of the pernicious misconceptions that can arise when people engage in such an introverted enterprise as a scientific study of human cognition. It is the case of the mind studying itself.

Psychology in Germany

The date usually cited as marking the beginning of psychology as a science is 1879, when Wilhelm Wundt established the first psychology laboratory in Leipzig, Germany. Wundt's psychology was cognitive psychology (in contrast to other major divisions of psychology, such as physiological, comparative, clinical, or social), although he had far-ranging views on many subjects. The method of inquiry used by Wundt, his students, and a large portion of the early psychologists was *introspection*. In this method, highly trained observers reported the contents of their consciousness under carefully controlled conditions. The basic belief was that the workings of the mind should be open to self-observation. Thus, to develop a theory of cognition, a psychologist had only to develop a theory that accounted for the contents of introspective reports.

Let us consider a sample introspective experiment. Mayer and Orth (1901) had their subjects perform a free-association task. The experimenters spoke a word to the subjects and then measured the amount of time the subjects took to generate responses to this word. Subjects then reported all their conscious experiences from the moment of stimulus presentation until the response was generated. To get a feeling for this method, try to generate an associate to each of the following words; after each association try to introspect on the contents of your consciousness during the period between reading the word and making your association:

coat

book

dot

bowl

In Mayer and Orth's experiment, many reports were given of rather nondescribable conscious experiences. Whatever was in consciousness, it did not seem to involve sensations, images, or other things that subjects in these laboratories were accustomed to reporting. This result started a debate on the issue of *imageless thought*—whether conscious experience could really be devoid of concrete content. As we will see in Chapters 4 and 5, this issue is still very much with us.

Psychology in America

Introspective psychology was not well accepted in America. Psychology in America at the turn of the century was largely an armchair avocation, in which the only self-inspection was casual and reflective rather than intense and analytic. William James's (1890) *Principles of psychology* reflects the best of this tradition, and many of its proposals are still relevant and cogent today. The mood of America was determined by the philosophical doctrines of pragmatism and functionalism. Many of the psychologists of the time were involved in education, and the demand was for an "action-oriented" psychology that would be capable of practical application. The intellectual climate in America was not receptive to a psychology focused on such questions as whether or not the contents of consciousness were sensory.

One of the important figures of early American scientific psychology was Edward Thorndike, who developed a theory of learning that was directly applicable to school situations. Thorndike was interested in such basic questions as the effects of reward and punishment on rate of learning. To him, conscious experience was just excess baggage that could be largely ignored. As often as not, his experiments were done on infrahuman animals such as cats. Animals involved fewer ethical constraints than humans with regard to experimenting, and Thorndike was probably just as happy that such subjects could not introspect.

While introspection was being ignored at the turn of the century in America, it was getting into trouble on the Continent. Different laboratories were reporting different types of introspections—each type matching the theory of the particular laboratory from which it emanated. It was becoming clear that introspection did not give one a clear window onto the workings of the mind. Much that was important in cognitive functioning was not open to conscious experience.

These two factors, the "irrelevance" of the introspective method and its apparent contradictions, set the groundwork for the great behaviorist revolution in American psychology, which occurred around 1920. John Watson and other behaviorists led a fierce attack, not only on introspectionism, but also on any attempt to develop a theory of mental operations. Psychology, according to the behaviorists, was to be entirely concerned with external behavior and was not to try to analyze the workings of the mind that underlay this behavior:

> Behaviorism claims that consciousness is neither a definite nor a usable concept. The Behaviorist, who has been trained always as an experimentalist, holds further that belief in the existence of consciousness goes back to the ancient days of superstition and magic. (Watson, 1930, p. 2)

> . . . The Behaviorist began his own formulation of the problem of psychology by sweeping aside all medieval conceptions. He dropped from his scientific vocabulary all subjective terms such as sensation, perception, image, desire, purpose, and even thinking and emotion as they were subjectively defined. (Watson, 1930, p. 5–6)

The behaviorist program and the issues it spawned all but eliminated any serious research in cognitive psychology for 40 years. The rat supplanted the human as the principal laboratory subject, and psychology turned to finding out what could be learned by studying animal learning and motivation. Quite a bit was discovered, but little was of direct relevance to cognitive psychology. Perhaps the most important lasting contribution of behaviorism is a set of sophisticated and rigorous techniques and principles for experimental study in all fields of psychology, including cognitive psychology.

In retrospect, it is hard to understand how behaviorists could have taken an antimental stand and clung to it so long. Just because introspection proved to be unreliable did not mean that it was impossible to develop a theory of internal structure and process. It only meant that other methods were required. In physics, a theory of atomic structure was developed, although that structure could not be directly observed but only inferred. But behaviorists argued that a theory of internal structure was not necessary to an understanding of human behavior, and in a sense they may have been right (see Anderson & Bower, 1973, pp. 30–37). However, a theory of internal structure makes understanding human beings much easier. The success of cognitive psychology during the past 35 years in analyzing complex intellectual processes testifies to the utility of such concepts as mental structures and processes.

In both the introspectionist and the behaviorist programs, we see the human mind struggling with the effort to understand itself. The introspectionists held a naive belief in the power of self-observation. The behaviorists were so afraid of falling prey to subjective fallacies that they refused to let themselves think about mental processes. Modern cognitive psychologists seem to be much more at ease with their subject matter. They have a relatively detached attitude toward human cognition and approach it much as they would any other complex system.

The Reemergence of Cognitive Psychology

Three main influences account for the modern development of cognitive psychology. The first was the development of what has been called the *information-processing approach,* which grew out of human-factors work and information theory. *Human factors* refers to research on human skills and performance. This field was given a great boost during World War II, when practical information on these topics was badly needed. *Information theory* is a branch of communication sciences that provides an abstract way of analyzing the processing of knowledge. The work of the British psychologist Donald Broadbent at the Applied Psychology Research Unit in Cambridge was probably most influential in integrating ideas from these two fields and developing the information-processing approach. He developed these ideas most directly with regard to perception and attention, but the analyses now pervade all of cognitive psychology. The characteristics of the information-processing approach are discussed later in this chapter. Although other types of analysis in cognitive psychology exist, information processing is the dominant viewpoint and the main one presented in this book.

Closely related to the development of the information-processing approach were developments in computer science, particularly artificial intelligence, which tries to get computers to behave intelligently. Allen Newell and Herbert Simon at Carnegie-Mellon University have spent 35 years educating cognitive psychologists in the implications of artificial intelligence (and educating workers in artificial intelligence about the implications of cognitive psychology). The direct influence of computer-based theories on cognitive psychology has always been minimal. The indirect influence, however, has been enormous. A host of concepts has been taken from computer science and used in psychological theories. Probably more important, observing how we could analyze the intelligent behavior of a machine has largely liberated us from our inhibitions and misconceptions about analyzing our own intelligence.

The third field of influence on cognitive psychology is linguistics. In the 1950s, Noam Chomsky, a linguist at the Massachusetts Institute of Technology, began to develop a new mode of analyzing the structure of language. His work showed that language was much more complex than had previously been believed and that many of the prevailing behavioristic formulations were incapable of explaining these complexities. Chomsky's linguistic analyses proved critical in enabling cognitive psychologists to fight off the prevailing behavioristic conceptions. George Miller, at Harvard University in the 1950s and early 1960s, was instrumental in bringing these linguistic analyses to the attention of psychologists and in identifying new ways of studying language.

Cognitive psychology has grown rapidly since the 1950s. A very important event was the publication of Ulric Neisser's *Cognitive psychology* in 1967. This book gave a new legitimacy to the field. It consisted of six chapters on perception and attention and four chapters on language, memory, and thought. Note that this chapter division contrasts sharply with that of this book, which has one chapter on perception and eleven on language, memory, and thought. The chapter division in my book reflects the growing emphasis on higher mental processes. Following Neisser's work, another important event was the beginning of the journal *Cognitive Psychology* in 1970. This journal has done much to give definition to the field.

More recently there has emerged a new field, called *cognitive science*, which attempts to integrate research efforts from psychology, philosophy, linguistics, neuroscience, and artificial intelligence. This field can be dated from the appearance of the journal *Cognitive Science* in 1976. The fields of cognitive psychology and cognitive science overlap. It is not profitable to try to define precisely the differences, but cognitive science makes greater use of methods such as computer simulation of cognitive processes and logical analysis, while cognitive psychology relies heavily on experimental techniques that grew out of the behaviorist era for studying behavior. This book draws on all methods but, as its title suggests, it makes most use of cognitive psychology's experimental methodology.

The Methods of Cognitive Psychology

The Need for an Abstract Analysis

How do we go about studying human cognitive functioning? An obvious but naive answer is that we study the physiological mechanisms that underlie the behavior. For example, in this context, to understand how people do mathematics, why not simply inspect their brains and determine what goes on there when they are solving mathematics problems? Serious technical obstacles must be overcome, however, before the physiological basis of behavior can be studied in this way. But even assuming that these obstacles could be properly overcome, the level of analysis required is simply too detailed to be useful. The brain is composed of perhaps 100 billion nerve cells. Millions are probably involved in solving a mathematics problem. Suppose we had a listing that explained the role of each cell in solving the problem. Since this listing would have to describe the behavior of millions of individual cells, it would not offer a very satisfactory explanation for how the problem was solved. A neural explanation is too complex and detailed to adequately describe sophisticated human behavior. We need a level of analysis that is more abstract.

Computers offer an interesting analogy to help us understand the need for an abstract analysis. Like the brain, a computer consists of millions of components. For any interesting computer task — for example, solving a problem in mathematics such as integration — trying to understand the overall behavior of the machine by studying the behavior of each of its physical components is hopeless. However, high-level programming languages exist for specifying the behavior of the computer. The computer has an *interpreter* for converting each statement in the high-level language into a large number of low-level statements that specify what the physical components of the computer should do. These high-level programming languages can be quite abstract and thus obviate the need to consider many of the physical details of the computer. A person can often obtain a good understanding of the behavior of the computer by studying the high-level computer program. A cognitive theory should be like a computer program. That is, it should be a precise specification of the behavior, but offered in terms sufficiently abstract to provide a conceptually tractable framework for understanding the phenomenon.

As an example of an abstract term in a high-level programming language, consider the LISP programming language, used in creating artificial-intelligence programs, in which there is an associative-retrieval function called GET. This function can be used to retrieve concepts related to other concepts. For instance, to retrieve the capital of the United States, a person might evoke the function GET, giving it the terms USA and CAPITAL (called arguments). The function will return WASHINGTON (called a value). The person need not specify the detailed machine operations that underlie this act. The GET function identifies that portion of the computer's memory which stores information about the United States, searches that portion for the name of the capital, and then returns the answer WASHINGTON. This GET function is the sort of concept that would be useful in a cognitive theory. To a large degree, cognitive psychology has been engaged in a search for the right set of higher-level concepts with which to describe human intelligence.

While it is necessary to study cognition at an abstract level to understand it, it is also interesting to inquire how these cognitive abstractions are realized in the brain. Cognitive psychologists believe their concepts can be explained in physiological terms, even as computer scientists believe that their programming constructs can be explained in terms of the machine's components. Cognitive psychology is to physiological psychology much as computer science is to electrical engineering. As this book will give witness, some cognitive psychologists spend a great deal of effort trying to map the relationship between the brain and cognitive processes.

An understanding of the physiological basis of cognition can set useful constraints on cognitive theories. For instance, knowledge about the amount of information the brain can store could serve to rule out certain theories of memory as impossible. Chapter 2 will consider some of the ways knowledge of neural functioning can influence cognitive theorizing.

Information-Processing Analysis

In this chapter the phrase *information processing* has already been bandied about, and you may well have encountered it elsewhere in psychology. What does it really mean? Again, let us begin to answer the question with an analogy. Suppose we followed a letter in a successful passage through the postal system. First, the letter would be put in a mailbox; the mailbox would be emptied and its contents brought to a central station. The letters would be sorted according to region, and the letters for a particular region shipped off to their destination. There they would be sorted again as to area within the postal district. Letters having the same destination would be given to a carrier, and the carrier would deliver the letter to the correct address.

Now, just as we traced the letter through the postal system, let us follow this question as it is processed through the human mind:

Where does your grandmother live?

First, you must identify each word and retrieve its meaning. Then you must determine the meaning of this configuration of words; that is, understand the question being asked. Next, you must search your memory for the correct answer. Upon finding the answer in memory, you have to formulate a plan for generating the answer in words, and then transform the plan into the actual answer:

She lives in San Francisco[2]

What we did in this example was to trace the flow of information through the mind. We use the term *information* to refer to the various mental objects operated on—the question, the representation of its meaning, the memory of where your grandmother lives, the plan for generating an answer, and so on. These objects, although mental and abstract, are analogous to the letter in the postal example. An important aspect of the analogy is that there is a clear *sequence* or *serial ordering* to the mental operations just as there is to the postal operations. The important characteristic of an information-processing analysis, then, is that it involves a tracing of a sequence of mental operations and their products (information) in the performance of a particular cognitive task.

Such analyses are often given in flowchart form. A flowchart is a sequence of boxes, each of which reflects a stage of processing. Arrows from one box to another indicate the temporal sequencing (flow) of the stages. Figure 1-1 is a sample flowchart specifying how students should process the information in a chapter in this text. Each chapter begins with a short summary of the information found there. The first box in the figure specifies the process of studying this summary. In box 2, readers ask themselves if they are interested in learning more about these points. If they are not, an arrow goes from the box to the instruction to quit (in many class situations students will not have this option). If interested, they go on. Note the decision boxes (diamonds in this figure), where students must decide between a number of different paths for further processing. The existence of decision boxes indicates that a fixed sequence of steps will not always be taken.

In the third box, students are to make up a set of questions from the summary to keep in mind while reading the chapter. For instance, one of the summary points for this chapter is

> The study of cognitive psychology is motivated by scientific curiosity, by the desire for practical applications, and by the need to provide a foundation for other fields of social science.

----

[2]The fact that your grandmother probably does not live in San Francisco may not be the only inaccurate part of this example. The serial stages described would be somewhat controversial. This example is meant to illustrate the process of information processing, not specific stages.

13

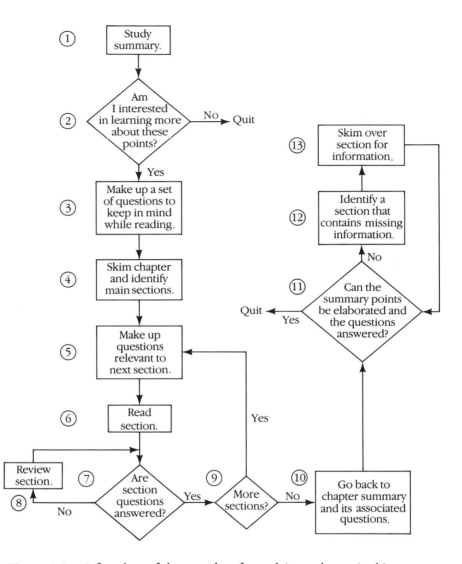

Figure 1-1. A flowchart of the procedure for studying a chapter in this text.

In box 3, students might ask

What are the practical applications of cognitive psychology?

In box 4, students are to skim the chapter to identify the major sections. Then to each section, they apply steps 5 through 9. They make up specific questions for the section to be read (box 5); for example, a question for this section on the information-processing approach might be:

How do I interpret a flowchart such as Figure 1-1?

Next, students read the section fairly carefully (box 6) and determine whether the section questions can be answered (box 7). If not, students review the section (box 8) until the questions can be answered. If all the section questions can be answered, students go on, making up more questions if more sections remain to be read (box 9).

The final portion of the flowchart (boxes 10 through 13) involves an end-of-chapter review. Students check to see whether they can answer the questions written for the chapter (boxes 10 and 11). If they cannot, they go back and skim the sections containing the information relevant to the unanswered questions (boxes 12 and 13). Thus, this flowchart provides at a rather global level (in contrast to specifying how to read each sentence) a prescription for sequencing the processing of information in a chapter.

How To Use This Book

We turn now to the substance of Figure 1-1 as a guide to study rather than as an example of information processing. Obviously, you will be the final judge of how best to study this book, but I recommend that you seriously consider following the scheme outlined in the figure. The chapter summaries are extremely important in this approach. Students have a natural tendency to skip over summaries and get to the "meat" of a text right away. However, research in our laboratory (Reder & Anderson, 1980) suggests that memory for a text is facilitated by initial study of a summary. The summaries are written in a deliberately terse style. Each point is central to the material, and each one is numbered. Take time to consider each point in the summary fully before starting the chapter text.

The summaries represent the most important points covered in the text. If you do not acquire and retain the information in the summary, there has been a serious failure of learning. Of course, I hope you will learn more than this from the chapters. However, what more you should learn should depend, in part, on your purposes.

The summaries serve three functions. First, they reflect the overall structure in each chapter. If you have learned a summary, you will know how the more specific points in the chapter relate to one another. Second, they serve to identify and define the most important new concepts and principles. The first stages of Figure 1-1 are intended to enable you to fix in memory these summary points and to prepare yourself for how the text will relate to the summary. Third, the summaries provide criteria against which you can test your learning of the material. The last stages (11, 12, and 13) of the figure are concerned with this function.

To use these summaries to the greatest advantage, you are advised to make up a set of questions, based on the summaries, to keep in mind as you read the text. When you finish a chapter, you should be able to answer these questions and be capable of elaborating each sentence of the summary with at least three or four sentences of additional detail. This question-generation process will encourage you to think deeply about the text and to be aware of your goals in reading it. Another function of the process is to introduce some spacing into your study of the text. You are encouraged first to study the main points, then to skim the chapter, next to read each section carefully and to review each section, and finally to review the chapter. This pattern will allow you to review major points throughout your study of the chapter. In Chapter 7, where learning from reading is covered in detail, the importance of question making and spaced study will be discussed more fully.

Organization of This Book

The next two chapters will set the stage for the information-processing analysis of cognition. In Chapter 2 we will address the question of how information processing is implemented in the brain. Chapter 3, on perception and attention, will address the question of how information is selected from the environment and processed.

The key construct in an information-processing analysis is *knowledge*. Cognition proceeds by utilizing in various ways the knowledge we have acquired from our experience. A prerequisite to understanding how knowledge is utilized is understanding how it is represented in the mind. Knowledge representation is the subject of Chapters 4 and 5. It proves profitable to make a distinction between the factual knowledge we have and knowledge about how to do things. The former is called declarative knowledge and the latter, procedural knowledge. Chapters 6 and 7, on human memory, concern themselves with declarative knowledge and how it is encoded in memory, how it is retained over long periods, and

16

how it is retrieved. Chapters 8 and 9, on cognitive skills, are concerned with procedural knowledge and its close connection to problem solving.

The remaining chapters of the book try to apply the analysis to some of the major aspects of cognition. Chapter 10 is devoted to human reasoning. Chapters 11 and 12 are concerned with language, which proves to be one of the more controversial fields of cognition. Chapter 13 looks at how our cognitive capabilities develop in childhood. Chapter 14 returns to the concept of intelligence and asks what we know about the property that supposedly distinguishes our species from the others.

Remarks and Suggested Readings

Boring's (1950) book is a classic review of the early history of psychology. A broad up-to-date survey of current theory and research in cognitive science is *Foundations of cognitive science* edited by Posner (1989). A textbook introduction to cognitive science was put together by Stillings, Feinstein, Garfield, Rissland, Rosenbaum, Weisler, and Baker-Ward (1987). A popular review of cognitive science is Morton Hunt's (1982) *The universe within.* Another very readable book is Gardner's (1985) *The mind's new science: A history of the cognitive revolution.*

There are a great many journals containing research relevant to cognitive psychology, but particularly important are the journals *Cognition; Cognitive Psychology; Cognitive Science; Journal of Experimental Psychology, General; Journal of Experimental Psychology: Learning, Memory, and Cognition; Journal of Experimental Psychology: Human Perception and Performance; Journal of Memory and Cognition;* and *Quarterly Journal of Experimental Psychology. Psychological Review* publishes important papers from all areas of psychology.

·2·

The Neural Basis of Cognition

Summary

1. Neurons are the most important cells in the brain for neural information processing. They receive electrochemical messages on their dendrites and send messages to other neurons along their axons. The connection from one axon to a dendrite is called a *synapse*.

2. Information is represented in terms of continuously varying electrochemical activity of neurons. Neurons can increase the activity of other neurons on which they synapse (excitation) or decrease the activity (inhibition).

3. Cognition is achieved by patterns of neural activation in large sets of neurons. Permanent memories are encoded by changing the synaptic connections among neurons so that a pattern of activation in one set of neurons will produce a pattern in another set.

4. The cortex is the most evolutionarily advanced part of the brain. The left half of the cortex receives sensory input about the right side of the world. The right half of the cortex receives sensory input about the left side.

5. Various parts of the cerebral cortex appear to be specialized for different cognitive functions. Different aspects of the same cognitive function often have different neural locations.

6. Light falls on the retina of the eye and is converted into neural energy by a photochemical process. This information is sent by various neural paths to the visual cortex of the brain.

7. Low-level cells in the visual system detect simple patterns of spots of light and darkness in the visual field. These are combined at higher cortical levels of the visual system to form bar and edge detectors.

8. *Connectionism* is an effort in cognitive science to explain the computational mechanisms by which higher-level cognition might arise from connections among basic neural elements.

A broad band of fibers, called the *corpus callosum,* connects the right and left halves of the brain. The corpus callosum has been surgically severed in some patients to prevent epileptic seizures. The operation is typically successful and patients seem to function fairly well. However, careful psychological research has found differences between such patients and subjects who have not had this surgery. In one experiment, the word *key* was flashed on the left side of a screen the patient was looking at. When asked what was presented on the screen he was not able to say. However, the patient's left hand (but not the right) was able to pick out a key from a set of objects hidden from view.

This experiment, the background of which we will discuss in more detail later, illustrates the obvious point that the brain underlies cognition and that physical operations on the brain affect cognition. Perhaps more surprising than the problems these patients experienced is the fact that they did not have more serious cognitive deficits after such a major surgical procedure.

We are just beginning to understand the role of the brain in cognition. Usually, the more primitive the cognitive function, the more we understand about how the nervous system achieves it. We have a much greater degree of understanding of the role of the nervous system in simple sensation, motor control, and autonomic regulation than of its role in memory, problem solving, and language. However, we are slowly acquiring understanding in all areas of cognition. In some cases, this under-standing takes the form of basic descriptive statements (for instance, such-and-such an area of the brain is involved in language). In other cases, this understanding takes the form of quite speculative proposals; for instance, we will discuss how memory and judgment might be imple-mented in the brain.

A great deal of research has been done on neural information process-ing, and this chapter will not attempt anything like an exhaustive review. Rather, the goal here is to sketch a few of the connections between neural processing and cognition so that you can get an idea of how cognition may actually be physically implemented in the human brain. At this stage in the development of the science, we cannot expect to fully understand the neural basis of cognition; however, even a fragmentary understanding provides an important perspective on the nature of cognition.

The Nervous System

The nervous system refers to more than just the brain. It refers to the various sensory systems that gather information from parts of the body and the motor system that controls movement. In some cases, the infor-mation processing that takes place outside the brain is considerable. From an information-processing point of view, the most important compo-nents of the nervous system are the neurons.[1] The human brain itself contains roughly 100 billion neurons, each of which may have roughly the processing capability of a medium-sized computer.[2] A considerable fraction of the 100 billion neurons are active simultaneously and do much of their information processing through interactions with one another. Imagine the information-processing power in 100 billion interacting computers! According to this view of the brain, there is more computa-tional power in one 3-pound brain than in all the computers in the world. Lest you become overwhelmed by the brain, we note that it is not good at doing some things the computer does well. There are many tasks, like finding square roots, at which a hand calculator can outperform all 100 billion neurons. Understanding the strengths and weaknesses of the

---

[1]Neurons are by no means the majority of cells in the nervous system; there are many others, such as glial cells, whose main function is thought to be supportive of the neurons.

[2]For instance, according to one view, each neuron computes on the order of 1000 multiplications and additions of real numbers every 10 milliseconds.

human nervous system is a major goal in understanding the nature of human cognition.

The Neuron

Neurons come in all shapes and sizes, depending on their exact location and function. (Figure 2-1 illustrates some of the variety.) There is, however, a generally accepted notion of what the prototypical neuron is like, and individual neurons match up with this prototype to greater or lesser degrees. This prototype is illustrated in Figure 2-2. The main body of the neuron is called the *soma*. Typically, the soma is 5–100 microns (μm, millionths of a meter) in diameter. Extending from the soma are a set of short branches called *dendrites*. Also attached to the soma is a long tube called the *axon*. The axon can vary in length from a few millimeters to a meter.

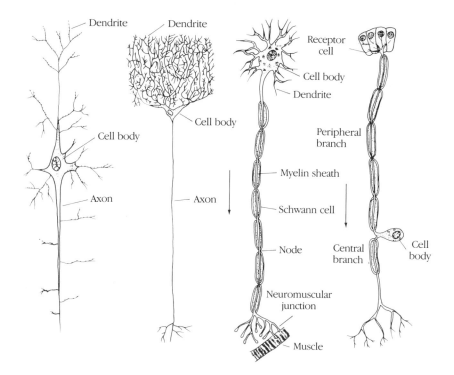

Figure 2-1. Some of the variety of neurons. (From Keeton, 1980.)

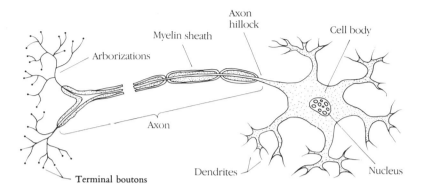

Figure 2-2. A schematic representation of a typical neuron. (From Katz, 1952.)

Axons provide the fixed paths by which neurons communicate with each other. The axon of one neuron extends toward the dendrites of others. At its end, the axon branches into a large number of terminal *arborizations*. Each arborization ends in terminal *boutons* that almost make contact with the dendrite of the other neuron. The gap separating the terminal bouton and the dendrite is typically in the range of 10–50 nanometers (a nanometer is one-billionth of a meter). This near contact between axon and dendrite is called a *synapse*. The most typical means of communication between neurons is that the axon terminal on one side of the synapse releases chemicals, called *neurotransmitters*, that act on the membrane of the receptor dendrite to change its polarization, or electrical potential. The inside of the membrane covering the entire neuron tends to be 70 millivolts (mV; a millivolt is one-thousandth of a volt, or .001 V) more negative than the outside due to the greater concentration of negative chloride ions inside and positive sodium and potassium ions outside. Depending on the nature of the neurotransmitter, the potential difference can decrease or increase. Synaptic connections that decrease the potential difference are called *excitatory* and synapses that increase the difference are called *inhibitory*.

In a mature adult the synaptic connections among neurons have all grown in, and new synapses are not formed among neurons. The average soma and dendrite have about 1000 synapses from other neurons and the average axon synapses to about 1000 neurons. The change in electrical potential due to any one synapse is rather small, but the individual excitatory and inhibitory effects can sum (the excitatory effects positive in the summation and the inhibitory effects negative). If there is enough net excitatory input, the potential difference in the soma can drop sharply. If the reduction in potential is large enough, a depolarization will occur at the *axon hillock*, where the axon joins the soma (see Figure 2-2). The inside of the neuron momentarily (for a millisecond) becomes more positive than the outside. This sudden change, referred to as an *action potential* (or *spike*), will propagate down the axon. That is, the potential difference will suddenly and momentarily change down the axon. The rate at which this change travels down the neuron can vary from .5 meter per second (m/s) to 130 m/s, depending on the characteristics of the axon—such as the degree to which the axon is covered by a myelin sheath (the more myelination, the faster the transmission). When the nerve impulse reaches the end of the axon, it will cause neurotransmitters to be released from the terminal boutons, thus completing the cycle.

To review, potential changes accumulate on a cell body, reach threshold, and cause an action potential to propagate down an axon. This pulse in turn causes neurotransmitters to be transmitted from the axon terminal to the body of a new neuron, causing changes in its membrane potential. It should be emphasized that this sequence is almost all there is to neural information processing, yet intelligence arises from this simple system of interactions. A major challenge to cognitive science is to understand how.

The time for this neural communication to complete the path from one neuron to another is roughly 10 milliseconds—definitely more than 1 millisecond, and definitely less than 100; the exact speed depends on the characteristics of the neurons involved. This is much slower than the millions of operations that can be performed in 1 second by a computer. There are, however, billions of these activities occurring simultaneously throughout the brain.

Neural Representation of Information

Information in the brain is represented in terms of continously varying quantities. There are two such quantities. First, the membrane potential can range more or less negative. Second, the axon can vary in terms of the number of nerve impulses it transmits per second. This is referred to as its *rate of firing*. It is usually the number, not the pattern, of impulses along a single axon that is important. There can be hundreds of nerve impulses per second. The greater the rate of firing, the more effect the axon will have on the cells to which it synapses. Information representation in the brain is to be contrasted with information representation in a computer, where individual memory cells or "bits" can have just one of two values

—off and on, or 0 and 1. There is not a continuous variation in a typical computer cell as there is in a typical neural cell.

There is a general way to conceptualize the interactions among neurons that captures the many specific variations on information transfer in the nervous system. This is to think of a neuron as having an "activation level" that corresponds roughly to its firing rate on the axon or to the degree of depolarization on the dendrite and soma. Neurons interact by driving up the activation level of other neurons (excitation) or driving down their activation level (inhibition). All neural information processing takes place in terms of these excitatory and inhibitory effects; they are what underlies human cognition.

It is an interesting question just how these neurons represent information. There is evidence that individual neurons respond to specific features of a stimulus. For instance, we will be discussing later in this chapter that there are neurons which are maximally active when there is a line in the visual field at a particular angle. There is some evidence that neurons exist which respond to more complex sets of features. For instance, neurons in the monkey brain appear to respond maximally to faces (Bruce, Desimone, & Gross, 1981; Desimone, Albright, Gross, & Bruce, 1984; Perrett, Rolls, & Caan, 1982). However, it is not possible that we have single neurons encoding all the concepts and shades of meaning we possess. Moreover, a single neuron's firing cannot represent the complexity of structure in a face.

If a single neuron cannot represent the complexity of our cognition, how is it represented? How can the activity of neurons represent our concept of baseball; how can they result in our solution of an algebra problem; how can they result in our feeling of frustration? Similar questions can be asked of computer systems, which have been shown to be capable of answering questions about baseball, solving algebra problems, and displaying frustration. Where in the millions of off-and-on bits in a computer does the concept of baseball lie; how does a change in a bit result in the solution of an algebra problem or in a feeling of frustration? The answer in every case is that these questions are failing to see the forest for the trees. The concepts of baseball, problem solution, and emotion occur in large patterns of bit changes. Cognition resides in patterns of the primitive elements of computers. Similarly, we can be sure that human cognition is achieved through large patterns of neural activity.

We do not really know how the brain encodes cognition in neural patterns, but the evidence is strong that it does. There are computational arguments that this is the only way to achieve cognitive function (see McClelland & Rumelhart, 1986). There is also a fair amount of evidence suggesting that human knowledge is not localized in any single neuron, but is distributed over the brain in large patterns of neurons. Damage to any small area of the brain generally does not result in the loss of specific memories. On the other hand, massive damage to large areas of the brain will result in temporary or permanent loss of a large set of memories.

It is informative to consider how the computer stores information. Consider a simple case: the spelling of a word. Most computers have codes by which individual patterns of binary values (1s and 0s) represent letters. Table 2-1 illustrates the use of one coding scheme, called ASCII; it contains a pattern of 0s and 1s that codes the words "cognitive psychology."

Similarly, information in the brain can be represented in terms of patterns of neural activity rather than simply as cells firing. The code in Table 2-1 includes certain redundant bits that allow the computer to correct errors should certain bits be lost (note that each column has an even number of 1s). Like the computer case, it seems that the brain codes information redundantly so that even if certain cells are missing, it can still determine what the pattern is encoding. It is generally thought that the brain uses very different schemes for encoding information and achieving redundancy than the computer. It also seems that the brain utilizes a much more redundant code than the computer. This is because individual neurons are not particularly reliable in their behavior. We will

Table 2-1 *Coding of Cognitive Psychology in ASCII*

1	1	1	1	1	1	1	1	1
0	0	0	0	0	0	0	0	0
0	0	0	0	0	1	0	1	0
0	1	0	1	1	0	1	0	0
0	1	1	1	0	1	0	1	1
1	1	1	1	0	0	0	1	0
1	1	1	0	1	0	1	0	1
1	1	0	0	1	1	1	0	1

1	1	1	1	1	1	1	1	1	1
0	0	0	0	0	0	0	0	0	0
1	1	1	0	0	0	0	0	0	1
0	0	1	0	1	1	1	1	0	1
0	0	0	0	0	1	1	1	1	0
0	1	0	1	0	1	0	1	1	0
0	1	1	1	0	1	0	1	1	1
0	0	0	1	0	1	1	1	0	0

also see in the later section on connectionism that there might be computational advantages in such distributed representations.

Coding of Permanent Memories

So far we have talked only about patterns of neural activation. However, such patterns are transitory. The brain does not maintain the same pattern for minutes, let alone days. This means that these patterns cannot encode our permanent knowledge about the world. The frequent belief, for which there is some evidence (Eccles, 1979), is that memories are encoded by changes in the synaptic connections among neurons. There is little evidence for growth of new synapses in the adult, but synapses can change in their effectiveness in response to experience. There is evidence that synaptic connections do change during learning with both increased release of neurotransmitters (Kandel & Schwartz, 1984) and increased sensitivity of dendritic receptors (Lynch & Baudry, 1984).

Organization of the Brain

Having reviewed some of the basic principles of neural information processing, we will look at the overall structure of the central nervous system and then focus on the nature of information processing in the visual system. The central nervous system consists of the brain and the spinal cord. the major function of the spinal cord is to carry neural messages from the brain to the muscles and sensory messages from the body back to the brain.

Figure 2-3 shows a cross section of the brain with some of the more prominent neural structures labeled. The lower parts of the brain are evolutionarily more primitive. The higher portions are well developed only in the higher species. Correspondingly, it appears that the lower portions of the brain are responsible for more basic functions. The medulla controls breathing, swallowing, digestion, and heartbeat. The cerebellum plays an important role in motor coordination and voluntary movement. The thalamus serves primarily as a relay station for motor and sensory information from lower areas to the cortex. The hypothalamus regulates expression of basic drives.

The cerebral cortex, or neocortex, is the most recently evolved portion of the brain. Although it is quite small and primitive in many mammals, it accounts for three-fourths of the neurons in the human brain. In the

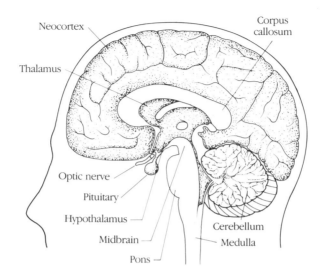

Figure 2-3. Some of the major components of the brain. (From Keeton, 1980.)

human, this cerebral cortex can be thought of as a rather thin neural sheet about 1 m square. To fit this neural sheet into the skull, it has to be highly convoluted. The amount of folds and wrinkles on the cortex is one of the striking physical differences between the human brain and those of lower mammals.

Neural Localization of Function

The neocortex is divided into left and right hemispheres. One of the interesting curiosities of anatomy is that the right part of the body tends to be connected to the left hemisphere and the left part of the body tends to be connected to the right hemisphere. Thus, motor control and sensation in the right hand are controlled by the left hemisphere. The right ear is most strongly connected to the left hemisphere. The neural receptors in either eye that receive input from the left part of the visual world are connected to the right hemisphere. The left and right hemispheres communicate by several pathways, the most prominent of which is the *corpus callosum*.

Each hemisphere can be divided into four lobes: frontal, parietal, occipital, and temporal (see Figure 2-4). Major folds or fissures on the cortex separate the areas. The frontal lobe is primarily involved with motor functions and contains an area, called the *prefrontal association cortex*,

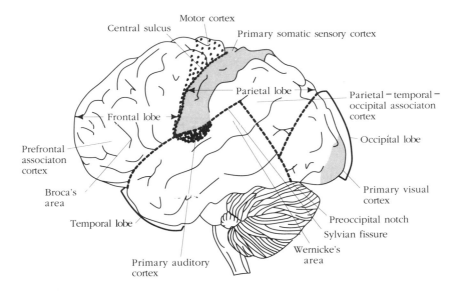

Motor cortex
Central sulcus
Primary somatic sensory cortex
Parietal lobe
Parietal – temporal – occipital associaton cortex
Frontal lobe
Occipital lobe
Prefrontal associaton cortex
Broca's area
Primary visual cortex
Temporal lobe
Preoccipital notch
Sylvian fissure
Wernicke's area
Primary auditory cortex

Figure 2-4. A side view of the cerebral cortex with the major components identified. (From Kandel & Schwartz, 1984. Reprinted by permission of the publisher. Copyright 1984 by Elsevier Science Publishing Co., Inc.)

that is thought to be involved in higher-level processes like planning. The occipital lobe contains the primary visual areas. The temporal lobe has the primary auditory areas and is also involved in the recognition of objects. The parietal lobe is concerned with some sensory functions, particularly those involving spatial processing.

In general, we are only beginning to understand where higher-level cognitive functions occur in the brain, let alone how they are achieved. We do know that a number of cortical areas are important in the processing of language. There are areas in the left frontal lobe, called *Broca's area* and *Wernicke's area*, that seem critical for speech, since damage to them results in severe impairment to speech. They may not be the only neural areas involved in speech, but they certainly are important.

Different language deficits appear depending on whether the damage is to Broca's area or Wernicke's area. People with Broca's aphasia (i.e., damage to Broca's area) speak in short, ungrammatical sentences. For instance, when one patient was asked whether he drives home on weekends, he replied:

> Why, yes . . . Thursday, er, er, er, no, er, Friday . . . Bar-
> ba-ra . . . wife . . . and, oh, car . . . drive . . . purnpike . . .
> you know . . . rest and . . . teevee. (Gardner, 1975, p. 61)

In contrast, patients with Wernicke's aphasia speak in fairly grammatical sentences that are almost devoid of meaning. Such patients have difficulty with their vocabulary and generate "empty" speech. The following is the answer given by one such patient to the question "What brings you to the hospital?"

> Boy, I'm sweating, I'm awful nervous, you know, once in a while I
> get caught up, I can't mention the tarripoi, a month ago, quite a
> little, I've done a lot well. I impose a lot, while, on the other hand,
> you know what I mean, I have to run around, look it over, trebbin
> and all that sort of stuff. (Gardner, 1975, p. 68)

It appears that the two hemispheres are somewhat specialized for different types of processing. As we already noted, the so-called language areas are localized in the left hemisphere. In general, the left hemisphere seems more associated with symbolic and analytic processing, while the right hemisphere is more associated with perceptual and spatial processing. Much of the evidence for the difference between the hemispheres comes from split-brain patients, such as the ones discussed earlier in this chapter.

By severing the connections between the left and right hemispheres in epileptic patients, surgeons have created a situation in which psychologists can study the spearate functions of the right and left hemispheres. Commands can be presented to the patients in their right ears (and hence to their left brains) or in their left ears (and hence to their right brains). The right hemisphere can comprehend only the simplest linguistic commands, whereas the left hemisphere displays full comprehension to produce spatial patterns. A quite different result is obtained when the ability of the right hand (hence left hemisphere) is compared with that of the left hand (hence right hemisphere). In this situation, the right hemisphere clearly outperforms the left hemisphere.

There is increasing evidence that different aspects of cognitive function are localized in different places in the brain. One example of this is the apparent separation of grammar in one region (Broca's area), and vocabulary in another (Wernicke's area). Research by Posner, Peterson, Fox, and Raichie (1988) on the localization of different components of the reading process is a demonstration of the differential localization of different components. They used a method called positron emission to-pography to measure changes in blood flow in various regions of the cortex to determine which areas were involved in a particular activity. For instance, they looked at what areas of the brain are involved in reading a word. Figure 2-5 illustrates their results. The triangles in the visual cortex represent areas that were active when subjects were just passively looking at concrete nouns. The squares are areas that became active when subjects were asked to engage in the semantic activity of generating uses for these nouns. The triangles are located in the occipital lobe while the squares are located in the frontal lobe. Thus, the data indicate that the processes of visually perceiving a word take place in a different part of the brain than the processes of thinking about the meaning of a word.

Topographic Organization of Brain Areas

In many areas of the cortex, information processing is organized spatially in what is called a topographic organization. For instance, in the visual area at the back of the cortex, adjacent areas represent information from

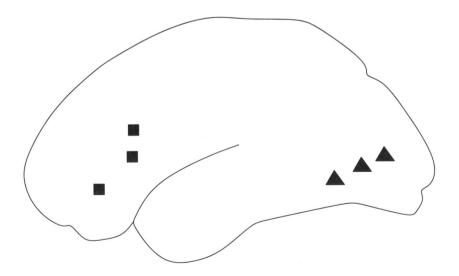

Figure 2-5. Areas activated in visual word reading in the lateral aspect of the cortex. Triangles refer to the passive visual task while squares refer to the semantic task. (From Posner, Peterson, Fox, & Raichle, 1988. Copyright 1988 by the AAAS.)

adjacent areas of the visual field. A similar principle of organization governs the representation of the body in the motor cortex and the somato-sensory cortex along the central fissure. Adjacent parts of the body are represented adjacently in the neural tissue. Figure 2-6 illustrates the representation of the body along the somato-sensory cortex. Note that the body is distorted, with certain areas receiving a considerable overrepresentation. It turns out that the overrepresented areas correspond to those that are more sensitive. Thus, for instance, we can make more subtle discriminations among tactile stimuli on the hands and face than on our back or thigh. Also in the visual cortex there is an overrepresentation of the visual field at the center of our vision, where we have the greatest visual activity.

Presumably, the reason for topographic maps is so that neurons processing similar regions can interact with one another (Crick & Asanuma, 1986). This may be related to an aspect of neural information processing called course-coding. If one records the neural activity from a single neuron in the somato-sensory cortex it does not respond when only a single point of the body is stimulated but rather responds when any point

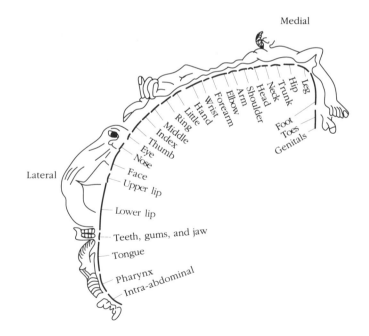

Figure 2-6. A cross section of the somatosensory cortex, showing a map of the human body. (From Kandel & Schwartz, 1984. Reprinted by permission of the publisher. Copyright 1984 by Elsevier Science Publishing Co., Inc.)

on a large patch of the body is stimulated. How, then, can we know exactly what point has been touched? That information is recorded quite accurately but not in the response of any particular cell. Rather, different cells will respond to different overlapping regions of the body and any point will evoke a different set of cells. Thus, the location of a point is reflected by the pattern of activation. This reinforces the idea that neural information tends to be represented in patterns of activation.

The Visual System

Our understanding of the neural underpinnings of higher-level cognitive systems is still in its infancy. We have a much firmer grasp of the neural information processing underlying the low-level aspects of vision. This knowledge is worth reviewing as a model of what neural information processing is like. It is also an area where artificial intelligence and psychological research have recently made major advances.

Figure 2-7 is a schematic representation of the eye. Light passes through the lens and the vitreous humor and falls on the retina at the

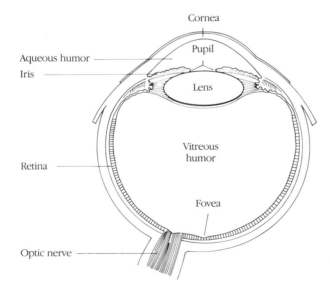

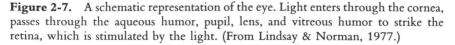

Figure 2-7. A schematic representation of the eye. Light enters through the cornea, passes through the aqueous humor, pupil, lens, and vitreous humor to strike the retina, which is stimulated by the light. (From Lindsay & Norman, 1977.)

back of the eye. The retina contains the light-sensitive cells that actually respond to the light. It should be pointed out that light is scattered slightly in passing through the vitreous humor, so the image falling on the back of the retina is not perfectly sharp. One of the important functions of early visual processing is, as we will see, to sharpen that image.

Light is converted into neural energy by a photochemical process. There are two distinct types of photoreceptors in the eye — rods and cones. Cones are involved in color vision and show high resolution and acuity. Less light energy is required to trigger a response in the rods, but they are associated with poorer resolution. As a consequence, they are principally responsible for the less acute, black-and-white vision we experience at night. Cones are especially concentrated in a small area of the retina called the *fovea*. When we fixate on an object, we move our eyes so that the object falls on the fovea. This enables us to maximize the high resolution of the cones in perceiving the object. Foveal vision is concerned with detection of fine details. The rest of the visual field, the *periphery*, is responsible for detection of more global information, including movement.

The receptor cells synapse onto bipolar cells and these onto ganglion cells, whose axons leave the eye and form the optic nerve, which goes to the brain. Altogether there are about 800,000 ganglion cells in the optic nerve from each eye. Each ganglion cell encodes information from a small region of the retina. The amount of neural firing on a ganglion axon will typically encode the amount of light stimulation in that region of the retina.

Figure 2-8 illustrates the neural paths from the eye to the brain. The optic nerves from both eyes meet at the optic chiasma, and the nerves from the nasal side of the retina cross over and go to the other side of the brain, while the nerves from the outside of the retina continue to the same side of the brain as the eye. This means that the right halves of both eyes are connected to the right brain. Since the left part of the visual field falls on the right half of each eye, information about the left part of the visual field goes to the right brain; similarly, information about the right side of the visual field goes to the left brain. We have already discussed this in considering research with split-brain patients.

The fibers from the ganglion cells synapse onto cells in either the lateral geniculate nucleus or the superior colliculus. Both of these are areas below the cortex in the brain. It is thought that the lateral geniculate nucleus is important in perceiving details and recognizing objects whereas the superior colliculus is involved in the localization of objects in space. Both of these neural structures are connected to the visual cortex.

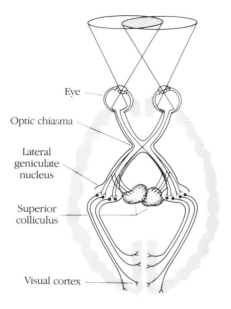

Eye

Optic chiasma

Lateral
geniculate
nucleus

Superior
colliculus

Visual cortex

Figure 2-8. Neural paths from the eye to the brain. (From Keeton, 1980.)

There are similar divisions in the cortex, with certain areas responsible for recognzing what an object is and other areas responsible for recognizing where an object is.

Information Coding in Visual Cells

Kuffler's (1953) research showed how information is encoded by the ganglion cells. These cells generally have a spontaneous rate of firing. For some ganglion cells, if light falls on a small region of the retina, there will be an increase from these spontaneous rates of firing. If light is presented in the region just around this sensitive center, however, the spontaneous rate of firing will go down. Light farther from the center elicits no response at all. These are known as on-off cells. There are also off-on ganglion cells, where light at the center suppresses the spontaneous rate of firing and light in the surround increases the rate of firing. Figure 2-9 illustrates the receptive fields of these cells. Cells in the lateral geniculate nucleus respond in the same way.

Hubel and Wiesel (1962), in their study of the visual cortex in the cat, found that visual cortical cells responded in a more complex manner than these lower cells. Figure 2-10 illustrates four of the patterns that have

On-off cell   Off-on cell

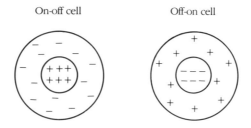

Figure 2-9. On-off and off-on receptive fields of ganglion cells and the cells in the lateral geniculate nucleus.

been observed in cortical cells. As can be seen, all of these receptive fields have an elongated shape, in contrast to the on-off cells. Types (a) and (b) are edge detectors. They respond positively to light on one side of a line and negatively to light on the other side. They will respond maximally if there is an edge of light lined up so as to fall at the boundary point. Types (c) and (d) are bar detectors. They respond positively to light in the center and negatively to light at the periphery, or vice versa. Thus, a bar with a positive center will respond maximally if there is a bar of light just covering its center.

Both edge and bar detectors are specific with respect to position, orientation, and width. That is, they respond only to stimulation in a small area of the visual field, to bars and edges of small range of orientations, and to bars and edges of certain widths. Thus, a striped pattern like

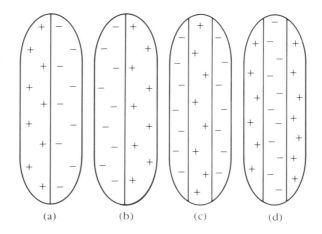

Figure 2-10. Response patterns of cortical cells.

the one in Figure 2-11 will excite a particular bar detector only if the stripes are of the appropriate orientation and width for that detector. However, different detectors seem tuned to different widths and orientations, so some subset of bar detectors would be stimulated by this pattern.

One of the interesting features of edge and bar detectors is that they respond if stimulation is presented to the corresponding visual region of either eye. Thus, visual information from corresponding points in either eye must converge on the same detector.

Figure 2-12 illustrates how a number of on-off and off-on cells might combine to form bar or edge detectors. Note that no single on-off cell is sufficient to stimulate a detector. Rather, the detector is responding to *patterns* of the on-off cells, so even at this low level we see the nervous system processing information in terms of patterns of neural activation.

David Marr's Work

We have described so far what various parts of the visual system do. Cognitive scientists are not content with this. They also want to know how the various parts are put together to enable us to actually perceive things. This is referred to as the issue of *neural computation*—how information is combined to enable us to perceive objects. This research is often done by developing computer models that try to simulate the information

Figure 2-11. A pattern that excites detectors of a particular width and orientation.

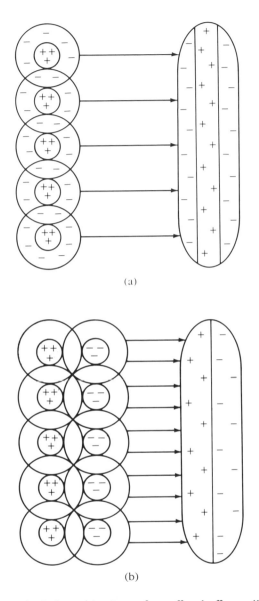

(a)

(b)

Figure 2-12. Hypothetical combinations of on-off and off-on cells to form (a) bar detectors and (b) edge detectors.

processing which is taking place in the visual system. The goal is to get these computer programs to see in a visual scene what a human sees.

The late David Marr developed a computer model of how information from the on-and-off cells could be used to yield a useful analysis of the visual image. Figure 2-13 shows a typical image that a computer might be asked to process. It is an image of the end of a bar. This image is a 128 × 128 grid where the lightness of each dot represents the intensity of light information at that point. However, it is not particularly easy to circumscribe the boundaries of the image. There are similar problems with the image that falls on the human retina. A major information-processing problem, then, is to identify the boundaries of an object in an image.

Marr and Hildreth (1980) combined the output of off-on detectors to calculate bars and edges of various widths and orientations. Wherever an edge or bar was detected, a symbolic description was created. Thus, the following descriptions might be created:

> There is an edge with coordinates (184,23), orientation 128°, contrast 25, length 32, and width 4.

> There is a bar with coordinates (118,134), orientation 105°, contrast 76, length 16, and width 6.

Where the coordinates are the horizontal and vertical position of the object, orientation measures the degree of rotation from the horizontal, contrast the intensity of brightness change, length the length of the bar, and width the width of the detectors.

Figure 2-14 illustrates the application of Marr's procedure to a figure (a). Part (b) shows the output of the on-off detectors adjusted to a particular width; each dark point is an on-off detector of that width. The output of the edge detectors is shown in part (c); each line reflects a particular edge. Finally, part (d) shows the bars detected in the image. The information in parts (c) and (d) of the figure is still quite low level, and the representation of this information Marr calls the *raw primal sketch*. To recognize an image, Marr must put the various edges and bars together. His system does this on the basis of similarity. So, suppose Marr's system has formed the following symbolic descriptions:

> 1. There is an edge with coordinates (112,39), orientation 118°, contrast 82, length 12, and width 4.

> 2. There is an edge with coordinates (107,48), orientation 119°, contrast 79, length 10, and width 5.

> 3. There is an edge with coordinates (102,58), orientation 117°, contrast 81, length 15, and width 4.

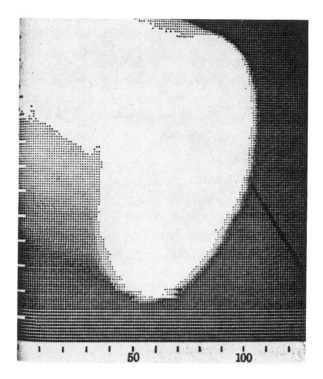

Figure 2-13. A typical visual image that is processed in computer vision. Problems in processing these images are typical of problems in processing an image on the retina of the eye. (From Marr, 1976.)

It would assume that these descriptions were all part of one edge, and would put them together. Figure 2-15 illustrates various stages of the analysis of the bar in Figure 2-13. The dots in part (a) reflect various symbolic statements. The connected points in part (b) reflect statements his system has put together because of similarity. We still have not identified the contour. A second-order analysis is required to put together similar lines to come up with a contour representation like that in part (c).

Marr's system had some successes at identifying the boundaries of objects in real images, a difficult problem in computer vision. There is some evidence that the visual system does an analysis somewhat like Marr's. There are so-called complex and hypercomplex cells in the visual cortex that seem to combine the output of the simple bar and edge cells, just as Marr's system combines the symbolic description to identify the contour of an object. However, the exact character and connections of the complex and hypercomplex cells remain a little obscure.

(a)

(b)

(c)

(d)

Figure 2-14. (a) The original image processed by Marr and Hildreth (1980); (b) the output of the on-off detectors; (c) the output of the edge detectors; (d) the output of the bar detectors.

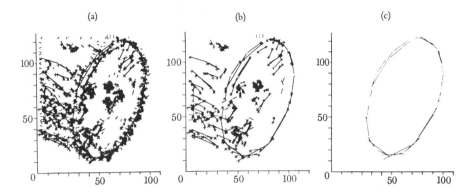

Figure 2-15. Analysis of the image of a bar in Figure 2-13 by Marr's system: (a) the symbolic description in the raw primal sketch; (b) and (c) different levels of aggregation into larger segments.

It is still some distance from the recognition of lines and boundaries to the recognition of object identity. The next chapter, on perception, will discuss some of the work that has been done in this area.

Connectionism

Hopefully, this chapter has given you some sense of where we are in understanding the cognitive bases of cognition—we know quite a bit about how basic neural elements operate, we have fairly good ideas about how they might be put together to perform relatively low-level processes such as basic vision, and we are getting some idea about how more advanced cognitive processes are organized and localized in the brain. However, there are great gaps in our knowledge. The contrast is glaring between what we can say about how we perceive a line versus how we can remember facts about people and judge their character. In the first case we can present relatively detailed neural models; in the second case we cannot. As discussed in Chapter 1, much progress has been made on understanding these higher-level processes but at a level abstracted away from the neural underpinnings. Much of the remainder of this book will be devoted to discussing this more abstract work.

There is a movement afoot in cognitive science to try to develop models of higher-level processes that are better grounded in our understanding of neural processing. Given that our knowledge of the relevant facts of the brain is still thin these attempts start, not by asking how the brain does achieve the higher processing, but by asking how it might. As in the case of Marr, they are concerned with the issue of neural computation. They start from our general knowledge of how neurons work and ask the question, How could higher-level function be achieved by connecting together basic elements like neurons? This approcah is therefore called *connectionism* because it is concerned with ways of connecting neural elements together to account for higher-level cognition. Connectionist models have had some degree of success in accounting for various aspects of human cognition, which we will discuss in later chapters. Here I would like to just present an example of how such models are developed.

Jay McClelland and David Rumelhart have developed one of the existing frameworks for such connectionist models. They call their framework parallel distributed processing, or PDP for short. McClelland, Rumelhart, and Hinton (1986) describe a PDP model of the following situation. They ask one to imagine living in an unsavory neighborhood dominated by two gangs, called the Jets and the Sharks, and meeting the people described in Table 2-2. They propose a neural-like model of how one might represent such knowledge and answer questions about the individuals in the neighborhood. They suggest someone might set up a network of neural elements to represent these people, such as that illustrated in Figure 2-16 (which represents only part of the information — McClelland et al. actually built a structure representing all of Table 2-2). One might think of each element as a neuron and the links between elements as connections among neurons. Each element in the central "cloud" represents what they call an "instance unit" that stands for one of the gang members. It is linked by excitatory connections to units that represent all of that fellow's properties. Thus, there is one element connected to the name Lance, the age 20, the occupation burglar, the status married, the gang Jets, and the educational level junior high.

Suppose one wants to retrieve information about Lance. The way this would be done in such a network is to activate the unit corresponding to Lance's name. This would in turn activate the instance unit for Lance, which would then activate the other properties for Lance, thereby creating a pattern of activation over the neural network corresponding to Lance. In effect, one has retrieved a representation of Lance from the neural network.

One can answer questions such as "Who do you know who is a Shark and in his 20s?" This would be done by activating the Sharks and 20s units and observing the pattern of activation that results. As it turns out,

Table 2-2 *Characteristics of a Number of Individuals Belonging to Two Gangs, the Jets and the Sharks.*

Name	Age	Education	Marital Status	Occupation
		Jets		
Art	40s	J.H.	Sing.	Pusher
Al	30s	J.H.	Mar.	Burglar
Sam	20s	Col.	Sing.	Bookie
Clyde	40s	J.H.	Sing.	Bookie
Mike	30s	J.H.	Sing.	Bookie
Jim	20s	J.H.	Div.	Burglar
Greg	20s	H.S.	Mar.	Pusher
John	20s	J.H.	Mar.	Burglar
Doug	30s	H.S.	Sing.	Bookie
Lance	20s	J.H.	Mar.	Burglar
George	20s	J.H.	Div.	Burglar
Pete	20s	H.S.	Sing.	Bookie
Fred	20s	H.S.	Sing.	Pusher
Gene	20s	Col.	Sing.	Pusher
Ralph	30s	J.H.	Sing.	Pusher
		Sharks		
Phil	30s	Col.	Mar.	Pusher
Ike	30s	J.H.	Sing.	Bookie
Nick	30s	H.S.	Sing.	Pusher
Don	30s	Col.	Mar.	Burglar
Ned	30s	Col.	Mar.	Bookie
Karl	40s	H.S.	Mar.	Bookie
Ken	20s	H.S.	Sing.	Burglar
Earl	40s	H.S.	Mar.	Burglar
Rick	30s	H.S.	Div.	Burglar
Ol	30s	Col.	Mar.	Pusher
Neal	30s	H.S.	Sing.	Bookie
Dave	30s	H.S.	Div.	Pusher

From Retrieving General and Specific Knowledge From Stored Knowledge of Specifics by J. L. McClelland, 1981, *Proceedings of the Third Annual Conference of the Cognitive Science Society*, Berkeley, CA. Copyright 1981 by J. L. McClelland. Reprinted by permission.

Ken (not shown in Figure 2-16) is the only individual who fits the description and his name unit would be most active in the network and could be retrieved as the answer.

This model has a number of features that enable it to display a certain degree of intelligence. For instance, suppose we ask it who is 20 years old,

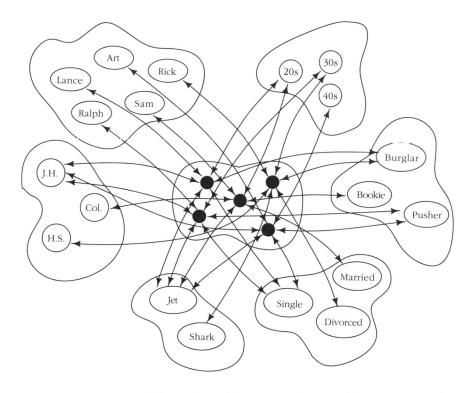

Figure 2-16. Some of the units and interconnections needed to represent the individuals shown in Table 2-2. The units connected with double-headed arrows are mutually excitatory. All the units within the same "cloud" are mutually inhibitory. (From Retrieving General and Specific Knowledge From Stored Knowledge of Specifics by J. L. McClelland, 1981. *Proceedings of the Third Annual Conference of the Cognitive Science Society.* Berkeley, CA. Copyright 1981 by J. L. McClelland. Reprinted by permission.)

a Shark, married, and a bookie. Inspection of Table 2-2 will reveal that no person matches this description but Ken comes closest. This system would most activate the Ken unit and would retrieve it as an answer. Thus, it can make judgments about closeness of match of a description to an individual.

Such a system can also make inferences based on similarity. For instance, suppose we do not know Lance's profession. If we ask what Lance's profession is, we can activate the Lance unit, which will in turn activate the properties we know about Lance—such as that he is in his

20s, is a Jet, and has a junior high education. These properties will in turn activate other people who share these properties and activate their profession. It turns out that all Jets in their 20s with junior high education are burglars. Correspondingly, this network will most activate burglar and make the reasonable inference that this is Lance's profession, even if that is not represented in the network. Such a network will also allow us to make generalizations about categories. So if we ask about what Jets are like, the nodes for single, 20s, and junior high will become active because most Jets have these features. So the system is capable of making spontaneous judgments about the character of various groups.

What McClelland et al. have provided for us, then, is a demonstration of how neural mechanisms might underlie some of the subtle memory judgments one might make. In many cases the behavior produced by such mechanisms also corresponds to the behavioral details of how people actually make these judgments. We will review a number of such situations in later chapters.

Right now such connectionist models are regarded in cognitive psychology as displaying considerable promise in finally bridging the gap that has existed between the brain and higher-level cognition. For examples of connectionist models other than PDP, read Schneider and Oliver (1988) and Grossberg (1987).

Remarks and Suggested Readings

A number of books, including Carlson (1985) and Kandel and Schwartz (1984), provide good discussions of the work in neuropsychology. Crick and Asanuma (1986) and Sejnowski and Churchland (in press) provide reviews of neuropsychology with an eye to its significance for cognitive psychology. A paper by Gazzaniga (1983) discusses the different character of the left and right hemispheres of the brain. The books by Gardner (1975) and Sacks (1985) provide some interesting case studies of the cognitive consequences of damage to various parts of the brain.

There has been a surge of interest in the computational character of neural processing. A two-volume series by McClelland and Rumelhart (1986) and Rumelhart and McClelland (1986) provides a good discussion of this material. Fodor (1975) should be read for a critique of neural considerations in cognitive psychology. More recent critiques by Pinker and Prince, Fodor and Pylyshyn, and Lachlter and Bever have appeared in a 1988 volume of the journal *Cognition*.

There is a great deal of work on computer vision, some of it based on human models and some of it not. This work tends to be published in proceedings of meetings such as the International Joint Conference on Artificial Intelligence, the American Association for Artificial intelligence, and the International Conference on Pattern Recognition. Marr's (1982) book gives a good discussion of his research on vision. The new journal *Neural Computation* carries recent work on neural networks.

·3·

Perception and Attention

Summary

1. When information first enters the human system, it is registered in
sensory memories. These sensory memories include an iconic
memory for visual information and an echoic memory for auditory
information. Sensory memories can store a great deal of
information, but only for brief periods of time.

2. Attention is a very limited mental resource that can be allocated to
at most a few cognitive processes at a time. The more frequently
that processes have been practiced, the less attention they require;
eventually they can be performed without interfering with other
cognitive processes. Processes that are highly practiced and require
little or no attention are referred to as *automatic*. Processes that
require attention are called *controlled*.

3. Recognizing a complex pattern involves a feature analysis in which
the overall pattern is decomposed into a set of primitive features,
the individual features are recognized, and then the combination of
features is recognized to identify the pattern.

4. A set of Gestalt principles determines how we break an overall
pattern into subunits or features.

5. Combining features in order to recognize a pattern requires attention. The amount of attention required decreases with the familiarity of the pattern.

6. Pattern recognition involves an integration of bottom-up processing and top-down processing. Bottom-up processing is the use of sensory information in pattern recognition. Top-down processing is the use of the context of the pattern as well as general knowledge in recognition.

In the preceding chapter we discussed how information is processed by the visual system. We noted how information works its way through the visual system to the point where lines are detected and contours of objects are identified. However, a great deal more information processing than this is required before we can recognize objects. An interesting demonstration of this fact concerns a soldier who suffered brain damage due to accidental carbon monoxide poisoning. He could recognize objects through their feel, smell, or sound, but was unable to distinguish a circle from a square or recognize faces or letters (Benson & Greenberg, 1969). On the other hand, he was able to discriminate light intensities and colors and tell in what direction an object was moving. Thus, his system was able to register visual information, but somehow his brain damage resulted in a loss of the ability to combine visual information into perceptual experience. This case shows that perception is much more than simply the registering of sensory information. In this chapter we will review what is known about the ways sensory information is processed and patterns are recognized, as well as the role of attention in guiding these information-processing activities.

Sensory Memory

Visual Sensory Memory

Many studies of visual information processing have involved determining what a subject can extract from a brief visual presentation. A typical trial in such an experiment begins with the subject's fixating on a dot in a blank white field. By having the subject so fixate, the experimenter can control where the subject is focusing during stimulus presentation. The stimulus, perhaps a set of letters, is visually projected where the subject is looking. After a brief exposure (e.g., 50 milliseconds), the stimulus is removed.

A number of studies have been concerned with the capacity of the memory that first registers this sensory information. In such experiments, displays of letters such as that in Figure 3-1 are presented briefly and subjects are then asked to report as many items as they can recall. Usually, subjects are able to report three, four, five, or at most six items. Many subjects report that they saw more items but that the items faded away before they could be reported.

An important methodological variation on this task was performed by Sperling (1960). He presented an array consisting of three rows of four letters, as shown in Figure 3-1. Immediately after this stimulus was turned off, the subject was cued to report just one row of the display. The cues were in the form of differential tones (high tone for top row, medium for middle, and low for bottom). Sperling's method was called the *partial-report procedure* in contrast with the *whole-report procedure*, which had been used until then.

By using the number of letters that the subject was able to report from a particular row, Sperling was able to estimate the number of letters the subject had available the instant the display was turned off. Subjects were able to recall a little more than three items from a row of four. Because subjects did not know beforehand which row would be cued, they had to have more than three items available from each of the three rows. The total number of items available, then, would be three rows times more than three items per row, which is more than nine items. This result contrasts sharply with the four or five items subjects typically recall in the whole-report procedure. So, subjects were correct in their claims that they could see more items than they could report before the items faded from the image of the display. Indeed, they probably could see all 12 letters. Sperling's estimate was less than 12, however, probably due to subjects' failures to use the partial-report procedure perfectly.

X	M	R	J
C	N	K	P
V	F	L	B

Figure 3-1. An example of the kind of display used in a visual-report experiment. This display is presented briefly to subjects, who are then asked to report the letters it contains.

In the procedure just described, the tone cue was presented immediately after offset of the display. Sperling also varied the length of the delay between the offset of the display and the tone. The results he obtained in terms of numbers of letters available out of 12 are presented in Figure 3-2. (Recall that our estimate of the number of letters available is three times the number reported from a row.) As the delay increases to 1 second, subjects' performance decays back to the original whole-report level of four or five items. Thus, it appears that the memory for the actual display decays very rapidly and is essentially gone by the end of 1 second. All that is left after a second is what the subject has had time to more permanently encode.

Sperling's experiments indicate the existence of a brief *visual sensory store*—a memory that can effectively hold all the information in the visual display. While information is being held in this store, it can be processed by higher-level mental routines such as those involved in making a report of the display's content. This sensory store appears to be particularly visual in character. In one experiment showing the visual character of the sensory store, Sperling (1967) varied the postexposure field (the visual field after the display). He found that when the postexposure field was light the sensory information remained for only a second, but when the field was dark it remained for a full 5 seconds. Thus, a bright postexposure field tends to "wash out" memory for the display. Further, following the display with another display of characters effectively "overwrites" the first display and so destroys the memory for the letters. The brief visual memory revealed in these experiments was called an *icon* by Neisser (1967). Without such a visual icon, perception would

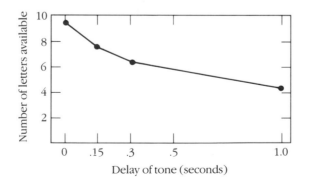

Figure 3-2. Results from Sperling's experiment. As the tone that signals the row to report is delayed, the number of items reported decreases. (Adapted from Sperling, 1960.)

be much more difficult. Many stimuli are of very brief duration. In order to recognize them, the system needs some means of holding on to them for a short while until they can be analyzed.

Auditory Sensory Memory

Evidence for an auditory sensory memory similar to the visual memory comes from experiments by Moray, Bates, and Barnett (1965) and by Darwin, Turvey, and Crowder (1972). The setup of the Darwin, Turvey, and Crowder study is illustrated in Figure 3-3. Subjects listened to a recording over stereo headphones, hearing three lists of three items read simultaneously. Because of stereophonic mixing, one list seemed to come from the left side of the subject's head, one from the middle, and one from the right side. The investigators compared results derived from a whole-report procedure, in which subjects were instructed to report all nine items, with a partial-report procedure, in which they were cued visually after the presentation of the lists as to whether they should report the items coming from the left, middle, or right locations.

A greater percentage of the letters were reported in the partial-report procedure than in the whole-report procedure. Thus, as with iconic memory, it appears that more information is immediately available in auditory memory than can be reported. Neisser has called this auditory

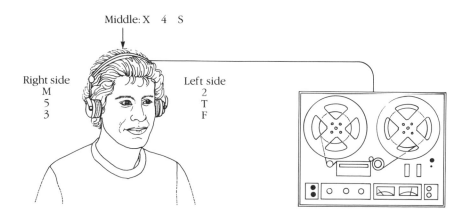

Figure 3-3. The experimental situation in the Darwin, Turvey, and Crowder experiment. By stereophonic mixings, lists of digits and letters are simultaneously presented to the left, middle, and right of the subject's head. (From Loftus & Loftus, 1976. Courtesy of Lawrence Erlbaum Associates, Inc., Publishers.)

51

memory the *echoic memory*. It is clear that we need such a memory to process many aspects of speech information. Neisser (1967, p. 201) gives the example of a foreigner who is told, "No, not zeal, seal." Foreigners would not be able to benefit from this information if they could not retain the *z* long enough to compare it with the *s*.

Attention and Sensory Information Processing

A Model of Attention

The types of studies described above on sensory memory show that a large amount of information gets into sensory memory, but that it is quickly lost if not attended to. Thus, attention plays an important role in selecting sensory information for further processing.

A great many theories of attention have been developed in cognitive psychology. In this section we describe a theory that has been quite successful in accounting for a wide range of attentional phenomena (Kahneman, 1973; LaBerge & Samuels, 1974; Norman & Bobrow, 1975; Posner & Snyder, 1975; Shriffin & Schneider, 1977; Schneider & Shiffrin, 1977). Attention is conceived of as being a very limited mental resource. Numerous metaphors can help us think about the limited-resource characteristic of attention. One is energy—imagine an energy limitation, as if attention were powered by a fixed electrical current. Given the fixed energy supply, attention would be allocable to only so many tasks. (If allocated to more, the performance would degrade or a fuse would blow.) A second metaphor is spatial—think of attention as a workspace in which only so many tasks can be performed. A third metaphor is animate—think of attention as a small set of agents, often called *demons*, that can perform tasks, but only one at a time; thus, attention cannot be assigned to more tasks than there are demons.

Attention is sometimes thought of as being single-minded. In terms of the metaphors just cited, this single-mindedness would mean that only enough energy, only enough workspace, or only a single attention demon was available for one task or process. Evidence for this single-minded character of attention is the fact that performing two attention-demanding tasks at once is difficult. For instance, it is difficult if not impossible to simultaneously do two addition problems, or to hold two conversations, or to hold a conversation and do an addition problem. Rather than thinking of attention as single-minded, however, it is probably more accurate to think of it as not having the capacity to perform two *demanding* tasks simultaneously. Tasks that are practiced to the point at which they do not make excessive demands can be performed simultaneously. For instance, we can walk and talk at the same time. Perhaps the reason we cannot simultaneously do mental addition and carry on a conversation is that each activity in itself involves multiple attention-demanding subcomponents. For instance, addition may involve reading, retrieving addition facts from memory, and writing—all three activities that make separate demands on attention. In any case, it is clear that whether or not attention is truly single-minded, its capacity is severely limited.

The limited capacity of attention is the root cause of the reporting limitations demonstrated in visual- and auditory-reporting tasks. All the information gets into sensory memory, but to be retained, each unit of information must be attended to and transformed into some more permanent form. Given that attention has a limited capacity, all the elements in sensory memory cannot be attended to before they are lost. If subjects are immediately cued to report only a subset, they can attend to these items before they fade from memory. However, if the cue is delayed until the terms have faded from memory, subjects will be able to report only those elements of the subset they were able to attend to and transform into a more permanent form.

Divided-Attention Studies

Considerable research has been done on how subjects select what sensory input they attend to. Much of this research has involved a dichotic listening task. In a typical dichotic listening experiment, illustrated in Figure 3-4, subjects wear a set of headphones. They hear two messages, one entering each ear, and are asked to "shadow" one of the two messages (i.e., report the words from one message as they hear them). Most subjects are able to attend to one message and tune out the other.

Psychologists (e.g., Cherry, 1953; Moray, 1959) have discovered that very little about the unattended message is processed in a shadowing task. Subjects can tell if the unattended message was a human voice or a noise; if human, whether male or female; and whether the sex of the speaker changed. However, this information is about all they can report. They cannot tell what language was spoken or report any of the words spoken, even if the same word was repeated over and over again. An analogy is often made between performing this task and being at a cocktail party, where a guest tunes in to one message (a conservation) and filters out others.

53

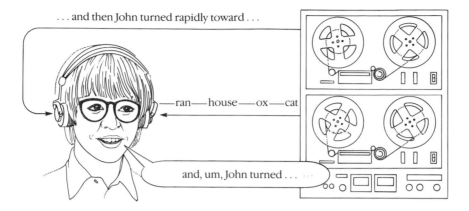

Figure 3-4. A typical shadowing task. Messages are presented to the left and right ears and the subject attempts to shadow one ear. (From Lindsay & Norman, 1977.)

We might think that the subject simply "turns one ear off," but a number of experiments have shown that this is not always the case. A couple of undergraduates at Oxford, Gray and Wedderburn (1960), demonstrated that subjects were quite successful in following a message that jumped back and forth between ears. Figure 3-5 illustrates the subjects' task in their experiment. Suppose that part of the meaningful message which subjects were to shadow was "dogs scratch fleas." The message to one ear might be "dogs six fleas," while the message to the other might be "eight scratch two." Instructed to shadow the meaningful message, subjects will report "dogs scratch fleas." Thus, subjects are capable of shadowing a message on the basis of meaning rather than physical ear.

Treisman (1960) looked at a situation in which subjects were instructed to shadow a particular ear. The result is illustrated in Figure 3-6. The message in the to-be-shadowed ear was meaningful until a certain point, at which it turned into a random sequence of words. Simultaneously, the meaningful message switched to the other ear—the one to which the subject had not been attending. Some subjects switched ears, against instructions, and continued to follow the meaningful message. Thus, it seems that messages from both ears get into sensory memory, and that subjects choose certain features for selecting what to attend to in sensory memory. If subjects use meaning as the criterion (either according to or in contradiction to instructions), they will switch ears to follow the message. If subjects use ear of origin in deciding what to attend to, they will shadow the proper ear. The conclusion is that a lot of informa-

Figure 3-5. An illustration of the shadowing task in the Gray and Wedderburn experiment. The subject follows the meaningful message as it moves from ear to ear. (Adapted from R. L. Klatzky, *Human memory*, 1st ed., W. H. Freeman and Company, copyright 1975.)

Figure 3-6. An illustration of the Treisman experiment. The meaningful message moves to the other ear, and the subject sometimes continues to shadow it against instructions. (Adapted from R. L. Klatzky, *Human memory*, 1st ed., W. H. Freeman and Company, copyright 1975.)

tion gets into sensory memory, but that only a small portion of it is attended to and only that portion is later remembered.

Automaticity

Recall that the capacity of attention for separate tasks is limited and must be divided up among competing processes. The amount of attention required by a process depends on how practiced that process is. The more a process has been practiced, the less attention it requires, and there is speculation that highly practiced processes require no attention at all. Such highly practiced processes that require little attention are referred to as *automatic.* Although it is probably more correct to think of automaticity as a matter of degree rather than as a well-defined category, it is useful to classify cognitive processes into two distinct types — *automatic processes*, which do not require attention, and *controlled processes*, which do (LaBerge & Samuels, 1974; Shiffrin & Schneider, 1977). Automatic processes complete themselves without conscious control by the subject. In the visual- and auditory-report tasks reviewed earlier, the registering of the stimuli in sensory memory is an automatic process. Many aspects of driving a car and comprehending language appear to be automatic. Controlled processing seems to require conscious control. In the report studies, reporting a row of items in the visual task or a spatial location in the auditory task is a controlled process. Many higher cognitive processes, such as performing mental arithmetic, are controlled.

A nice demonstration of the way practice affects attentional limitations is the study reported by Underwood (1974) on the psychologist Neville Moray, who has spent many years studying shadowing. In that time, Moray practiced shadowing a great deal. Unlike most subjects, he has a good ability to report what is contained in the nonattended channel. Through a great deal of practice, the process of shadowing has become partially automated, and Moray now has capacity left over to attend to the nonshadowed channel.

Schneider and Fisk (1982), Schneider and Shiffrin (1977), Shiffrin and Dumais (1981), and Shiffrin and Schneider (1977) performed a series of studies contrasting controlled processing with automatic processing. They addressed this issue in an experimental paradigm that requires subjects to scan visual arrays. Figure 3-7 illustrates the Schneider and Shiffrin paradigm. Subjects are given a target letter or number and are instructed to scan a series of visual displays for the target. The displays consist of 20 different frames flashed on a screen; subjects are to report if the target occurred in one of these frames. Two factors are varied. First,

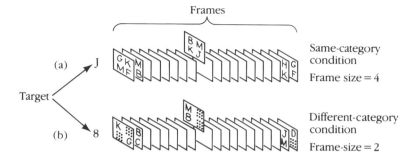

Figure 3-7. Two examples of positive trials in the Schneider and Shiffrin experiment: (a) the same-category condition, in which the target is a letter (J), as are the distractors; (b) the different-category condition, in which the target is a digit (8) and the distractors are letters. (Adapted from Schneider & Shiffrin, 1977. Copyright 1977 by the American Psychological Association. Reprinted by permission.)

each frame has one, two, or four characters on it. This factor is referred to as *frame size*. The other important variable is the relationship between the target item and the items on the frames. In the same-category condition the target is a letter, as were all items on the frames. In the different-category condition the target is always a number and all nontargets on the frames are letters. Thus, in the different-category condition, either one number appears on 1 of the 20 frames, in which case it is the target and the subject is to respond *yes*, or no number occurs on any of the frames, in which case the subject is to respond *no*.

As reported in Schneider and Shiffrin (1977), performance was strikingly different between the conditions. In the different-category condition subjects required an exposure of only 80 milliseconds per frame to achieve 95 percent accuracy, but in the same-category condition they needed 400 milliseconds per frame to achieve the same degree of accuracy. In the different-category condition the number of items per frame had little effect on performance, but in the same-category condition subjects' performance deteriorated dramatically as the number of items per frame increased.

Schneider and Shiffrin argue that before coming into the laboratory, subjects were so well practiced at detecting a number among letters that this process was automatic. In contrast, when subjects had to identify a letter among letters, controlled processing was needed. In this situation, subjects had to attend separately to each letter in each frame and compare it with the target. All these steps took time, and thus, subjects were able to inspect each frame properly and achieve respectable levels of performance only when the slides were presented slowly. Also, the more letters that were in a frame, the more slowly the frames had to be presented, since subjects had to check each letter in the frame separately. In contrast, subjects could check all items simultaneously in the different-category situation to see if any were numbers. They were able to perform this processing simultaneously because the detection process was automatic.

Schneider and Shiffrin's results in the same-category condition are similar to Sperling's study reviewed earlier. Just as Sperling found limitations on ability to report, so Schneider and Shiffrin found limitations on ability to detect letters among other letters. However, when the task was a letter-number discrimination, subjects were able to revert to an automatic process that was not limited as to capacity.

Shiffrin and Schneider (1977) ran another experiment similar to the one just described but in which the target always came from one set of letters (B, C, D, F, G, H, J, K, L) and the distractors always came from another set (Q, R, S, T, V, W, X, Y, Z). After 2100 trials, subjects were at the same levels of performance as in the different-category condition of the previous experiment. Thus, subjects need 2100 trials of practice before discriminating between two different sets of letters had become as automatic as discriminating numbers from letters. This result demonstrates that processes can become automatic with enough practice. When they do, devoting attention to them is no longer necessary and performance is no longer affected by the number of processes being performed simultaneously.

Pattern Recognition

Thus far we have considered how sensory information is first recorded and selected for processing by attentional mechanisms. We are now in a position to answer the critical question for a theory of perception: How is this information recognized for what it is? Much of this research has focused on the question of how we recognize the identity of letters. For instance, how do we recognize a presentation of the letter *A* as an instance of the pattern *A*?

Template-Matching Models

Perhaps the most obvious way to recognize a pattern is by means of template matching. The template-matching theory of perception assumes that a retinal image of an object is faithfully transmitted to the brain, and that an attempt is made to compare it directly to various stored patterns. These patterns are called *templates*. The basic idea is that the perceptual system tries to compare the letter to templates it has for each letter and reports the template that gives the best match. Figure 3-8 illustrates various attempts to make template matching work. In each case, an attempt is made to achieve a correspondence between the retinal cells stimulated by the *A* and the retinal cells specified for a template pattern.

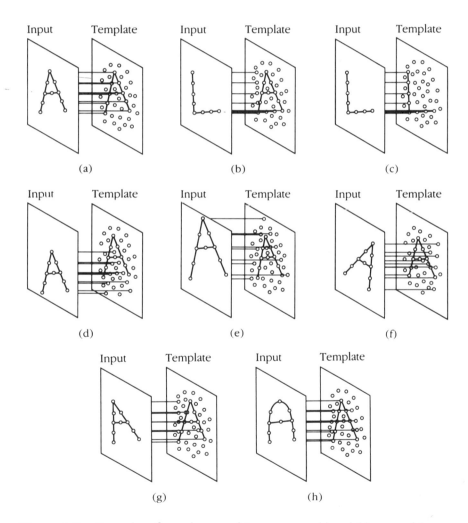

Figure 3-8. Examples of template-matching attempts: (a) and (c) successful template-matching attempts; (b) and (d)–(h) failed attempts. (Adapted from Neisser, 1967.)

Diagram (a) shows a case in which a correspondence is achieved and an *A* is recognized. The second diagram, (b), shows that no correspondence is reached between the input of an *L*, and the template pattern for an *A*. But *L* is matched in diagram (c) by the *L* template. However, things can go wrong very easily with a template. Diagram (d) shows a mismatch that occurs when the image falls on the wrong part of the retina, and diagram (e) shows the problem when the image is a wrong size. Diagram (f) shows what happens when the image is in a wrong orientation, and diagrams (g) and (h) show the difficulty when the images are nonstandard *A*'s. There is no known way to correct templates for all these problems.

A common example of template matching involves the account numbers printed on checks, which are read by check-sorting machines used by bank computers. Figure 3-9 shows my check blank (actually from a former account). The account number is the bottom line. A great deal of effort has gone into making the characters in this number maximally discernible. To assure standardization of size and position, they must be printed by machine; a check-sorter would not recognize hand-printed numbers. The very fact that a standardized system is needed for template matching to work reduces the credibility of this process as a model for human pattern recognition. In humans, pattern recognition is very flexible; we can recognize LARGE characters and small characters; characters in the wrong place; in strange o$^{r}_{i}$e^{n}t$_{a}$t$^{i}_{o}$ns; in unusual SHaPes; blurred or broken characters, and even, with some effort, ǝpᴉsdn uʍop characters.

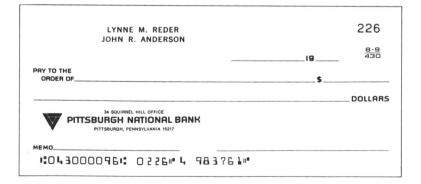

Figure 3-9. A typical blank check, with specially designed account numbers to permit successful template matching.

Feature Analysis

Partly because of the difficulties posed by template matching, psychologists have proposed that pattern recognition occurs through feature analysis. In this model, stimuli are thought of as combinations of elemental features. The features for the alphabet might consist of horizontal lines, vertical lines, lines at approximately 45° angles, and curves. Thus, the capital letter *A* can be seen as consisting of two lines at 45° angles (/ and \) and a horizontal line (—). The pattern for the letter *A* consists of these lines plus a specification as to how they should be combined. These features are very much like the output of edge and bar detectors in the visual cortex (discussed in Chapter 2).

You might wonder how feature analysis represents an advance beyond the template model. After all, what are the features but minitemplates? However, the feature model has a number of advantages over the template model. First, since the features are simpler, it is easier to see how the system might try to correct for the kinds of difficulties caused by template models. A second advantage of the feature-combination scheme is that it is possible to specify those relationships among the features that are most critical to the pattern. Thus, for *A* the critical point is that the two approximately 45° lines intersect (or almost intersect) at the top and that the cross bar intersects both of these. Many other details are unimportant. Thus, all the following patterns are *A*'s: A, *A, A,* A, *A.* A final advantage is that use of features rather than larger patterns will reduce the number of templates needed. In the feature model, we would not need a template for each possible pattern but only for each feature. Since the same features tend to occur in many patterns, this would mean a considerable savings.

There is a fair amount of behavioral evidence for the existence of features as components in pattern recognition. For instance, if letters have many features in common—as with *C* and *G*—evidence suggests that subjects are particularly prone to confuse them (Kinney, Marsetta, & Showman, 1966). When such letters are presented for very brief intervals, subjects often misclassify one stimulus as the other. So, for instance, subjects in the Kinney et al. experiment made 29 errors when presented with the letter G. Of these errors, 21 involved misclassification as *C*, 6 misclassification as *O*, 1 misclassification as *B*, and 1 misclassification as 9. No other errors occurred. It is clear that subjects were choosing items with similar feature sets as their responses. Such a response pattern is what we would expect if a feature-analysis model were used. If subjects could extract only some of the features in the brief presentation, they would not be able to decide among stimuli that shared these features.

Speech Recognition

Up to this point we have considered only the recognition of written characters. Recognition of a spoken message poses some new problems. One major problem is segmentation. Speech is not broken up into discrete units the way printed text is. Well-defined gaps seem to exist between words in speech, but often this is an illusion. If we examine the actual physical speech signal, we often find undiminished sound energy at word boundaries. Indeed, a cessation of speech energy is as likely to occur within a word as between words. This property of speech becomes clear when we listen to a foreign language that we do not know. The speech appears to be a continuous stream of sounds with no obvious word boundaries. It is our familiarity with our own language that leads to the illusion of word boundaries.

Even within a single word, segmentation problems exist. These intra-word problems involve the identification of *phonemes*. Phonemes are the basic vocabulary of speech sounds; it is in terms of them that we recognize words. A phoneme is defined as the minimal unit of speech that can result in a difference in the spoken message. To illustrate, consider the word *bat*. This word is analyzed into three phonemes: [b], [a], and [t]. Replacing [b] by the phoneme [p], we get *pat*; replacing [a] by [i] we get *bit*; replacing [t] by [n], we get *ban*. Obviously, a one-to-one correspondence does not always exist between letters and phonemes. For example, the word *one* consists of the phonemes [w], [ə], and [n], *school* consists of the phonemes [s], [k], [ú], and [l]; and *night* consists of [n], [ī], and [t]. It is the lack of perfect letter-to-sound correspondence that makes English spelling so difficult.

A segmentation problem arises when the phonemes composing a spoken word are to be identified. The difficulty is that speech is continuous, and phonemes are not discrete the way letters are on a printed page. Segmentation at this level is like recognizing a written (not printed) message, where one letter runs into another. Also, as in the case of writing, different speakers vary in the way they produce the same phonemes. The variation among speakers is dramatically clear, for instance, when a person first tries to understand a speaker with a strong and unfamiliar dialect—as when an American listener tries to understand an Australian speaker. However, examination of the speech signal will reveal that even among speakers with the same accent considerable variation exists. For instance, the voices of women and children normally have a much higher pitch than those of men.

Feature-analysis and feature-combination processes seem to underlie speech perception much as they do visual recognition. As with individual letters, individual phonemes can be analyzed as consisting of a number of features. It turns out that these features refer to aspects of how the phoneme is generated. Among the features for phonemes are the consonantal feature, voicing, and the place of articulation (Chomsky & Halle, 1968). *Consonantal* is the quality in the phoneme of having a consonant-like property (in contrast to vowels). *Voicing* is the sound of a phoneme produced by the vibration of the vocal cords. For example, compare the ways you produce *sip* and *zip*. The [s] in *sip* is voiceless but the [z] in *zip* is voiced. You can detect this difference by placing your fingers on your larynx as you generate these sounds. The larynx will vibrate for a voiced consonant.

Place of articulation refers to the place at which the vocal track is closed or constricted in the production of a phoneme. (It is closed at some point in the utterance of most consonants.) For instance [p], [m], and [w] are considered *bilabial* because the lips are closed during their generation. The phonemes [f] and [v] are considered *labiodental* because the bottom lip is pressed against the front teeth. Two different phonemes are represented by [th] — one in *thy* and the other in *thigh*. Both are *dental* because the tongue presses against the teeth. The phonemes [t], [d], [s], [z], [n], [l], and [r] are all *alveolar* bcause the tongue presses against the alveolar ridge of the gums just behind the upper front teeth. The phonemes [sh], [ch], [j], and [y] are all *palatal* because the tongue presses against the roof of the mouth just behind the alveolar ridge. The phonemes [k] and [g] are *velar* because the tongue presses against the soft palate, or velum, in the rear roof of the mouth.

Consider the phonemes [p], [b], [t], and [d]. All four share the feature of being consonants. However, the four can be distinguished according to voicing and place of articulation. Table 3-1 classifies these four consonants according to these two features.

Considerable evidence exists for the role of such features in speech perception. For instance, Miller and Nicely (1955) had subjects try to recognize consonants such as [b], [d], [p], and [t] when presented in noise.

Table 3-1 *The Classification of [b], [p], [d], and [t] According to Voicing and Place of Articulation*

Place of Articulation	Voicing	
	Voiced	Voiceless
Bilabial	[b]	[p]
Alveolar	[d]	[t]

Subjects exhibited confusion, thinking they had heard one sound in the noise when actually another sound had been presented. The experimenters were interested in what sounds subjects would confuse with what. It seemed likely that subjects would most often confuse consonants that were distinguished by just a single feature, and this prediction was confirmed. To illustrate, when presented with [p], subjects more often thought that they heard [t] than that they heard [d]. The phoneme [t] differs from [p] only in terms of place of articulation, whereas [d] differs in both place of articulation and voicing. Similarly, subjects presented with [b] more often thought they heard [p] than [t].

This experiment is an earlier demonstration of the kind of logic we saw in the Kinney, Marsetta, and Showman study on letter recognition. When the subject can identify only a subset of the features underlying a pattern (in this case the pattern is a phoneme), the subject's responses will reflect confusion among the phonemes sharing the same subset of features.

Voice-Onset Time

The features of phonemes refer to properties by which they are articulated. What are the properties of the acoustic stimulus that encodes these articulatory features? The issue has been particularly well researched in the case of voicing. In the pronunciation of such consonants as [b] and [p], two things happen: The closed lips are opened, releasing air, and the vocal cords begin vibrating (voicing). In the case of the voiced consonant [b], the release and the vibration of the vocal cords are nearly simultaneous. In the case of the unvoiced consonant [p], the release occurs 60 milliseconds before the vibration begins. What we are detecting when we perceive a voiced versus an unvoiced consonant is the presence or absence of a 60-millisecond interval between release and voicing. This period of time is referred to as *voice-onset time*. The difference between [p] and [b] is illustrated in Figure 3-10. Similar differences exist in other voiced-unvoiced pairs, such as [d] and [t]. Again, the factor controlling the perception of a phoneme is the delay between the release of closure and vibration of the vocal cords.

Lisker and Abramson (1970) performed experiments with artificial (computer-generated) stimuli in which the delay between release of closure and voicing was varied from −150 milliseconds (voicing 150 milliseconds before release) to +150 milliseconds (voicing 150 milliseconds after release). The task was to identify which sounds were [b]'s and which were [p]'s. Figure 3-11 plots the percentage of [b] identifications and [p] identifications. Throughout most of the continuum, subjects agreed 100

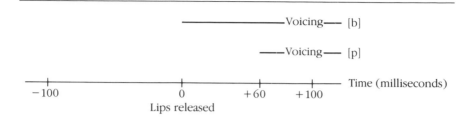

Figure 3-10. The difference between [b] and [p], the delay between the release of the lips and voicing in the case of [p]. (From *Psychology and language* by Herbert H. Clark and Eve E. Clark. Copyright 1977 by Harcourt Brace Jovanovich. Reproduced by permission of the publisher.)

percent on what they heard, but there is a sharp switch from [b] to [p] at about 25 milliseconds. At a 10-millisecond voice onset, subjects are in nearly unanimous agreement that the sound is a [b]; at 40 milliseconds they are in nearly unanimous agreement that the sound is a [p]. Because of this sharp boundary between the voiced and unvoiced phoneme, perception of this feature is referred to as *categorical*.

Other evidence for categorical perception of speech comes from discrimination studies (see Studdert-Kennedy, 1976, for a review). Subjects are very poor at discriminating between a pair of [b]'s or a pair of [p]'s that

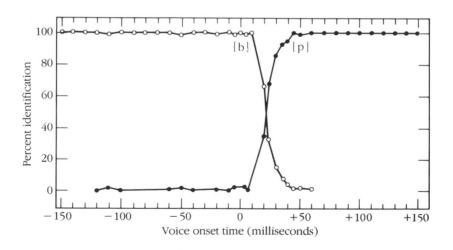

Figure 3-11. Percentage identification of [b] versus [p] as a function of voice-onset time. A sharp shift in these identification functions occurs at about 25 milliseconds. (From Lisker & Abramson, 1970.)

differ in voice-onset time. However, they are good at discriminating pairs that have the same difference in voice-onset time but where one is identified as a [b] and the other is identified as a [p]. It seems that subjects can only identify the phonemic category of a sound and are not able to make acoustic discriminations within that phonemic category. Thus, subjects are able to discriminate two sounds only if they fall on different sides of a phonemic boundary.

Another line of research showing evidence for such features in speech recognition involves an *adaptation paradigm*. Eimas and Corbit (1973) had their subjects listen to repeated presentations of *da*. This sound involves a voiced consonant, [d]. The experimenters reasoned that this constant repetition of the voiced consonant might fatigue, or *adapt*, the feature detector that responded to the presence of voicing. They then presented subjects with a series of artificial sounds that spanned the acoustic continuum — such as that between *ba* and *pa* (as in the Lisker and Abramson study mentioned earlier). Subjects had to indicate whether each of these artificial stimuli sounded more like *ba* or more like *pa*. (Remember, the only feature difference between *ba* and *pa* is voicing.) Eimas and Corbit found that some of the artificial stimuli which subjects would normally have called the voiced *ba* they now called the voiceless *pa*. Thus, the repeated presentation of *da* had fatigued the *voiced* feature detector and raised the threshold for detecting voicing in *ba*, making many former *ba* stimuli sound like *pa*.

Gestalt Principles of Organization

The preceding discussion of pattern recognition left open an important issue: When we recognize an *E* as made up of various vertical and horizontal bars, how did we decide to put those features together to recognize the pattern? Consider the four stimuli in Figure 3-12. Stimuli (a) and (c) are very easy to recognize because the letters are segmented by spaces. However, consider what happens when we run the letters together, as in (b) and (d). *BEAD* in (b) is still quite recognizable, whereas *FEEL* in (d) is extremely difficult to perceive.

Various principles determine how we segment an object into components. Only after the segmentation does perceptual pattern matching come into play. In Chapter 2 we discussed Marr's ideas for aggregating various lines and images into segments. Principles such as those he used for segmentation are very similar to what have been referred to as *Gestalt principles of perceptual organization*, after the Gestalt psychologists who documented many of them. Consider the various parts of Figure 3-13. In

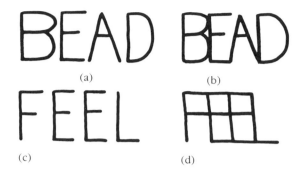

Figure 3-12. Illustrations of where Gestalt principles facilitate perceptual segmentation of letters and where they do not.

part (a) we perceive four pairs of lines rather than eight separate lines. This picture illustrates the principle of *proximity*: elements close together tend to organize into units. Part (b) illustrates the principle of *similarity*. Even though elements in a column are closer, we tend to see this array as five rows of alternating O's and X's. Objects that look alike tend to be grouped together. Part (c) illustrates the principle of *good continuation*. We

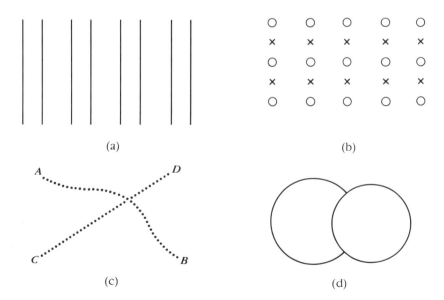

Figure 3-13. Illustrations of the Gestalt principles of organization: (a) the principle of proximity; (b) the principle of similarity; (c) the principle of good continuation; (d) the principle of closure.

perceive two lines, one from *A* to *B* and the other from *C* to *D*, although there is no reason why this sketch could not represent another pair of lines, one from *A* to *D* and the other from *C* to *B*. However, the line from *A* to *B* displays better continuation than the line from *A* to *D*, which has a sharp turn. Part (d) illustrates the principles of *closure* and *good form*. We see the drawing as one circle occluded by another, although the occluded object could have many other possible shapes.

These principles will tend to organize even completely novel stimuli into units. Palmer (1977) studied subjects' recognition of figures such as the ones in Figure 3-14. He first showed subjects stimuli such as (a) and then asked them to decide whether fragments (b)–(e) were part of the original figure. Stimuli (a) tends to organize itself into a triangle (closure) and a bent letter *n* (good continuation). Palmer found that subjects could recognize the parts most rapidly when they were the segments predicted by the Gestalt principles. So, stimuli (b) and (c) were recognized more rapidly than (d) and (e). Thus, we see that recognition depends critically on the initial segmentation of the figure. Recognition can be impaired when this Gestalt-based segmentation contradicts the actual pattern structure. FoRiNsTaNcEtHiSsEnTeNcEiShArDtOrEaD. The reasons for the difficulty are that the Gestalt principle of similarity is influencing you to perceive nonadjacent letters together, and that the proximity cues have been eliminated by removing the spaces between words.

Object Perception

So far we have focused on the perception of the linguistic stimuli of letters and sounds. The reason for the extensive research on these stimuli is that it is fairly easy to identify what the features might be that underlie

(a)   (b)   (c)   (d)   (e)

Figure 3-14. Examples of stimuli used by Palmer (1977) for studying segmentation of novel figures: (a) the original stimulus that subjects saw; (b)–(e) the subparts presented for recognition. Stimuli (b) and (c) are good subparts; (d) and (e) are bad subparts.

their recognition. We have reviewed the evidence that their recognition is mediated by first segmenting these stimuli into sets of features and then recognizing the feature combinations.

One of the exciting new developments in the field of perception is the increasing evidence that the same processes might underlie the recognition of such familiar categories of objects as horses or cups. The basic idea is that a familiar object can be seen as a known configuration of simple components. Figure 3-15 illustrates a proposal by Marr (1982) for how familiar objects can be seen as configurations of simple pipelike components. For instance, an ostrich has a horizontally oriented torso attached to two long legs and a long neck.

Biederman (1987) has proposed that there are three stages in our recognition of an object as a configuration of simpler components. First, the object is segmented into a set of basic subobjects. These subobjects are

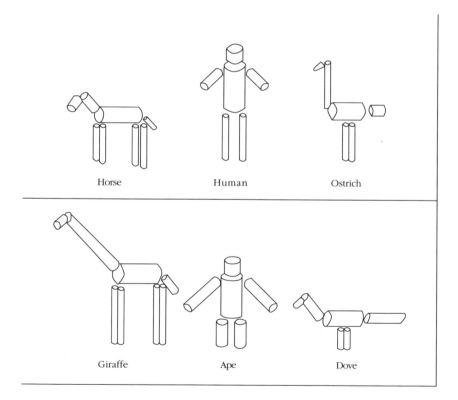

Horse Human Ostrich

Giraffe Ape Dove

Figure 3-15. Segmentation of some familiar objects into basic cylindrical shapes. (Adapted from Marr and Nishihara, 1978.)

defined by their line contours. In Chapter 2 we discussed some of the principles by which the visual system might extract lines and boundaries that define these subobjects. Hoffman and Richards (1985) argue that Gestalt-like principles can be used to segment an outline representation of an object into subobjects. Figure 3-16 illustrates their basic proposal. They observe that where one segment joins another there is typically a concavity in the line outline. Basically, people exploit the Gestalt principle of good continuation—the lines at the points of concavity are not good continuations of one another and so they do not group these parts together.

Second, once an object has been segmented into basic subobjects, one can classify the category of each subobject. Biederman (1987) argues that there are 36 basic categories of subobjects, which he calls *geons* (an abbreviation of "geometric ions"). Figure 3-17 shows some examples. We can think of the cylinder as being created by a circle as it is moved along a straight line (the axis) perpendicular to its center. We can gener-

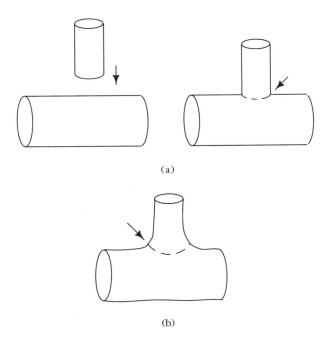

(a)

(b)

Figure 3-16. Segmentation of an object into subobjects: (a) when one piece of stovepipe is stuck into another, the joint between them, marked by a dotted line, is a concave crease. In general, such creases identify boundaries between parts; (b) in many cases the part boundary can be identified with a contour that follows points of maximum concave curvature. (Stillings, 1987. Based on Hoffman & Richards, 1985.)

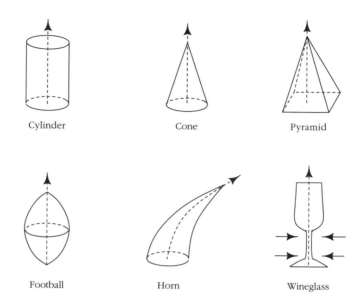

Cylinder Cone Pyramid

Football Horn Wineglass

Figure 3-17. Generalized cylinders. In each object the dashed line represents the central axis of the object. The objects can be described in terms of the movement of a cross-sectional shape along an axis. Cylinder: a circle moves along a straight axis. Cone: a circle contracts as it moves along a straight axis. Pyramid: a square contracts as it moves along a straight axis. American football: a circle expands and then contracts as it moves along a straight axis. Horn: a circle contracts as it moves along a curved axis. Wineglass: a circle contracts and then expands, creating concave segmentation points marked by arrows. (From Biederman, 1985.)

alize this basic cylinder shape to other shapes by varying some of the properties of its generation. We can change the shape of the object we are moving. If it is a rectangle rather than a circle that we move along the axis we get a block rather than a cylinder. We can curve the axis and get objects that curve. We can vary the size of the shape we are moving and get objects like the pyramid or wine glass. Altogether Biederman proposes there are some 36 geons that can be generated in this manner and that they serve as an alphabet for composing objects, much as letters or phonemes serve as the alphabet for building up words.

Third, having identified the pieces out of which the object is composed and their configuration, one recognizes the object as the pattern composed from these pieces. Thus, recognizing an object is like recognizing a letter; the subobjects become the features. As in the case of letter recognition there are many small variations on the underlying features or geons that should not be critical for recognition. For example, one need only determine whether an edge is straight or curved (in discriminating, say, a brick from a cylinder) or whether edges are parallel or not (in discriminating, say, a cylinder from a cone). It is not necessary to determine precisely how curved an edge might be.

Only edges are needed to define geons. Color, texture, and small detail should not matter. This predicts that schematic line drawings of complex objects which allow the basic geons to be identified should be recognized as quickly as detailed color photographs of the objects. Biederman and Ju (1988) confirmed that this is true—that is, schematic line drawings of objects like telephones provide all the information needed for quick and accurate recognition.

The critical assumption in this theory is that object recognition is mediated by recognition of the components of the object. Biederman, Beiring, Ju, and Blickle (1985) performed a test of this prediction with

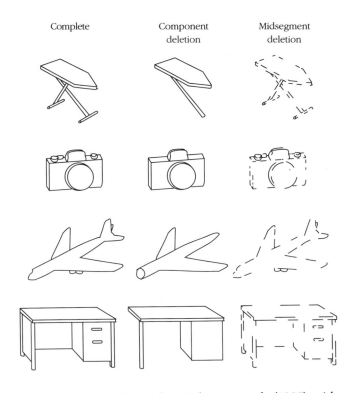

Figure 3-18. Sample stimuli used by Biederman et al. (1985) with equivalent proportion of contours removed either at midsegments or as whole components. (Copyright 1985 by the American Psychological Association. Adapted by permission.)

objects such as those in Figure 3-18. Some objects had whole components deleted while others had all the components present but segments of these components were deleted. They presented these two types of degraded figures to subjects for various brief intervals and asked them to identify the objects. The results are shown in Figure 3-19. At very brief presentations (65 or 100 milliseconds) subjects were more accurate at the recognition of figures with component deletion than segment deletion; this reversed for the longer 200 millisecond presentation. Biederman et al. reasoned that at the very brief intervals subjects were not able to identify the components with segment deletion and so had difficulty in recognizing the objects. With 200 millisecond exposure, however, subjects were able to recognize all the components in either condition. Since there were more components in the condition with segment deletion they had more information as to object identity.

Attention and Pattern Recognition

We have reviewed the evidence that pattern recognition is performed by recognizing combinations of primitive features. There is evidence that attention is required in order to combine the features to perceive the

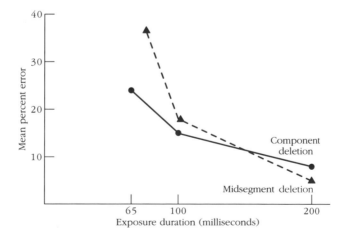

Figure 3-19. Results from Biederman et al. (1985): Mean percent errors of object naming as a function of the nature of contour removal (deletion of midsegments or components) and exposure duration. (Copyright 1985 by the American Psychological Association. Adapted by permission.)

73

pattern. One experiment demonstrating this was performed by Treisman and Gelade (1980). They had subjects try to detect a *T* in an array of 30 *I*'s and *Y*'s, such as in Figure 3-20(a). They reasoned that subjects could do this by simply looking for the cross-bar feature of the *T* that distinguishes it from all *I*'s and *Y*'s. Subjects took about 800 milliseconds to make this decision. Treisman and Gelade also asked subjects to detect a *T* in an array of *I*'s and *Z*'s, such as in Figure 3-20(b). In this condition, they could not use just the vertical bar or just the horizontal bar of the *T*; they would have to look for the conjunction of these features, performing the feature combination required in pattern recognition. It took subjects more than 1200 milliseconds to make their decision. Thus, a condition

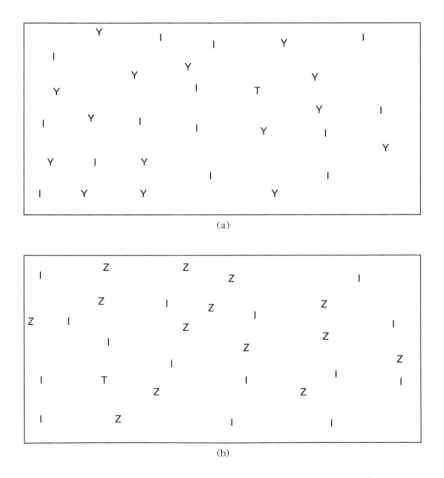

(a)

(b)

Figure 3-20. Stimuli used by Treisman and Gelade (1980). Subjects find it easier to detect a *T* in an array like (a) than in an array like (b).

requiring them to recognize the conjunction of features took about 400 milliseconds longer than one in which perception of a single feature was sufficient. Moreover, when Treisman and Gelade varied the size of the display they found that subjects were much more affected by display size in the condition that required recognition of the conjunction of features. Figure 3-21 shows these results. Subjects showed little difference between the single-feature and the conjunction condition for displays containing fewer than five letters. Only with displays presenting more distractors did subjects' attention become substantially overloaded.

It might seem surprising that attention is required to detect patterns of features that define common letters. We have the experience of automatically recognizing letters. It should be noted, however, that for familiar letters the deficit in perception of feature conjunctions only becomes apparent with large displays. Only then does the processing load get large enough to expose attention deficits.

Context and Pattern Recognition

Consider the example in Figure 3-22. We perceive these symbols as *THE CAT* even though the *H* and the *A* are identical. The general context provided by the words forces the appropriate interpretation. When con-

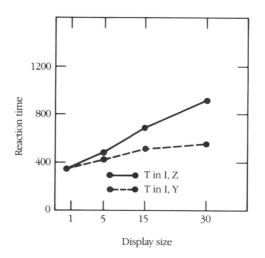

Figure 3-21. Results from Treisman and Gelade: Reaction time to detect a target as a function of number of distractors and whether the distractors contain separately all the features of the target. (Adapted from Treisman & Gelade, 1980.)

75

TAE CAT

Figure 3-22. A demonstration of context. The same stimulus is perceived as an *H* or an *A*, depending on the context. (From Selfridge, 1955.)

text or general world knowledge guides perception, we refer to the processing as *top-down* processing, because high-level general knowledge determines the interpretation of the low-level perceptual units.

One important line of research on top-down, or contextual, effects comes from a series of experiments on letter identification, starting with those of Reicher (1969) and Wheeler (1970). Subjects were given a very brief presentation of either a letter (such as *D*) or a word (such as *WORD*). Immediately afterward they were given a pair of alternatives and instructed to report which they had seen. (The initial presentation was sufficiently brief that subjects made a good many errors in this identification task.) If they had been shown *D*, subjects might be presented with *D* or *K* as alternatives. If they had been shown *WORD*, they might be given *WORD* or *WORK* as alternatives. Note that the two-word choices differ only in the *D* or *K* letter. Subjects were about 10 percent more accurate in the word condition. Thus, they more accurately discriminated between *D* and *K* in the context of a word than as letters alone, even though, in a sense, they had to process four times as many letters in the word context. This phenomenon is known as the *word superiority effect*.

Rumelhart and Siple (1974) have provided one explanation for why subjects are more accurate in the word condition. Suppose subjects are able to identify the first three letters as *WOR*. Now consider how many four-letter words are consistent with a *WOR* beginning: *WORD*, *WORK*, *WORM*, *WORN*, *WORT*. Suppose subjects only detect the bottom curve (⌣) in the fourth letter. In the *WOR* context, they know the stimulus must have been *WORD*. However, when the letter is presented alone and subjects detect the curve, they will not know whether the letter was *B, D, C, O,* or *Q*, since each of these letters is consistent with the curve feature. Thus, in the *WOR* context subjects need only detect one feature (e.g., the ⌣) in order to perceive the fourth letter, but when the letter is presented alone they must identify a number of features. Note that the Rumelhart and Siple analysis implies that perception is a highly inferential process. In the context of *WOR*, it is not that the subject sees the *D* better; rather the subject is better able to infer that *D* is the fourth letter. However, the subject is not conscious of these inferences; rather the subject is said to make *unconscious inferences* in the act of perception. Note in particular that the subject in this example does not have conscious access to the fact that the bottom curve (⌣) was detected or it would have been possible to choose between *D* and *K*. Rather the subject only has conscious access to the word or letter that the perceptual system has inferred.

This example illustrates the *redundancy* of many complex stimuli such as words. These stimuli consist of many more features than are required to distinguish one stimulus from another. Thus, perception can proceed successfully when only some of the features are recognized, with context filling in the remaining features. In language, this redundancy exists on many levels besides the feature level. For instance, redundancy occurs at the letter level. We do not need to perceive every letter in a string of words to be able to read it. To xllxstxatx, I cxn rxplxce xvexy txirx lextex of x sextexce xitx anx, anx yox stxll xan xanxge xo rxad xt—ix wixh sxme xifxicxltx. (This example is adapted from Lindsay & Norman, 1977.)

Figure 3-23 illustrates just a part of a pattern-recognition network that McClelland and Rumelhart (1981) have implemented to model our use of word structure to facilitate recognition of individual letters. In this model, individual features are combined to form letters and individual letters are combined to form words. This is a connectionist model like the one we discussed in Chapter 2; it depends heavily on excitatory and inhibitory activation processes. Activation spreads from the features to excite the letters and from the letters to excite the words. Alternative letters and words inhibit each other. Activation can also spread down from the words to excite the component letters. In this way a word can support the activation of a letter and hence promote its recognition.

In such a system, activation will tend to accumulate at one word and it will repress the activations of other words through inhibition. The dominant word will support the activation of its component letters, and these letters will repress activation of alternative letters. The word superiority effect is due to the support a word gives to its component letters. The computation proposed by McClelland and Rumelhart's interactive activation model is extremely complex, as is the computation of any model that simulates neural processing. However, they are able to reproduce many of the results on word recognition in their system. Their success encourages us in the belief that we are beginning to make some headway in understanding how neural processing underlies pattern recognition.

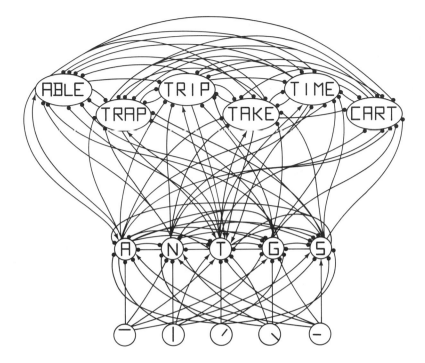

Figure 3-23. Part of the pattern-recognition network proposed by McClelland and Rumelhart (1981) to perform word recognition by performing calculations on neural activation values. Connections with arrowheads (→) indicate excitatory connections from the source to the head. Connections with rounded heads (——•) indicate inhibitory connections from the source to the head.

Effects of Sentence Context

Effects similar to the Reicher–Wheeler effect have been shown at the multiword level in an experiment by Tulving, Mandler, and Baumal (1964). The following are examples of the material they used:

Countries in the United Nations form a military *alliance.*

The political leader was challenged by a dangerous *opponent.*

A voter in municipal elections must be a local *resident.*

The huge slum was filled with dirt and *disorder.*

Each sentence provides an eight-word context preceding a critical word. Subjects were given either none, four, or eight of the context words and then shown the target word for a brief period. So, in the various conditions subjects would see the following:

0 context	disorder
4 context	*Filled with dirt and* disorder
8 context	*The huge slum was filled with dirt and* disorder

where the italicized words constitute the context first studied and *disorder* the critical word, presented after the context for a very brief period. The experimenters manipulated the duration of this critical word from 0 to 140 milliseconds. They were interested in how *bottom-up* information (manipulated by exposure duration) interacted with context (manipulated by number of words).

Figure 3-24 presents the results of the experiment. It can be seen that the probability of a correct identification increases both as the amount of context increases and as the exposure duration increases. Note that subjects benefit from context even in the 0-millisecond exposure condition, where they are clearly guessing. In this exposure condition, subjects are performing 16 percent better with an eight-word context than with a zero-word context. Note, however, that this benefit of context is larger with longer exposures—more than 40 percent at a 60-millisecond exposure and about 30 percent at the longest exposure, 140 milliseconds. (The effect diminishes somewhat between 60 and 140 milliseconds because subjects in the eight-word context condition are performing almost perfectly and show little benefit of further exposure, whereas subjects in the zero-word condition continue to benefit from the longer exposure.) These results indicate that subjects can take advantage of the context to improve their identification of the words. As was the case in the Reicher–Wheeler letter-identification paradigm, subjects are using the context to reduce the amount of perceptual information they need in order to identify the word.

The experiment by Tulving et al. shows that we can use sentence context to help identify words. With context we need to extract less information the word itself in order to identify it. In fact, we can use context to fill in words that did not even occur, as the previous sentence illustrates. Presumably, you were able to fill in the missing *from* as you read the sentence, and perhaps you did not even notice that it was missing. (This example is also adapted from Lindsay & Norman, 1977.)

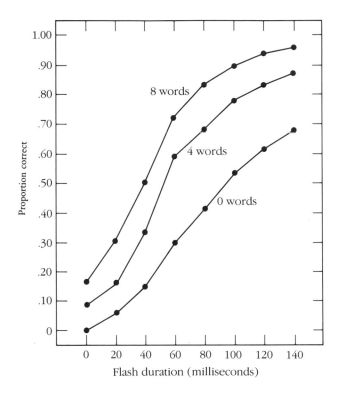

Figure 3-24. Percentage of correct identifications of word strings as a function of the duration of a string's exposure and the number of preceding context words. (From Tulving et al., 1964. Copyright 1964 by the Canadian Psychological Association. Reprinted by permission.)

Context and Speech

Equally good evidence exists for the role of context in the perception of speech. A nice illustration is the *phoneme-restoration effect*, demonstrated in an experiment by Warren (1970). He had subjects listen to the sentence "The state governors met with their respective legislatures convening in the capital city," with a 120-milliseconds pure tone replacing the middle *s* in *legislatures*. However, only 1 in 20 subjects reported hearing the pure tone, and that subject was not able to locate it correctly.

A nice extension of this first study is an experiment by Warren and Warren (1970). They presented subjects with sentences such as the following:

It was found that the *eel was on the axle.

It was found that the *eel was on the shoe.

It was found that the *eel was on the orange.

It was found that the *eel was on the table.

In each case, the * denotes a phoneme replaced by nonspeech. For the four sentences above, subjects reported hearing *wheel, heel, peel,* and *meal,* depending on context. The important feature to note about each of these sentences is that the sentences are identical through the critical word. The identification of the critical word is determined by what occurs after it. Thus, the identification of words is often not instantaneous but can depend on the perception of subsequent words.

Context and the Recognition of Faces and Scenes

So far, our discussion has focused on the role of context in the perception of printed and spoken material. When we process other highly over-learned patterns, such as faces, the same kind of interaction seems to take place between features and context that occurs with linguistic stimuli. Consider Figure 3-25, which is derived from work by Palmer (1975). He pointed out that in the context of a face, very little feature information is required for recognition of the individual parts, such as nose, eye, ear, or

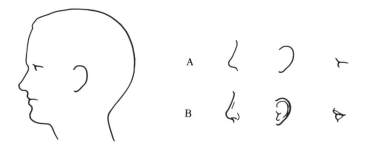

Figure 3-25. Facial features in the context of a face and out of context. Minimal information is necessary in context, but the same minimal features are not easily recognized in row A. More of the features' internal structure must be provided to permit recognition, as in row B. (Adapted from Palmer, 1975.)

(a)

(b)

Figure 3-26. Scenes used in the study by Biederman et al. (1973): (a) a coherent scene; (b) a jumbled scene. It is harder to recognize the fire hydrant in the jumbled scene. (From Biederman et al., 1973. Copyright 1973 by the American Psychological Association. Reprinted by permission.)

lips. In contrast, when these parts are presented in isolation, considerably more visual detail is required to permit their recognition.

Context also appears to be important for visual stimuli that are not highly overlearned patterns. Biederman, Glass, and Stacy (1973) have looked at perception of objects in novel scenes. Figure 3-26 illustrates the two kinds of scenes presented to their subjects. Part (a) of the figure is a normal scene, whereas in part (b) the same scene is jumbled. The scene was briefly presented to subjects on a screen, and immediately after the presentation an arrow was shown that pointed to a position where an object had been. Subjects were asked to identify the object that had been in that position in the scene. So, in the example scene, the object pointed to might have been the fire hydrant. Subjects were considerably more accurate in their identification with the coherent than with the jumbled pictures. Thus, as with their processing of written text or speech, subjects are able to recruit context in a visual scene to help their identification of an object.

Conclusions

An enormous amount of sensory information comes into our system every moment. The major problem facing the perceptual system is that it must, with only limited resources, process this great load of information in such a way that the environment makes sense. Unless sensory information is encoded quickly, it is very rapidly lost from iconic and echoic stores. The system utilizes various pattern recognizers and some basic Gestalt principles of organization to structure this sensory input. The pattern recognizers appear to combine both sensory features and contextual information in identifying familiar configurations.

Figure 3-27 is an attempt to sketch out this overall flow of information in an abstract way, combining ideas from this chapter and Chapter 2. Perception begins with energy, such as light or sound, from the external environment. Receptors, such as those on the retina, transform this energy to neural information. Early sensory processing is concerned with making initial sense of the information. The output of this system is a feature description of the stimulus and some segmentation of the stimulus into units or bundles. The Gestalt principles have already operated in producing this initial segmentation. This representation of the stimulus as bundles of features is what resides in the iconic and echoic memories. The various pattern recognizers attempt to identify these feature bundles. This process of pattern recognition is attention demanding, especially

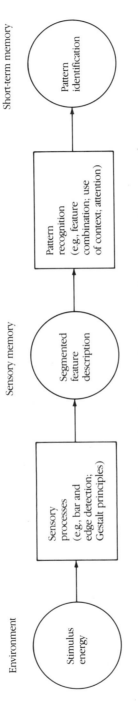

Figure 3-27. The flow of information from the environment to its perceptual representation. The information indicated in the circles is operated upon by the sensory and perceptual processes indicated in the boxes.

when the patterns are unfamiliar. Context has a strong impact on this recognition process.

Remarks and Suggested Readings

The topics covered in this chapter are easily expanded into a full course; most colleges offer at least one course on this material. Such courses focus particularly on what is known about the elemental sensory processes. A fair amount of physiological evidence is available about these processes, and direct connections can be made between physiology and psychological experience. (We reviewed a small amount of that evidence in Chapter 2.) Among the standard texts providing extensive surveys of the research on sensation and perception are those of Rock (1984), Sekuler and Blake (1985), and Goldstein (1989).

James Gibson (e.g., 1950, 1966, 1979) has developed a very influential theory of perception, quite different from the one presented here. Ideas from this theory are beginning to appear in analyses of other higher-level cognitive phenomena. For instance, Turvey and Shaw (1977), in their analysis of human memory, have been strongly influenced by Gibson. Neisser (1976) presents a view of perception, attention, and cognition that also shows the influence of Gibson.

A number of texts dealing with human information processing provide somewhat different, and also often more extensive, discussions of perception and attention. You should not think that the model of attention presented here is the only one in cognitive psychology. For discussions of a number of alternative attention models, read Massaro (1975) and Norman (1976). Other texts on attention and perception include those of Klatzky (1979), Lindsay and Norman (1977), Rumelhart (1977), and Wickelgren (1979).

The book by Spoehr and Lehmkuhle (1982) is a good discussion of many aspects of visual information processing. That by Clark and Clark (1977) contains good discussions of speech generation and perception. Very current research can be found in an annual series titled *Attention and Performance*. Another set of readings on attention is Parasuraman and Davies (1984). For information on attempts at making computers see, read Ballard and Brown (1982) and Marr (1982).

Perception-Based Knowledge Representations

Summary

1. Perception-based knowledge representations store memories of the perceptual structure of events and appear to be processed in neural regions close to where the original perceptions were processed.

2. Two types of perception-based knowledge representations are images that encode the spatial structure of items and linear orderings that encode the sequence of items.

3. When asked to perform a mental transformation on an image, such as rotating it 180°, subjects imagine the image moving through the intermediate states in the transformation. The greater the transformation that must be performed, the longer subjects take to perform it.

4. When subjects are asked to compare two mental objects with regard to a dimension such as magnitude, they engage in a process similar to that of comparing two physically presented objects.

5. There appear to be two types of mental imagery—one that preserves visual detail and one, not tied to the visual modality, that encodes spatial relationships.

6. Both spatial images and linear orderings have a hierarchical organization in which subimages or sublists can occur as elements in larger images or lists.

7. Subjects have more rapid access to the first and last elements of a linear ordering, and they tend to search linear orderings from beginning to end. They can more rapidly judge the order of elements in a linear ordering the farther the elements are apart.

This chapter and the next will be concerned with the different ways in which information is represented in memory. Chapter 3 discussed the evidence for sensory memories—repositories that can store sensory representations for a few seconds at most. Beyond the first few seconds, information must be transformed, or encoded, into more permanent representations. Some of these permanent representations tend to preserve much of the structure of the original perceptual experience. Others, however, are quite abstracted from the perceptual details and encode the meaning of the experience. This chapter will focus on perception-based representations; Chapter 5 will focus on meaning-based representations.

In this chapter we will consider two types of knowledge representation—images and linear orderings—that partially preserve the structure of perceptions. Images preserve information about the position of objects in space and other visual properties of objects. Linear orderings preserve information about the sequence of events, such as the order of words in a sentence. A linear ordering represents events by organizing them sequentially, like beads on a string.

A famous theory in cognitive psychology, called the *dual-code theory* (Bower, 1972; Paivio, 1971), is concerned with a spatial and a linear knowledge representation. The dual-code theory ties the spatial code to the visual modality and the linear code to the verbal modality. The dual-code theory has proven to be quite controversial in the connections it makes between these two representations and two modalities. We will discuss the evidence, pro and con, for the connection of these knowledge representations to particular sensory modalities.

Spatial versus Linear Representations

An experiment by Santa (1977) nicely illustrates the difference between spatial and linear representations. The two conditions of Santa's experiment are illustrated in Figure 4-1. In the geometric condition, subjects

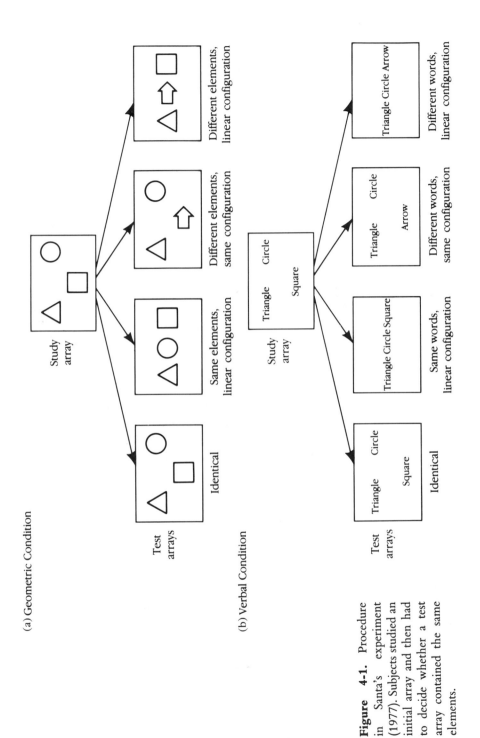

Figure 4-1. Procedure in Santa's experiment (1977). Subjects studied an initial array and then had to decide whether a test array contained the same elements.

studied a spatial array of three geometric objects, two geometric objects above and one below. As the figure shows, this array had a facelike property—without much effort we can see eyes and a mouth. After subjects studied it, this array was removed and subjects were immediately presented with one of a number of test arrays. The subjects' task was to verify that the test array contained the same elements, although not necessarily in the same spatial configuration, as the study array. Thus, subjects should respond positively to the first two test arrays and negatively to the other two arrays. Interest was focused on the contrast between the two positive test arrays. The first array is identical to the study array, but in the second array the elements are arrayed linearly. Santa predicted that subjects would make a positive judgment more quickly in the first case, where the configuration was identical, since, he hypothesized, the visual memory for the study stimulus would preserve spatial information. The results for the geometric condition are displayed in Figure 4-2. As can be seen, Santa's predictions were confirmed. Subjects were faster when the geometric test array preserved the configuration information in the study array.

The results from the geometric condition are more impressive when they are contrasted with the results from the verbal condition, illustrated in Figure 4-1(b). Here subjects studied words arranged in spatial configurations identical with geometric objects in the geometric condition. However, because it involved words, the study stimulus did not suggest a face or have any pictorial properties. Santa speculated that subjects would encode the word array according to normal reading order—that is, left to right and top to bottom. So, given the study array, subjects would encode

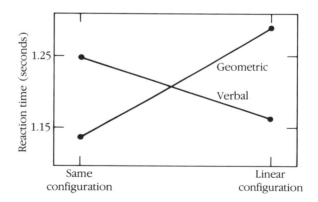

Figure 4-2. Reaction times for Santa's experiment (1977), showing an interaction between type of material and test configuration.

it "triangle, circle, square." Following the study one of the test arrays was presented. Subjects had to judge whether the words were identical. All the test stimuli involved words, but otherwise they presented the same possibilities as the tests in the geometric condition. In particular, the two positive stimuli exhibited the same configuration and a linear configuration, respectively. Note that the order of words in the linear array is the same as that in which Santa predicted subjects would encode the study stimulus. Santa predicted that, since subjects had encoded the words linearly from the study array, they would be fastest when the test array was linear. As Figure 4-2 illustrates, his predictions were again confirmed. The verbal and the geometric conditions display a sharp interaction.

In conclusion, Santa's experiment indicates that some information, such as geometric objects, tends to be stored according to spatial position, whereas other information, such as words, tends to be stored according to linear order.

A very different sort of data for the difference between spatial and linear representations comes from the research of Roland and Friberg (1985). They had subjects either mentally rehearse a word jingle or mentally rehearse finding their way from their house and around streets in their neighborhood. Then, as in the research of Posner et al. (1988), described in Chapter 2, Roland and Friberg measured changes in blood

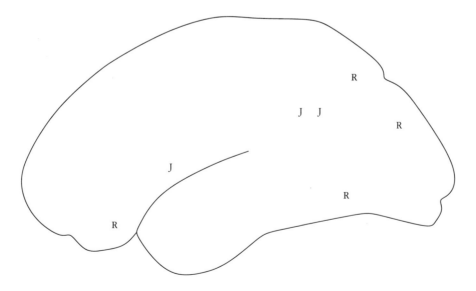

Figure 4-3. Results from Roland and Friberg (1985) showing regions of the left cortex with increased blood flow when imagining a verbal jingle (*J*) and when imagining a spatial route (*R*).

flow in various parts of the cortex. Figure 4-3 shows the regions of the left cortex that were activated by one mental process versus the other. *R*'s indicate areas with increased activity in the spatial route task while *J*'s indicate areas with increased activity during the verbal jingle task. It is apparent that different neural regions are involved when we process verbal versus spatial information. Moreover, these appear to be the regions that are involved in the actual processing of spoken and seen (rather than imagined) material. The occipital and temporal areas involved in the route-finding task are the same areas involved in vision. Among the areas involved in the jingle task is Broca's area, which, as we saw in Chapter 2, has a major role in the processing of speech. This would seem evidence for tying the two representations to the two modalities, as Paivio's dual-code hypothesis claimed. However, as we will see shortly, the situation is considerably more complicated with respect to the issue of whether imagery is really tied to the visual modality or not. (There is not yet much research on whether linear representations are really tied to the verbal modality.)

Mental Imagery

Many times when we are thinking about a scene or an object no longer present, we experience an image of that scene or object. People often refer to this as "seeing in their mind." There has been a great deal of research during the last 25 years on the nature of the knowledge representations that underlie such mental imagery. These representations are typically referred to as *mental images*. Much of this research has been concerned with the types of mental processes that can be performed on spatial images.

Mental Rotation

Among the most influential research on mental images is the long series of experiments on mental rotation performed by Roger Shepard and his colleagues. The first experiment was that of Shepard and Metzler (1971). Subjects were presented with pairs of two-dimensional representations of three-dimensional objects like those in Figure 4-4. Their task was to determine if the objects were identical except for orientation. The two figures in parts (a) and (b) are identical; they are just presented at different orientations. Subjects report that to match the two shapes they rotated one of the objects in each pair mentally until it was congruent with the other object. Part (c) is a foil pair: There is no way of rotating one object so that it is identical with the other.

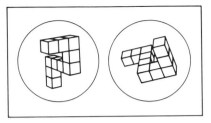

(a)

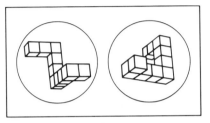

(b)

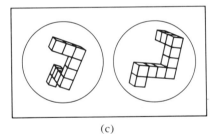

(c)

Figure 4-4. Stimuli in the Shepard and Metzler study on mental rotation (1971): (a) the objects differ by an 80° rotation in the picture plane; (b) the objects differ by an 80° rotation in depth; (c) the pair cannot be rotated into congruence. (From Metzler & Shepard, 1974.)

The graphs in Figure 4-5 show the time required for subjects to decide that the members of pairs such as those in Figure 4-4(a) and (b) were identical. The reaction times are plotted as a function of the angular disparity between the two objects presented to the subject. This angular disparity represents the amount one object would have to be rotated in order to match the other object in orientation. Note that the relationship is linear—for every equal increment in amount of rotation, an equal increment in reaction time is required. Reaction time is plotted for two different kinds of rotation. One is for two-dimensional rotations (Figure 4-4a), which can be performed in the picture plane (i.e., by rotating the page). The other is for depth rotations (Figure 4-4b), which require the

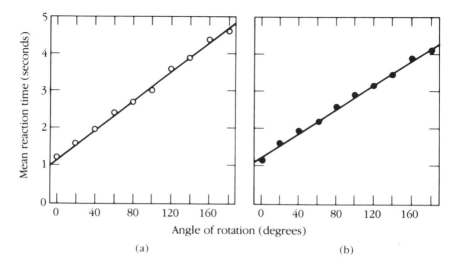

Figure 4-5. Mean time to determine that two objects have the same three-dimensional shape as a function of the angular difference in their portrayed orientations. (a) Plot for pairs differing by a rotation in the picture plane. (b) Plot for pairs differing by a rotation in depth. (From Metzler & Shepard, 1974.)

subject to rotate the object *into* the page. Note that the two functions are very similar. Processing an object in depth (in three dimensions) does not appear to take longer than processing in the picture plane. Hence, subjects must be operating on three-dimensional representations of the objects in both the picture-plane condition and the depth condition.

These data might seem to indicate that subjects rotate the object in a three-dimensional space within their heads. The greater the angle of disparity between the two objects, the longer subjects take to complete the rotation. Of course, subjects are not actually rotating an object in their heads. However, whatever the actual mental process is, it appears to be analogous to physical rotation.

Image Scanning

Researchers have looked at a number of other tasks which seem to show that when subjects are performing certain mental computations they are operating on a visual image the way a person might perform continuous operations on a physical object. An experiment by Kosslyn, Ball, and Reiser (1978) shows that it takes time to scan between two locations on a mental image. These investigators presented subjects with a map of a fictitious island (see Figure 4-6) containing a hut, a tree, a rock, a well, a lake, sand, and grass. Subjects were trained on this map until they could draw it with great accuracy. Then an object was named aloud and subjects were asked to picture the map mentally and focus on the object named. Five seconds later, a second object was named. Subjects were instructed to scan the map for this second object and to press a button when they had mentally focused on it.

Figure 4-7 presents the times subjects needed to perform this mental operation as a function of the distance between the two objects in the original map. There are 21 possible pairs of points, and each point is represented. The abscissa gives the distance between each pair. The farther apart the two objects were, the greater was the reaction time. Clearly, subjects did not have the actual map in their heads and therefore were not moving from one location in their heads to a second location.

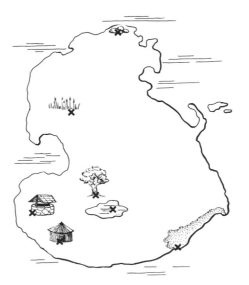

Figure 4-6. The fictitious map used by Kosslyn et al. (1978) to determine differences in processing time relative to the distance between images to be recalled. Subjects had to commit this map to memory and then mentally scan from point to point in the map. (Copyright 1978 by the American Psychological Association. Reprinted by permission.)

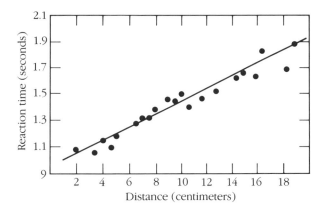

Figure 4-7. Time to scan between two points in Figure 4-6 as a function of the distance between the points. (From Kosslyn et al., 1978. Copyright 1978 by the American Psychological Association. Reprinted by permission.)

However, they were going through a process analogous to this physical operation.

Both the Shepard and Metzler and Kosslyn et al. experiments make the same point: When people operate on mental images they appear to go through a process analogous to actually operating on a physical object. In both the case of rotation and scanning, we saw that the time needed to perform the mental operation increased with the amount of time needed to perform the analogous physical operation. These findings leave open the issue of how close the similarity is between a mental image and a physical object. The next set of studies that we will review is concerned with whether mental images are tied to the visual modality.

Interference and Image Scanning

Brooks (1968) performed an important series of experiments on the scanning of visual images. He had subjects scan imagined diagrams such as the one in Figure 4-8. For example, the subject was to scan around an imagined block *F* from a prescribed starting point and in a prescribed direction, categorizing each corner as a point in the extreme top or bottom (assigned a yes response) or as a point in between (assigned a no response). In the example, the correct sequence of responses is yes, yes, yes, no, no, no, no, no, no, yes. For a nonvisual contrast task, Brooks also

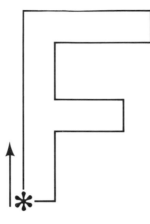

Figure 4-8. An example of a simple block diagram used by Brooks (1968) to study the scanning of mental images. The asterisk and arrow showed the subject the starting point and the direction for scanning the image. (Copyright 1968 by the Canadian Psychological Association. Reprinted by permission.)

gave subjects sentences such as *A bird in the hand is not in the bush*. Subjects had to scan through such a sentence while holding it in memory, classifying each word as a noun or not. A second experimental variable was how subjects made their responses. Subjects either (1) said yes and no; (2) tapped with the left hand for yes and the right hand for no; or (3) pointed to successive *Y*'s or *N*'s on a sheet such as that in Figure 4-9. The two variables of stimulus material (diagram or sentence) and output mode were crossed to yield six conditions.

Table 4-1 gives the results of Brooks's experiment in terms of the mean time spent in classifying the sentences or diagrams in each output condition. The important result for our purposes is that subjects took much longer for diagrams in the pointing condition than in any other condition. This was not the case for sentences. Apparently, scanning a sheet like the one in Figure 4-9 conflicted with scanning a mental array. Thus, this result strongly reinforces the conclusion that when subjects are scanning a mental array, they are scanning a representation that is analogous to physical aray. Requiring the subject to simultaneously engage in a conflicting scanning action on an external physical array causes great interference to the mental scan.

It is sometimes thought that Brooks's result was due to the conflict between engaging in a visual pointing task and scanning a visual image. However, subsequent results make it clear that the interference is not due to the visual character of the task. Rather, the problem is more abstract,

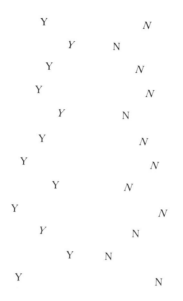

Figure 4-9. A sample output sheet for the pointing condition in Brooks (1968) for mental image scanning. The letters are staggered to force careful visual monitoring of pointing. (Copyright 1968 by the Canadian Psychological Association. Reprinted by permission.)

arising from the conflicting directions in which subjects had to scan the physical array versus the mental image. For instance, in another experiment, Brooks found evidence of similar interference when subjects had their eyes closed and indicated yes and no by scanning an array of raised *Y*'s and *N*'s, as in Figure 4-9, with their fingers. In this case the actual stimuli were tactile, not visual. Thus, the conflict is *spatial*, not visual per se.

Baddeley and Lieberman (reported in Baddeley, 1976) performed an experiment that strongly supports the view that the nature of the inter-

Table 4-1 *Mean Classification Times in Brooks, 1968 (Seconds)*

Stimulus Material	Output		
	Pointing	Tapping	Vocal
Diagrams	28.2	14.1	11.3
Sentences	9.8	7.8	13.8

ference in the Brooks task is spatial rather than visual. Subjects were required to perform two tasks simultaneously. All subjects performed the Brooks letter-image task. However, subjects in one group simultaneously monitored a series of stimuli of two possible brightnesses. Subjects had to press a key whenever the brighter stimulus appeared. This task involved the processing of visual but not spatial information. Subjects in the other condition were blindfolded and seated in front of a swinging pendulum. The pendulum emitted a tone and contained a photocell. Subjects were instructed to try to keep the beam of a flashlight on the swinging pendulum. Whenever they were on target, the photocell caused the tone to change frequency, thus providing auditory feedback. This test involved the processing of spatial but not visual information. The spatial-auditory tracking task produced far greater impairment in the image-scanning task than did the brightness-judgment task. This result also indicates that the nature of the impairment in the Brooks task was spatial, not visual. These results reinforce the conclusion that an image is an abstract analog of a spatial structure.

Two Types of Imagery

Research such as that just reviewed lends support to the view that imagery is spatial but not visual in character. Recently, however, Farah, Hammond, Levine, and Calvanio (1988) have made the suggestion that there might be two kinds of imagery, one that involves visual properties and one that involves spatial properties. In Chapter 2 we noted that tasks which involved recognition of visual objects and patterns seemed to be performed in the temporal lobe while visual or tactile tasks that involved the location of objects tended to be performed in the parietal lobe. Farah et al. argue that these same cortical regions are used in imagery tasks that do not involve any external stimuli. They argue that imagery tasks which involve spatial judgments will be performed in the parietal region and will not show modality-specific effects. In contrast, imagery tasks that require access to visual details will be performed in the temporal region and will show modality-specific effects.

Farah et al. provide some supportive data that was collected from a subject who had suffered bilateral temporal damage. They compared his performance on a wide variety of imagery tasks to that of normal subjects. They found that he had problems only on a subset of these tasks: tasks where he had to make judgments about color (what is the color of a football?), where he had to judge sizes (which is bigger, a popsicle or a pack of cigarettes?), where he had to judge lengths of animals' tails (does a kangaroo have a long tail?), and where he had to judge whether two states in the United States had similar shapes. In contrast, he did not show any deficit on tasks that seemed to involve a substantial amount of spatial processing—mental rotation, image scanning, letter scanning (as in Figure 4-9), or judgments of where one state was relative to another state. Thus, temporal damage seemed only to affect those image tasks that required access to visual detail and not those that required spatial judgments. It would seem that spatial information can be represented in a modality-free way during imagery but that we have a separate imagery system which comes into play when we have to process distinctly visual information.

Comparisons of Visual Quantities

There has been a fair amount of research concerned with how subjects judge the visual details of objects in their mental images. One line of research has asked subjects to discriminate between objects on some dimensions such as size. This research has shown that, when subjects try to discriminate between two objects, their time to make this discrimination decreases continuously with the amount of difference between the two objects.

An experiment illustrating this result was performed by Moyer (1973). He was interested in the speed with which subjects could judge the relative size of two animals from memory. For example, *Which is larger, moose or roach?* and *Which is larger, wolf or lion?* Many people report that in making these judgments, particularly for the items that are similar in size, they experience images of the two objects and seem to compare the size of the objects in their image.

Moyer also asked subjects to estimate the absolute size of these animals. He plotted the reaction time for making a mental-size-comparison judgment between two animals as a function of the difference between the two animals' estimated sizes. Figure 4-10 reproduces these data. The individual points represent comparisons between pairs of items. In general, the judgment times decrease as the difference in estimated size increases. The graph shows that a fairly linear relation exists between the scale on the abscissa and the scale on the ordinate. Note, however, that on the abscissa the differences have been plotted logarithmically. (A log-difference scale makes variations among small differences large relative to

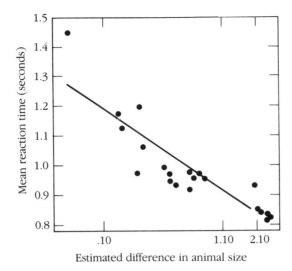

Figure 4-10. Results from Moyer (1973): Mean time to judge which of two animals is larger as a function of the estimated difference in size of the two animals. The difference measure is plotted on the abscissa in a logarithmic scale.

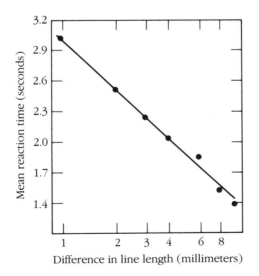

Figure 4-11. Results from Johnson (1939): Mean time to judge which of two lines is longer as a function of the difference in line length. The difference measure is plotted on the abscissa in a logarithmic scale.

the same variations among large differences.) Thus, the linear relationship in the figure means that increasing the size difference has a diminishing effect on reaction time.

Significantly, very similar results are obtained when subjects make comparisons of actual physical magnitudes. For instance, Johnson (1939) had subjects judge which of two simultaneously presented lines were longer. Figure 4-11 plots subject judgment time as a function of the log difference in line length. Again a linear relation is obtained. It is reasonable to expect perceptual judgments to take longer the more similar the quantities being compared are, since discriminating accurately is more difficult in such circumstances. The fact that similar functions are obtained when mental objects are compared indicates that making mental comparisons involves difficulties of discrimination similar to those involved in perceptual comparisons.

Hierarchical Structure of Images

Complex mental images tend to be organized into pieces where each piece represents part of the whole structure. Consider Figure 4-12(a), which illustrates this point. Reed presented subjects with such forms and asked them to hold images of the forms in their minds (Reed, 1974; Reed & Johnsen, 1975). The form was removed and subjects were presented with parts of the form, as in (b–d). Subjects were able to identify forms (b) and (c) as parts of form (a) 65 percent of the time but were successful with form (d) only 10 percent of the time. The reason for the difference was that subjects' image of form (a) consisted of parts such as forms (b)

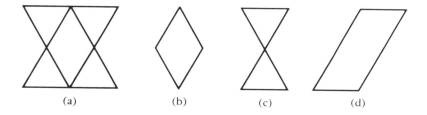

(a) (b) (c) (d)

Figure 4-12. Forms used by Reed in his studies concerning the components of images. Forms (b), (c) and (d) are all contained in form (a). However, subjects appear to see forms (b) and (c) as part of form (a) more easily than they can see form (d) as part of form (a). (From Reed, 1974.)

and (c) but not form (d). A picture would not show this property. All parts of form (a) would be equally represented in a physical picture. A physical picture is just ink on paper; the ink does not know which portions go together—that segmentation is in the mind of the perceiver. The human perceiver creates a mental image that is segmented. One of the serious problems in artificial-intelligence efforts to get computers to see is similarly going from raw pictures to such segmented images.

Complex images can be formed from a hierarchy of units. For instance, consider a schematic image of a house such as the one illustrated in Figure 4-13. At one level, it consists of a square and a triangle. However, the images of the squares and angles themselves consist of units—namely, lines. The term *chunk* is frequently used in cognitive psychology to refer to a unit like the triangle (e.g., Miller, 1956; Simon, 1974). At one level a chunk combines a number of primitive units. At another level it is a basic unit in a larger structure.

Mental Maps

Subjects' memory for maps appears to have the hierarchical structure associated with spatial images. Consider your mental map of the map of the United States. It is probably divided into regions, and these regions

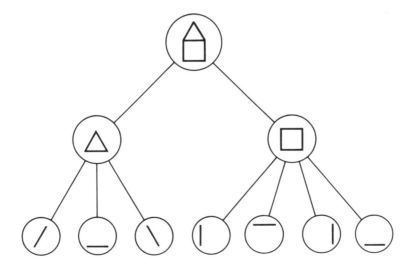

Figure 4-13. The house figure has a hierarchical representation.

into states, and cities are presumably pinpointed within the states. It turns out that certain systematic distortions arise because of the hierarchical structure of these mental maps. Stevens and Coupe (1978) documented a set of misconceptions people have about North American geography. Consider the following questions taken from their research:

Which is farther east: San Diego or Reno?

Which is farther north: Seattle or Montreal?

Which is farther west: The Atlantic or the Pacific entrance to the Panama Canal?

The first choice is the correct answer in each case, but most people hold the wrong opinion. Reno seems to be farther east because Nevada is east of California, but this reasoning does not account for the curve in California's coastline. Montreal seems to be north of Seattle, since Canada is north of the United States, but the border dips in the east. And the Atlantic is certainly east of the Pacific, but consult a map if you need to be convinced about the Panama Canal. The geography of North America is quite complex, and subjects resort to abstract facts about relative locations of large physical bodies (e.g., California and Nevada) to make judgments about smaller locations (e.g., San Diego and Reno).

Stevens and Coupe were able to demonstrate such confusions with experimenter-created maps. Figure 4-14 illustrates the maps that different groups of subjects learned. The important feature of the incongruent maps is that the relative location of the Alpha and Beta counties is inconsistent with the X and Y cities. After learning the maps, subjects were asked a series of questions about the locations of cities, including *Is X east or west of Y?* for the left-hand maps, and *Is X north or south of Y?* for the right-hand maps.

Subjects were in error 18 percent of the time on the $X-Y$ question for the congruent maps and 15 percent for the homogeneous maps, but they were in error 45 percent of the time for the incongruent maps. Subjects were using information about the location of the counties to help them remember the city locations. This reliance on "higher order" information led them to make errors, just as similar reasoning can lead to errors in questions about North American geography.

An image may not be a picture but the distinctions between them can be frustratingly subtle. Like pictures, images are capable of representing continuously varying quantities, such as size. We can perform operations on images, such as scanning, which we also can on pictures. However, it appears that there may be two image systems—one that contains the

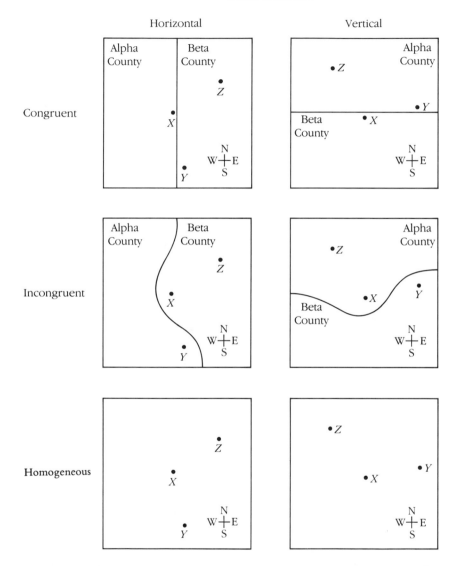

Figure 4-14. Maps studied by subjects in the experiments of Stevens and Coupe (1978), which demonstrated the effects of "higher order" information (location of county lines) on subjects' recall of city locations.

continuously varying information and one that contains the spatial information. Only the continuously varying information seems tied to the visual modality. The spatial information appears modality independent. Finally, images appear to have a hierarchical structure that pictures per se do not (although our perception of pictures may well also see the discussion in Chapter 3).

Linear Orderings

Another kind of representational structure encodes the linear order of a set of elements. Most of the research on linear representations has used a memory paradigm of one sort or another. Subjects commit or try to commit to memory elements in a fixed order. By looking at subjects' ability to access this information, it is possible to make inferences about the structure of that information in memory. Consider an experiment from my laboratory: We had subjects learn sequences of four consonants. So, subjects might learn the consonant string *KRTB*. They also learned to associate a digit to the consonant string. Thus, they might learn that 7 is the digit associated to *KRTB*. After this learning phase, they were presented with four consonants, and they had to recall the digit associated to the consonants. We were interested in how fast they could make their recall, which we interpreted as a measure of how long it took to recognize the consonant string. The major experimental manipulation involved the order in which the four consonants were presented. They were not always presented in the order in which they had been studied. For instance, subjects had to recognize *RTKB* as a variation of the string *KRTB* that they had studied. Below are some of the orders that were tested and reaction times for these orders:

(a) identical *KRTB*	1.55 seconds
(b) same first two letters: *KRBT*	1.55 seconds
(c) same first letter: *KTBR*	1.59 seconds
(d) same last two letters: *RKTB*	1.59 seconds
(e) same last letter: *TKRB*	1.64 seconds
(f) totally different: *TKBR*	1.74 seconds

As can be seen, reaction time is quickest when the first two letters of the string are in the same order as in the study string. There is little difference between the conditions when all letters match, case (a), and when just the first two match, case (b). The next fastest condition is when just the first letter matches, case (c). Reaction times are as fast when just the first letter matches, case (c), as when the last two letters match, case (d), but slower when only the last letter matches, case (e). Reaction times are a good bit slower when there is no match at the beginning or end, case (f). These data show two major effects governing access to ordinal structure. The first, called *front anchoring*, concerns the fact that subjects have better access to the structure from the beginning of the string. The second, called *end anchoring*, is less pronounced, but there is some advantage when the end of the string matches.

Angiolillo-Bent and Rips (1982) report similar reaction-time data from the recognition of three consonant strings. They indicate that the memory for these strings is not like a visual image. For instance, there is little effect of whether the case of the letters at study matches the case of the letters at test. That is, if subject study *PRB*, they can quickly recognize *prb*.

An experiment by Sternberg (1969) also shows the importance of front anchoring in a linear ordering. He had subjects memorize strings of up to seven digits and asked them to generate the next item in the string after a probe digit. Thus, a subject might be given 38926 and be asked for the

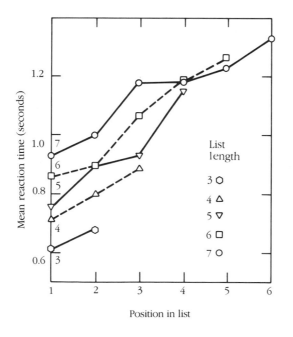

Figure 4-15. Time to generate the next digit in a string of digits as a function of the ordinal position in the string and the length of the list. (From Sternberg, 1969.)

digit after 9, in which case the answer would be 2. Figure 4-15 illustrates the results from his experiment as a function of the position of the probe digit in the sequence of digits for lists of varying lengths. Note that subjects are fastest to access the first digit and get progressively slower toward the end of the string. It has been suggested that subjects answer such questions by starting at the beginning of the string, searching forward until they find the probe, and then generating the next digit.

Hierarchical Encoding of Orderings

So far we have discussed the representation of rather short sequences of elements. What happens with longer sequences? There is considerable evidence that subjects store these hierarchically, with subsequences as units in larger sequences. So, for instance, consider how people might represent the order of the 26 letters in the alphabet. A possible hierarchical representation, based on the "Alphabet Song," is illustrated in Figure 4-16. This song is in turn based on the rhythm and melody of "Twinkle, Twinkle Little Star," and this correspondence is also illustrated in the figure. Thus, the alphabet is a hierarchical structure whose major constituents are ABCD, EFG, HIJK, LMNOP, QRS, TUV, WXYZ. In the "Alphabet Song" there are pauses, as indicated here by the commas, between the sublists.

Klahr, Chase, and Lovelace (1983) did an experiment to look for effects of this hierarchical structure on time to generate the next letter in the alphabet. Thus, the subject might be given K and asked to generate the next letter (L). Figure 4-17 shows the generation times for each letter in the alphabet. Note that generation times are fastest at the beginning of a major constituent and get progressively slower toward the end of the constituent. Thus, within a constituent, subjects' judgment times show the same front-anchoring effect found by Sternberg. Klahr et al. theorize that subjects have access to the beginning of a sublist and search forward for the target letter.

The research of Johnson (1970) provides more evidence for the reality of the hierarchical structure of long lists. He had subjects commit to memory random strings of letters, but used spacing to encourage a particular hierarchical organization. So, he might present his subjects with the following string to memorize:

DY JHQ GW

He assumed subjects would set up hierarchies in which the individual phrases would be strings like *JHQ*, as dictated by the spacing. He looked at subjects' later recall of these strings and found that they tended to recall

107

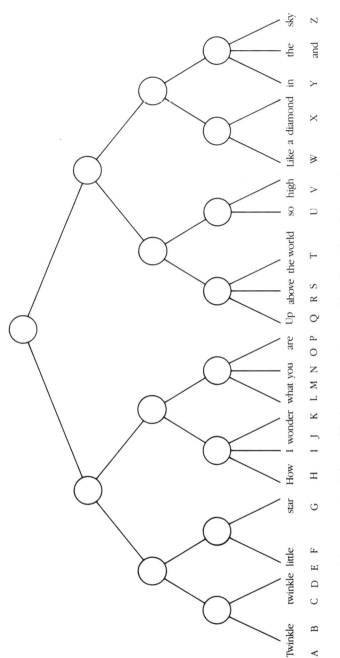

Figure 4-16. A hierarchical representation encoding the order of the 26 letters in the alphabet. This representation is based on the song learned in early childhood. This structure is in turn based on the hierarchical structure of "Twinkle, Twinkle, Little Star."

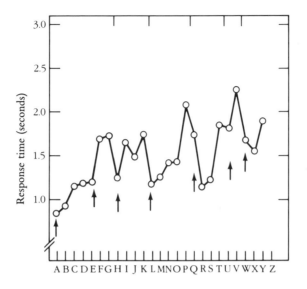

Figure 4-17. Time to generate the next letter in the alphabet. Arrows indicate beginning of new major constituents in the hierarchical encoding. (From Klahr et al., 1983. Copyright 1983 by the American Psychological Association. Adapted by permission.)

these substrings as units. If subjects recalled the first letter of a substring, there was a 90 percent probability of recalling the next letter. For instance, if they recalled the *J*, they would be very likely to recall the *H*. There was not the same tendency across unit barriers. For instance, if the subjects recalled *Y* in the foregoing string, there was only a 70 percent probability of recalling the *J* that follows.

Judgments of Linear Order

Another issue that has been explored concerns how people judge the relative order of items in a list of items. For instance, which comes first in the alphabet, *J*, or *L*? This issue is usually studied experimentally by having subjects commit to memory a set of facts specifying the order of various pairs of items. For instance, subjects are asked to learn such information as the following:

John is taller than Fred.

Fred is taller than Bill.

109

Bill is taller than Herb.

Herb is taller than Dave.

Dave is taller than Alex.

After having committed these pairs to memory, subjects are able to recite the order of all of the items:

John, Fred, Bill, Herb, Dave, and Alex

Thus, they commit this information to memory as a list of items. Subjects are then asked to answer questions such as *Who is taller, Dave or Fred?* — that is, they are asked to make judgments about which item is more extreme in the linear ordering. Many such experiments have been performed using linear orderings, such as those of Potts (1972, 1975) and Trabasso and Riley (1975). The results of an experiment by Woocher, Glass, and Holyoak (1978), in which subjects were asked to learn quite long linearly ordered lists, are typical. Subjects learned about the linear ordering on the dimension of height of 16 people, referred to by name, and were asked to judge the relative heights of various pairs of items in the list. Interest focused on the amount of time subjects took to answer these questions as a function of the distance between the two items in the list. The latter varied from a distance of no intervening items (members of the pair were adjacent in the ordering) to a distance of six intervening items. Figure 4-18 plots subjects' reaction times as a function of this distance. Note that a decreasing function was obtained, similar to that obtained when subjects make magnitude estimates of natural categories (as in Figure 4-10). A particularly striking feature of these data concerns the results for pairs with no intervening items. These are the pairs subjects were trained on to learn the linear orderings. Although directly trained on only these pairs, they were slowest in judging these pairs.

This distance effect for linear orderings is like the distance effect for sizes of images (p. 99). In that case we found that subjects found it easier to judge the relative size of two objects the greater the difference in the actual size of the objects.

Remarks and Suggested Readings

Paivio (1971) and Yuille (1983) should be consulted for Paivio's dual-code theory and particularly his theory on imagery. Kosslyn (1980) has developed an extensive theory of the mental image. Kosslyn (1983) is a

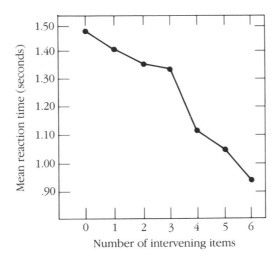

Figure 4-18. Data from a study of linear ordering by Woocher et al. (1978). The graph shows mean reaction times for judging the order of pairs of items as a function of the number of intervening items in the linear ordering.

more readable version of this work. Recent papers by Farah (1988) and Finke (1985) discuss the issue of what images and visual perception have in common. Other recent books on imagery are Richardson (1980) and Shepard and Cooper (1983). For papers critical of this research, consult Pylyshyn (1973, 1981).

A fair amount of research has been concerned with how mental images are used to encode maps of our environment. For two representative papers, read Hintzman, O'Dell, and Arndt (1981) and Thorndyke and Stasz (1980). An interesting book is *Maps and minds* by Downs and Stea (1977). McNamara (1986) has done research on how our representation of our environment combines spatial and hierarchical information.

Lee and Estes (1981), Ratcliff (1981), and Wickelgren (1967) have been concerned about how we represent linear orders. I (Anderson, 1983; Chapter 2) have written about the relation between spatial and ordinal representations and the meaning-based representations to be discussed in the next chapter.

Meaning-Based Knowledge Representations

Summary

1. Meaning-based knowledge representations encode what is significant about an event and omit many of the unimportant perceptual details.

2. Initial memory for an event contains both verbal and visual details. However, information about these details tends to be rapidly forgotten within the first minute following the event, leaving only memory for the meaningful information in the event.

3. Because memory for meaning is longer lasting than memory for physical details, individuals can improve their memories by converting meaningless to-be-remembered information into a more meaningful form.

4. The meaning of a sentence or picture can be represented as a network of propositions. Often propositions enter into hierarchical relationships in which one proposition occurs as part of another proposition. Propositional networks reveal in graphical form the associative connections between concepts.

5. The closer together the concepts in a propositional network are, the better cues they are for each other's recall.

6. *Schemas* are large, complex units of knowledge that encode properties which are typical of instances of general categories and omit properties which are not typical of the categories. An important function of schemas is to enable a person to infer unseen information from what is seen.

7. Schemas are organized according to a set of *slots*, or attributes. One type of slot indicates schemas more general than the current schema. Another type of slot indicates schemas that define parts of the current schema.

8. Individual instances of natural categories, such as birds or fruits, vary in how well they match the schema for their category.

9. Schemas can represent stereotypic sequences of actions, such as going to a restaurant. Such event schemas are referred to as *scripts*. Scripts play an important role in the understanding of stories.

Recall a wedding you attended a while ago. Presumably, you can remember who married whom, probably where the wedding was, many of the people at the wedding, and some of the things that happened. However, you would probably be hard pressed to say exactly what all the participants wore, exactly what was said, how many steps the bride took walking down the aisle, etc.—although you probably registered all of these details. It seems we have the ability to remember the gist of an event without recalling any of its exact details.

The previous chapter was concerned with knowledge representations that retain much of the detail of the original event. This chapter will be concerned with knowledge representations that try to extract out what is significant about an event and discard many of the unimportant perceptual details. Knowledge representations that achieve this kind of abstraction are called *meaning-based representations* to contrast them with the *perception-based representations* of the previous chapter. A fair amount of research in cognitive psychology has been devoted to documenting the importance of such meaning-based memories and establishing that they are different from perception-based memories. We will review that research and then consider two types of meaning-based representations: propositional structures that encode the significant information about a particular event and schemas that represent categories of events and objects in terms of their typical properties.

Memory for Verbal Information

In the last chapter we discussed the linear orderings that store information about the exact order of elements. There is no doubt that we use such a representation to encode some verbal information—that is, sometimes we can remember verbatim lines from poems, songs, plays, and speeches. However, considerable doubt exists as to whether all or even most of our memory for verbal communication can be accounted for in terms of memory for the verbatim (auditory or written) message.

An experiment by Wanner (1968) illustrates circumstances in which people do and do not remember information about exact wording. Wanner had subjects come into the laboratory and listen to tape-recorded instructions. For one group of subjects, "the warned group," the tape began this way:

> The materials for this test, including the instructions, have been recorded on tape. Listen very carefully to the instructions because you will be tested on your ability to recall particular sentences which occur in the *instructions*.

The second group received no such warning and so had no idea that they would be responsible for the verbatim instructions. After this point, the instructions were the same for both groups. At a later point in the instructions, one of four possible critical sentences occurred:

> 1. When you score your results, do nothing to correct your answers but mark carefully those answers which are wrong.
>
> 2. When you score your results, do nothing to correct your answers but carefully mark those answers which are wrong.
>
> 3. When you score your results, do nothing to your correct answers but mark carefully those answers which are wrong.

4. When you score your results, do nothing to your correct answers but carefully mark those answers which are wrong.

Immediately after presentation of this sentence, all subjects (warned or not) heard the following conclusion to the instructions:

To begin the test, please turn to page 2 of the answer booklet and judge which of the sentences printed there occurred in the instructions you just heard.

On page 2 they found the critical sentence they had just heard plus a similar alternative. Suppose they had heard sentence 1. They might have to choose between 1 and 2 or between 1 and 3. Both pairs differ in the ordering of two words. However, the difference between 1 and 2 does not contribute critically to the meaning of the sentences; the difference is just stylistic. On the other hand, sentences 1 and 3 clearly do differ in meaning. Thus, by looking at subjects' ability to discriminate between different pairs of sentences, Wanner was able to measure their ability to remember the meaning versus the style of the sentence and to determine how this ability interacted with whether or not they were warned. The relevant data are in Figure 5-1.

The percentage of correct identifications of sentences heard is displayed as a function of whether subjects had been warned. The percentages are plotted separately for subjects who were asked to discriminate a meaningful difference in wording and for those who were asked to

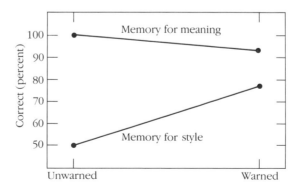

Figure 5-1. Ability of warned versus unwarned subjects to remember a wording difference that affected meaning versus style. (Adapted from Wanner, 1968).

discriminate a stylistic difference. If subjects were just guessing, they would have scored 50 percent correct by chance; thus we would not expect any values below 50 percent.

The implications of Wanner's experiment are clear. First, memory is better for changes in wording that result in changes of meaning than for changes in wording that result just in changes of style. The superiority of memory for meaning indicates that people normally extract the meaning from a linguistic message and do not remember its exact wording. Moreover, memory for meaning is equally good whether subjects are warned or not. (The slight advantage for unwarned subjects does not approach statistical significance.) Thus, subjects retain the meaning of a message as a normal part of their comprehension process. They do not have to be especially cued to memorize the sentence. In Chapter 7 we will see more evidence showing that intention to learn is often irrelevant to good memory.

The second implication of these results is that the warning did have an effect on memory for the stylistic change. Subjects were almost at chance in remembering stylistic change when unwarned, but they were fairly good at remembering when warned. This result indicates that we do not naturally retain much information about exact wording, but that we can do so when we are especially cued to pay attention to such information. Even with such a warning, however, memory for stylistic information is poorer than memory for meaning.

Memory for Visual Information

On many occasions, our memory capacity seems much greater for visual information than for verbal information. A representative experiment was reported by Shepard (1967) in which he had subjects study a set of magazine pictures one picture at a time. After studying the pictures, subjects were presented with pairs of pictures consisting of one they had studied and one they had not studied. The subjects' task was to recognize which of each pair was the studied picture. This task was contrasted with a verbal situation in which subjects studied sentences and were similarly tested on their ability to recognize studied sentences when presented with pairs containing one new and one studied sentence. Subjects exhibited 11.8 percent errors in the sentence condition but only 1.5 percent errors in the picture condition. Recognition memory was fairly high in the sentence condition, but it was virtually perfect in the picture condition. There have been a number of experiments like Shepard's. His experiment involved 600 pictures. Perhaps the most impressive demonstration of visual memory is the experiment by Standing (1973), who showed that subjects could remember 73 percent of 10,000 pictures!

You might think that such high memory for pictures means people show very high retention of spatial images such as those discussed in Chapter 4. However, the evidence is that subjects are not likely to remember the exact visual details or spatial relations in a picture. Instead, they are remembering some rather abstract representation that captures the picture's meaning. That is, it proves useful to distinguish between the meaning of a picture and the physical picture, just as it proves important to distinguish between the meaning of a sentence and the physical sentence. A number of experiments point to the utility of this distinction with respect to picture memory and to the fact that we tend to remember the picture's meaning, not the physical picture.

For instance, consider an experiment by Mandler and Ritchey (1977). The experimenters had subjects study pictures of scenes, such as the classroom scenes in Figure 5-2. After studying eight such pictures for 10 seconds each, subjects were tested for their recognition memory. They were presented with a series of pictures and instructed to identify which pictures they had studied in the series. The series contained the exact pictures they had studied as well as distractor pictures. A distractor such as (b) in the figure was called *token distractor*. It differs from the target only with respect to the pattern on the teacher's dress, a visual detail relatively unimportant to the meaning of the picture. In contrast, the distractor in (c) involves a *type change* — from a world map to an art picture used by the teacher. This visual detail is relatively more important to the meaning of the picture, since it indicates the subject being taught. All eight pictures shown to subjects contained possible token changes and type changes. In each case, the type change involved a more important change to the picture's meaning than did the token change. There was no systematic difference in the amount of physical change involved in a type versus a token change. Subjects were able to recognize the original pictures 77 percent of the time, reject the token distractors only 60 percent of the time, but reject the type distractors 94 percent of the time. Chance guessing performance would have been 50 percent.

The conclusion in this study is very similar to that in the Wanner experiment reviewed earlier. Just as Wanner found that subjects were much more sensitive to meaning-significant changes in a sentence, so Mandler and Ritchey found that subjects are sensitive to meaning-significant changes in a picture. It may be that subjects have better memory for the meanings of pictures than for the meanings of sentences, but that they have poor memory for the physical details of both.

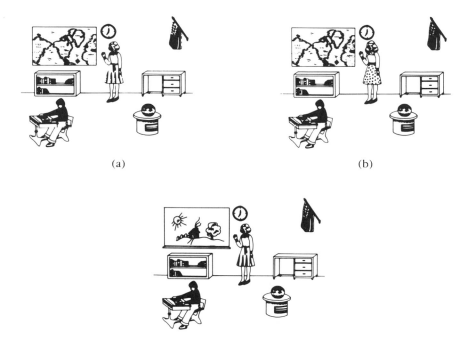

Figure 5-2. Pictures similar to those used by Mandler and Ritchey (1977). Subjects studied the target picture (a). Later they were tested with a series of pictures that included the target (a) along with token distractors such as (b) and type distractors such as (c). (Copyright 1977 by the American Psychological Association. Reprinted by permission.)

An interesting demonstration of just how poor memory for visual detail can be was provided by Nickerson and Adams (1979). Try to draw a picture of the face side of the American penny. Before checking the accuracy of your drawing by looking at a coin, try to recognize which is the correct penny in Figure 5-3. What Nickerson and Adams found (and presumably what you experienced) is that, while people remember some things quite well, such as Abraham Lincoln's face and a date, they are virtually at chance guessing when trying to remember such details as which way the head is pointed and whether it is "In God we trust" or "United States of America" which appears on that side of the coin.

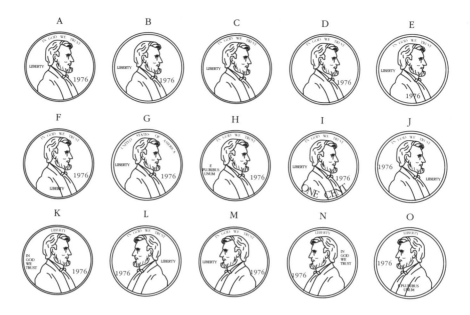

Figure 5-3. Which is the "honest" penny? (After Nickerson & Adams, 1979. Courtesy of Academic Press, Inc.)

Retention of Perception-based versus Meaning-based Knowledge Representations

There is evidence that subjects initially encode verbatim information about a sentence and exact spatial information about a picture, but they tend to quickly forget this information. Once the perceptual information is forgotten, subjects retain only information about the meaning.

Memory for orientation of a picture is one of the visual details that appears to decay rapidly, as demonstrated in an experiment by Gernsbacher (1985). Subjects were shown pictures such as the ones in Figure 5-4. After studying one of these pictures they were asked to judge which of the pair they had seen. At a 10-second delay subjects displayed 79 percent accuracy in making their judgment, showing a considerable retention of information about left-right orientation. However, after 10 minutes their accuracy in judgment had fallen to 57 percent (50 percent would reflect chance guessing). On the other hand, their memory for what the picture was about remained high over that period of time.

Figure 5-4. Example picture from an experimental story displayed in one orientation (top) and the reverse (bottom). (From Gernsbacher, 1985. Original illustration from *One Frog Too Many* by Mercer and Mariana Meyer. Copyright © 1975 by Mercer and Mariana Meyer. Reprinted by permission of the publisher, Dial Books for Young Readers.)

An experiment by Anderson (1974b) made the same point in the verbal domain. Subjects listened to a story that contained various critical sentences which would be tested; for instance:

    1. The missionary shot the painter.

Later, subjects were presented with one of the following sentences and asked whether it followed logically from the story they had heard. They were also asked to judge which sentence they had actually heard.

    2. The missionary shot the painter.

    3. The painter was shot by the missionary.

4. The painter shot the missionary.

5. The missionary was shot by the painter.

The first two sentences require a positive response to the logical judgment and the last two require a negative response. Subjects were tested either immediately after hearing the sentence or a delay of about 2 minutes.

The delay had little effect on the accuracy of their logical judgment — 98 percent immediately and 96 percent at a delay. However, when they were asked to judge which sentence they had heard (2 or 3 above) there was a dramatic effect of delay. Subjects were 99 percent correct immediately but only 56 percent correct at a delay.

Implications of Good Memory for Meaning

It has been shown over and over again that meaningful information is better remembered than meaningless information. If people have a choice about whether to commit information to memory meaningfully or non-meaningfully, they are well advised to go to the meaningful route. Unfortunately, many people are unaware of this fact and their memory performance suffers as a consequence.

I can still remember the traumatic experience I had in my first paired-associate experiment. It was part of a sophomore class on experimental psychology. For reasons I have long since forgotten, we had designed a class experiment that involved learning 16 memorable pairs such as DAX—GIB. That is, our task was to be able to recall GIB when prompted with the cue DAX. I was determined to outperform other members of my class. My personal theory of memory at that time, which I intended to apply, was basically that if you try hard and intensely you will remember well. In the impending experimental situation, this meant that during the learning period I would say (as loud as was seemly) the paired associates over and over again, as fast as I could. My theory was that by this method the paired associates would be forever burned into my mind. To my chagrin, I wound up with the worst score in the class.

My theory of "loud and fast" was directly opposed to the true means of improving memory. I was trying to commit a meaningless auditory pair to memory. But the material in this chapter suggests that we have best memory for meaningful information, not meaningless verbal information. I should have been trying to convert my memory task into something more meaningful. For instance, DAX is like *dad* and GIB is the first part of *gibberish*. So I might have created an image of my father speaking some gibberish to me. This would have been a simple *mnemonic* (memory-assisting) *technique* and would have worked quite well as a means of associating the two.

We do not often have the need to learn pairs of nonsense syllables outside the laboratory situation. However, in many situations we have to associate various combinations of terms that do not have much inherent meaning. We have to learn shopping lists, names for faces, telephone numbers, rote facts in a college class, vocabulary items in a foreign language, and so on. In all cases, we can improve memory if we transform the task into one of associating the items meaningfully. Transforming meaningless information into meaningful information is a prime trick of the memory experts who perform in nightclubs.

One mnemonic technique that can help in the classroom is the *key-word method* for learning vocabulary items. Consider, for instance, the Italian *formaggio* (pronounced FOR MODGEJO), which means "cheese." No inherently meaningful connection exists between the Italian and English equivalents, but the key-word method forces one. The first step is to transform the foreign word into some English soundalike phrase — for example, FOR MODGEJO sounds like "for much dough." The second step is to invent a meaningful connection between the two. In this case, we might imagine an expensive cheese that sold for much money, or "for much dough." Or consider *carciofi* (pronounced CAR CHOH FEE), which means "artichokes." We might transform CAR CHOH FEE into "car trophy" and imagine a winning car at an auto show with a trophy shaped like an artichoke. Atkinson and Raugh (1975) studied such a key-word technique in language learning and showed it to be very effective. They claimed that as students become familiar with a foreign language, their consciousness of the key words drops out. Thus, it appears that the key word provides a helpful crutch for getting started but does not stay around to clutter up memory.

Summary of Research on Memory for Meaning

Representations that do not preserve the exact perceptual structures of the events remembered are the mainstay of long-term memory. It is important to appreciate that these meaning representations are neither linguistic nor pictorial. Rather, they can encode the meaning of pictures and linguistic communications. There remains the question of how to represent that meaning. *Propositional representations* are often used for this purpose.

Propositional Representations

Analysis into Propositions

The idea that information is represented in terms of propositions is currently the most popular concept of how meaning is represented in memory. In a propositional analysis, only the meaning of an event is represented. The unimportant details—details that humans tend not to remember—are not represented. This idea has been incorporated into such contemporary theories as Anderson (1976), Anderson and Bower (1973), Clark (1974), Frederiksen (1975), Kintsch (1974), and Norman and Rumelhart (1975). The concept of a *proposition*, borrowed from logic and linguistics, is central to this analysis. A proposition is the smallest unit of knowledge that can stand as a separate assertion; that is, the smallest unit about which it makes sense to make the judgment true or false. Propositional analysis most clearly applies to linguistic information, and it is with respect to this information that the topic is developed here.

Consider the following sentence:

1. Nixon gave a beautiful Cadillac to Brezhnev, who was the leader of the USSR.

This sentence can be seen to be composed from the following simpler sentences:

2. Nixon gave a Cadillac to Brezhnev.

3. The Cadillac was beautiful.

4. Brezhnev was the leader of the USSR.

If any of these simple sentences were false, the complex sentence would not be true. These sentences closely correspond to the propositions that underlie the meaning of sentence 1. Each simple sentence expresses a primitive unit of meaning. One condition that our meaning representations must satisfy is that each separate unit in them correspond to a unit of meaning.

However, the propositional-representation theory does not claim that a person remembers in exact sentences such as 2 through 4. Past research indicates that subjects do not remember the exact wording of such underlying sentences any more than they remember the exact wording of the original sentences. For instance, Anderson (1972) showed that subjects would demonstrate poor ability to remember whether they heard sentence 2 or another sentence, labeled 5:

5. Brezhnev was given a Cadillac by Nixon.

Thus, it seems that information is represented in memory in a way that expresses the meaning of the primitive assertions but does not preserve exact wording. A number of propositional notations represent information in this abstract way. One, used by Kintsch (1974), represents each proposition as a list containing a *relation* followed by an ordered list of *arguments*. The relations correspond to the verbs (in this case, *give*), adjectives (*beautiful*), or other relational terms (*is the leader of*) in the sentences, while the arguments correspond to the nouns (*Nixon, a Cadillac, Brezhnev,* and *USSR*). The relations assert connections among the entities referred to by these nouns. As an example, sentences 2 through 4 would be represented by these lists:

6. (*Give*, Nixon, Cadillac, Brezhnev, Past)

7. (*Beautiful*, Cadillac)

8. (*Leader-of*, Brezhnev, USSR, Past)

Kintsch standardly embeds a list of relations plus arguments in parentheses, as above. Note that *Past* is represented as an argument to the propositions in lists 6 and 8 to denote the fact that both propositions were true in the past.

Whether the subject had heard sentence 1 or 9,

9. The leader of the USSR, Brezhnev, was given a Cadillac by Nixon and it was beautiful.

the meaning of the message would be represented by lists 6 through 8. Note that various relations take different numbers of arguments. For instance, the relation *give* is assumed to take four arguments — the agent of the giving, the object of the giving, the recipient of the giving, and the time of the giving.

An interesting demonstration of the psychological reality of propositional units was provided by Bransford and Franks (1971). They had subjects study 12 sentences, including the following:

The ants ate the sweet jelly which was on the table.
The rock rolled down the mountain and
  crushed the tiny hut.
The ants in the kitchen ate the jelly.
The rock rolled down the mountain and
  crushed the hut beside the woods.
The ants in the kitchen ate the jelly which was on the table.

The tiny hut was beside the woods.
The jelly was sweet.

These sentences are all composed from two sets of four propositions. One set of four propositions can be represented:

(Eat, Ants, Jelly, Past)
(Sweet, Jelly)
(On, Jelly, Table, Past)
(In, Ants, Kitchen, Past)

The other set of four propositions can be represented:

(Roll-down, Rock, Mountain, Past)
(Crush, Rock, Hut, Past)
(Beside, Hut, Woods, Past)
(Tiny, Hut)

Bransford, and Franks looked at subjects' recognition memory for the following three kinds of sentences:

OLD: The ants in the kitchen ate the jelly.
NEW: The ants ate the sweet jelly.
NONCASE: The ants ate the jelly beside the woods.

The first kind of sentence was actually studied, the second was not but is a combination of propositions that were studied, while the third consists of words that were studied but cannot be composed from the propositions studied. Bransford and Franks found that subjects had almost no ability to discriminate between the first two kinds of sentences and were equally likely to say that they had actually heard either. On the other hand, subjects were quite confident that they had not heard the third noncase sentence.

Their experiment shows that subjects remember quite well what propositions they encounter but are quite insensitive to the actual combination of propositions. Indeed subjects were most likely to say they heard a sentence consisting of all four propositions, such as:

The ants in the kitchen ate the sweet jelly which was on the table.

even though they had in fact not studied this sentence.

Propositional Networks

There is another way to represent the meaning of the sentence, which is by means of a *propositional network*.[1] Figure 5-5 illustrates the structure of a propositional network that encodes the sentence "Nixon gave a beautiful Cadillac to Brezhnev, who was the leader of the USSR," which was used earlier to illustrate the Kintsch propositional analysis. In such a network, each proposition is represented by an ellipse, which is connected by labeled arrows to its relation and arguments. The propositions, the relations, and the arguments are called the *nodes* of the network, and the arrows are called the *links* because they connect nodes. For instance, the ellipse labeled 6 in the figure represents proposition 6. This ellipse is connected to the relation *give* by a link labeled *relation* (to indicate that it is pointing to the relation node) to *Nixon* by an *agent* link, to *Cadillac* by an *object* link, to *Brezhnev* by a *recipient* link, and to *Past* by a *time* link. The three network structures in parts (a–c) represent the individual propositions 6 through 8 listed on p. 124. Note that these different networks contain the same nodes; for example, parts (a) and (b) both contain *Cadillac*. This overlap indicates that these networks are really interconnected parts of a larger network, which is illustrated in part (d).

The spatial location of elements in a network is totally irrelevant to the interpretation. A network can be thought of as a tangle of marbles connected by strings. The marbles represent the nodes, and the strings represent the links between the nodes. The network represented on a two-dimensional page is that tangle of marbles laid out in a certain way. We try to lay the network out in a way that facilitates its understanding, but any order is possible. Thus, part (e) of Figure 5-5 is another way of representing the network shown in part (d). All that matters is which elements are connected to which, not where the components lie.

We now have two ways of representing the same propositional information: with a set of linear propositions, as in propositions 6 through 8, or with a network, as in Figure 5-5. Since the information represented is abstract, either notational convention will work. The linear representation is somewhat neater and more compact, but the network representation reveals the connections among elements. As we will see, this connectivity proves useful for understanding certain memory phenomena.

---

[1]The propositional-network representation used here is a slight variant of a system proposed by Rumelhart, Lindsay, and Norman (1972). Many variations on and sophistications of these ideas exist (e.g., Anderson, 1976; Anderson & Bower, 1973; Norman & Rumelhart, 1975; Quillian, 1969), but this system has the virtue of simplicity.

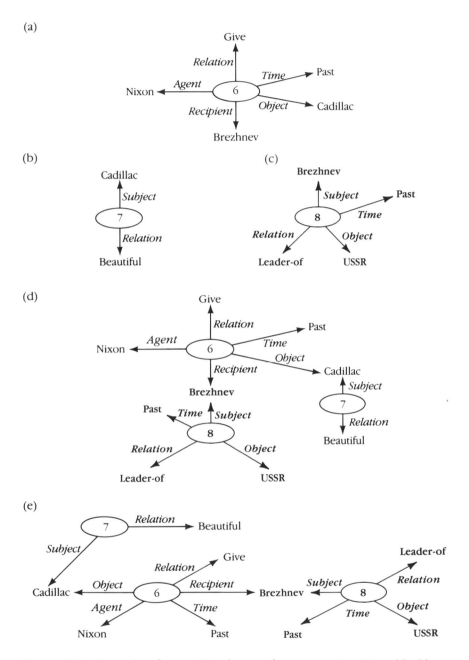

Figure 5-5. Examples of propositional-network representations. Parts (a)–(c) represent propositions 6–8. Part (d) illustrates the combined networks (a)–(c). Part (e) is another way of displaying the network in part (d).

Besides the basic propositional structure, some other structures are needed to create adequate meaning representations. Suppose we wanted to represent the following three sentences:

   10.   Nixon gave Brezhnev a Cadillac.

   12.   Fred owns a Cadillac.

   12.   Fred shouts "Nixon."

(We will assume that Fred is the same person in sentences 11 and 12.) Given the representational concepts discussed so far, we would represent this information with the network in Figure 5-6(a). However, this network exhibits a number of inadequacies. First, it is not the case that the object of Fred's shouting in sentence 12 is the same as the agent of the giving in sentence 10. In one case we are dealing with the person, and in the other case we are dealing with his name. Therefore, we need to distinguish between words and the concepts they refer to. This distinction is made in part (b), where words and concepts have different nodes. In this network (and as a general rule) words are written within quotation marks, whereas concepts are represented by words without quotation marks. A link labeled *Word* indicates the connection between the concept and the word.

Another problem with part (a) is that only one node exists for Cadillac, which implies that the Cadillac Nixon gave is the one Fred owns. This example illustrates the need for a distinction between specific objects, such as the particular Cadillacs, and general classes, such as the category *Cadillac*. In part (b), the distinction is made: Two instance nodes, *X* and *Y*, stand for the two Cadillacs. Links labeled *Isa* indicate that each node is a Cadillac.

Hierarchical Organization of Propositions

One of the important features about propositions is that, like spatial images and linear orderings, they are capable of entering into hierarchical relationships where one proposition occurs as a unit within another proposition. Parts (a) and (b) of Figure 5-7 illustrate the propositional representations for the following two sentences:

   John bought some candy because he was hungry.

   John believed Russia would invade Poland.

Note in Figure 5-7 that both the proposition *John bought some candy* and the proposition *John was hungry* occur as arguments within a larger propo-

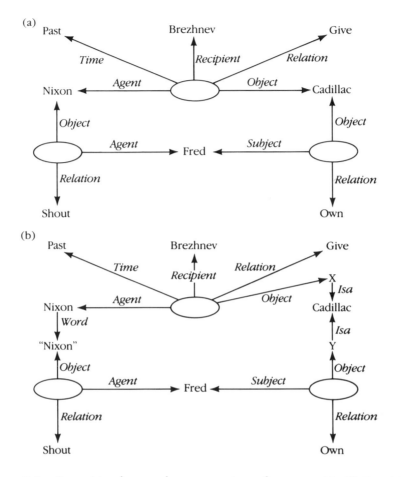

Figure 5-6. Propositional-network representations of sentences 10–12. Part (a) is inadequate; part (b) is more adequate because it distinguishes between words and concepts and between classes and instances.

sition which asserts that the first proposition is caused by the second. Similarly, the proposition *Russia would invade Poland* occurs as the object of the proposition about John's believing.

Propositional Networks as Associative Structures

It is useful to think of the nodes in a semantic network as ideas and to think of the links between the nodes as associations between the ideas, as a number of experiments suggest. Consider an experiment by Weisberg

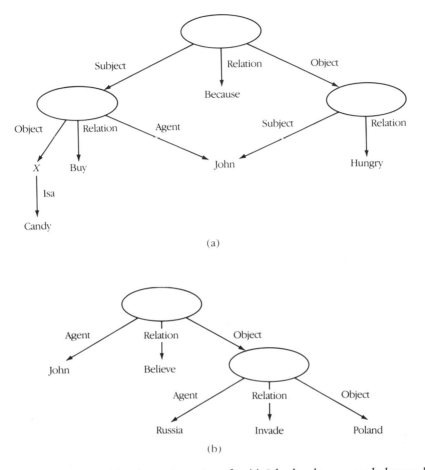

Figure 5-7. Propositional representations for (a) *John bought some candy because he was hungry* and (b) *John believed Russia would invade Poland.*

(1969) that used a constrained association task. He had subjects study and commit to memory such sentences as *Children who are slow eat bread that is cold.* The propositional-network representation for this sentence is illustrated in Figure 5-8. After learning a sentence, subjects were administered free-association tasks in which they were given a word from the sentence and asked to respond with the first word from the sentence that came to mind. Subjects cued with *slow* almost always free-associated *children* and almost never *bread*, although *bread* is closer to *slow* in the sentence than *children*. However, the figure shows that *slow* and *children* are nearer each other (three links) than *slow* and *bread* (five links). Similarly, subjects cued with *bread* almost always recalled *cold* rather than *slow*, although in the

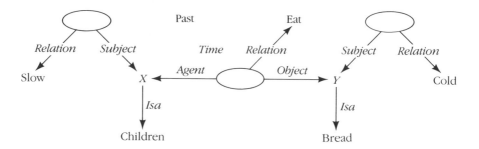

Figure 5-8. A propositional-network representation of the sentence *Children who are slow eat bread that is cold.*

sentence *bread* and *slow* are closer than *bread* and *cold.* This is because *bread* and *cold* are closer to each other (three links) in the network than are *bread* and *slow* (five links). (A similar point has been made in an experiment by Ratcliff & McKoon, 1978.)

Retrieval from Propositional Networks

This associative analysis of propositional structures has proven to be very useful in understanding variations in the times subjects take to retrieve information from memory. Collins and Quillian (1969) had subjects judge the truth of assertions about concepts such as the following:

1. Robins eat worms.

2. Robins have feathers.

3. Robins have skin.

Subjects were shown facts such as these as well as false assertions, such as *Apples have feathers.* They were asked to judge whether a statement was true or false by pressing one of two buttons. The time from presentation of the statement to the button press was measured.

Figure 5-9 illustrates the kind of network structure that Collins and Quillian assumed represented the information in subjects' memories. Sentence 1 is directly stored with *robin.* However, sentence 2 is not directly stored at the *robin* node. Rather, the *have feathers* property is stored with *bird*, and sentence 2 can be inferred from the directly stored facts that *a robin is a bird* and *birds have feathers.* Again, sentence 3 is not directly stored with *robin*; rather, the *have skin* predicate is stored with *animal*. Thus, sentence 3 can be inferred from the facts *a robin is a bird* and *a bird is an animal* and *animals have skin*. Thus, with sentence 1, all the requisite information for its verification is stored with *robin*; in the case of sentence 2, subjects must traverse one link from *robin* to *bird* to retrieve the requisite information; and in sentence 3, subjects would have to traverse two links from *robin* to *animal*.

If our memories were structured like Figure 5-9, we would expect statement 1 to be verified more quickly than statement 2, which would be verified more quickly than statement 3. This is just what Collins and Quillian found. Subjects required 1310 milliseconds to make judgments about statements like statement 1, 1380 milliseconds for questions like 2, and 1470 milliseconds for statements like 3. Subsequent research on the retrieval of information from memory has somewhat complicated the

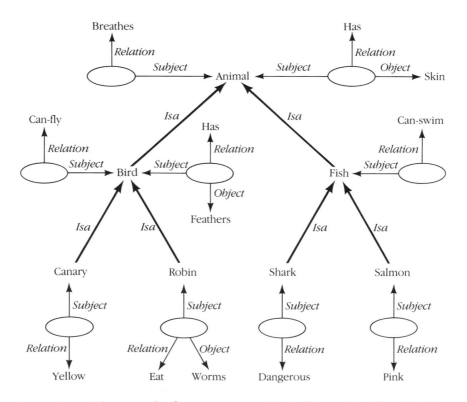

Figure 5-9. The network of concepts assumed by Collins and Quillian (1969) in their experiment to compare reaction times in making true-or-false judgments about statements. A hierarchy of concepts and associated properties can be seen.

132

conclusions drawn from the initial Collins and Quillian experiment. The frequencies with which facts are experienced have been observed to have strong effects on retrieval time (e.g., Conrad, 1972). Some facts, such as *Apples are eaten*, for which the predicate could be stored with an intermediate concept such as food, but which are experienced quite frequently, are verified as fast as or faster than facts such as *Apples have dark seeds*, which must be stored more directly with the *apple* concept. It seems that if a fact about a concept is frequently encountered, it will be stored with that concept even if it is also stored with a more general concept. The following statements about the organization of facts in propositional memory and their retrieval times seem to be valid conclusions from the research:

1. If a fact about a concept is frequently encountered, it will be stored with that concept even if it could be inferred from a more distant (in the network) concept.

2. The more frequently encountered a fact about a concept is, the more strongly that fact will be associated with the concept. And the more strongly associated with concepts facts are, the more rapidly they are verified.

3. Verifying facts that are not directly stored with a concept but that must be inferred takes a relatively long time.

Thus, both the strength of the connections between facts and concepts (determined by frequency of experience) and the distance between them propositionally have effects on retrieval time. We will have much more to say about the strength factor in Chapter 6, which discusses memory retrieval.

Schemas

Propositions are a useful way to represent meaning that abstracts away from perceptual information about an event to what is significant about an event. On the other hand, when representing the knowledge we have about various categories, it is useful to be able to encode the information that certain features are typical of a category while others are not. Here the abstraction is from specific instances to generalizations about the category from which these instances come.

Consider, for instance, our knowledge of what a house is like. We know many things about houses, such as the following:

Houses are a type of building.

Houses have rooms.

Houses can be built of wood, brick, or stone.

Houses serve as human dwellings.

Houses tend to have rectilinear and triangular shapes.

Houses are larger than 100 square feet and smaller than 10,000.

Just to list such facts, however, does not capture their interrelational structure. The basic insight is that concepts like *house* are defined by a configuration of features, and each of these features involves specifying a value the object has on some attribute. The schema representation is the way to capture this basic insight. *Schemas* represent the structure of an object according to a *slot* structure, where slots specify values that the object has on various attributes. So, we have the following partial schema representation of a house:

> *House*
>
> superset: building
>
> parts: rooms
>
> materials: wood, brick, stone
>
> function: human dwelling
>
> shape: rectilinear, triangular
>
> size: $100 - 10,000$ ft^2

In this list, terms like *materials* or *shape* are the *attributes*, or *slots*, and terms like *wood, brick,* or *rectilinear* are the *values*. Each pair of a slot and a value specifies a typical feature. The fact that houses are typically built of materials like wood and brick does not exclude such possibilities as cardboard.

Note that certain of these features—such as that houses serve as human dwellings—are basically propositional while other information —such as that about shape and size—is basically perceptual. Thus, schemas are not simply an extension of propositional representations. Rather they are ways of encoding regularities in categories, whether these regularities are perceptual or propositional. They are abstract in the sense that they encode what is generally true rather than what is true about a specific instance. Thus, our schema is for houses in general, not a particular house. Hence, we do not represent information that is true only of a specific house, such as its color or whether it is in Pittsburgh. So, whereas propositions can represent what is important about specific things, schemas can represent what specific things have in common.

A special slot in each schema is its superset schema. Basically, unless contradicted, a concept inherits the features of its superset. Thus, stored with the schema for *building*, the superset of *house*, we would have features such as that it has a roof and walls and is found on the ground. This information is not represented in the above schema for *house* because it can be inferred from *building* (actually other information such as materials could probably also be inferred from *building*). These supersets are basically the *isa hierarchies* that we saw with semantic networks. In the case of schemas, they are sometimes called *generalization hierarchies*.

Schemas have another type of hierarchy, called a *part hierarchy*. Thus, parts of houses, such as walls and rooms, have their own schema definitions. Stored with schemas for *walls* and *rooms* we would find that these have windows and ceilings. Thus, using the part relationships, we would be able to infer that houses have windows and ceilings.

Schemas are designed to facilitate making inferences about the concepts. If we know something is a house, we can use the schema definition to infer that it is probably made of wood or brick, and that it has walls, windows, and the like. However, the inferential processes for schemas must be able to deal with exceptions. So, we can still understand what a house without a roof is. Also, it is necessary to understand the constraints between slots of a schema. So, if we hear of a house that is underground, we can infer that it will not have windows.

Psychological Reality of Schemas

Brewer and Treyens (1981) provided an interesting demonstration of the effects of schemas in memory inferences. Thirty subjects were brought individually to the room shown in Figure 5-10. They were told that this was the office of the experimenter, and they were asked to wait there while the experimenter went to the laboratory to see if the previous subject had finished. After 35 seconds the experimenter returned and took the waiting subject to a nearby seminar room. Here the subject was asked to write down everything he or she could remember about the experimental room. What would you be able to recall?

Brewer and Treyens argued that their subjects' recall would be strongly influenced by their schema of what an office contains. Subjects would do very well recalling items that are part of that schema; they should do much less well at recalling office items that are not part of the schema; they should falsely recall things that are part of the typical office but not of this one. This is just the pattern of results that Brewer and Treyens found. For instance, 29 of the 30 subjects recalled that the office

Figure 5-10. The experimental room used in the memory experiment of Brewer and Treyens (1981).

had a chair, a desk, and walls. However, only 8 subjects recalled that it had a bulletin board or a skull. On the other hand, 9 subjects recalled that it had books, which it did not. Thus, we see that a subjects memory for location is strongly influenced by that person's schema for the location.

Schemas as a formalism for representing knowledge were developed in the field of artificial intelligence, where they have proven very useful for organizing and reasoning about large and complex knowledge bases (Bobrow & Winograd, 1977; Minsky, 1975; Schank & Abelson, 1977). Winston (1984) provides a readable discussion of their use in artificial intelligence. We are still in the process of trying to understand the psychological significance of this representational construct (see discussions by Abelson, 1981, and Rumelhart & Ortony, 1977). Although experiments such as those of Brewer and Treyens indicate that humans have knowledge representations like schemas, it is not clear that human schemas have all and only the properties associated with schemas as they are used in artificial intelligence.

Schemas Represent Natural Categories

One of the important features of schemas is that they allow variation in the objects that might fit a particular schema. There are constraints on what typically occupies various slots of a schema, but there are few absolute prohibitions. This suggests that if schemas encode our knowledge about various object categories, we ought to see a shading from less typical to more typical members of the category as the features of the members better satisfy the schema constraints. There is now considerable evidence that natural categories like *birds* have the kind of structure that would be expected of a schema.

Much of the research documenting such variation in category membership has been done by Rosch. In one experiment (1973), she had subjects rate the typicality of various members of a category on a 1 to 7 scale, where 1 meant very typical and 7 meant very atypical. Subjects consistently rated some members as more typical than other members. In the bird category, *robin* got an average rating of 1.1 and *chicken* a rating of 3.8. In reference to sports, *football* was thought to be very typical (1.2), whereas *weightlifting* was not (4.7). *Murder* was rated a very typical crime (1.0), whereas *vagrancy* was not (5.3). *Carrot* was a very typical vegetable (1.1); *parsley* was not (3.8).

Rosch (1975) asked subjects to judge actual pictures of objects rather than to judge words. Subjects are faster to judge a picture as an instance of a category when it presents a typical member of the category. For instance, apples are more rapidly seen as fruits than are watermelons, and robins are more rapidly seen as birds than are chickens. Thus, typical members of a category appear also to have an advantage in perceptual recognition.

Rosch (1977) demonstrated another way in which central members of a category are more typical. She had subjects compose sentences for category names. For *bird*, subjects generated sentences such as these:

I heard a bird twittering outside my window.

Three birds sat on the branch of a tree.

A bird flew down and began eating.

Rosch replaced the category name in these sentences with a central member (robin), a less central member (eagle), or a peripheral member (chicken) and asked subjects to rate the sensibleness of the resulting sentences. Sentences involving central members got high ratings, sentences with less central members got lower ratings, and sentences with peripheral members got the lowest ratings. So, the evidence is that when people think of a category member, they generally think of typical instances of that category.

A prediction that derives from the schematic structure of categories is that they do not have fixed boundaries. People should have great difficulty and should be quite inconsistent in judging whether items at the periphery of a category are actually members of that category. McCloskey and Glucksberg (1978) looked at people's judgments as to what were or were not members of various categories. They found that although subjects did agree on some items, they disagreed on many. For instance, whereas all 30 subjects agreed that *cancer* was a disease and *happiness* was not, 16 thought *stroke* was a disease and 14 did not. Again, all 30 subjects agreed that *apple* was a fruit and *chicken* was not, but 16 thought *pumpkin* was and 14 disagreed. Once again, all subjects agreed that a *fly* was an insect and a *dog* was not, but 13 subjects thought a *leech* was and 17 disagreed. Thus, it appears that subjects do not always agree among themselves. McCloskey and Glucksberg tested the same subjects a month later and found that many had changed their mind about the disputed items. For instance, 11 out of 30 reversed themselves on *stroke*, 8 reversed themselves on *pumpkin*, and 3 reversed themselves on *leech*. Thus, disagreement as to category boundaries does not just occur *among* subjects. Subjects are very uncertain *within* themselves exactly where the boundaries of a category should be drawn.

Figure 5-11 illustrates a set of materials used by Labov (1973). He was interested in which items subjects would call cups and which they would not. Which do you consider to be cups? The interesting point is that these concepts do not appear to have clear-cut boundaries. In one experiment, Labov used the series of items 1 through 4. These items reflect an increasing ratio of width of the cup to depth. For the first item that ratio is 1, while for item 4 it is 1.9. Labov also used an item (not shown) where the ratio was 2.5 to 1. Figure 5-12 shows the percentage of subjects calling each of the five objects a cup and the percentage calling it a bowl. The solid lines indicate the classifications when subjects were simply presented with pictures of the objects (the neutral context). As can be seen, the percentages of *cup* responses gradually decreased with increasing width, but there is no clear-cut point where subjects stopped using *cup*. At the extreme 2.5-width ratio, about 25 percent of the subjects still used the *cup* response, while another 25 percent used *bowl*. (The remaining 50 percent used other responses.) The dotted lines give classifications when subjects were asked to imagine the object filled with mashed potatoes and placed on a table. In this context, fewer *cup* responses and more *bowl* responses were given, but the data show the same gradual shift from *cup*

Figure 5-11. The various cuplike objects used in the experiment by Labov (1973) studying the boundaries of the *cup* category. (Reprinted with permission from W. Labov. "The Boundaries of Words and Their Meanings." In *New ways of analyzing variations in English*. Edited by C.-J. N. Bailey and R. W. Shuy. Washington, DC: Georgetown University Press. Page 354. Copyright 1973 by Georgetown University.)

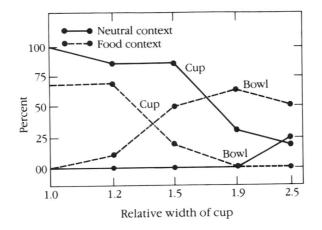

Figure 5-12. The percentage of subjects who used the terms *cup* or *bowl* to describe the objects shown in Figure 5-1 as a function of the ratio of cup width to cup depth imagined. The solid lines are for the neutral-context condition; the dotted lines are for the food-context condition. (Reprinted with permission from W. Labov. "The Boundaries of Words and Their Meanings." In *New ways of analyzing variations in English*. Edited by C.-J. N. Bailey and R. W. Shuy. Washington, DC: Georgetown University Press. Page 356. Copyright 1973 by Georgetown University.)

to *bowl*. Thus, it appears that subjects' classification behavior varies continuously not only with the properties of an object but also with the context in which the object is imagined or presented.

Event Schemas

It is not just objects and concepts that can be encoded by schemas. It is also possible to represent events as schemas. That is, we can encode our knowledge about stereotypic events, such as going to a movie, according to their parts—for instance, going to the theater, buying the ticket, buying refreshments, seeing the movie, and returning from the theater. Each of these can be divided into its parts. So, as with object schemas, we have part hierarchies. We also can have generalization hierarchies— going to a drive-in theater is a special case of going to a movie, which is a special case of an entertainment event. The slots associated with a story schema also include typical participants (ticket-takers in movies) and typical objects (e.g., a movie screen). As with objects, slots of event schemas have typical values or constraints. For instance, the typical

140

choice for refreshments is popcorn and soda, whereas the means of going is typically the same as the means of leaving and typically involves a vehicle (e.g., car, bus).

Schank and Abelson (1977) at Yale University have worked extensively on event schemas that they call *scripts*. They pointed out that many circumstances involve stereotypic sequences of actions. For instance, the list below shows their hunch as to what stereotypic aspects of dining at a restaurant might be, and represents the components of a script for such an occasion.

Scene I: Entering
Customer enters restaurant
Customer looks for table
Customer decides where to sit
Customer goes to table
Customer sits down

Scene 2: Ordering
Customer picks up menu
Customer looks at menu
Customer decides on food
Customer signals waitress
Waitress comes to table
Customer orders food
Waitress goes to cook
Waitress gives food order to cook
Cook prepares food

Scene 3: Eating
Cook gives food to waitress
Waitress brings food to customer
Customer eats food

Scene 4: Exiting
Waitress writes bill
Waitress goes over to customer
Waitress gives bill to customer
Customer gives tip to waitress
Customer goes to cashier
Customer gives money to cashier
Customer leaves restaurant

Bower, Black, and Turner (1979) report a series of experiments in which the psychological reality of the script notion was tested. They had subjects name what they considered the 20 most important events in an episode such as going to a restaurant. With 32 subjects, they failed to get complete agreement on what these events were. No action was listed as part of the episode by all of the subjects. However, considerable consensus was reported. Table 5-1 lists the events named. The items in roman were listed by at least 25 percent of the subjects. The italicized items were named by at least 48 percent of the subjects, and the items in capitals were given by at least 73 percent. Using the 73 percent as a criterion, we find the stereotypic sequence was *sit down, look at menu, order, eat, pay bill,* and *leave.*

Bower et al. went on to show a number of effects of such action scripts on memory for stories. They had subjects study stories that included some

Table 5-1 *Empirical Script Norms at Three Agreement Levels*

Going to a Restaurant
Open door
Enter
Give reservation name
Wait to be seated
Go to table
BE SEATED
Order drinks
Put napkins on lap
LOOK AT MENU
Discuss menu
ORDER MEAL
Talk
Drink water
Eat salad or soup
Meal arrives
EAT FOOD
Finish meal
Order dessert
Eat dessert
Ask for bill
Bill arrives
PAY BILL
Leave tip
Get coats
LEAVE

Adapted from Bower et al. (1979).

but not all of the typical events from a script. Subjects were then asked to recall the stories (in one experiment) or to recognize (in another experiment) whether various statements came from the story. When recalling these stories, subjects tended to report statements that were part of the script but that had not been presented as part of the stories. Similarly, in the recognition test, subjects thought they had studied script items that had not actually been in the stories. However, subjects showed a greater tendency to recall actual items from the stories or to recognize actual items than to falsely recognize foils not in the stories, despite the distortion in the direction of the general schema.

In another experiment, these investigators read to subjects stories composed of 12 prototypical actions in an episode. Eight of the actions occurred in their standard temporal position, but four were rearranged. Thus, in the restaurant story the bill might be paid at the beginning and the menu read at the end. In recalling these stories, subjects showed a strong tendency to put the events back in their normal order. In fact, about half of the statements were put back. This experiment serves as another demonstration of the powerful effect of general schemas on memory for stories.

These experiments indicate that new events are encoded with respect to these general schemas and that subsequent recall is influenced by the schemas. We have talked about these effects as if they were "bad"; that is, as if subjects were misrecalling the stories. However, it is not clear that these results should be classified as acts of misrecall. Normally, if a certain standard event such as paying a check is omitted in a story, we are supposed to assume it occurred. Similarly, if the storyteller says the check was paid at the beginning of the restaurant episode, we have some reason to doubt the storyteller. Scripts or schemas exist because they encode the predominant sequence of events in a particular kind of situation. Thus, they can serve as valuable bases for predicting missing information and for correcting errors in information.

Conclusions

We have reviewed meaning-based representations at two levels. Propositions represent the atomic units of meaning and can be used to represent the meaning of sentences and pictures. The interconnections among propositions define a network that can be profitably used to understand memory phenomena. In this chapter we discussed a few examples of how these networks can be used to understand memory phenomena (e.g.,

Weisberg's constrained association task). The next two chapters on memory will make extensive use of this network representation.

However, there are features of our knowledge that cannot be represented simply by the network structures defined by propositions. Certain sets of propositions cohere together in larger-order units called schemas. For instance, part of our knowledge about restaurants is not just that certain events happen there, but that they tend to occur together in certain sequences. Thus, schemas represent our knowledge about how features tend to go together to define objects or how events tend to go together to define episodes. This knowledge about what tends to occur with what is very important to our ability to predict what we will encounter in our environment.

A natural inference from the structure of this chapter is that the units that make up schemas are propositions. However, this is not always the case. For instance, some of the components that make up a house include spatial information about object shape as well as propositional information about the function of a house. Similarly, a major part of an event schema is information about the order of subevents. Spatial information is encoded by images and order information by linear orderings, as discussed in Chapter 4. Thus, we see that schemas encode the co-occurrence relations among propositions, spatial images, and linear orderings.

Remarks and Suggested Readings

The exact details of the propositional network given in this chapter differ from those described in any of the specific proposals in the literature. See Anderson (1976), Anderson and Bower (1973), Kintsch (1974), and Norman and Rumelhart (1975) for some of these specific proposals about how propositional information is represented. Lindsay and Norman (1977) provide another introductory exposition of propositional networks.

In the 1970s there was a debate between dual-code theorists, who believed only in spatial and verbal codes, and propositional theorists. Key papers in this debate include those of Pylyshyn (1973), Kosslyn and Pomerantz (1977), Palmer (1978), Paivio (1975), and Anderson (1978). Researchers are now moving to a more eclectic viewpoint, which allows all representations. (However, read Pylyshyn, 1984.) In this assessment I may be biased because I have strongly argued for multiple representations (Anderson, 1983). That book can also be consulted for proposals about how these representational types should be combined into schemas.

Any number of popular books on mnemonic techniques are available. Perhaps the best is by Harry Lorayne and Jerry Lucas (1974), but be warned that the techniques detailed there are at times difficult to acquire and that some of the recommendations might be simply incorrect. For a historical perspective on mnemonic techniques, read Yates (1966). For examples of the scientific study of mnemonic techniques, see Bower (1970a) or Atkinson and Raugh (1975).

A great many of the ideas about schemas have come from artificial intelligence, where they have proven very useful. For artificial-intelligence research on schemas and related concepts, consult Bobrow and Winograd (1977), Minsky (1975), Schank and Abelson (1977), and Schank (1982). For more psychologically oriented research on schemas, read Bower et al. (1979), Rumelhart and Norman (1978, 1981), and Rumelhart and Ortony (1977). Alba and Hasher (1983) provide a thorough review of the psychological evidence for a schematic theory of memory.

Human Memory: Basic Concepts and Principles

Summary

1. Memory structures vary in their level of activation, which determines how rapidly and successfully we can access the memories. Unless attended a memory structure's activation level will decay away in a matter of seconds. To be accessed again, the memory structure needs to be reactivated.

2. We can maintain things in an active state by rehearsing them. The number of things one can keep active is determined by the rate at which we can rehearse them.

3. Memory structures also vary in terms of their long-term strength. Strength determines our long-term retention of a memory.

4. To be recalled or retrieved from long-term memory, information must be activated. Activation spreads along paths through a long-term network of associations from the currently active portion of memory to the to-be-retrieved portion.

5. The level of activation spread to a knowledge structure depends directly on the strength of the path along which the activation spreads and inversely on the number of competing paths. The

detrimental effect of competing paths on the amount of activation spread down a path is referred to as *associative interference.*

6. The strength of a knowledge structure increases with practice of the structure, but there is diminishing benefit from practice. The form of this practice effect conforms to a *power function.*

7. If the level of activation of a knowledge structure is low, because of either low strength or associative interference, there will be failure of recall.

8. The strength of a knowledge structure decreases with the retention interval, but the rate of decrease slows down with time. The form of this forgetting process conforms to a power function.

The First Memory Experiment

Hermann Ebbinghaus, an early experimental investigator of human memory, published a significant research monograph in 1885. The research reported in this monograph was probably the first rigorous experimental investigation of human memory. No pools of subjects were available when Ebbinghaus was doing his research. Therefore, he used himself as his sole subject. He taught himself series of nonsense syllables, consonant-vowel-consonant trigrams such as DAX, BUP, and LOC. In one of his many experiments, Ebbinghaus required himself to learn lists of 13 syllables to the point of being able to repeat the lists twice in order without error. Then he tested his retention for these lists at various delays. He counted the amount of time he took to relearn the lists, using the same criterion of two perfect recitations. Of interest was how much faster the second learning was than the first. Suppose it took him 1156 seconds to learn the list initially and only 467 seconds to relearn the list. This meant he had saved 1156 − 467 = 689 seconds in the relearning. This savings can be expressed as a percentage of the original learning: 689/1156 = 64.3 percent. Ebbinghaus used percent-savings scores as the standard measure of his retention. Figure 6-1 plots these percent-savings scores as a function of retention intervals. As this figure clearly shows, rapid forgetting occurs initially, but some forgetting still occurs up to 30 days following the learning of the material.

Using a 24-hour retention interval, Ebbinghaus considered what would happen if, after learning the list to the criterion of two perfect

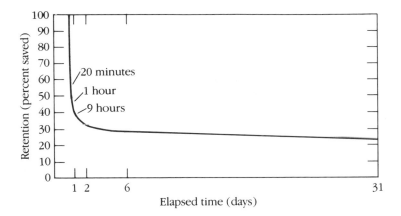

Figure 6-1. Ebbinghaus's (1885) forgetting function. Retention of nonsense sylla-bles is measured by savings in relearning. Retention decreases as the retention interval (the time between initial learning and the retention time) increases, but the rate of forgetting slows down.

recitals, he rehearsed it 30 additional times. Without this overlearning, Ebbinghaus achieved a savings score of 33.8 percent, but with this amount of overlearning, his savings on a subsequent 24-hour retention test was 64.1 percent. So, the additional study trials resulted in increased savings on a subsequent retention test.

Over the decades, the basic experimental results of Ebbinghaus have been reproduced by many other researchers using a large variety of techniques and measures. In all cases, subjects show rapid initial forget-ting of the material they have learned. The effect of extra study time is to protect the memory against the process of forgetting.

Although Ebbinghaus was correct in identifying delay and amount of study as two important determinants of recall, his research left many important factors undiscovered. Also, he was not very successful at iden-tifying the mechanisms underlying the effects of study time and retention interval. In this chapter, we will review the more recent research and theories that serve to broaden the picture of the mechanisms underlying the retention of information in memory.

The Two-Concept Theory of Memory

While it certainly is not the case that there is unanimous agreement about all aspects of human memory, many current theories (Anderson, 1983; Baddeley, 1986; Gillund & Shiffrin, 1984; Eich, 1982; Hintzman, 1986;

Murdoch, 1982; Ratcliff, 1978; see Ratcliff & McKoon, 1989; for a discussion of these various theories) do seem to agree in stressing two concepts in understanding human memory. One concept refers to some transient factor that determines the momentary availability of the memory trace and the other determines the long-term durability of that trace. I will refer to the first concept as *activation* although in some theories it is called degree of match and can play a slightly different role. Activation can be thought of in neural terms although not all memory theorists want to commit themselves to a particular neural realization. In Chapter 2, under Connectionism, we discussed the idea that neural activation might determine the availability of knowledge.

The second concept, which has been called *strength*, refers to the long-term durability of the memory. Any particular experience we have can be cross-classified according to its activation and strength. Table 6-1 illustrates such a cross classification where we have dichotomized activation into high and low levels and dichotomized strength into high and low levels. Let us first consider memories that have high activation and high strength. These are well-learned things that we are currently thinking about. For instance, if you are currently recalling the members of your immediate family you are probably dealing with memories from this cell. Memories in the high-activation, low-strength cells tend to be things that you have just encountered. Thus, if someone tells you a phone number and you rehearse it while dialing it, this would be a case of a high-activation memory. However, it is also low strength as witnessed by your inability to recall it an hour later. The low-activation, high-strength cell refers to all those things that you have well learned but are not thinking about at the time. Thus, if you are not thinking about it you would be a little slower (probably no more than a second slower) to say who wrote *Romeo and Juliet*, but most people with exposure to English

Table 6-1 *A Representation of the Two-Concept Theory of Memory*

	High Strength	Low Strength	
High activation	Well-learned things we are currently thinking about	Things we have just encoded	} Working memory
Low activation	Well-learned memories we are not thinking about	Things we cannot recall	

Long-term memory

literature would have no difficulty in retrieving the answer. Finally, there is the sad cell of low-activation, low-strength memories, which are all the experiences and facts that we can no longer recall. In this chapter we will discuss the intriguing question of whether they have been truly forgotten.

Activation controls the speed and reliability of access to the memories. While they are in an active state we can access them quickly and reliably. Strength determines the degree to which we can *reactivate* old memories. Strong memories can easily be reactivated or returned to a high level of activation. Thus, activation is defined in terms of our access to memories while strength has a second-order definition in terms of activation. One of the important features that distinguishes activation and strength is their durability. We will discuss the evidence that activation can decay from a high level to a low level in seconds. In contrast, it takes some memories years to decay in their strength.

The memories that are currently active are often referred to as *working memory*[1] (Baddeley, 1986) because they are the knowledge which we can currently work with. Memories which have sufficiently strong encodings that they can be reactivated are referred to as *long-term memory* because they can be recalled at long delays. In this chapter we will be concerned first with discussing working memory and the activation processes that support it. Then we will examine long-term memory and what determines the strength of a memory trace and how the strength of a trace relates to our ability to reactivate it.

Working Memory

Perhaps the most characteristic feature about information in working memory is that if we do not do something special to keep it active, its activation will rapidly decay away and we will lose access to the information. Now classical experiments by Brown (1958) and Peterson and Peterson (1959) illustrate the transient character of short-term memory. Peterson and Peterson had subjects study three letters and then asked for recall of the letters after various intervals of time up to 18 seconds. Normally, subjects would have no difficulty performing this task perfectly. However, to prevent them from rehearsing the material, Peterson and Peterson had subjects count backward by threes during the retention interval. Thus, following presentation of the letters, subjects might be

---

[1]The term *short-term memory* is often used to refer to a concept quite similar to working memory.

asked to count backward by threes as fast as possible from 418: 415, 412, and so on. Figure 6-2 illustrates recall at various retention intervals up to 18 seconds from a similar experiment by Murdock (1961). At 18 seconds, subjects are recalling less than 20 percent of the three letters—or an average of less than 1 letter. The decay in recall to this level is rapid, largely complete after only 9 seconds. After this point the recall level appears to approach an asymptote; that is, it does not decrease much more. We can conclude from these results that when subjects are distracted from rehearsing, they will lose information very rapidly. People are only able to keep a telephone number in short-term memory when they can rehearse it to themselves.

The asymptotic level of recall reflects what subjects are able to reactivate from long-term memory. The very poor performance (20 percent recall) displayed in Figure 6-2 at a 9-second delay is not found in the first trials (Keppel & Underwood, 1962). It seems that repeated testing causes interference to the long-term representation of the items (interference is a topic we will return to later in this chapter).

A second feature of working memory is that it is difficult to maintain information in working memory. The most dramatic illustration of this is the typical memory span task. Try it out with a friend. Read each other lists of random digits (0 to 9) and try to repeat them back after hearing them. Try different lengths of digits from 5 to 10. Most people can repeat back 5 digits reliably and cannot repeat back 10. Most people's memory span breaks down somewhere around 7 or 8 digits. Thus, typical Ameri-

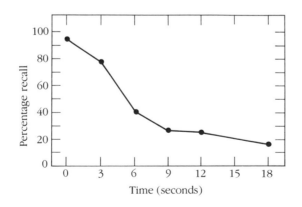

Figure 6-2. Decrease in recall as a function of duration of interpolated activity. This graph shows the rapid loss of information from short-term memory. (From Murdock, 1961).

can telephone numbers (7 digits long) are just short enough to fit within people's memory span.

What controls the amount of information we can maintain in working memory? An obvious theory is that our working memories have a fixed number of slots (say, 7) and that once we fill these up we can hold no more. More than 20 years ago this was a very popular idea in psychology but it has since fallen into disfavor. One problem with this theory is that the momentary capacity of our working memories is very high — we can be aware of a great many things in our environment. Thus, the problem is not the instantaneous capacity of our working memories, it is with the ability to maintain information in a high state of activation once it is no longer present in the environment. The problem is that information rapidly decays in its level of activation.

Baddeley (1986) proposes that to maintain information in working memory we have to be able to rehearse it. He proposes that for verbal material such as words we typically rehearse these by covertly saying them over and over again to ourselves. He calls this the *articulatory loop*. By saying the words over and over again we keep them active. We may not always be aware of such rehearsals but the evidence is quite strong that we do.

One of the most compelling pieces of evidence concerns the word length effect (Baddeley, Thomson, & Buchanan, 1975). Read the 5 words below and then try to repeat them back without looking at the page:

Chad, Burma, Greece, Cuba, Malta

Most people can do this. Baddeley et al. found that subjects were able to repeat back an average of 4.17 words out of 5. Now read and try to repeat back the following 5 words:

Czechoslovakia, Somaliland, Nicaragua, Afghanistan, Yugoslavia

Subjects were able to recall only an average of 2.80 words out of 5. The crucial factor appears to be how long it takes to say the word.

Vallar and Baddeley (1982) looked at recall for words that varied from 1 to 5 syllables. They also measured how many words of the various lengths subjects could say in a second. Figure 6-3 shows the results. Note that the percent correct exactly mirrors the reading rate.

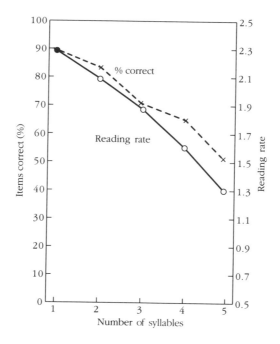

Figure 6-3. Mean reading rate and percentage correct recall of sequences of five words as a function of length. (From Baddeley, 1986.)

Trying to maintain information in working memory is analogous to the circus act that involves spinning plates on a reed. The circus performer will get one plate spinning on one reed, then another on another reed, then another, etc. He has to run back to the first before it slows down and falls off. He respins it and then respins all the rest. There are only so many plates he can keep spinning. Baddeley proposes that it is the same situation with respect to working memory. If we try to keep too many items in working memory, by the time we get back to rehearse the first one its level of activation will have sunk to the point where it takes too long to retrieve and re-rehearse. Baddeley proposes that we can keep about 1⅓ seconds worth of material rehearsed in the articulatory loop.

There is considerable evidence that this articulatory loop truly involves speech. Some of the original research was performed by Conrad (1964). He showed that when subjects misremembered something from a memory span task they tended to recall something that sounded similar. Thus, in his experiment subjects may be asked to recall a string of letters such as

HBKLMW. They were much more likely to misrecall *B* as a sound alike *V* than as an *S*, which does not sound similar. Conrad also found that subjects had a harder time recalling a string of letters which had a high proportion of rhyming letters (such as BCTHVZ) than one which did not (such as HBKLMW).

The articulatory loop is not the only mechanism we have for rehearsing material. Baddeley also proposes that we have what he calls a visuospatial sketchpad for rehearsing images of the kind we discussed in Chapter 4. He argues that these are two separate "slave" systems for maintaining information in working memory and speculates that there might be more.

When presented with subspan lists of words that can all be rehearsed, subjects display near perfect ability to remember them for long periods of time as long as their attention is devoted to rehearsing. However, one would expect a difference in the mean level of activation of subspan lists depending on how long they are. A list of 2 digits can be rehearsed more often than a list of 4 digits. This should mean that they can be kept in a more active state and should be more accessible.

A classic series of experiments by Sternberg (1969) has shown the effect of list length on access to the items in a subspan list. He presented subjects with a *memory set* of digits (e.g., 3, 4, 8, 1) to hold in short-term memory. He then presented a test digit, and subjects were required to determine whether it was in the memory set. Sternberg varied the size of the memory set from 1 digit to 6. Figure 6-4 displays the results of his manipulation in terms of the time it took to recognize targets (digits in the memory set) and to reject foils (digits not in the memory set). As can be seen, there is a nearly linear relationship between memory-set size and judgment time. With each additional digit in the memory set, judgment time increases by about 38 milliseconds. Thus, increasing the number of items that a subject must keep in memory increases the time to access any item. This is one of the most robust and well-studied phenomena in cognitive psychology. The size of the memory set slows down judgment time whether the items are letters, words, colors, and so on, with all kinds of subject populations, and in all kinds of mental states.

These results have attracted a wide range of theoretical interpretations. An early and dominant theory is the one proposed by Sternberg himself: Subjects had to search through their working memories to see if the test digit was there. He theorized that subjects serially considered one digit after another, and that it required about 38 milliseconds to consider each digit in working memory. Of course, a search of 38 milliseconds per item is much too rapid to be open to conscious inspection; but by assuming this

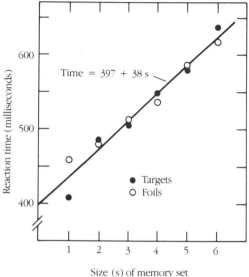

Figure 6-4. Time to recognize a digit increases with the number of items in the memory set. The straight line represents the linear function that fits the data best. (From Sternberg, 1969.)

search of working memory, Sternberg was able to explain why reaction time increased 38 milliseconds with each additional item the subject was holding in short-term memory.

Sternberg's theory has been criticized on many grounds, although none of the criticisms have proven definitive. J. A. Anderson (1973) argued that it was implausible to suppose that our brains worked fast enough to perform a comparison in every 38 milliseconds. Recall the earlier evidence that our brains are parallel devices, quite unlike the serial computer, and that they compute many relatively slow operations simultaneously.

An alternative to Sternberg's *serial theory* is a *parallel theory*, which holds that each item in the memory set is simultaneously being compared to the test item. Numerous parallel theories have been proposed, but a common one (e.g., Baddeley & Ecob, 1973) holds that the rate at which these comparisons can be performed is a function of how active the items are. Basically, the more digits one is rehearsing in working memory the less active any one digit will be.

Working Memory: A Summary

The following properties appear to be true of working memory:

1. The items in working memory are defined by a high level of activation, which enables reliable and rapid access to them.

2. If unattended the items in working memory will rapidly decay away in their level of activation.

3. One can maintain items in working memory by rehearsing them and keeping them in a highly active state.

4. There are limitations on how many items one can maintain in working memory. These limitations are determined by how many items one can rehearse before they decay away.

5. As items in working memory decay in level of activation the speed of our access to them slows.

Long-Term Memory

So far we have been concerned with the transient characteristics of information that we are currently processing. Typically, although not always, research on working memory has used information that we have just learned. Now we will turn to considering research that is concerned with the long-term fate of our memories. What happens to them when they drop out of a state of high activation? What determines whether and how fast we can get access to them again?

Not only does activation determine probability of access to memory, it also controls rate of access. This can be demonstrated by looking at the speed with which we can retrieve well-learned (i.e., strong) information that is in working memory versus well-learned information that is not. An experiment by Loftus (1974) nicely illustrates this. She looked at the time subjects required to retrieve well-learned information about categories such as fruit. She had subjects retrieve instances of a category that began with a certain initial letter. For instance, subjects might have to retrieve a fruit beginning with *p*. She found that they took an average of 1.53 seconds to perform this task the first time they were asked about a category. Then after varying delays she asked subjects to retrieve from the same category another member beginning with a different letter. Thus, she might ask subjects to retrieve a fruit beginning with *b*. She manipulated delay by inserting tests on other unrelated categories between the two tests on a category. For instance, during a two-item delay, subjects might be asked to retrieve a breed of dog that begin with *c* and a country that began with *r*. Looking at zero, one, and two intervening items, she found retrieval times of 1.21 seconds, 1.28 seconds, and 1.33 seconds, respectively. The first time they were tested, subjects took 1.53 seconds to generate an associate. So, relative to this initial retrieval time, we see strong facilitation if the category is tested again immediately, when the information about the category is still active in working memory. With increasing delay, however, the activation decays, producing longer and longer retrieval times.

One factor that ought to affect access to our memories is how much we have practiced the memory. An experiment from my laboratory (Anderson, 1976) illustrates how speed of retrieval varies with practice. In the first phase of this experiment, subjects committed to memory facts about locations of various people. For instance, they might learn the following sentences:

> The sailor is in the park.
>
> The lawyer is in the church.

Subjects were drilled over and over again on these sentences until they knew them by heart. Later, they were presented with sentences and asked to say whether each was among the sentences they had studied. Thus, subjects might see:

> The sailor is in the park.

This would require a positive response. Negative items were created by recombining people and locations in ways that had not been studied. For example, subjects might be presented with the following negative test item:

> The sailor is in the church.

Subjects had not studied this sentence and therefore were required to give a negative response. Since they knew the material well enough to be correct almost all the time, we were interested only in the speed with which they made their correct recognition judgments.

We were interested in two variables. One was differences in the amount of study applied to different sentences before testing. Some sentences were studied twice as frequently as others. We would expect frequency to be related to the strength of the encoding of a sentence, and hence that more frequently encountered information would be retrieved more quickly from long-term memory. The second variable was the delay between any two presentations of a particular sentence. We compared the situation in which zero to two items intervened between repetitions and the sentence was still likely to be active in working memory with the situation in which three or more items intervened and the sentence probably had to be reactivated. We were interested in the effect of this delay between tests on recognition time for the second presentation of a sentence. The difference between the short delay and the long delay is a measure of the amount of time that it takes to reactivate the information.

Table 6-2 displays judgment times for the second sentence in a repetition classified according to these two variables. After short test delays, frequency of study had very little effect on recognition time. On the other hand, following a long delay between repetitions, subjects were considerably faster on the more frequently studied sentence. Time to activate a sentence in long-term memory can be estimated as the difference between three or more intervening items and zero to two intervening items. Using this estimate, it takes $1.53 - 1.11 = .42$ seconds to activate the less frequently studied items from long-term memory, but only $1.38 - 1.10 = .28$ seconds to activate the more frequently studied items. Thus, as expected, it takes longer to reactivate the weaker memories.

The effects of practice on memory retrieval are extremely regular and very large. In one study, Anderson (1983) had subjects practice sentences like the ones displayed earlier for 25 days and looked at the effects of this practice on time to recognize a sentence. Figure 6-5 illustrates the result

Table 6-2 *Effects of Delay of Repetition and Frequency of Exposure on Recognition Time for Second Presentation of a Sentence*

	Delay	
Degree of Study	Short (0 to 2 Intervening Items)	Long (3 or More Intervening Items)
Less study	1.11 seconds	1.53 seconds
More study	1.10 seconds	1.38 seconds

From Anderson, 1976.

of this manipulation. As can be seen, subjects sped up from about 1.6 seconds to .7 seconds, cutting their retrieval time by more than 50 percent. The figure also shows that the rate of improvement decreases with more practice. The data are nicely fit by a power function[2] of the form

$$RT = .36 + .96(D - \tfrac{1}{2})^{-.36}$$

where RT is the reaction time and D is the number of days of practice. We will have more to say about such practice functions in Chapter 9, where the development of expertise is discussed.

At the beginning of this chapter we saw in Ebbinghaus's research that frequency of exposure affected probability of recall. The data in Table 6-2 and Figure 6-5 show that frequency also affects retrieval time. These effects on retrieval time and effects on retention are probably manifestations of the same underlying memory mechanisms. One view is that failure to recall is just the result of an extreme retrieval time — that the item is still in memory, but its retrieval is just too slow. We will return to this point later in the chapter.

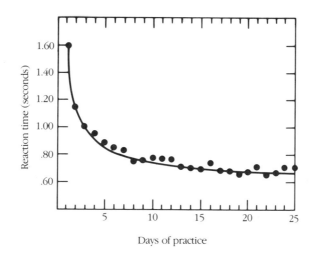

Figure 6-5. Time to recognize a sentence as a function of the number of trials of practice.

---

[2]*Power functions* define the dependent variable (in this case, RT) by raising the independent variable (in this case, D) to an exponent. The simplest form of a power function is $y = ax^b$

Spread of Activation

It is informative to think about the activation concept within the network framework developed in Chapter 5. Consider Figure 6-6, which illustrates part of the propositional network surrounding the concept *dog*. Note that *dog* is connected to the concept *bone*. Thus, when the word *dog* is presented to the subject, not only will that concept become active, but activation should spread to the concepts surrounding *dog*, so that terms such as *bone* become active as well. An unpublished experiment by Perlmutter and Anderson illustrates the kind of evidence that exists for this spreading activation process. Subjects were presented with a sequence of words and asked to generate associates that began with specific letters. We were interested in contrasting such sequences as the following two:

Priming	*Control*
dog – c	gambler – c
bone – m	bone – m

In the first case, the subject might generate *cat* as the associate to *dog* and then be presented with *bone* and generate *meat* as an associate. In the second case, the control condition, the responses might be *card* and *meat*. The important feature of the priming condition is that an already existing associative path leads from *dog* to *bone* and to *meat*. Therefore, activating the network structure to answer the first associate should help activate the structure needed to answer the second. The first associate (dog – c)

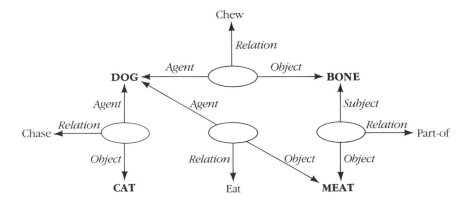

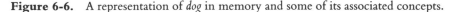

Figure 6-6. A representation of *dog* in memory and some of its associated concepts.

160

serves to prime the second (bone – m). In contrast, no priming connection exists in the control case. Therefore, subjects were expected to generate the second associate faster in the priming condition. This expectation was confirmed: Subjects took 1.41 seconds to generate an associate in the priming case, as contrasted with 1.53 seconds in the control case.

The notion of *spread of activation*, illustrated in this and other experiments, is fundamental to an understanding of recall from long-term memory. Activation spreads through long-term memory from active portions to other portions of memory, and this spread takes time. Consider the results in Table 6-2, drawn from the experiment in which subjects were required to recognize sentences of the form *A sailor is in the park.* Figure 6-7 is the propositional-network representation of such a sentence. This sentence, presented as a test probe, should activate the words *sailor, in,* and *park.* Activation spreads from link to link through the structure shown in Figure 6-7 like water flowing through irrigation channels. Before the sentence can be recalled, the whole structure in the figure must be activated. Thus, the time spent in the retrieval of a memory structure would reflect the time taken for the spread of activation through that structure.

Note that the spread-of-activation process is not entirely under an individual's control. For example, when subjects generated an associate to *dog* in the Perlmutter and Anderson experiment described earlier, they had no reason to *want* to activate the *bone – meat* association. Still, some

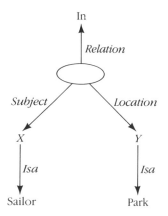

Figure 6-7. A propositional-network representation for the statement *A sailor is in the park.* This structure must be activated in order for the proposition to be recognized.

activation spread to this part of the network and helped to prime knowledge of the connection between *bone* and *meat*. Many experiments in cognitive psychology have demonstrated this unconscious priming — called *associative priming* — of knowledge through spreading activation.

Associative Priming

Meyer and Schvaneveldt (1971) performed what has become a classic demonstration of associative priming. They had subjects judge whether or not pairs of items were words. Table 6-3 shows examples of the materials used in their experiments and subjects' judgment times. The items were presented one above the other. If either item in a pair was a nonword, subjects were to respond no. It appears from examining the negative pairs that subjects judged first the top item and then the second. Where the top item was a nonword, subjects were faster to reject the pair than when only the second item was a nonword. Where the top item was not a word, subjects did not have to judge the second item and so could respond sooner.

The major interest in this study was in the positive pairs. There were unrelated items such as *nurse* and *butter*, and pairs with an associative relation such as *bread* and *butter*. Subjects were 85 milliseconds faster on the related pairs. This result indicates that because subjects judged the first item to be a word, activation spread from that word and primed information about the second, associatively related, item. If a subject is to make a judgment about whether an item is a word, the representation of the word has to be active in short-term memory. The implication of this result is that the associative spreading of activation through memory can facilitate the rate at which words are read. Thus, we can read material that has a strong associative coherence more rapidly than incoherent material in which the words are unrelated.

Table 6-3 *Examples of the Pairs Used to Demonstrate Associative Priming*

Positive Pairs		Negative Pairs		
Unrelated	Related	Nonword First	Nonword Second	Both Nonwords
Nurse	Bread	Plame	Wine	Plame
Butter	Butter	Wine	Plame	Reab
940 msec	855 msec	904 msec	1087 msec	884 msec

From Meyer and Schvaneveldt, 1971.

Ratcliff and McKoon (1981) report a rather different priming demonstration of spreading activation. They had subjects commit to memory sentences such as *The doctor hated the book.* After committing these sentences to memory, subjects were transferred to a word-recognition paradigm where they saw nouns from the sentences and had to recognize whether the nouns came from the studied sentences. So, if subjects saw a word such as *book*, which was in the memorized sentences, they would respond yes.

Sometimes, before presenting the target (e.g., *book*), Ratcliff and McKoon presented a prime noun that came from the same sentence (i.e., *doctor*). They found subjects faster in this primed condition compared to a control condition that did not have the prime noun. Subjects took 667 milliseconds in the control condition compared to 624 milliseconds in the primed condition. Thus, Ratcliff and McKoon demonstrated that experimentally learned associates could prime a recognition judgment.

Ratcliff and McKoon varied the delay between the prime (*doctor*) and the target (*book*) from 50 to 300 milliseconds. All of these intervals were too short for subjects to develop any conscious expectations. So, we are looking at the effects of automatic spread of activation. The interesting issue is how the priming effect grew over the 300 millisecond interval. Figure 6-8 shows how reaction time in the priming condition decreased over this interval. This decrease in reaction time reflects the growth in the level of activation.

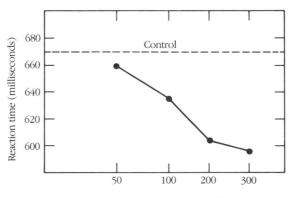

Delay between prime and target (milliseconds)

Figure 6-8. Difference between primed and control conditions as a function of the interval between priming word and target word.

The priming effect appears very rapidly. Subjects are somewhat faster in the primed condition than in the control condition even when there are just 50 milliseconds between prime and target. The priming essentially reached asymptotic levels in 200 milliseconds. Thus, it appears that activation can spread very rapidly.

Summary: Relation of Activation to Processing Time

For information to be used in a task such as a recognition judgment, it must first be activated and then inspected. When information is in long-term memory but not currently in working memory, activation must spread to it, which takes some amount of time, as we saw in the McKoon and Ratcliff study. Once activated, the time to inspect the information will depend on its level of activation, as was illustrated in the Sternberg experiment.

Interference

The Fan Effect

Various factors can affect the amount of activation that is spread to a knowledge structure. From the results reviewed before (Table 6-2 and Figure 6-5), we can infer that strength of encoding has an effect such that more strongly encoded information receives greater activation. Another factor, to be discussed here, is the number of alternative network paths down which activation can spread. In one experiment (Anderson, 1974a) we had subjects memorize 26 facts, again of the form *A person is in a location*. Some persons were paired with only one location and some locations with only one person. Other persons were paired with two locations and other locations were paired with two persons. For instance, suppose that subjects studied these sentences:

1. The doctor is in the bank. (1-1)

2. The fireman is in the park. (1-2)

3. The lawyer is in the church. (2-1)

4. The lawyer is in the park. (2-2)

Each statement is followed by two numbers, reflecting the number of facts associated with the subject and the location. For instance, sentence 3 is labeled 2-1 because its subject occurs in two sentences (sentences 3 and 4) and its location occurs in one (sentence 3).

Subjects were drilled on this material until they knew it quite well. Before beginning the reaction-time phase, subjects were able to recall all the locations associated with a particular type of person (e.g., *doctor*) and all the people associated with a particular location (e.g., *park*). Then they began a speeded-recognition phase of the experiment, during which they were presented with sentences and had to judge whether they recognized them from the study set. New foil sentences were created by the repairing of people and locations from the study set. The reaction times involving sentences such as those listed above are displayed in Table 6-4, which classifies the data as a function of the number of facts associated with a person and a location. As can be seen, recognition time increases as a function of both the number of facts studied about the person and the number of facts studied about the location.

Figure 6-9 shows the network representation for sentences 1 through 4.[3] By applying the activation concept to this representation, we can nicely account for the increase in reaction time. Consider how the subject might recognize such a probe as *A lawyer is in the park.* First, suppose that the presentation of the terms *lawyer, in,* and *park* serves to activate their representations in memory. Then activation will spread from these nodes

Table 6-4 *Mean Recognition Time for Sentences as a Function of Number of Facts Learned About Person and Location*

Number of sentences Using a Specific Location	Number of Sentences About a Specific Person	
	1 Sentence	2 Sentences
1 sentence	1.11 sec	1.17 sec
2 sentences	1.17 sec	1.22 sec

From Anderson, 1974a.

[3]For simplicity, we have not represented the distinction between instances and concepts in the figure. As indicated in Chapter 5, this distinction can be important. Therefore, the representation in Figure 6–9 is only an approximation of the true underlying representation. However, the figure highlights the features of the propositional network that are significant for an understanding of this experiment.

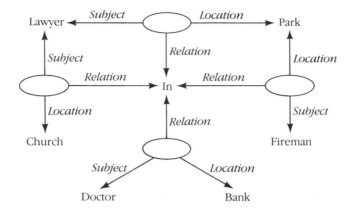

Figure 6-9. Network representations for four sentences used in the experiment of Anderson (1974a). The sentences are *The doctor is in the bank; The fireman is in the park; The lawyer is in the church;* and *The lawyer is in the park.*

to activate the target proposition and enable it to be recognized. The critical assumption is that the amount of activation reaching the proposition is inversely related to the number of links leading from it. So, given a structure like Figure 6-9, subjects should be slower to recognize a fact involving *lawyer* and *park* than one connecting *doctor* and *bank* because more paths emanate from the first set of concepts. That is, in the *lawyer* and *park* case two paths point from each of the concepts to the two propositions in which each was studied, whereas only one path leads from each of the *doctor* and *bank* concepts.

This is one experiment among many that point to a *limited-capacity feature* of the spreading-activation process. The nodes, such as *lawyer* and *park*, from which the spread of activation starts can be called *source nodes*. A source node has a certain fixed capacity for emitting activation. This capacity is divided among all the paths emanating from that node. The more paths that exist, the less activation will be assigned to any one path and the slower will be the rate of activation. The *fan effect* is the name given to this increase in reaction time related to an increase in the number of facts associated with a concept. It is so named because the increase in reaction time is related to an increase in the fan of facts emanating from the network representation of the concept.

Interference is the more general term used to refer to such phenomena. The term conveys the fact that additional information about a concept interferes with memory for a particular piece of information. As we will see, such interference affects a wider range of measures than just recognition time. The term *fan effect* is reserved for interference effects as measured by reaction time.

Interference and Historical Memories

An experiment by Lewis and Anderson (1976) investigated whether the fan effect could be obtained with material the subject knew before the experiment. We had subjects learn fantasy facts about public figures — for example, *Napoleon Bonaparte was from India*. Subjects studied from zero to four such fantasy facts about each public figure. After learning these "facts," they proceeded to a recognition-test phase. In this phase they saw three types of sentences: (1) statements they had studied in the experiment; (2) true facts about the public figures (such as *Napoleon Bonaparte was an emperor*); and (3) statements about the public figure that were false both in the experimental fantasy world and in the real world. Subjects had to respond to the first two types of facts as true and to the last type as false.

Figure 6-10 presents subjects' reaction time in making these judgments as a function of the number of fantasy facts (the fan) studied about the person. Note that reaction time increased with fan for all types of facts. Also note that subjects responded much faster to actual truths than to experimental truths. The advantage of actual truths can be explained, because these true facts would be much more strongly encoded in memory than the fantasy facts because of greater prior exposure. The most important result to note in Figure 6-10 is that the more fantasy facts subjects have learned about an individual such as Napoleon Bonaparte, the longer subjects take to recognize a fact that they already know about the individual; for example, *Napoleon Bonaparte was an emperor*. Thus, we can produce interference with preexperimental material. For further research on this topic, see Peterson and Potts (1982).

Interference and Retention

So far, we have considered how interference from other information associated with a concept can slow down the speed with which the fact can be retrieved. The effects have been a matter of a few hundred milliseconds. We will now consider what happens as these interfering effects get more extreme — either because the to-be-recalled fact is very weak or because the interference is very strong. There is evidence that the

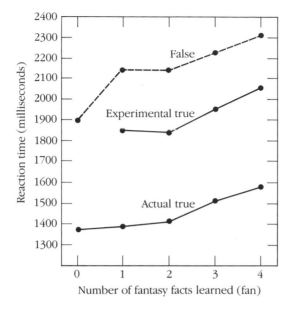

Figure 6-10. Reaction times from Lewis and Anderson (1976). The task was to recognize true and fantasy facts about a public figure and to reject statements that were neither true nor fantasy facts. This figure shows that the time subjects took to make all three judgments increased as they learned more fantasy facts about public figures.

subject simply fails to remember the information under both conditions. Results showing such failures of memory have traditionally been obtained with paired-associate material, although similar results have been obtained with other material.

In the typical interference experiment, two critical groups are defined (these are illustrated in Table 6-5). The $A-D$ experimental group learns two lists of paired associates, the first list designated $A-B$ and the second designated $A-D$. The lists are so designated because they share common stimuli (the A terms). For example, among the pairs that the subject studies in the $A-B$ list might be *cat–43* and *house–61*, and in the $A-D$ list *cat–82* and *house–37*. The $C-D$ control group also first studies the $A-B$ list, but then studies a different second list, designated $C-D$, which does not contain the same stimuli as the first list. For example, in the $C-D$ list subjects might study *bone–82* and *cup–37*. After learning their respective second lists, both groups are retested for their memory of their

Table 6-5 *Experimental and Control Groups Used in a Typical Interference Paradigm*

A–D Experimental		C–D Control	
LEARN	A–B	LEARN	A–B
LEARN	A–D	LEARN	C–D
TEST	A–B	TEST	A–B

first list, in both cases the $A-B$ list. Often this retention test is administered after a considerable delay, such as 24 hours or a week. In general, the $A-D$ group does not do as well as the $C-D$ group with respect to both rate of learning of the second list and retention of the original $A-B$ list.

These results are to be expected given our understanding of interference. Figure 6-11 shows the network representation of the knowledge structures for the two groups. Part (a) illustrates the assumed memory structure for the experimental group. Members of this group have A stimuli in both lists and so have learned interfering associations to these stimuli. Part (b) of the figure illustrates the assumed memory structure for the control group. There were different stimuli in the two lists — in list 1 subjects associated *43* to *cat*, while in list 2 they associated *82* to *bone*. Thus, the experimental group has an extra list 2 association to interfere with the *cat–43* memory while the control group does not. In the reaction-time experiments discussed earlier, such interference (two associations rather than one) resulted in increased reaction time, but not failure to recall. In those experiments, however, the items had been highly overlearned before reaction time was tested. In the interference experiments, subjects are tested as they are learning the paired associates. Here the strengths of associations are much weaker. When the exposure to the pairs has been minimal and their associations barely learned, the interference of associates learned in the second list can result in failure to recall. The implication is that failure to recall is the extreme case of a long retrieval time. Thus, it is not the case that the forgotten information is not in memory, but rather that it is in memory but is too weak to be activated in the face of the interference from other associations. In this view, forgetting is not actual loss of information from memory but rather loss of the ability to activate that information.

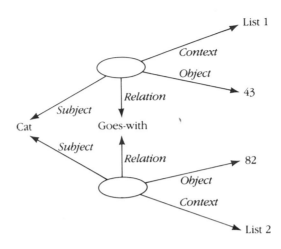

(a) Lists *A–B, A–D*

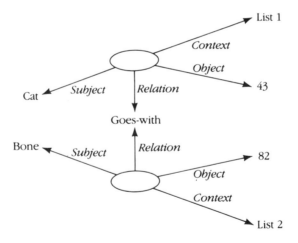

(b) Lists *A–B, C–D*

Figure 6-11. Network representations for the two conditions identified in Table 6-5: (a) network representing the encodings of the *A–B* and *A–D* associations in the experimental condition; (b) network representing the encodings of the *A–B* and *C–D* associations in the control condition.

170

Recall versus Recognition

Consistent with the hypothesis that there exists in memory information that we cannot recall is the fact that we can recognize many things we cannot recall.[4] This phenomenon suggests that information can be in memory even though it cannot be activated in the recall-test situation. The memory-network analysis we have been developing makes clear the reason that recognition often works even when recall fails. For example, let us compare the efforts of students trying to answer the following questions:

1. Who was the president after Wilson?

2. Was Harding the president after Wilson?

Figure 6-12 illustrates the memory structure that is being addressed by the questions. The first question, a recall question, provides subjects with *Wilson* as a probe from which to search memory. The question requires that subjects access memory from *Wilson* and activate the memory structures 1, 2, and 3, which contain the information relating *Wilson* to *Harding*. It is possible that the activation from *Wilson* is not enough to achieve this. However, the second, recognition question also provides the

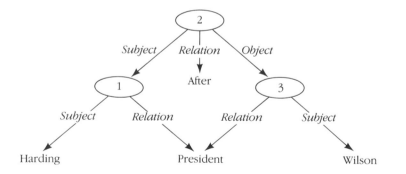

Figure 6-12. A propositional-network representation of the information that Harding was president after Wilson.

---

[4]There are, however, situations where performance on a recall test can be better than performance on a recognition test, as we will discuss in the next chapter.

answer, *Harding*, as a second source of activation. The combined activation spreading from *Wilson* and *Harding* might be sufficient to activate the requisite memory structures 1, 2, and 3.

Note that this analysis says that recognition is typically better than recall because a recognition test typically provides more sources for activating memory. However, this is not always the case. In the next chapter, under Effects of Encoding Context, we will discuss where recall is better than recognition because the recall test provides better sources for activating the relevant memory.

Decay Processes in Forgetting

Although interference is an important cause of forgetting, it seems unlikely that interference is the only cause. Memories appear to decay very systematically with delay, independent of any interference. Much of the research documenting this fading has been done by Wickelgren. In one recognition experiment (1975), he presented subjects with a sequence of words to study and then looked at their probability of recognizing the words after delays ranging from 1 min to 14 days. Figure 6-13 shows performance as a function of delay. The performance measure Wickelgren used is called *d'*; it is derived from probability of recognition and is thought to be a measure of memory strength.

We see that performance systematically deteriorates with delay. However, these changes are *negatively accelerated*—that is, the rate of change gets smaller and smaller with delay. In Figure 6-13 part (b) I have replotted the data, plotting the logarithm of the performance measure and the logarithm of delay. Marvelously, the function becomes linear. Log performance is a linear function of delay; that is,

$$log(d') = A - b \log D$$

This equation can be transformed to become

$$d' = A^*D^{-b}$$

where $A^* = 10^A$. That is, these performance measures are power functions of delay. Interestingly, the Ebbinghaus retention function in Figure 6-1 can also be shown to be a power function.

A very dramatic example of the retention function was produced by Bahrick (1984), who looked at subjects' retention of Spanish-English

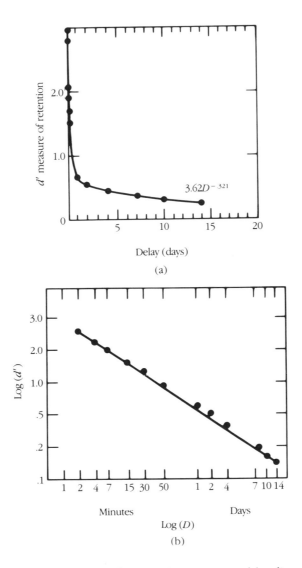

$$3.62D^{-.321}$$

Figure 6-13. (a) Success at word recognition as measured by d' as a function of delay (D); (b) the data in (a) replotted on a log–log scale. (Adapted from Wickelgren, 1975.)

vocabulary items anywhere from immediately to 50 years after they had completed courses in high school and college. Figure 6-14 plots their scores out of 15 items as a function of the logarithm of the time since course completion. Separate functions are plotted for students who had 1, 3, or 5 courses. The data clearly show a slow decay of knowledge with

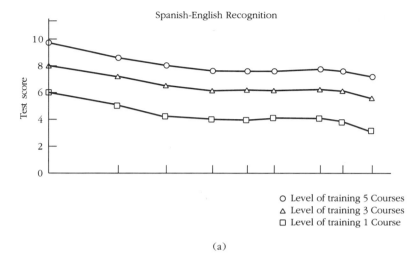

Figure 6-14. The effect of level of training on the retention of recognition vocabulary. (From Bahrick, 1984. Copyright 1984 by the American Psychological Association. Reprinted by permission.)

time combined with a substantial practice effect. In Bahrick's data the retention functions are nearly flat between 3 and 25 years with some further drop-off from 25 to 49 years.

These forgetting functions are highly systematic and appear to describe forgetting in the absence of any apparent interference. There has been a long-standing controversy in cognitive psychology about whether such retention functions reflect decay in the absence of any interference or whether they reflect interference from unidentified sources. Objections have been raised to decay theories because they do not identify the psychological factors producing the forgetting, but rather assert that forgetting occurs spontaneously with time. It may be possible, however, that there is no explanation of decay at the purely psychological level. The explanation may be physiological. It has been shown that synaptic efficacy deteriorates with lack of use, and apparently this deterioration also follows a power law (Barnes & McNaughton, 1980). Thus, it may be that the mechanism underlying the very lawful functions in Figures 6-13 and 6-14 may be neural. Just as our muscles will atrophy with lack of use, so will neural connections. This analogy to muscles also suggests that our memories may not be lost because of decay; the memories may still be encoded in our brains but are too weak to be retrieved.

Are Forgotten Memories Truly Lost?

An interesting possibility is that we never do really lose our memories — that forgotten memories are still there but are too weak to be revived. The results reported by Penfield (1959) are consistent with this notion. As part of a neurosurgical procedure, Penfield electrically stimulated portions of patients' brains and asked them to report what they experienced (patients were conscious during the surgery but the stimulation technique was painless). In this way Penfield was able to determine the function of various portions of the brain. Stimulation of the temporal lobes led to reports of memories that patients were unable to report in normal recall—for instance, events from their childhood. It was as if Penfield's stimulation activated portions of the memory network that spreading activation could not reach. Unfortunately, it is hard to know whether the patients' memory reports were accurate, since going back in time to check on whether the events reported actually occurred was nearly impossible. Therefore, although suggestive, the Penfield experiments are generally discounted by memory researchers.

A better experiment, conducted by Nelson (1971), also indicates that "forgotten" memories still exist. He had subjects learn 20 number–noun paired associates; they studied the list until they reached a criterion of one errorless trial. Subjects returned for a retest two weeks later, recalling 75 percent of the items on this retention test. However, interest focused on the 25 percent of the items for which the subjects were unable to recall the noun response to the digit stimulus. Subjects were given new learning trials on the 20 paired associates. The paired associates they had missed were either kept the same or changed. In the changed case, a new response was associated to an old stimulus. If subjects had learned *43 – dog*, but failed to recall the response to *43*, they might now be trained on either *43 – dog* (unchanged) or *43 – house* (changed). They were tested after studying the new list once. If subjects had lost all memory for the forgotten pairs, there should be no difference between changed and unchanged pairs. However, subjects correctly recalled 78 percent of the unchanged items formerly missed but only 43 percent of the changed items. This large advantage for unchanged items indicates that subjects had retained something about the paired associates even though they had been unable to recall them initially. This retained information was reflected in the savings displayed in relearning.

Nelson (1978) also looked at the situation in which the retention test involved recognition. Four weeks after learning, subjects failed to recognize 31 percent of the paired associates they had learned. As in the previous experiment, Nelson had subjects relearn the missing items. For half the stimuli the responses were changed and for the other half they were left unchanged. After one relearning trial, subjects recognized 34 percent of the unchanged items but only 19 percent of the changed items. The recognition-retention test should have been very sensitive to whether subjects have anything in memory. However, even when subjects fail this sensitive test, there appears to be some evidence that a record of the items is still in memory—the evidence that relearning was better for the unchanged than the changed pairs. The implication of the Nelson studies is that if we can come up with a sufficiently sensitive measure, we can show that apparently forgotten memories are still there.

Remarks and Suggested Readings

There are a good many texts on human memory, including those of Baddeley (1976), Crowder (1976), and Klatzky (1979). The book by Anderson and Kosslyn (1984) contains a series of essays surveying the current state of literature in the field.

Many different views have been expressed regarding the nature of working memory or the related concept of short-term memory. Baddeley (1986) and Crowder (1982) provide good reviews of the research and opinions. Atkinson and Shiffrin (1968) should be consulted for a very elegant model that represented the viewpoint nearly 25 years ago.

The concept of spreading activation became popular in cognitive psychology with work on computer-simulation models by Quillian (1966, 1969) and Reitman (1965). A comprehensive statement of the application of Quillian's ideas to psychological issues is to be found in Collins and Quillian (1972) and Collins and Loftus (1975). I gave a review of this topic in Anderson (1984).

Interference in long-term memory has had a very long research tradition, and many current issues could not be considered in this chapter. For discussions of the current ideas about forgetting, see the relevant chapters in Anderson and Bower (1973) and Crowder (1976). See also the papers by Postman (1971), Postman and Underwood (1973), and Wickelgren (1976).

Human Memory: Elaborations and Distinctions

Summary

1. When information is committed to memory it is often elaborated with additional information. Those elaborations facilitate recall by providing additional retrieval paths and by permitting recall by inference and reconstruction.

2. Memory for a piece of information can be improved by manipulations that increase the amount of elaboration performed by a subject.

3. Intention to learn is irrelevant to the amount learned. What is relevant is the way in which the information is processed.

4. People often recall by inferring what is plausible given what they can remember. Such inferential recall will cause subjects to recall what they did not study but will also help them recall more of what they did study and more rapidly.

5. Schemas are a major mechanism for elaborating material during study, and they are a major mechanism for reconstructing memories at test. Recall will be distorted to fit the schemas that a subject has.

6. Memory performance improves the more closely the context at test matches the context at study. This has been shown to be true with respect to physical context (e.g., location), internal context (e.g., mood), and the context provided by other study materials.

7. Studying material at widely spaced intervals tends to lead to better long-term retention because the material is learned in more different contexts.

8. Methods like the *PQ4R method* for studying textbooks are effective because they impose a retrieval structure on the text, because they enforce spaced study, and because they promote more elaborate processing of the text.

9. People can have implicit memories of which they are not conscious. These implicit memories manifest themselves in the performance of cognitive tasks as varied as word identification and problem solving.

Elaborations and Their Network Representations

In Chapter 6, we assumed, for simplicity's sake, a rather impoverished conception of the material that is typically committed to memory. Now, consider an experiment where a subject must commit to memory the following sentence:

    1.   The doctor hated the lawyer.

Figure 7-1 part (a) illustrates the kind of memory-network representation that we have been assuming for such a sentence. However, a subject presented with sentence 1 is unlikely to deposit only this structure in memory. Figure 7-1 part (b) is a network representation of what a subject might really think while studying the sentence. The difference between this structure and the simplified one is that the subject has elaborated upon the sentence with new thoughts or propositions. Since the subject thinks these propositions upon being presented with the sentence, they might be committed to memory—just as the studied proposition is. In such a case, in addition to the studied proposition, the subject would have stored the following information:

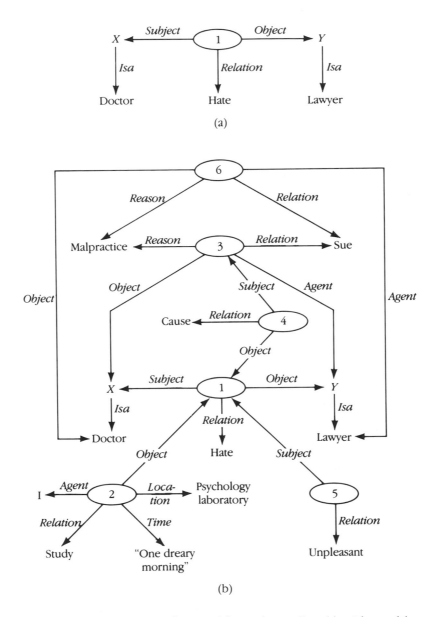

Figure 7-1. A comparison of an unelaborated encoding (a) with an elaborated encoding (b) of the sentence *The doctor hated the lawyer.*

2. The subject studied this sentence in the psychology laboratory one dreary morning.

3. The lawyer had sued the doctor for malpractice.

4. The malpractice suit was the source of the doctor's hatred.

5. This sentence is unpleasant.

Another fact representing some relevant information was probably already in memory:

6. Lawyers sue doctors for malpractice.

Such structures as that in part (b) of Figure 7-1 — called *elaborated structures*, since they incorporate *elaborations* on the original proposition — can have profound effects on memory. The function of this chapter is to review research that studies these effects.

One effect we would expect is that memory for any event would improve the more it is elaborated. Elaborations can lead to better memory in at least two ways. First, they provide redundant retrieval routes for recall. To see this, contrast parts (a) and (b) of Figure 7-1. Suppose the link from node X (the doctor node) to the target proposition (node 1) is too weak to be revived at recall. If this were true and if the subject had only structure (a), he or she would be unable to recall proposition 1 when prompted with *doctor*. On the other hand, in representation (b), even if the first link were too weak, there are other ways of retrieving the target proposition. For instance, the subject could recall from X the proposition that the lawyer sued the doctor for malpractice (node 3). From proposition node 3, the subject could recall the proposition that the malpractice suit led to the doctor's hating the lawyer (node 4). From here the subject would be able to recall node 1, which he or she had been unable to recall directly from X. That is, although the subject could not traverse the direct path from X to 1, he or she would be able to go from X to 3 to 4 to 1. Thus, this elaborated structure would help recall by providing the subject with *alternate retrieval routes* through the network to be used should the more direct ones fail.

Now, suppose the subject completely failed to encode target proposition 1. Then, no matter what the attempts, recall would fail. However, if the subject were able to recall the elaborations on the target proposition, his or her knowledge state would be following:

> I cannot remember the target sentence but I can remember conjecturing that it was caused by the lawyer's suing the doctor for malpractice and I can remember it was a negative sentence.

With this information the subject might infer that the target sentence was *The doctor hated the lawyer.* Thus, a second way in which elaboration aids memory is that it helps individuals to infer what they can no longer actually remember.

Both of these processes can be said to work because elaborations increase the *redundancy* with which information is encoded in memory. *Redundant elaboration* means that additional information is encoded in memory, which provides more paths for retrieving and bases for inferring the to-be-remembered information. We would predict that experimental manipulations which increase the amount of redundant elaboration should increase the amount of recall.

The interference manipulations that we studied in Chapter 6 showed that a subject's memory was poorer the more information that was learned about a concept. Here the argument is that memory is being improved by redundant elaborations. The difference is that in the former case the additional information is irrelevant. An experiment by Bradshaw and Anderson (1982) illustrates the contrasting effects of relevant versus irrelevant information. They looked at subjects' ability to learn some little-known information about some famous people. In one condition they had subjects study just a single fact:

> Newton became emotionally unstable and insecure as a child.

In the irrelevant condition they had subjects learn a target fact plus two unrelated facts about the individual:

> Locke was unhappy as a student at Westminister.
> *plus*
> Locke felt fruits were unwholesome for children.
> Locke had a long history of back trouble.

In the third, relevant condition subjects learned two additional facts that were causally related to the target fact:

> Mozart made a long journey from Munich to Paris.
> *plus*
> Mozart wanted to leave Munich to avoid a romantic entanglement.
> Mozart was intrigued by musical developments coming out of Paris.

Subjects were tested for their ability to recall the target facts immediately after studying a set of facts such as these and at a week's delay. They were presented with names like Newton, Mozart, and Locke and asked to recall what they had studied. The results are displayed in Table 7-1. Comparing the irrelevant condition with the single condition we see the standard interference effect, which is that recall is worse when there are more facts to be learned. However, the conclusion is quite different when we compare the relevant condition to the single condition. Here, particularly at a week's delay, recall is better when the subject had to learn additional facts causally related to the target facts.

Elaborateness of Processing

Representative Studies

A number of experiments have appeared in the literature that can be interpreted as illustrating that more fully elaborated material results in better memory. These experiments have sometimes been viewed as illustrating the principle of *depth of processing*. Fergus Craik at the University of Toronto has promoted the term (e.g., see Craik & Lockhart, 1972), but a great many independent researchers have been involved. They have shown in various ways that manipulations to increase the depth with which information is processed result in better memory. *Depth* here is used as an intuitive term to reflect how fully the subject processes the meaning of the material to be learned. It is probably best interpreted as referring to the number of elaborations the learner generates. Therefore, we will refer to this factor as *elaborateness of processing*.

A classic demonstration of elaborateness of processing comes from the 1969 experiments of Bobrow and Bower. They had subjects try to commit to memory simple subject-verb-object sentences. There were two conditions of interest. In condition 1 subjects were provided with sen-

Table 7-1 *Percentage of Recall as a Function of Condition and Time Intervals*

	Immediate Recall	Recall at a Week
Single fact	92	62
Irrelevant facts	80	45
Relevant facts	94	73

From Bradshaw and Anderson,1982.

tences written by the experimenters. In condition 2 subjects had to generate sentences to connect the subject nouns and object nouns. After studying the sentences, subjects were prompted with the first (*subject*) noun and where required to generate the second (*object*) noun.

In condition 1 (sentences provided by the experimenters), subjects recalled 29 percent of the nouns; in condition 2 (sentences generated by subject), they recalled 58 percent. Presumably, in generating their own sentences subjects had to think more carefully about the meaning of the two nouns and their possible interrelationships. They probably considered a number of tentative connections between the two nouns before they chose one. This extra mental effort or deeper processing would have led to more elaborations of the nouns, and particularly to more elaborations that served to connect them. Similar demonstrations of the advantage of generation have been provided by Jacoby (1978) and Slamecka and Graf (1978).

A number of devices are known to improve subjects' memory for sentences provided by an experimenter. One is to ask the subject to generate a logical continuation to the sentence. So, given the sentence *The fireman stabbed the dancer*, a subject might continue *in a lovers' quarrel*. Another technique is simply to ask subjects to develop a vivid visual image of the situation described by the sentence. As with the Bobrow and Bower manipulation, both of these techniques encourage the subject to process the sentence more deeply and more elaborately.

A series of experiments by Stein and Bransford (1979) shows why self-generated elaborations are often better than experimenter-provided elaborations. In one of these experiments, subjects were to remember 10 sentences, such as *The fat man read the sign*. There were four conditions of study. In the base condition, subjects studied just the sentence. In the self-generate condition, subjects were to generate an elaboration of their own. In the imprecise elaboration condition, subjects were presented with a continuation of the sentence, such as *that was two feet tall*. In the precise elaboration condition, they were presented with a continuation, such as *warning about the ice*. After studying the material, subjects in all conditions were presented with sentence frames like *The   man read the sign*, and they had to recall the missing adjective. Subjects recalled 4.2 of the 10 adjectives in the base condition and 5.8 when they generated their own elaboration. Thus, self-generated elaborations helped. They could recall only 2.2 of the adjectives in the imprecise elaboration condition, replicating the typical inferiority found for experimenter-provided elaborations relative to self-generated ones. However, subjects recalled the most—7.8—adjectives in the precise elaboration condition. So, by careful choice of elaboration, experimenter elaborations can be made better than subject elaborations. (For further research on this topic read Pressley, McDaniel, Turnure, Wood, & Ahmad, 1987.)

Thus, it appears that the critical factor is not whether the subject or the experimenter generates the elaborations. Rather, it is whether the elaborations are such that they constrain the to-be-recalled material. Subject-generated elaborations are quite effective because these elaborations reflect the idiosyncratic constraints of the particular subject's knowledge. However, as Stein and Bransford demonstrate, it is possible for the experimenter to construct elaborations that are even more precise in their constraints. Thus, elaborations help to the degree that they are an effective means of redundancy and so provide a means for reconstructing the to-be-remembered information.

These sorts of results are not limited to sentences. One important experiment, reported by Hyde and Jenkins (1973), involved memory for individual words. Subjects saw groups of 24 words presented at the rate of 3 seconds per word. One group of subjects was asked to check whether each word had an *e* or a *g*. The other group of subjects was asked to rate the pleasantness of the words. These two tasks were called *orienting tasks*. It is reasonable to assume that the pleasantness rating involved deeper and more elaborate processing than the letter-verification task. Another manipulation was whether subjects were told that the true purpose of the experiment was to learn the words. Half the subjects in each group were told the true purpose of the experiment. These subjects were said to be in the intentional-learning condition. The other half in each group, who thought the true purpose was to rate the words or check for letters, were said to be in the incidental-learning condition. Thus, there are altogether four conditions: pleasantness intentional, pleasantness incidental, letter-checking intentional, and letter-checking incidental.

After studying the list, all subjects were asked to recall as many words as they could. Table 7-2 presents the results from the Hyde and Jenkins

Table 7-2 *Percentage of Words Recalled as a Function of Orienting Task and Whether Subjects Were Aware of Learning Task*

Learning-purpose Conditions	Orienting Task	
	Rate Pleasantness	Check Letters
Incidental	68	39
Intentional	69	43

Adapted from Hyde and Jenkins, 1973

experiment in terms of percentage of the 24 words recalled. Two results are noteworthy. First, subjects' knowledge of the purpose of learning the words (of whether they would be tested for recall) had relatively little effect. Second, a large elaborateness-of-processing effect was demonstrated; subjects showed much higher recall in the pleasantness-rating condition independent of whether they expected to be tested on the material later. In rating a word for pleasantness, subjects had to think about its meaning, which gave them an opportunity to elaborate upon the word. For instance, a subject presented with *duck* might think, "Duck— oh yes, I used to feed the ducks in the park; that was a pleasant time."

Incidental Versus Intentional Learning

The Hyde and Jenkins experiment illustrates an important finding that has been proven over and over again in the research on intentional versus incidental learning: Whether a person intends to learn or not really does not matter (see Postman, 1964, for a review). What matters is how the person processes the material during its presentation. If the individual engages in identical mental activities when not intending as when intending to learn, he or she gets identical memory performance in both conditions. People typically show better memory when they intend to learn because they are likely to engage in activities more conducive to good memory, such as rehearsal and elaborative processing. The small advantage of intentional subjects in the Jenkins and Hyde experiment may reflect some small variation in processing. Experiments that take great care to control processing find that intention to learn or amount of motivation to learn has no effect (see Nelson, 1976).

Nonmeaningful Elaborations

The studies we have discussed to this point have confounded processing material in a more *meaningful* way with processing in a more *elaborate* way. More recent research has indicated that the important variable is really elaborateness of processing. For instance, Slamecka and Graf (1978) found improved memory when subjects had to generate rhymes like *save–cave* rather than read them. Similarly, Nelson (1979) has shown that phonemic rather than semantic processing will improve memory. Apparently, the process the subject goes through in generating the rhyme leaves traces behind in memory. The traces of rhyme generation are elaborations of the memory just as much as traces of sentence continua-

186

tion. These process traces provide a redundant means for reconstructing the memory.

Some psychologists, such as Kolers (1979), have argued that the entire depth-of-processing literature is to be accounted for in terms of memory for the processes involved in the original study of the material. Kolers has looked at subjects' memory for sentences that are read in normal form versus sentences that are printed upside down, and has found that subjects can remember more about the upside-down sentences. He argues that the extra processing involved in processing the typography of upside-down sentences provides the basis for the improved memory. Again, it is not a case of more meaningful processing but rather of more elaborate processing.

Text Material

Frase (1975) has found evidence for the benefit of elaborative processing with text material. He compared two groups of subjects on their memory for a text: one that had been given topics to think about before reading the text, and a control group that simply studied the text without advance topics. (The topics given to the test group were similar to the summaries beginning the chapters in this book.) Sometimes called *advance organizers*, the topics were in the form of questions that the subjects had to answer.[1] The subjects were to find answers to the advance questions as they read the text. This requirement should have forced them to process the text more carefully and to think about its implications. The advance-organizer group answered 64 percent of the questions correctly in a subsequent test, while the control group answered 57 percent correctly. The questions in the final test could be divided into those relevant to the advance organizers and those not relevant. For instance, if a test question was about an event that precipitated America's entry into World War II, it would be considered relevant if the advance questions directed the subject to learn why America entered the war. Such a test question would be considered not relevant if the advance question directed students to learn about the economic consequences of World War II. The advance-organizer group answered 76 percent of the relevant questions correctly and 52 percent of the irrelevant. Thus, they did only slightly worse than the control group on those topics for which they had not been given advance

---

[1]Ausubel (1968) introduced the term *advance organizers* to refer to general statements of information such as those in the chapter summaries here.

187

warning, but much better on topics for which they had been given advance warning.

Summary

The evidence is quite clear that elaborative processing produces better memory for all sorts of material. This conclusion would be expected from the network model described earlier. Thus, students should elaborate on the material that they are learning in a course. This recommendation should please most instructors, because it coincides with the recommendation that students think about the implications of what they are learning.

Inferential Reconstruction in Recall

Let us return to the discussion of a subject's memory for this sentence:

  1. The doctor hated the lawyer.

Elaborations improve memory for this sentence by increasing the redundancy of its encodings. Note that redundancy is not created by the subject's simply making multiple mental copies of the sentence. Rather, redundancy is created by the storing of additional propositions that weakly or strongly imply the target sentence, as the following propositions do:

  2. The lawyer sued the doctor for malpractice.

  3. The doctor cursed the lawyer in court.

  4. The doctor glared at the lawyer.

  5. The lawyer assailed the doctor with a stream of questions.

Suppose subjects are no longer able to remember the studied sentence at test, but are able to recall two of their elaborations, say:

  2. The lawyer sued the doctor for malpractice.

  4. The doctor glared at the lawyer.

In this case, the subject might well infer that the doctor hated the lawyer. Note, however, that this inference need not be true. For instance, the doctor and lawyer might be in cahoots, trying to defraud the doctor's malpractice-insurance company. Thus, when people do try to recall by inference, there always is the possibility that their recall will be in error.

Bransford, Barclay, and Franks (1972) reported an experiment that demonstrates how inference can lead to incorrect recall. They had subjects study one of the following sentences:

1.   Three turtles rested beside a floating log, and a fish swam beneath them.

2.   Three turtles rested on a floating log, and a fish swam beneath them.

Subjects who had studied sentence 1 were later asked whether they had studied this sentence:

3.   Three turtles rested beside a floating log, and a fish swam beneath it.

Not many subjects thought they had studied this. Subjects who had studied sentence 2 were tested with:

4.   Three turtles rested on a floating log, and a fish swam beneath it.

Many more subjects thought they had studied this sentence than thought they had studied sentence 3. Of course, sentence 4 is implied by sentence 2, whereas sentence 3 is not implied by sentence 1. Thus, subjects thought that they had actually studied what was implied by the studied material.

A study by Sulin and Dooling (1974) provides an illustration of how inference can bias subjects' memory for a text. They had subjects read the following passage:

Carol Harris's Need for Professional Help

Carol Harris was a problem child from birth. She was wild, stubborn, and violent. By the time Carol turned eight, she was still unmanageable. Her parents were very concerned about her mental health. There was no good institution for her problem in her state. Her parents finally decided to take some action. They hired a private teacher for Carol.

A second group of subjects read the same passage except that the name *Helen Keller* was substituted for *Carol Harris*. A week after reading the passage, subjects were given a recognition test in which they were presented with a sentence and asked to judge whether it had occurred in the passage. One of the critical sentences was *She was deaf, dumb, and blind*. Only 5 percent of the subjects who read the Carol Harris passage accepted this sentence, but a full 50 percent of the Helen Keller subjects thought they had read the sentence. This is just what we would expect. The second group of subjects had elaborated the story with facts they knew about Helen Keller. Thus, it would seem reasonable to them at test that this sentence had appeared in the studied material, but in this case their inference would have been wrong.

It is interesting to inquire whether such an inference as *She was deaf, dumb, and blind* was made while the subject was studying the passage or only at the time of the test. This is a subtle issue to get at, and subjects certainly do not have reliable intuitions about the matter. However, a couple of techniques are generally considered to yield evidence that inferences are being made at test. One is to determine whether the inferences increase in frequency with delay. With delay, subjects' memory for the studied passage should deteriorate and they will have to do more reconstruction, which will lead to more inferential errors. Both Dooling and Christiaansen (1977) and Spiro (1977) have found evidence for increased inferential intrusions with increased delay of testing.

Dooling and Christiaansen used another technique with the Carol Harris passage to show that inferences were being made at test. They had the subjects study the passage and told them a week later, just before test, that Carol Harris really was Helen Keller. In this situation, subjects also made many inferential errors, accepting such sentences as *She was deaf, dumb, and blind*. Since they did not know Carol Harris was Helen Keller until test, they must have made such inferences at test. Thus, it seems that subjects do make reconstructive inferences at time of test.

Plausible Retrieval

In the foregoing analysis we spoke of subjects as making errors when they recalled or recognized facts that were not explicitly presented. In real life, however, such acts of recall would often not be regarded as errors, but as intelligent inferences. Reder (1982) has argued that much of recall in real life involves plausible inference rather than exact recall. For instance, in deciding that Darth Vader was evil in *Star Wars* a person does not search memory for the specific proposition that Darth Vader was evil, although the proposition may well have been directly asserted in the movie. The person infers that Darth Vader was evil from memories about his behavior.

Reder has demonstrated that subjects will display very different behavior, depending on whether they are asked to engage in exact retrieval or plausible retrieval. She had subjects study passages such as the following:

> The heir to a large hamburger chain was in trouble. He had married a lovely young woman who had seemed to love him. Now he worried that she had been after his money after all. He sensed that she was not attracted to him. Perhaps he consumed too much beer and french fries. No, he couldn't give up the fries. Not only were they delicious, he got them for free.

Then she had subjects judge sentences such as the following:

> 1. The heir married a lovely young woman who had seemed to love him.
>
> 2. The heir got his french fries from his family's hamburger chain.
>
> 3. The heir was very careful to eat only healthy food.

The first sentence was studied; the second was not studied, but is plausible; and the third was neither studied nor plausible. Subjects in the exact condition were asked to make exact recognition judgments, in which case they were to accept the first sentence and reject the second two. Subjects in the plausible condition were to judge if the sentence was plausible given the story, in which case they were to accept the first two and reject the last. Reder tested subjects immediately after studying the story, 20 minutes later, or 2 days later.

She was interested in judgment time for subjects in the two conditions, exact versus plausible. Figure 7-2 shows the results from Reder's experiment as a function of delay. Plotted in the figure are the average judgment times for sentence types 1 and 2. As might be expected, subjects get slower with delay in the exact condition. However, they get faster in the plausible condition. They start out slower in the plausible than in the exact condition, but this is reversed after 2 days. Reder argues that subjects get worse in the exact condition because the exact traces are getting weak. However, a plausibility judgment is not dependent on any particular trace, and so is not similarly vulnerable to forgetting. Subjects get faster in the plausible condition with delay because they no longer try to use inefficient exact retrieval, but use plausibility, which is faster.

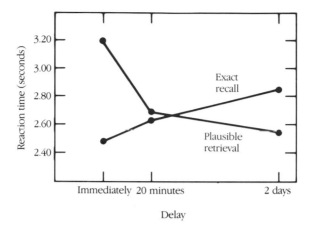

Figure 7-2. Time to make exact versus plausible recognition judgments of sentences as a function of delay since study of a story. (From Reder, 1982.)

Reder and Ross (1983) compared exact versus plausible judgments in another paradigm. They had subjects study sentences such as the following:

> Alan bought a ticket for the 10:00 A.M. train.
>
> Alan heard the conductor call "All aboard."
>
> Alan read a newspaper on the train.
>
> Alan arrived at Grand Central Station.

They manipulated the number of sentences that subjects had to study about a particular person such as Alan. Then they looked at subjects' times to recognize sentences such as:

1. Alan heard the conductor call "All aboard."
2. Alan watched the approaching train from the platform.
3. Alan sorted his clothes into colors and whites.

In the exact condition subjects had to judge whether the sentence had been studied. So, given the foregoing material, subjects would accept test sentence 1 and reject test sentences 2 and 3. In the plausible condition subjects had to judge whether it was plausible that Alan was involved in the activity, given what they had studied. Thus, subjects would accept sentences 1 and 2 and reject 3.

In the exact condition, Reder and Ross found that subjects took longer the more facts they studied about Alan. This is basically a replication of the fan effect discussed in Chapter 6. In the plausible condition, however, subjects were faster the more facts they had learned about Alan. The more facts they knew about Alan, the more ways there were to judge a particular fact plausible. Thus, plausibility judgment did not have to depend on retrieval of a particular fact.

The Interaction of Elaboration and Inferential Reconstruction

We have discussed inferential processes by which subjects elaborate a memory at study and inferential processes by which they reconstruct the memory at test. We would expect that the more a subject embellished a sentence at study, the more inferential reconstruction would be possible at test. In fact, to use elaborations at study to improve memory performance, subjects often have to go from these elaborations to inferences about what was studied. Thus, we expect elaborative processing to lead to both an improvement in memory for what was studied and an increase in the number of inferences recalled. An experiment by Owens, Bower, and Black (1979) confirms this prediction. Subjects studied a story that followed the principal character, a college student, through a day in her life: making a cup of coffee in the morning, visiting a doctor, attending a lecture, going shopping for groceries, and attending a cocktail party. The following is a passage from the story:

> Nancy went to see the doctor. She arrived at the office and checked in with the receptionist. She went to see the nurse, who went through the usual procedures. Then Nancy stepped on the scale and the nurse recorded her weight. The doctor entered the room and examined the results. He smiled at Nancy and said, "Well, it seems my expectations have been confirmed." When the examination was finished, Nancy left the office.

Two groups of subjects studied the story. The only difference between the groups was that the theme group had read the following additional information at the beginning:

Nancy woke up feeling sick again and she wondered if she really were pregnant. How would she tell the professor she had been seeing? And the money was another problem.

College students who read this additional passage characterized Nancy as an unmarried student who is afraid she is pregnant as a result of an affair with a college professor. Subjects who had not read this opening passage had no reason to suspect that there is anything special about Nancy. We would expect subjects in the theme condition to make many more theme-related elaborations of the story than subjects in the neutral condition.

Subjects were asked to recall the story 24 hours after studying it. Those in the theme condition introduced a great many more inferences that had not actually been studied. For instance, subjects often reported that the doctor told Nancy she was pregnant. Intrusions of this variety are expected if subjects reconstruct the story on the basis of their elaborations. Table 7-3 reports some of the results from the study. Many more inferences are added in recall for the theme condition than for the neutral condition. However, a second important observation is that subjects in the theme condition also remembered more of the propositions they had actually studied. Thus, because of the additional elaborations made by subjects in the theme condition, they may be able to recall more of the story.

We might question whether subjects really benefited from their elaborations, since they also "misrecalled" many things that did not occur in the story. However, it is wrong to characterize the intruded inferences as errors. Given the theme information, subjects were perfectly right to make calling inferences and to recall them. In a nonexperimental setting (e.g., recalling information on an exam) we would expect these subjects to treat such inferences as facts that were actually studied.

Table 7-3 *Number of Propositions Recalled*

	Theme Condition	Neutral Condition
Studied propositions	29.2	20.2
Inferred propositions	15.2	3.7

Adapted from Owens et al., 1979

Advertisers often capitalize on our tendency to embellish what we hear with plausible inferences. Consider the following portion of a Listerine commercial:

"Wouldn't it be great," asks the mother, "if you could make him coldproof? Well, you can't. Nothing can do that. [Boy sneezes.] But there is something that you can do that may help. Have him gargle with Listerine Antiseptic. Listerine can't promise to keep him cold-free, but it may help him fight off colds. During the cold-catching season, have him gargle twice a day with full-strength Listerine. Watch his diet, see he gets plenty of sleep, and there's a good chance he'll have fewer colds, milder colds this year."

A verbatim text of this commercial, with the only change that of the product name to "Gargoil," was used by Harris (1977). After hearing this commercial, all 15 of his subjects checked that "gargling with Gargoil Antiseptic helps prevent colds," although this assertion was clearly not made in the commercial. The Federal Trade Commission explicitly forbids advertisers from making false claims, but does the Listerine ad make a false claim? In a potentially landmark case, the courts have ruled against Warner-Lambert, makers of Listerine, for implying false claims in this commercial.

Use of Schemas

In Chapter 5 we discussed the role of schemas in guiding the interpretation of a story. To review, schemas are organized sets of facts, such as beliefs about what goes on in a restaurant. Subjects use schemas to infer that certain unobserved and unmentioned elements must be present. Thus, a subject who heard, "Fred ordered a duck. He drank red wine with his meal. He left a generous tip," would tend to infer that Fred ate the duck. It seems that schemas are a major mechanism for elaborating material during study, and are also a major mechanism for reconstructing memories at test. Some striking evidence for the role of schemas in memory was obtained by Bartlett (1932, p. 65) in research with English subjects before World War I. He used a story called "The War of the Ghosts." It has been used in research on many subsequent occasions and is still a popular research item today. The story is reproduced in its entirety here.

The War of the Ghosts

One night two young men from Egulac went down to the river to hunt seals, and while they were there it became foggy and calm. Then they heard war-cries, and they thought: "Maybe this is a war-party." They escaped to the shore, and hid behind a log. Now canoes came up, and they heard the noise of paddles, and saw one canoe coming up to them. There were five men in the canoe, and they said:

"What do you think? We wish to take you along. We are going up the river to make war on the people."

One of the young men said, "I have no arrows."

"Arrows are in the canoe," they said.

"I will not go along. I might be killed. My relatives do not know where I have gone. But you," he said, turning to the other, "may go with them."

So one of the young men went, but the other returned home.

And the warriors went on up the river to a town on the other side of Kalama. The people came down to the water, and they began to fight, and many were killed. But presently the young man heard one of the warriors say: "Quick, let us go home: that Indian has been hit." Now he thought: "Oh, they are ghosts." He did not feel sick, but they said he had been shot.

So the canoes went back to Egulac, and the young man went ashore to his house, and made a fire. And he told everybody and said: "Behold I accompanied the ghosts, and we went to fight. Many of our fellows were killed, and many of those who attacked us were killed. They said I was hit, and I did not feel sick."

He told it all, and then he became quiet. When the sun rose he fell down. Something black came out of his mouth. His face became contorted. The people jumped up and cried.

He was dead.

Presumably, you find this a rather bizarre story. Certainly, it appeared bizarre to Bartlett's subjects, accustomed as they were to the world of upper-class Edwardian England. This story, however, would be perfectly reasonable to the people from which it was taken. It was part of the oral literary tradition of Indians on the west coast of Canada a century ago. It fit in very well with their schemas for how the world worked. It does not fit in well with our cultural schemas nor with those of Bartlett's subjects.

Bartlett was interested in how subjects would remember a story that fit in so poorly with their cultural schemas. He had his subjects recall the story after various delays, from immediately after study to years later. To get a feeling for their task, you might put this book aside and try to write down all you can remember from the story.

Bartlett's subjects showed clear distortions in their memory for the story, and these distortions appeared to grow with time. Below is a representative recall (Bartlett, 1932, p. 66) given 20 hours after hearing the story:

> Two men from Edulac went fishing. While thus occupied by the river they heard a noise in the distance.
>
> "It sounds like a cry," said one, and presently there appeared some in canoes who invited them to join the party on their adventure. One of the young men refused to go, on the ground of family ties, but the other offered to go.
>
> "But there are no arrows," he said.
>
> "The arrows are in the boat," was the reply.
>
> He thereupon took his place, while his friend returned home. The party paddled up the river to Kaloma, and began to land on the banks of the river. The enemy came rushing upon them, and some sharp fighting ensued. Presently someone was injured, and the cry was raised that the enemy were ghosts.
>
> The party returned down the stream, and the young man arrived home feeling none the worse for his experience. The next morning at dawn he endeavored to recount his adventures. While he was talking something black issued from his mouth. Suddenly he uttered a cry and fell down. His friends gathered around him.
>
> But he was dead.

Subjects omitted much of the story, changed many of the facts, and imported new information. Such inaccuracies in memory are not particularly interesting in and of themselves. The important observation is that these inaccuracies were systematic: The subjects were distorting the story to fit with their own cultural stereotypes. For instance, "something black came from his mouth" in the original story became "he frothed at the mouth" or "he vomitted" in some stories. In the recall above, we find "hunting seals" changed to "fishing" and "canoe" changed to "boat." The hard-to-interpret aspects are omitted, including the hiding behind the log and the connection between the Indian's injury and the termination of the battle. Further, this subject has the role of the ghosts completely turned around. Thus, when subjects read a story that does not fit with their own schemas, they will exhibit a powerful tendency to distort the story to make it fit.

Organization and Recall

Hierarchical Structures and Other Organizations

Numerous manipulations have been shown to improve subjects' memory in recalling a long list of items. Many such devices involve organizing the material in such a way that subjects can systematically search their memories for the items. A nice demonstration of this use of organization is an experiment by Bower, Clark, Lesgold, and Winzenz (1969). They had subjects learn all the words in four hierarchies such as the one in Figure 7-3. Two conditions of learning were compared. In the organized condition, the four hierarchies were presented in upside-down trees, as in the figure. In the random condition subjects saw four trees, but the positions in the trees were filled by random combinations of words from the four categories. Thus, instead of seeing separate trees for animals, clothing, transportation, and minerals, subjects saw four trees, each containing some items from each category.

Subjects were given a minute to study each tree, and after studying all four trees they were asked to recall all the words in the four trees in any order. This study–test sequence was repeated four times. The performance of the two groups over the four trials is given in Table 7-4 in terms of number of words recalled. The maximum possible recall was 112. The

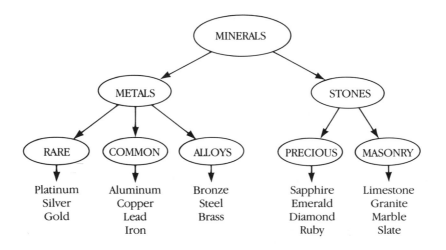

Figure 7-3. A hierarchical tree presented to subjects in the free-recall experiment of Bower et al. The relationships among the items in the tree are categorical. (From Bower et al., 1969).

Table 7-4 *Average Number of Words Recalled Over Four Trials as a Function of Organization*

| | Trials | | | |
Conditions	1	2	3	4
Organized	73.0	106.1	112.0	112.0
Random	20.6	38.9	52.8	70.1

Adapted from Bower et al., 1969.

organized group was shown to have an enormous advantage. Analysis of the order in which the organized group recalled the words indicated that subjects had organized their recall according to the tree hierarchies and recalled the words going down a tree from the top — for example, using Figure 7-3, first they would recall *minerals* and then *metals*.

The associative-network explanation of this result is straightforward: In the organized condition subjects were forming a memory network during the study phase similar to the hierarchy in Figure 7-3. To do this they had only to elaborate on connections already in memory. Thus, to return to the main topic of this chapter, another important function of elaborations can be imposing a hierarchical organization on memory. Such a hierarchical organization allows a person to structure the search of memory and to retrieve information more efficiently.

The implication for study habits of the results in Bower et al. is both important and clear. Course material can often be organized into hierarchies just as word lists can. Table 7-5 is a hierarchical organization for the material up to this point in the chapter. (In actually studying this material, students would be better off deriving their own organizations, since doing this will force deeper processing of the material.) For readability, levels of the hierarchy are represented by levels of indentation. Note that in this hierarchy the connections are often not categorical, unlike those in Figure 7-3. For instance, the relation of *network representation* to *elaborations and reconstructions* is not one of an instance to a category. Rather, *network representation* serves as an explanation of or a mechanism for describing a phenomenon.

Bower et al. have shown that an individual need not utilize a strict categorical organization in order to derive the benefits of hierarchical structure. They investigated hierarchies such as the one in Figure 7-4, where the organization involves a loose associative structure. The presentation of information in such a hierarchy resulted in a considerable advantage over a random presentation.

Table 7-5 *Chapter Outline to This Point*

Elaborations and reconstruction
  Network representation
    Inferences and embellishments
    Alternate retrieval routes
    Inferences at time of test
    Bradshaw and Anderson (relevant vs. irrelevant facts)

Elaborateness of processing
  Representative studies
    Bobrow and Bower (self-generation)
    Use of continuations
    Stein and Bransford (precision of elaborations)

  Incidental versus intentional learning
    Nonmeaningful elaborations
    Text material (Frase; advance organizers)
      Effect of questions on relevant material
      Effect of questions on irrelevant material

  Inference in recall
    Bransford, Barclay, and Franks (three turtles)
    Dooling's studies with the Helen Keller passage
    Plausible retrieval (Reder)
    Interaction between elaboration and reconstruction

  Use of schemas
    Barlett's "War of the Ghosts"

  Effects of organization
    Hierarchies
      Bower, Clark, Lesgold, and Winzenz
      This example

The Method of Loci

A classic mnemonic technique, the *method of loci*, has its effect by promoting good organization in recall situations. This technique, used extensively in ancient times when speeches were given without written notes, is still used today. Cicero (in *De Oratore*) credits the method to a Greek poet, Simonides. Simonides had delivered a lyric poem at a banquet. Following his delivery, he was called from the banquet hall by the gods Castor and Pollux, whom he had praised in this poem. While he was absent the roof fell in, killing all the participants at the banquet. The corpses were so mangled that relatives could not identify them. However, Simonides was able to identify each corpse according to where the person

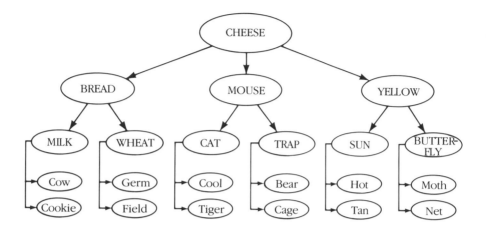

Figure 7-4. A second type of hierarchical tree presented to subjects in the free-recall experiment of Bower et al. Here the relationships among the items are general associative rather than strictly categorical, as in Figure 7-3. (From Bower et al., 1969.)

had been sitting in the banquet hall. This feat of total recall convinced Simonides of the usefulness of an orderly arrangement of locations into which a person could place objects to be remembered. This story may be rather fanciful, but whatever the true origin of the method of loci, it is well documented (e.g., Christen & Bjork, 1976; Ross & Lawrence, 1968) as a useful technique for remembering an ordered sequence of items, such as the points a person wants to make in a speech.

Basically, to use the method of loci the individual imagines a fixed path through a familiar area with some fixed locations along the path. For instance, if there were such a path on campus from the bookstore to the library, we might use it. To remember a series of objects, we simply mentally walk along the path, associating the objects with the fixed locations. As an example, consider a grocery list of six items — milk, hot dogs, dog food, tomatoes, bananas, and bread. To associate the milk with the bookstore, we might imagine a puddle of milk in front of the bookstore with books fallen into the milk. To associate hot dogs with the record shop (the next location in the path from the bookstore), we might imagine a package of hot dogs spinning on a record player turntable. The pizza shop is next, and to associate this with dog food we might imagine a pizza with dog food on it (well, some people even like anchovies). Then we come to the intersection; to associate this with tomatoes we can imagine an overturned vegetable truck and tomatoes splattered everywhere. Next we come to the administration building — and an image of the president coming out, wearing only a hula-type skirt made of bananas. Finally, we reach the library and associate it to bread by imagining a huge loaf of bread serving as a canopy under which we must pass to enter. To re-create the list, we need only take an imaginary walk down this path, reviving the associations to each location. This technique works well with very much longer lists; we only need more locations. There is considerable evidence (e.g., Christen & Bjork, 1976) that the same loci can be used over and over again in the learning of different lists.

Two important principles underlie the effectiveness of the method of loci. First, the technique imposes organization on an otherwise unorganized list. We are guaranteed that if we follow the mental path at time of recall, we will pass all the locations for which we created associations. The second principle is that generating connections between the locations and the items forces us to process the material elaboratively.

The Effects of Encoding Context

A clear implication of the network representation in Figure 7-1 part (b) is that reviving the experimental context in which items have been studied should aid recall. Note that such concepts as *psychology laboratory, one dreary morning,* and *unpleasant* are associated with the experimental memory. If at test such contextual stimuli and concepts could be revived, the subject would have additional ways to reactivate the target memory. There is ample evidence that context can greatly influence memory. This section will review some of the ways in which context influences memory. These context effects are often referred to as *encoding effects* because the context is affecting what is encoded into the memory trace that records the event.

Smith, Glenberg, and Bjork (1978) performed an experiment that showed the importance of physical context. In their experiment, subjects learned two lists of paired associates on different days and in different physical settings. On day 1, subjects learned the paired associates in a windowless room in a building near the University of Michigan campus. The experimenter was neatly groomed, dressed in a coat and a tie, and the paired associates were shown on slides. On day 2, subjects learned the paired associates in a tiny room with windows on the main campus. The experimenter was dressed sloppily in a flannel shirt and jeans (it was the same experimenter, but some subjects did not recognize him) and presented the paired associates via a tape recorder. A day later, subjects made their recall, half in one setting and half in the other setting. Subjects could recall 59 percent of the list learned in the same setting as tested, but only 46 percent of the list learned in the other setting. Thus, it seems that recall is better if the context at test is the same as the context at study.

Perhaps the most dramatic manipulation of context was performed by Godden and Baddeley (1975). They had divers learn a list of 40 unrelated words either on the shore or 20 feet under the sea. The divers were then asked to recall the list in either the same or a different environment. Figure 7-5 displays the results of this study. Subjects clearly showed superior memory when they were asked to recall in the same context in which they studied. So, it seems that contextual elements get associated to memories, and that memory is improved when subjects are provided with these contextual elements again.

The degree to which such contextual effects are obtained has proven to be quite variable from experiment to experiment. Fernandez and Glenberg (1985) report a number of failures to find a context dependence, and Saufley, Otaka, and Bavaresco (1985) report a failure to find such effects in a classroom situation. Eich (1985) argues that the magnitude of such contextual effects depends on the degree to which the subject integrates the context with the memories. In his experiment he read lists of nouns to two groups of subjects. In one condition subjects were instructed to imagine the referents of the nouns alone and in the other condition subjects were asked to imagine the referents integrated with the context. Eich found a much larger effect of a change of context when subjects were instructed to imagine the referents integrated with the context.

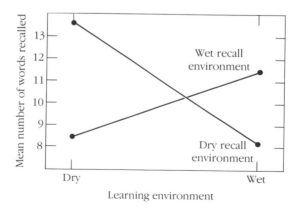

Figure 7-5. Mean number of words recalled as a function of environment in which learning took place. Word lists were recalled better in the same environment in which they were learned than in a different environment. (Data from Godden & Baddeley, 1975.)

Research by Bower, Monteiro, and Gilligan (1978) shows that emotional context can have the same effect as physical context. They also had subjects learn two lists. For one list they hypnotically induced a positive state by having subjects review a pleasant episode in their lives, and for the other list they hypnotically induced a negative state by having subjects review a traumatic event. A later recall test was given under either a positive or a negative emotional state (again hypnotically induced). Better memory was obtained when the emotional state at test matched the emotional state at study.

As an aside it is worth commenting that, despite popular reports, the best evidence is that hypnosis per se does nothing to improve memory (see Hilgard, 1968; Smith, 1982), although it can help memory to the extent that it can be used to re-create the contextual factors at the time of test. However, much of a learning context can also be re-created by nonhypnotic means, such as through free association about the circumstances of the to-be-remembered event.

A related phenomenon is referred to as *state-dependent learning*. People find it easier to recall information if they can return to the same emotional and physical state they were in when they learned the information. For instance, it is often casually claimed that heavy drinkers when sober are unable to remember where they hid their alcohol when drunk, and when drunk they are unable to remember where they hid their money when sober. In fact, some experimental evidence does exist for this state dependency of memory with respect to alcohol, but the more important factor seems to be that alcohol has a general debilitating effect on the acquisition of information (Parker, Birnbaum, & Noble, 1976). Marijuana has been shown to have similar state-dependent effects. In one experiment (Eich, Weingartner, Stillman, & Gillin, 1975), subjects learned a free-recall list after smoking either a marijuana cigarette or an ordinary cigarette. Subjects were tested 4 hours later—again after smoking either a marijuana cigarette or a regular cigarette. Table 7-6 shows

Table 7-6 *Interaction Between Effects of Drugged State at Study and Test*

		Test		
		Ordinary Cigarette	Marijuana Cigarette	Average
Study	Ordinary cigarette	25%	20%	23%
	Marijuana cigarette	12%	23%	18%

From Eich, Weingartner, Stillman, and Gillin, 1975.

the results from this study. There are two effects shown in this table, typical of the research on the effects of psychoactive drugs on memory. First there is a state dependent effect reflected by higher recall when state at test matched state at study. Second, there is an overall higher level of recall when the material was studied in a nonintoxicated state.

Encoding Specificity

The effects of general environmental and internal context are fairly easy to understand intuitively, but evidence suggests that there can be less obvious effects of the context in experimental situations. For example, there is now good evidence that memory for to-be-learned material can be heavily dependent on the context of other to-be-learned material in which it is embedded. Consider a recognition-memory experiment by Thomson (1972). He had subjects study pairs of words such as *sky blue.* Subjects were told that they were responsible only for the second item of the pair—in this case *blue*; the first word represented context. Later, they were tested by being presented with either *blue* or *sky blue.* In either case, they were asked whether they had originally seen *blue.* In the single-word case they recognized *blue* 76 percent of the time, while in the pair condition their recognition rate was 85 percent. This difference indicates a dependence of memory on the context in which a to-be-recognized item is studied.

A series of experiments (e.g., Tulving & Thompson, 1973; Watkins & Tulving, 1975) has dramatically illustrated how memory for a word can depend on how well the test context matches the original study context. Watkins and Tulving had subjects learn pairs of words such as *train–black* and told them that they were only responsible for the second word, referred to as the *to-be-remembered word* (again, the first word in the pairs served as the context). After this study phase, subjects were given words such as *white* and asked to generate four free associates to the word. So, a subject might generate *snow, black, wool,* and *pure.* The stimuli for the associate task were chosen to have a high probability of eliciting a to-be-remembered word. For instance, *white* has a high probability of eliciting *black.* Overall, the to-be-remembered word was generated 66 percent of the time as one of the four associates. After they had generated their associates, subjects were told to indicate which of the four associates was the one they had studied. They were forced to indicate a choice even if they thought they had not studied any of the words. In cases where the to-be-remembered word was generated, subjects correctly chose the word 54 percent of the time. Since subjects were always forced to indicate a choice, some of these correct choices must have been lucky guesses, meaning that true recognition was even lower. Following this test in which subjects free associated and then recognized study words, they were presented with the original context words and asked to recall the to-be-remembered words. Subjects recalled 61 percent of the words— higher than their recognition rate without any correction for guessing! Moreover, Watkins and Tulving found that 42 percent of the words recalled had not been recognized earlier when the subjects gave them as free associates.

As we saw in the previous chapter, recognition is generally superior to recall. Conversely, we would expect that if subjects could not recognize a word, they would be unable to recall it. Usually, we expect to do better on a multiple-choice test than on a recall-the-answer test. Experiments such as the one just described have provided some very dramatic reversals of such standard expectations. Their results can be understood in terms of the similarity of the test context to the study context. The context in which the word *white* and its associates were studied was quite different from that in which *black* had originally been studied. In contrast, in the cued-recall task, subjects were given the original context (*train*) with which they had studied the word. Thus, if the contextual factors are sufficiently weighted in favor of recall, as they were in these experiments, recall can be superior to recognition. Tulving offers these results as illustrating what he calls the *encoding-specificity principle*: The probability of recalling an item at test depends on the similarity of its encoding at test and its original encoding at study.

Encoding Variability and the Spacing Effect

When facts are studied on multiple occasions, their encodings will be slightly different on each occasion. An important factor determining the measure of difference among the various encodings is the measure of difference among the learning contexts on each occasion. An obvious factor influencing the differences among learning contexts is the spacing over time of these contexts. The importance of spacing is illustrated in an experiment by Madigan (1969), again on the free recall of single words. Forty-eight words were presented at the rate of 1.5 seconds per word. Some words were presented once and others twice. After study, subjects were asked to recall as many words as they could. They recalled 28 percent of the words that appeared once and 47 percent of the words that appeared twice. Figure 7-6 shows an analysis of Madigan's data in the twice-presented condition. The data are plotted as a function of *lag*, or the

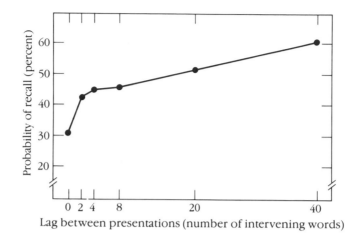

Figure 7-6. Recall probability of twice-presented words as a function of the lag between the two occurrences of the word. Memory improves as the lag between presentations increases. (From Madigan, 1969.)

number of intervening words between the two presentations. Probability of recall increases systematically with lag. There is a very rapid increase over the initial lag, and the benefit increases, if more slowly, to lags of 40 intervening items. This result is known as the *spacing effect*.

The spacing effect is an extremely robust and powerful phenomenon, and it has been repeatedly shown with many kinds of material. Spacing effects have been demonstrated in free recall, in cued recall of paired associates, in the recall of sentences, and in the recall of text material. It is important to note that these spacing results do generalize to textbook materials (Reynolds & Glaser, 1964; Rothkopf & Coke, 1963, 1966). Also the effect of spaced study can be very long-lasting. Bahrick and Phelps (1987) tested the long-term retention for Spanish vocabulary items 8 years after original learning. They contrasted students who spaced their study at 30-day intervals with students who massed all their study in a single day. The retention of subjects who received spaced presentations was approximately twice that of those who received massed presentations.

It is probable that a number of factors combine to produce the spacing effect. For instance, subjects may do poorly at short lags simply because of inattention. That is, they may regard a second study at such a short lag as unnecessary and ignore it. Rundus (1971) asked subjects to rehearse material out loud and found that they spent less rehearsal time on the second presentation of items after short lags. Although other factors are probably involved (e.g., see Hintzman, 1974), an important factor in the lag effect, especially after long lags, is that suggested at the start of this subsection: *encoding variability* due to change of context. Probability of recall depends in part on the study context matching the test context. At long lags, it is likely that the two study contexts will be quite different from each other. The greater the difference between the two study contexts, the greater is the probability that one of the contexts will overlap with the test context. On the other hand, at short lags the two study contexts will be more similar, and the probability of the study contexts matching the test context will be not much greater than in the single-presentation condition.

The importance of encoding variability to the spacing effect is nicely demonstrated in some of the other analyses reported by Madigan (1969). He presented subjects with pairs of words but told them they were responsible for remembering only the second—the first just provided context (as in the previously described studies of Thomson and of Watkins and Tulving). Some target words were presented twice and some only once. When items were repeated, they occurred each time either with the same context word or with different context words. For example, the target word *chill* might occur twice in a list, separated by a lag of four intervening items. In the different condition it might occur the first time with *fever* and the second time with *snow*. In the same condition it would occur both times with *fever*. Madigan found that subjects performed better in the different condition. Moreover, the different condition did not show as large a spacing effect as the same condition. That is, the advantage of long lags over short lags was smaller in the different condition.

Madigan's results would be expected from the encoding-variability interpretation of the spacing effect. By providing different context words, Madigan forced a change in the encoding context. This change should be particularly important at short lags when large variations in context do not occur naturally. Note that this experiment demonstrates that it is possible to make repetition at short lags more effective by taking measures to create a change in the context. The implications of these results for study habits are almost too obvious to require comment: We should space our study of particular material over time; and when such spacing is impossible, we should change the context of repetitive study. At a physical level, we can change the location in which we study. At a more abstract level, we can try to change the perspective we take on the to-be-learned material.

208

The encoding-variability analysis of the spacing effect does not imply that spaced study and variable encoding will always result in superior memory. What is really important is that one of the contexts in which the material is studied overlap with the context in which the material is tested. When students are not sure how the material is to be tested, they should study it in contexts as varied as possible. Spacing study is one way of ensuring a variety of contexts, but, as we have noted, other ways are also effective, such as changing the physical environment or the mental set. However, when students know the context in which they are to be tested, then variable encoding may not be such a good idea. In this case, the ideal study location would be the location in which the test is to be administered. Of course, with respect to college exams this ideal may be hard to achieve. Gaining access to an exam room is often difficult, and in any case, the difference between an empty exam room and one filled with anxious students and a monitor pacing slowly around the room is considerable.

Conclusions about Elaborative Processing

Consider again Figure 7-1, which compares the simplified conception of the information deposited in memory with an elaborated conception. The research reviewed in this chapter indicates that the elaborative conception is more accurate. Subjects elaborate the information they study with the following:

1. connections to prior knowledge

2. imaginings and inferences about the material

3. features from the current context

The evidence we have reviewed indicates that this process of elaboration leads to improved memory in the following ways:

1. It increases the redundancy of interconnections among the to-be-remembered information.

2. It imposes an organization on the information that can be used to guide the retrieval process.

3. It can increase the number of contextual elements that will overlap between study and test.

The PQ4R Method

Many college study-skills departments as well as private firms offer courses designed to improve students' memory for text material. These courses mainly teach study techniques for texts such as those used in the social sciences, not the more dense texts used in the physical sciences and mathematics nor less dense, literary materials such as novels. The study techniques from different programs are fairly similar, and their success has been documented to some extent. Two of the more publicized and publicly accessible techniques are the *SQ3R method* (Robinson, 1961) and the later *PQ4R method* (Thomas & Robinson, 1972). Other techniques are quite similar and are often adaptations of these methods. These methods are strongly supported by the ideas covered in this chapter. We will examine the PQ4R method as an example.

The PQ4R method derives its name from the six phases it advocates for studying a chapter in a textbook:

1. *Preview.* Survey the chapter to determine the general topics being discussed. Identify the sections to be read as units. Apply the next four steps to each section.

2. *Questions.* Make up questions about the section. Often, simply transforming section headings results in adequate questions. For example, a section heading might be *Encoding Variability*, resulting in such questions as "What is encoding variability?" and "What are the effects of encoding variability?"

3. *Read.* Read the section carefully, trying to answer the questions you have made up about it.

4. *Reflect.* Reflect on the text as you are reading it, trying to understand it, to think of examples, and to relate the material to prior knowledge.

5. *Recite.* After finishing a section, try to recall the information contained in it. Try answering the questions you made up for the section. If you cannot recall enough, reread the portions you had trouble remembering.

6. *Review.* After you have finished the chapter, go through it mentally, recalling its main points. Again try answering the questions you made up.

A slight variation on this technique for studying this text is detailed in Chapter 1. Clearly, one of the reasons for the success of this kind of technique is that all the passes through the material serve as spaced study of the material. Another probable effect is to make the student aware of the way the material is organized. As we have seen, organization leads to good memory, especially on free-recall-type tests.

The central feature of the PQ4R technique, however, is the question-generation and question-answering characteristics. There is reason to suspect that the most important aspect of this feature is that it encourages (perhaps *forces* would be a better word) deeper or more elaborative processing of the text material. Earlier, we reviewed the experiment by Frase that demonstrated the benefit of reading a text with a set of advance organizers in mind. It seems that the benefit of that activity was specific to test items related to the questions.

The distinction between test items related to the study questions and those not related is important. Suppose that a study question in a text on African economics was "What were the effects of the transition from colonialism on economic growth?" A *related* test question might then be "Did the rate of foreign investment decrease as a result of the transition from colonialism?" An *unrelated* test question might be "What factors limit the rate of development of the forestry industry in Africa?" Clearly, study questions related to test questions would be expected to aid memory more effectively than unrelated ones. Therefore, creating study questions that tap the most important topics is an important aspect of the study technique.

Another experiment by Frase (1975) compared the effects of making up questions and answering them. He had pairs of subjects study a text that was divided into halves. For one half, one subject in the pair read the passage and made up study questions as he or she went along. These questions were given to the second subject, who then read the text while trying to answer them. The subjects switched roles for the second half of the text. All subjects answered a final set of test questions about the passage. A control group, who just read without doing anything special, answered correctly 50 percent of the set of questions that followed. Experimental subjects, when they read to make up questions, answered correctly 70 percent of the test items that were relevant to their questions and 52 percent of the irrelevant test items. When they read to answer questions, experimental subjects answered correctly 67 percent of the relevant test items and 49 percent of the irrelevant items. Thus, it seems that both question generation and question answering contribute to good memory. If anything, question making contributes the most. T. H. Anderson (1978), in a review of the research literature, finds further evidence for the particular importance of question making.

In another study lending support to the PQ4R technique, Rickards (1976) looked at the effect of different types of questions as advance organizers for reading. He had subjects study a passage about a fictitious African nation called Mala. The experiment compared the effectiveness of conceptual questions, which required subjects to process a general issue such as exploitation of the people, and verbatim questions, which required subjects to recall a specific fact. Subjects responding to the conceptual questions showed better recall. Such results are the justification for prefacing each chapter in this book with general statements about the chapter contents. You should be using these statements to form general conceptual questions.

Reviewing the text with the questions in mind is another important component of the PQ4R technique. Rothkopf (1966) compared the benefit of reading a text with questions in mind and the benefit of considering a set of questions after reading the text, which enabled subjects to review the text. Rothkopf had subjects read a long text with questions interspersed every three pages. The questions were relevant to the three pages either following or preceding the questions. In the former condition, subjects were supposed to read the subsequent text with these questions in mind. In the latter condition, they were to review what they had just read and answer the questions. The two experimental groups were compared with a control group, which read the text without any special questions. This control group answered 30 percent of the questions correctly in a final test of the whole text. The experimental group whose questions previewed the text answered correctly 72 percent of the test items relevant to their questions and 29 percent of the irrelevant items—basically the same results as those Frase obtained in comparing the effectiveness of relevant and irrelevant test items. The experimental group whose questions reviewed the text answered correctly 72 percent of the relevant items and 42 percent of the irrelevant items. Thus, it seems that reviewing the text with questions in mind is more generally beneficial.

Implicit Memory

So far this chapter has focused on memories that subjects have conscious access to. However, some of the most interesting research in the field of memory concerns memories we are not conscious that we have. Occasionally, we will become aware that we know things which we cannot describe. One example that many people can relate to is memory for the keyboard of a typewriter. Many accomplished typists cannot recall the arrangement of the keys except by imagining themselves typing. Clearly, their fingers know where the keys are, but they just have no conscious access to this knowledge.

Cases of such clear dissociation of knowledge from conscious access are rare with normal humans. However, such cases are more common in amnesic patients who suffer certain memory deficits due to neural damage. One group of such patients are those who suffer from Korsakoff's syndrome. This is associated with chronic alcoholism and is a result of malnourishment and consequent brain damage. These patients seem unable to remember very much after the onset of Korsakoff's syndrome. Consider the following description of a patient:

> Only after long conversation with the patient, one may note that at times he utterly confuses events and that he remembers absolutely nothing of what goes on around him: he does not remember whether he had his dinner. On occasion the patient forgets what happened to him just an instant ago: you came in, conversed with him, and stepped out for one minute, then you come in again and the patient has absolutely no recollection that you had already been with him. Patients of this type read the same page over and over again, sometimes for hours, because they are absolutely unable to remember what they had read. (Oscar-Berman, 1980, p. 410)

However, research has indicated that amnesic patients have implicit memories of many experiences that they cannot consciously recall. For instance, Graf, Squire, and Mandler (1984) compared amnesic versus normal subjects with respect to their memory for a list of words. After studying these words, subjects were asked to recall the words. The results are shown in Figure 7-7. Amnesics did much worse than normals. Then subjects were given a word-completion task. They were shown the first three letters of a word they had studied and were asked to make an English word out of it. For instance, subjects might be asked to complete ban–. By chance, there is a less than 10 percent probability that subjects can guess the word they studied but, as shown in the figure, subjects in both groups were recalling more than 50 percent. Moreover, there was no difference between the amnesics and the normals in the word-completion task. So, the amnesics clearly did have memory for the word list. However, they could not gain conscious access to these memories in a free-recall task. Rather, they displayed implicit memory in the word-completion task.

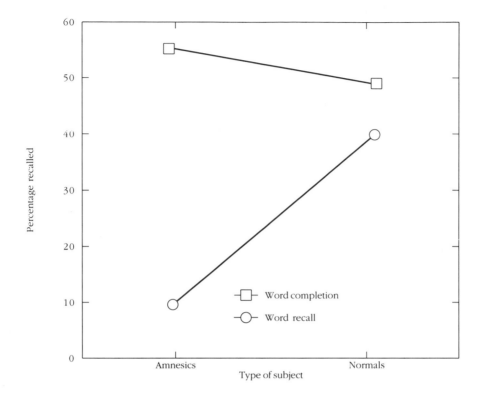

Figure 7-7. Ability of amnesic patients and normal subjects to recall words studied versus complete fragments of words studied. (From Graf, Squire, & Mandler, 1984.)

One of the most studied amnesics is a patient called H.M. H.M. had large parts of his temporal lobes removed in an attempt to cure epilepsy. He has one of the most profound amnesias and for more than 30 years has been almost totally unable to remember new events. However, he has been shown capable of acquiring implicit memories. For example, he is able to improve on various perceptual-motor tasks across days although each day he has no memory of the task from the previous day (Milner, 1962). He is also able to acquire complex cognitive skills.

Figure 7-8 shows the Tower of Hanoi task, which we will discuss at length in the next chapter on problem solving. There are three pegs and a

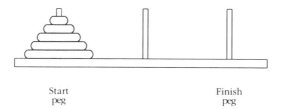

Start
peg

Finish
peg

Figure 7-8. A typical Tower of Hanoi problem.

number of different-sized disks with holes in them. Because of the holes
the disks can be stacked on the pegs. The disks start out all stacked on one
peg ordered by size. Subjects can move the disks one at a time from peg to
peg with the constraints that they can only move the top disk in a stack
and they cannot put a larger disk on a smaller disk. The subjects' task is to
get all the disks from the start peg to the finish peg. To solve this
problem requires a complex sequence of transferring the disks one by one
to and from all three pegs. This is a relatively hard task for both normal
and amnesic subjects. However, with practice people get better at it.
H.M. learns as fast as normals and was able to remember how to solve the
problem for up to a year (Cohen, 1984). Yet he has no memory of having
ever seen the problem.

A great deal of recent research (for reviews, read Schacter, 1987;
Richardson-Klavehn & Bjork, 1988) has looked at the dissociation between implicit and explicit memory in normal subjects. With this population it is often not possible to obtain the dramatic dissociation we see in
amnesics, where there is no conscious memory in the presence of considerable implicit memory. However, it has been possible to demonstrate
that one class of variables has different effects on tests of explicit memory
than on tests of implicit memory. For instance, Jacoby (1983) had subjects either just study a word such as *woman* alone (the no context
condition) or study it in the presence of an antonym *man–woman* (the
context condition) or generate the word as an antonym. In this last
condition subjects would see *man–???* and have to say *woman*.

The explicit memory test involved presenting subjects with a list of
words, some studied and some not, and asking them to recognize the old
words. The implicit memory test involved presenting the word for a brief
period (40 milliseconds) and asking them to identify the word. Figure 7-9
shows the results from these two tests as a function of study condition. As

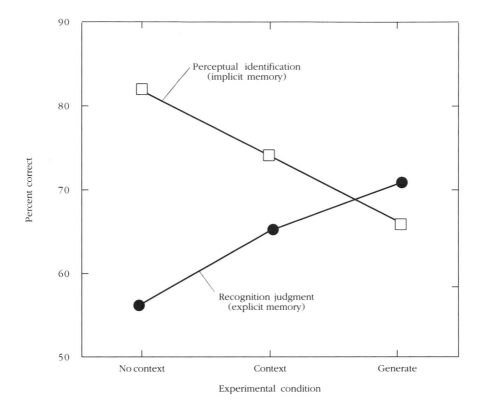

Figure 7-9. Ability to recognize a word in a memory test versus ability to identify it in a perceptual test as a function of how the word was originally studied. (From Jacoby, 1983.)

can be seen, performance on the explicit memory test is best in the condition that involves more semantic and generative processing — in line with earlier research we reviewed on elaborative processing. In contrast, performance on the implicit perceptual identification test gets worse. All three conditions show better perceptual identification than if the subject had not studied the word at all (only 60 percent in this condition, which is marginally worse than the generate condition). Jacoby argues that subjects produce best perceptual identification in the no context condition because this is the study condition in which they had to most rely on a perceptual encoding to identify the word. In the generate condition, subjects did not even have a word to read.

For specific words, particularly in the no context condition, there was a dissociation of explicit and implicit memory. That is, subjects were not able to recognize that they had seen a particular word but they were nonetheless helped in their perception of the word by the prior exposure. Thus, these normal subjects showed the influence in their word perception of experiences they were not aware of.

Research such as that just reviewed has convinced many researchers that there are at least two types of memory. Some people have called the explicit memory *declarative memory* because it contains the memories of which we are conscious and can declare. The other kind of memory is called *procedural memory* because it is implicit in our performing various kinds of procedures such as perceiving a word or solving a problem. The research in this chapter and the previous one has been mainly concerned with declarative memory. In the next two chapters we will be mainly concerned with procedural memory.

Remarks and Suggested Readings

The topics of this chapter are discussed more fully in a number of sources. The elaboration analysis comes from work by Reder and myself (Anderson, 1983, Chapter 5; Anderson & Reder, 1979; Reder, 1979, 1982). A survey of research and opinion about depth of processing is found in the book edited by Cermak and Craik (1979). Shaw and Bransford (1977) provide another perspective of the integrative and constructive nature of cognition. Graesser (1981) describes a general model of text comprehension and inference and relates it to memory. Alba and Hasher (1983) discuss evidence for the use of schema in memory research. Johnson and Raye (1981) discuss how people discriminate between what they actually heard and saw and what they inferred. Good reviews of research on organizational factors in memory are to be found in Bower (1970c) and Mandler (1967, 1972). Good sources for Endel Tulving's opinions on encoding and memory are the articles by Watkins and Tulving (1975) and Flexser and Tulving (1978) and Tulving's 1983 book. A recent book in honor of Endel Tulving edited by Roediger and Craik (1989) provides a set of current views on human memory. Crowder's 1976 and Underwood's 1983 memory texts provide excellent surveys of many of these topics, including the spacing effect. Squire's 1987 book is a good source for information on the neural basis of memory.

A number of papers set forth recommendations from memory research for learning and teaching techniques. Among these are Bower (1970a), Bjork (1979), Greeno (1976), and Norman (1973). Frase (1975), R. C. Anderson and Biddle (1975), and Rothkopf (1972) provide reviews of a good deal of research that is relevant to evaluating the PQ4R method. Gibson and Levin (1975, Chapter 11) provide a review of memory research relevant to reading. Also, the book by Thomas and Robinson (1972) sets forth the PQ4R method, and an earlier book by another Robinson (1961) describes the SQ3R method, which seems to have been the source for the PQ4R method. Higbee's 1988 book, *Your memory: How it works and how to improve it,* is a useful, popular self-help book.

Problem Solving

Summary

1. Declarative knowledge refers to knowledge about facts and things; procedural knowledge refers to knowledge about how to perform various cognitive activities. Procedural knowledge fundamentally has a problem-solving organization.

2. Problem solving can be conceived of as a search of a problem space. The problem space consists of physical states or knowledge states that are achievable by the problem solver. The problem-solving task involves finding a sequence of *operators* to transform the initial state into a goal state, in which the goal is achieved.

3. People often use general problem-solving methods for deciding what sequence of operators to use in solving a problem. These methods are called *heuristics* because they often lead to problem solution but are not guaranteed to succeed.

4. The *difference-reduction method* for problem solving involves choosing operators that reduce the difference between the current state and the goal state.

5. The *means–ends method* for problem solving involves selecting operators to reduce the differences between the current state and the goal state as well as setting subgoals to transform the current state so that needed operators can apply.

6. The *working-backward method* for problem solving involves breaking a goal into a set of subgoals whose solutions imply a solution of the original goal.

7. Problem solving by *analogy* involves using the structure of the solution to one problem to guide the solution to another problem.

8. The knowledge underlying problem solving can be formalized as a set of production rules that specify actions which will achieve goals under particular conditions.

9. The key to solving problems in many cases is to represent them in a way that the needed operators can apply. *Functional fixedness* is the failure to solve a problem because the person fails to represent an object as having a novel function so that it can be used in solving the problem.

10. The amount and type of knowledge available for solving a problem will vary with a person's problem-solving experience. Increasing the availability of relevant knowledge can facilitate problem solving; conversely, increasing the availability of irrelevant knowledge can inhibit problem solving. Effects of knowledge availability on problem solving are referred to as *set effects*.

This chapter represents a watershed in the book. To this point, we have concerned ourselves with how knowledge about the world gets into the system, how this knowledge is represented, and how it is stored in and retrieved from long-term memory. As discussed at the end of the last chapter, this kind of knowledge is frequently referred to as *declarative knowledge*—knowledge about facts and things. In this chapter we begin to consider *procedural knowledge*—knowledge about how to perform various cognitive activities. This chapter is about the knowledge underlying problem-solving activities. Later chapters will be concerned with the knowledge underlying reasoning, decision making, language comprehension, and language generation.

Procedural Knowledge and Problem Solving

In understanding procedural knowledge we start with problem solving because it seems that all cognitive activities are fundamentally problem solving in nature. The basic argument (Anderson, 1983; Newell, 1980; Tolman, 1932) is that human cognition is always purposeful, directed to achieving goals and to removing obstacles to those goals. In order to understand what this claim means, it is useful to understand what we mean when we say that a behavior is an instance of problem solving.

To get a perspective on what is meant by problem solving, we will look at one of the classic studies of problem solving in another species — apes (Köhler, 1927). Köhler, a famous German Gestalt psychologist who came to America in the 1930s, found himself trapped on Tenerife in the Canary Islands during World War I. On this island he found a colony of captive chimpanzees, which he studied, taking particular interest in the problem-solving behavior of the animals. His prize subject was a chimpanzee named Sultan. One problem posed to Sultan was to get some bananas that were outside his cage. Sultan had no difficulty if he was given a stick that could reach the bananas. He simply used the stick to pull the bananas into his cage. However, the critical problem occurred when Sultan was provided with two poles, neither of which would reach the food. After vainly reaching with the poles, the frustrated ape sulked in his cage. Suddenly, he went over to the poles and put one inside the other, creating a pole long enough to reach the food; with this extended pole, he was able to reach his prize (see Figure 8-1). This was clearly a creative problem-solving activity on the part of Sultan. Köhler used the term *insight* to refer to the ape's discovery.

What are the essential features that qualify this episode as an instance of problem solving? There seem to be three essential features:

1. *Goal directedness.* The behavior is clearly organized toward a goal — in this case, of getting the food.

2. *Subgoal decomposition.* If the ape could have gotten the food by simply reaching for it, the behavior would have been problem solving in only the most primitive sense. The essence of the problem solution is that the ape had to decompose the original goal into subtasks, or subgoals, such as getting the poles and putting them together.

Figure 8-1. Köhler's ape solving the two-stick problem: He combines two short sticks to form a pole long enough to reach the food. (From Köhler, 1956.)

3. *Operator selection.* Decomposing the overall goal into subgoals such as putting the sticks together is useful because the ape knows *operators* to achieve these subgoals. The term *operator* refers to an action that will transform the problem state into another problem state. The solution of the overall problem is a sequence of these known operators.

An interesting question is, What would have happened had Sultan been required to solve the same problem over and over again? Eventually, the whole situation would have become packaged as a single operation, and Sultan would have been able to achieve his goal without decomposing it into subgoals; he would simply breeze through the sequence of steps required to achieve the goal. One of the issues in the next chapter will be how the character of problem solving changes with repeated practice.

The Problem Space

States in the Problem Space

Frequently, problem solving is described in terms of searching a *problem space*, which consists of various states of the problem. The initial situation of the problem solver is referred to as the *initial state,* the situations on the way to the goal as *intermediate states*, and the goal as the *goal state.* Starting from the initial state, there are many ways the problem solver can choose to change his or her state. Sultan could reach for a stick, stand on his head, sulk, and so on. Suppose the ape reaches for the stick. Now he is in a new state. He can transform this to another state; for example, by letting go of the stick (thereby returning to the earlier state), reaching with the stick for the food, throwing the stick at the food, or reaching for the other stick. Suppose he reaches for another stick. Again he is in a new state. From this state Sultan can choose to try, say, walking on the sticks, putting them together, or eating the sticks. Suppose he chooses to put the sticks together. He can then choose to reach for the food, throw the sticks away, or undo them. If he reaches for the food, he will achieve his goal state.

Searching the Problem Space

The various states that the problem solver can achieve are referred to as defining a problem space, or state space. Problem-solving operators can be conceived of as changing one state in the space into another. The problem is to find some possible sequence of state changes that goes from the initial state to the goal state in the problem space. We can conceive of the problem space as a maze of states and of the operators as paths for moving among the states. In this conception, the solution to a problem is achieved through a *search* process; that is, the problem solver must find an appropriate path through a maze of states. This conception of problem solving as a search through a state space was developed by Allen Newell and Herbert Simon of Carnegie-Mellon University and has become the dominant analysis of problem solving, in both cognitive psychology and artificial intelligence.

A problem-space characterization consists of a set of states and operators for moving among states. A good problem for illustrating the problem-space characterization is the eight-tile puzzle, consisting of eight numbered, movable tiles set in a 3 × 3 frame. One cell of the frame is always empty, making it possible to move an adjacent numbered tile into the empty cell and thereby to "move" the empty cell as well. The goal is to achieve a particular configuration of tiles, starting from a different configuration. For instance, a problem might be to transform

The possible states of this problem are represented as configurations of tiles in the eight-tile puzzle. So, the first configuration shown is the initial state, and the second is the goal state. The operators that change the states are movements of tiles into empty spaces. Figure 8-2 reproduces an attempt of mine to solve this problem. This solution involved 26 moves, each move being an operator that changes the state of the problem. This sequence of operators is considerably longer than necessary. Try to find a shorter sequence of moves. (The shortest sequence possible is given at the end of the chapter, in Figure 8-16).

Often, discussions of problem solving involve the use of *search graphs* or *search trees*. Figure 8-3 gives a partial search tree for the following eight-tile problem:

Figure 8-3 is like an upside-down tree with a single trunk and branches leading out from that. This tree begins with the *start state*, represents all states reachable from this state, then all states reachable from those states, and so on. Any path through such a tree represents a possible sequence of moves that a problem solver might make. By generating a complete tree, we can also find the shortest sequence of operators between the start state and the goal state. Figure 8-3 illustrates some of the problem space. Frequently, in discussions of such examples, only the path through the problem space that leads to the solution is presented (for instance, in Figure 8-2). Figure 8-3 gives a better idea of the size of the space of possible moves that exist for a problem.

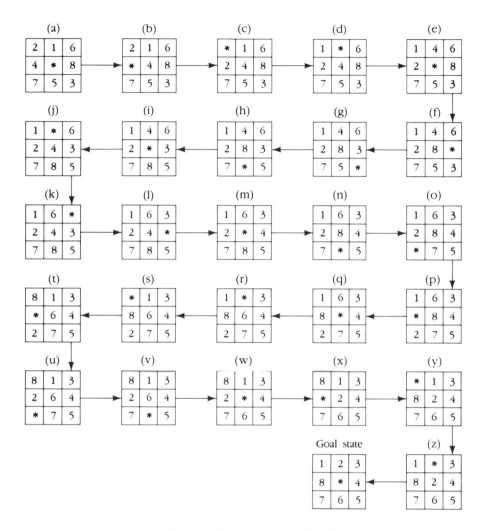

Figure 8-2. A sequence of moves for solving an eight-tile puzzle.

General Problem-Solving Methods

This search-space terminology is a descriptive way of characterizing possible steps that the problem solver might take. It does not explain the steps that the problem solver does take. Much of the theory of problem solving is concerned with identifying the principles that govern people's

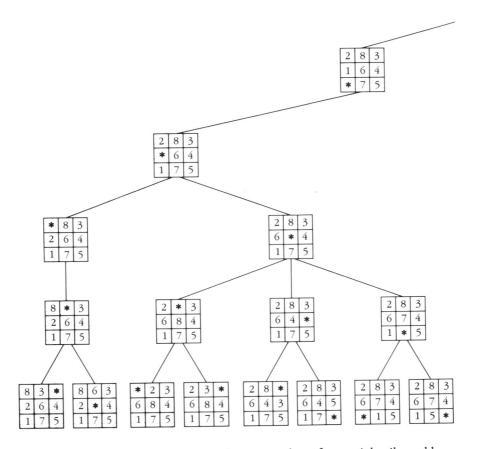

Figure 8-3. Part of the search tree, five moves deep, for an eight-tile problem. (From Nilsson, 1971.)

search through a problem space. These principles are concerned with how subjects select subgoals when they cannot directly achieve the whole goal. A major contribution of the research on cognitive science has been a cataloging of some of the methods people use.

In discussing methods for selecting subgoals, it is useful to make the distinction between *algorithms* and *heuristics*. Algorithms are procedures guaranteed to result in the solution of a problem. The procedure for

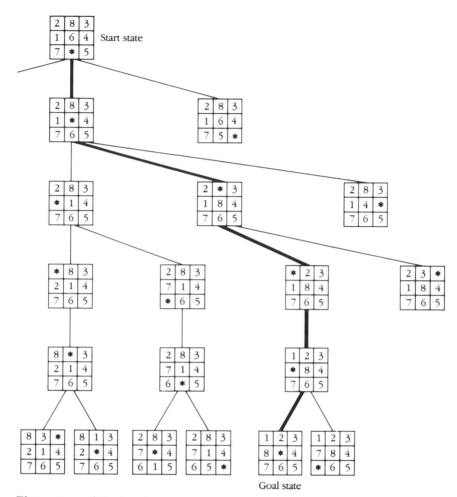

Figure 8-3. (*Continued*).

multiplication is an algorithm, because it identifies a series of subgoals that, if correctly achieved, will always result in the correct answer. In contrast, a heuristic is a rule of thumb that often (but not always) leads to a solution. For instance, most people in trying to solve the eight-tile puzzle wind up using heuristics of one sort or another. Often heuristics lead to more rapid solutions than algorithms. The problem-solving methods we will describe are all heuristics.

The Difference-Reduction Method

A frequent method of problem solving, particularly in unfamiliar domains, is to try to reduce the difference between the current state and the goal state. For instance, consider my solution to the eight-tile puzzle in Figure 8-2. There were four options possible for the first move. One possible operator was to move the 1 into the empty square, another was to move the 8, a third was to move the 5, and the fourth was to move the 4. I chose the last operator. Why? The answer is that it seemed to get me closer to my end goal. I was moving the 4 tile closer to its final destination. Human problem solvers are often strongly governed by *similarity*. They choose operators that transform the problem state into a state that resembles the goal state more closely than the initial state.

One of the ways problem solvers improve is by using more sophisticated measures of similarity. My move above was intended simply to get a tile closer to its final destination. After working with many tile problems, we begin to notice the importance of *sequence*—that is, whether noncentral tiles are followed by their appropriate successors. For instance, in state 0 of Figure 8-2, the 3 and 4 tiles are in sequence because they are followed by their successors 4 and 5, but the 5 is not in sequence because it is followed by 7 rather than 6. Trying to move tiles into sequence proves to be more important than trying to move them to their final destination. Thus, using sequence as a measure of similarity leads to more effective problem solving based on difference reduction (see Nilsson, 1971, for further discussion).

Where Similarity Is Misleading

The difference-reduction technique relies on evaluations of the similarity between the current state and the goal state. Although difference reduction probably works more often than not, it can also lead the problem solver astray. In some problem-solving situations, a correct solution involves going against the grain of similarity. A good example is called the hobbits and orcs problem:

> On one side of a river are three hobbits and three orcs. They have a boat on their side that is capable of carrying two creatures at a time across the river. The goal is to transport all six creatures across to the other side of the river. At no point on either side of the river can orcs outnumber hobbits (or the orcs would eat the outnumbered hobbits). The problem, then, is to find a method of transporting all six

creatures across the river without the hobbits ever being outnumbered.

Stop reading and try to solve this problem.

Figure 8-4 shows a correct sequence of moves for solution of this problem. Illustrated there are the locations of hobbits (H), orcs (O), and the boat (b). The boat, the three hobbits, and the three orcs all start on

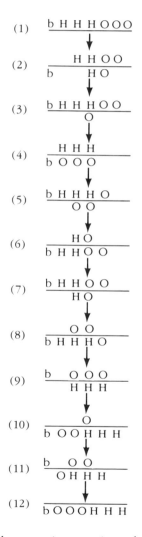

Figure 8-4. A diagram of the successive states in a solution to the hobbits and orcs problem.

one side of the river. This condition is represented in state 1 by the fact that all are above the line. Then, a hobbit, an orc, and the boat proceed to the other side of the river. The outcome of this action is represented in state 2 by placement of the boat (b), the hobbit (H), and the orc (O) on the other side of the line. In state 3, one hobbit has taken the boat back, and the diagram continues in the same way. Each state in the figure represents another configuration of hobbits, orcs, and boat. Subjects (e.g., those studied by Greeno, 1974) have a particular problem with the transition from state 6 to state 7 (see also Jeffries, Polson, Razran, & Atwood, 1977). One reason for this difficulty is that the action involves moving two creatures back to the wrong side of the river. The move seems to be away from a solution. At this point, subjects will often back up and look for some other solution.

Atwood and Polson (1976) provide another experimental demonstration of subjects' reliance on similarity and how that reliance can be beneficial or harmful. Subjects were given the following water-jug problem:

> You have three jugs, which we will call A, B, and C. Jug A can hold exactly 8 cups of water, B can hold exactly 5 cups, and C can hold exactly 3 cups. A is filled to capacity with 8 cups of water. B and C are empty. We want you to find a way of dividing the contents of A equally between A and B so that both have 4 cups. You are allowed to pour water from jug to jug.

Figure 8-5 illustrates two paths of solution to this problem. At the top of the figure all the water is in jug A — represented by $A(8)$; no water is in jug B or C — represented by $B(0)$ $C(0)$. The two possible actions are to pour A into C, in which case we get $A(5)$ $B(0)$ $C(3)$, or to pour A into B, in which case we get $A(3)$ $B(5)$ $C(0)$. From these two states more moves can be made. Numerous other sequences of moves are possible besides the two paths illustrated in the figure. However, it does illustrate the two shortest sequences to the goal.

Atwood and Polson used the representation in Figure 8-5 to analyze subjects' behavior. For instance, they asked which move subjects would prefer in starting from the initial state 1. That is, would they prefer to pour A into C and get state 2, or A into B and get state 9? The answer is that subjects preferred the latter move. Twice as many subjects moved to state 9 as moved to state 2. Note that state 9 is quite similar to the goal. The goal is to have 4 cups in both A and B, and state 9 has 3 cups in A and 5 cups in B. In contrast, state 2 has no cups of water in B. Throughout their problem, Atwood and Polson found a strong tendency for subjects

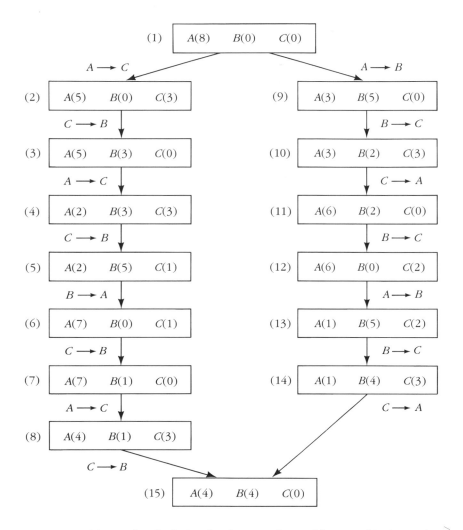

Figure 8-5. Two paths of solution for the water-jug problem posed in Atwood and Polson (1976). Each state is represented in terms of the contents of the three jugs. The transitions between states are labeled in terms of which jug is poured into which.

to move to states that were similar to the goal state. Usually, similarity was a good heuristic, but there are critical cases where similarity is misleading. For instance, the transitions from state 5 to state 6 and from state 11 to state 12 both lead to significant decreases in similarity to the goal. However, both transitions are critical to their solution paths. Atwood and Polson found that more than 50 percent of the time subjects deviated from the correct sequence of moves at these critical points.

Rather, subjects chose some move that seemed closer to the goal but actually took them away from the solution.

These examples illustrate the heuristic character of similarity. While it frequently does a good job in leading the problem solver to a solution, in some situations it does not work and can even be misleading. To repeat, heuristics are only rules of thumb and can be wrong on occasion.

Means – Ends Analysis

A more sophisticated method of subgoal selection is referred to as means–ends analysis. This method has been extensively studied by Newell and Simon, who have used it in a computer simulation program (called the General Problem Solver or GPS) that models human problem solving. The following is their description of means–ends analysis.

> The main methods of GPS jointly embody the heuristic of means–end analysis. Means–end analysis is typified by the following kind of common-sense argument:
>
> > I want to take my son to nursery school. What's the difference between what I have and what I want? One of distance. What changes distance? My automobile. My automobile won't work. What is needed to make it work? A new battery. What has new batteries? An auto repair shop. I want the repair shop to put in a new battery; but the shop doesn't know I need one. What is the difficulty? One of communication. What allows communication? A telephone . . . and so on.
>
> This kind of analysis—classifying things in terms of the functions they serve and oscillating among ends, functions required, and means that perform them—forms the basic system of heuristic of GPS. More precisely, this means–ends system of heuristic assumes the following:
>
> > 1. If an object is given that is not the desired one, differences will be detectable between the available object and the desired object.
> >
> > 2. Operators affect some features of their operands and leave others unchanged. Hence operators can be characterized by the changes they produce and can be used to try to

eliminate differences between the objects to which they are applied and desired objects.

3.   If a desired operator is not applicable, it may be profitable to modify the inputs so that it becomes applicable.

4.   Some differences will prove more difficult to affect than others.

It is profitable, therefore, to try to eliminate "difficult" differences, even at the cost of introducing new differences of lesser difficulty. This process can be repeated as long as progress is being made toward eliminating the more difficult differences. (Newell & Simon, 1972, p. 416)

Figure 8-6 displays in flowchart form the procedures used in the means–ends analysis employed by GPS. A general feature of this means–

Flowchart I   Goal: Transform current state into goal state

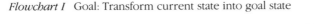

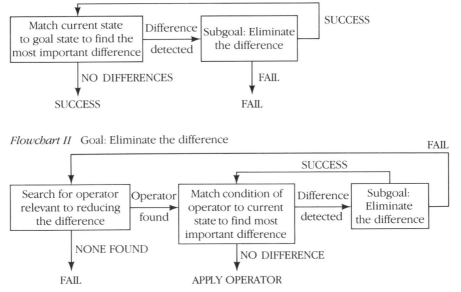

Figure 8-6.   The application of means–ends analysis by Newell and Simon's General Problem Solver (GPS). Flowchart I breaks a problem down into a set of differences and tries to eliminate each. Flowchart II searches for an operator relevant to eliminating a difference.

ends analysis is that it breaks a larger goal into subgoals. GPS creates subgoals in two ways. First, in flowchart I, GPS breaks the current state into a set of differences and sets the reduction of each difference as a separate subgoal. It chooses to try to eliminate first what it perceives as the most important difference. Second, in flowchart II, GPS tries to find an operator that will eliminate the difference. However, this operator may be unable to apply immediately because a difference exists between the operator's condition and the state of the environment. Thus, before the operator can be applied, eliminating another difference may be necessary. To eliminate the difference that is blocking the operator's application, flowchart II will have to be called again to find another operator relevant to eliminating that difference. In summary, means–ends analysis is like difference reduction with the added feature that if an operator to reduce a difference does not apply, the problem solver makes applying that operator the new subgoal. In contrast, in difference reduction the problem solver would simply abandon an operator if it could not be applied immediately.

The Tower of Hanoi Problem

Means–ends analysis has proved to be an extremely general and powerful method of problem solving. Ernst and Newell (1969) discuss its applications to the modeling of monkey and bananas problems (such as Sultan's predicament described at the beginning of the chapter), algebra problems, calculus problems, and logic problems. However, we will illustrate means–ends analysis here by applying it to the Tower of Hanoi problem. A simple version of this problem is illustrated in Figure 8-7. There are three pegs and three disks of differing sizes, *A, B,* and *C.* The disks have holes in them, so they can be stacked on the pegs. The disks can be moved from any peg to any other peg. Only the top disk on a peg can be moved,

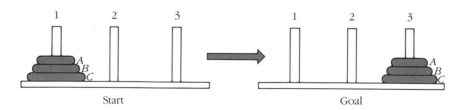

Figure 8-7. The three-disk version of the Tower of Hanoi problem.

and it can never be placed on a smaller disk. The disks all start out on peg 1, but the goal is to move them all to peg 3, one disk at a time, by means of transferring disks among pegs.

Figure 8-8 traces out the application of the GPS techniques to this problem. The first line gives the general goal of moving *A*, *B*, and *C* to peg 3. This goal leads us to the first flowchart of Figure 8-6. One difference between the goal and the current state is that *C* is not on 3. This difference is chosen first because GPS tries to remove the most important differences first, and we are assuming that the largest misplaced disk will be viewed as the most important difference. Therefore, a subgoal is set up to eliminate this difference. This takes us to the second flowchart of Figure 8-6, which tries to find an opertor to reduce the difference. The operator chosen is to *move C to 3*. The condition for applying a move operator is that nothing be on the disk. Since *A* and *B* are on *C*, there is a difference between the condition of the operator and the current state. Therefore, a new subgoal is created to reduce one of the differences — *B* on *C*. This subgoal gets us back to the start of flowchart II, but now with the goal of removing *B* from *C* (line 6 in Figure 8-8). Note that we have gone from use of flowchart I to use of II to a new use of II. This action is called *recursion* because to apply flowchart II to find a way to move *C* to 3 we need to apply flowchart II to find a way to remove *B* from *C*. Thus, one procedure is using itself as a subprocedure.

The operator chosen the second time in flowchart II is to *move B to 2*. However, we cannot immediately apply the operator of moving *B to 2*, since *B* is covered by *A*. Therefore, another subgoal is set up — that of removing *A* — and flowchart II is used to remove this difference. The operator relevant to achieving this is to *move A to 3*. There are no differences between the conditions for this operator and the current state. Finally, we have an operator we can apply (line 12 in Figure 8-8). Thus, we achieve the subgoal of moving *A* to 3. Now we return to the earlier intention of moving *B* to 2. There are no more differences between the operator for this move and the current state, so the action takes place. The subgoal of removing *B* from *C* is then satisfied (line 16 in Figure 8-8).

We have now returned to the original intention of moving *C* to 3. However, disk *A* is now on peg 3, which prevents the action. Thus, we have another difference to be eliminated between the now current state and the operator's condition. We move *A* onto peg 2 to remove this difference. Now the original operator of moving *C* to 3 can be applied (line 24 in Figure 8-8).

The state at this point is that disk *C* is on peg 3 and *A* and *B* are on peg 2. At this point, GPS returns to its original goal of moving the three disks to 3. It notes that another difference is that *B* is not on 3 and sets up

1. Goal: Move *A*, *B*, and *C* to Peg 3
2.   :Difference is that *C* is not on 3
3.   :Subgoal: Make *C* on 3
4.   :Operator is to move *C* to 3
5.   :Difference is that *A* and *B* are on *C*
6.   :Subgoal: Remove *B* from *C*
7.   :Operator is to move *B* to 2
8.   :Difference is that *A* is on *B*
9.   :Subgoal: Remove *A* from *B*
10.   :Operator is to move *A* to 3
11.   :No difference with operator's condition
12.   :Apply operator (move *A* to 3)
13.   :Subgoal achieved
14.   :No differences with operator's condition
15.   :Apply operator (move *B* to 2)
16.   :Subgoal achieved
17.   :Difference is that *A* is on 3
18.   :Subgoal: Remove *A* from peg 3
19.   :Operator is to move *A* to 2
20.   :No difference with operator's condition
21.   :Apply operator (move *A* to 2)
22.   :Subgoal achieved
23.   :No difference with operator's condition
24.   :Apply operator (move *C* to 3)
25.   :Subgoal achieved
26.   :Difference is that *B* is not on 3
27.   :Subgoal: Make *B* on 3
28.   :Operator is to move *B* to 3
29.   :Difference is that *A* is on *B*
30.   :Subgoal: Remove *A* from *B*
31.   :Operator is to move *A* to 1
32.   :No difference with operator's condition
33.   :Apply operator (move *A* to 1)
34.   :Subgoal achieved
35.   :No difference with operator's condition
36.   :Apply operator (move *B* to 3)
37.   :Subgoal achieved
38.   :Difference is that *A* is not on 3
39.   :Subgoal: Make *A* on 3
40.   :Operator is to move *A* to 3
41.   :No difference with operator's condition
42.   :Apply operator (move A to 3)
43.   :Subgoal achieved
44.   :No difference
45. Goal Achieved

Figure 8-8. A trace of the application of GPS to the Tower of Hanoi problem in Figure 8-7.

another subgoal of eliminating this difference. It achieves this subgoal by first moving *A* to 1 and then *B* to 3. This gets us to line 37 in the trace. The remaining difference is that *A* is not on 3. This difference is eliminated in lines 38 through 42. With this step, no more differences exist and the original goal is achieved.

Note that subgoals are created in service of other subgoals. For instance, to achieve the subgoal of moving the largest disk, a subgoal is created of moving the second largest disk, which is on top of it. We indicated this logical dependency of one subgoal on another in Figure 8-8 by indenting the processing of the dependent subgoal. At line 9 the figure, four goals and subgoals had to be remembered. As Simon (1975) has pointed out, the number of subgoals that must be remembered simultaneously will increase as we increase the number of disks. With every disk added to the problem, another subgoal will have to be maintained. From what we studied earlier about the limitations of working memory (Chapter 6), we can predict that subjects should have difficulty keeping many goals and subgoals active in working memory. In fact, the evidence is that when subjects try to use such problem-solving methods, they often fail because they lose track of the subgoals and how they interrelate.

Note that there are two problem-solving methods that subjects could bring to bear in solving the Tower of Hanoi problem. They could use a means–ends approach as illustrated in Figure 8-8 or they could use the simple difference-reduction method, in which case subjects never set as a subgoal to move a disk that currently cannot be moved. In the Tower of Hanoi problem, such a simple difference-reduction method would be disastrous as one needs to look beyond what is currently possible and have some more global plan of attack on the problem. Kotovsky, Hayes, and Simon (1985) did a study of how subjects actually approached the solution of the Tower of Hanoi problem. They found that there was an initial problem-solving period when subjects did adopt this fruitless difference-reduction strategy. Subjects then switched to a means–ends strategy, after which the solution to the problem came quickly.

Working Backward

A useful method of solving some problems is to work backward from the goal. This can be a particularly useful search heuristic in areas such as finding proofs in mathematics. Consider the geometry problem illustrated in Figure 8-9. The student is given that *ABDC* is a rectangle and is asked to prove that *AD* and *CB* are of the same length (are congruent). In

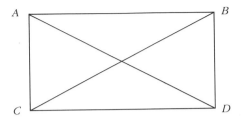

Figure 8-9. A geometry problem: Given that ▭*ABDC* is a rectangle, prove that $\overline{AD}$ and $\overline{CB}$ are congruent.

working backward, the student would ask, "What would prove that *AD* and *CB* are congruent? I could prove this if I could prove that the triangles *ACD* and *BDC* are congruent." Thus, the student would work backward from the goal of proving line congruence to that of proving triangle congruence. The next step is reasoning. "I could prove that triangles *ACD* and *BDC* are congruent if I could prove that two sides and an included angle (the side-angle-side postulate) are congruent." Thus, the student would reason back from this subgoal to another subgoal.

The key to working backward is to decompose the initial goal into a set of subgoals that imply solution of the original goal. The problem solver can then focus on solving each of the subgoals independently. The method runs into difficulty when solving one of the subgoals prevents solution of another goal—that is, when the subgoals prove not to be independent.

A good example of dealing with nonindependent subgoals is Sacerdoti's (1977) work on NOAH, an artificial-intelligence problem solver. Part (a) of Figure 8-10 illustrates the plan first generated by NOAH to solve the problem of painting a ladder and a ceiling green. It decomposed these goals into separate subgoals: (1) painting the ladder green and (2) painting the ceiling green. Painting the ladder was decomposed into getting the green paint and applying the green paint. Painting the ceiling was decomposed into getting the paint, using the ladder, and applying the paint to the ceiling. Unfortunately, applying the paint to the ladder made it unavailable for painting the ceiling. NOAH responds to such goal conflicts by reorganizing the goals in this case to the plan shown in part (b). Now the ceiling is painted first. Note, too, that the reorganized plan will get the green paint only once.

Many of the difficulties in our daily problem solving arise because of such nonindependence of goals. For instance, as a student, I often encountered problems because the Stanley Cup finals were always sched-

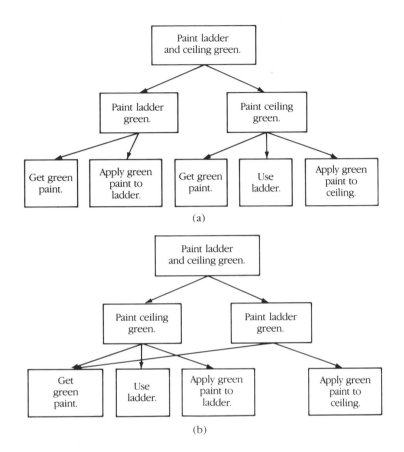

(a)

(b)

Figure 8-10. (a) Goal structure generated by working backward from the goal of painting the ladder and ceiling; (b) reorganization of the goal structure to deal with the conflicts between nonindependent goals in part (a). (Adapted from Sacerdoti 1977.)

uled around the time of final exams. I had to make difficult, but inventive, choices about how to satisfy both my need to watch hockey and my need to get good grades. Fortunately, it is not so much of a problem now that I give exams.

Problem Solving by Analogy

Another important method of solving a problem is by analogy. With this method, the problem solver attempts to use the structure of the solution to one problem to guide solutions to another problem. This method is frequently employed, for instance, in solving exercises in a mathematics text, where students will use the structure of one example worked out in the text to guide solutions to other problems. Here, the subgoals set are to transform the steps of the example into steps for the current problem.

An example of the power of analogy in problem solving is provided in an experiment of Gick and Holyoak (1980). They presented their subjects with the following problem, which is adapted from Duncker (1945):

> Suppose you are a doctor faced with a patient who has a malignant tumor in his stomach. It is impossible to operate on the patient, but unless the tumor is destroyed the patient will die. There is a kind of ray that can be used to destroy the tumor. If the rays reach the tumor all at once at a sufficiently high intensity, the tumor will be destroyed. Unfortunately, at this intensity the healthy tissue that the rays pass through on the way to the tumor will also be destroyed. At lower intensities the rays are harmless to healthy tissue, but they will not affect the tumor either. What type of procedure might be used to destroy the tumor with the rays, and at the same time avoid destroying the healthy tissue? (pp. 307–308)

This is a very difficult problem, and few subjects are able to solve it. However, Gick and Holyoak presented their subjects with the following story as an analogy for solution:

> A small country was ruled from a strong fortress by a dictator. The fortress was situated in the middle of the country, surrounded by farms and villages. Many roads led to the fortress through the countryside. A rebel general vowed to capture the fortress. The general knew that an attack by his entire army would capture the fortress. He gathered his army at the head of one of the roads, ready to launch a full-scale direct attack. However, the general then learned that the dictator had planted mines on each of the roads. The mines were set so that small bodies of men could pass over them safely, since the dictator needed to move his troops and workers to and from the fortress. However, any large force would detonate the mines. Not only would this blow up the road, but it would also destroy many neighboring villages. It therefore seemed impossible to capture the fortress. However, the general devised a simple plan. He divided his army into small groups and dispatched each group to the head of a different road. When all was ready he gave the signal and each group marched down a different road. Each group continued down its road to the fortress so that the entire army arrived together at the

fortress at the same time. In this way, the general captured the fortress and overthrew the dictator. (p. 351)

With this story as a hint nearly 100 percent of the subjects were able to develop an analogous solution to the tumor problem.

An interesting example of problem solving by analogy that did not quite work is a problem encountered by one geometry student whom we have studied. Part (a) of Figure 8-11 illustrates the steps of a geometry solution that the text gave as an example, and part (b) illustrates the student's attempts to use that worked-out proof to guide his solutions to a homework problem. In part (a), two segments of a line are given as equal length and the goal is to prove that two larger segments have equal length. In part (b) the student was given two segments with *AB* longer than *CD* and his task was to prove the same inequality for two larger segments, *AC* and *BD*.

Our subject noted the obvious similarity between the two problems and proceeded to develop the apparent analogy. He thought he could simply substitute points on one line for points on another, and inequality for equality. That is, he tried the following, simply substituting *A* for *R*, *B* for *O*, *C* for *N*, *D* for *Y*, and > for = . With these solutions he got the first line correct: Analogous to $RO = NY$, he wrote $AB > CD$. Then he had to write something analogous to $ON = ON$. He wrote $BC > BC$!

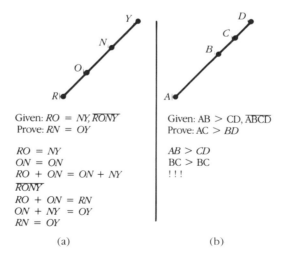

Given: $RO = NY$, $\overline{RONY}$
Prove: $RN = OY$

$RO = NY$
$ON = ON$
$RO + ON = ON + NY$
$\overline{RONY}$
$RO + ON = RN$
$ON + NY = OY$
$RN = OY$

(a)

Given: $AB > CD$, $\overline{ABCD}$
Prove: $AC > BD$

$AB > CD$
$BC > BC$
! ! !

(b)

Figure 8-11. (a) A worked-out proof problem given in a geometry text; (b) one student's attempt to use the structure of this problem's solution to guide his solution of a similar problem.

241

This example illustrates both how analogy can be used to guide problem solving, and that it requires a little sophistication to use analogy correctly.

Another difficulty with analogy is noticing that an analogy is possible. Gick and Holyoak did an experiment where they read subjects the general and the dictator story and then the Duncker ray problem (both given earlier). Very few subjects spontaneously noticed the relevance of the first story to solving the second. To achieve success, subjects had to be explicitly told to use the general and dictator story as an analogy for solving the ray problem.

When subjects do spontaneously use previous examples to solve a problem, they appear to be guided by superficial similarities. Thus, Ross (1984, 1987) taught subjects several methods for solving probability problems. These methods were taught with respect to specific examples, such as finding the probability that a pair of tossed dice will sum to 7. Subjects were then tested with new problems that were superficially similar to prior examples. This superficial similarity took the form of both example and problem involving the same content (e.g., dice) but not necessarily the same principle of probability. Subjects tried to solve the new problem by analogy to the superficially similar prior example. When that prior example illustrated the same principle as required in the current problem, subjects were able to solve the problem. When it did not, they were unable to solve the current problem. Reed (1987) has found similar results with algebra story problems.

In solving school problems students use temporal proximity as a cue to what examples to use in analogy. For instance, a student working physics problems at the end of a chapter expects that problems solved as examples in the chapter will use the same methods and so tries analogy to these (Chi, Bassok, Lewis, Riemann, & Glaser, 1989).

Production Systems: A General Problem-Solving Formalism

How to formalize the knowledge that underlies problem solving is an important issue. There is a general theoretical construct, called *production systems*, that has proven to be particularly useful in representing problem-solving knowledge. Production systems consist of a set of *productions*, which are rules for solving a problem. A typical problem-solving production (Anderson, 1983; Brown & Van Lehn, 1980; Card, Moran, & Newell, 1983) consists of a goal, some application tests, and an action. The following is a fairly simple production rule:

IF the goal is to drive a standard transmission car
   and the car is in first gear
   and the car is going more than 10 miles an hour
THEN shift the car into second gear

Such a production is organized into a condition and an action. The *condition* consists of a statement of the goal (i.e., to drive a standard transmission car) and of certain tests to determine if the rule is applicable to the goal. If these tests are met, the rule will apply and the *action* (i.e., shifting the car into second gear) will be performed.

Later chapters will illustrate the utility of such rules in modeling a wide range of cognitive behavior. For current purposes, however, it is important to note an important distinction between two types of production rules — *domain-general* and *domain-specific rules*. The foregoing rule is domain specific. It applies only in the context of driving a car. If we had only domain-specific production rules, we would be incapable of solving problems in novel domains. The various general problem-solving strategies or methods that we have just reviewed demand domain-general productions. For instance, consider the means–ends problem-solving strategy represented in Figure 8-6. It can be encoded by the following domain-general production rules:

P1   IF the goal is to transform the current state into the
             goal state
             and *D* is the largest difference between the states
      THEN set as subgoals
             1. To eliminate the difference *D*
             2. To convert the resulting state into the goal state

P2   IF the goal is to eliminate a difference *D*
             and *O* is an operator relevant to reducing the difference
      THEN set as a subgoal
             1. To apply *O*

P3   IF the goal is to apply an operator *O*
             and *D* is the most important difference between the
             application condition of *O* and the current state
      THEN set as subgoals
             1. To eliminate the difference *D*
             2. To apply the operator *O*

The first production rule selects differences to be reduced. The second production rule selects operators to apply. The third eliminates any features that prevent the operators from applying. Note that P2 sets a subgoal that can lead to P3, which sets a subgoal that can lead to P2. In this way, we get the embedding of goals as observed in Figure 8-6. Eventually, we get to a point where there are no more differences and operators can apply. In that case, the following rule would apply:

P4   IF the goal is to apply operator *O*
            and there are no differences between the application
            condition of *O* and the current state
            and operator *O* calls for action *A*
       THEN set as a goal to perform *A*

In the context of solving Tower of Hanoi problems, this production would lead to goals such as moving disk *A* to peg 3. Now domain-specific rules for moving objects can apply, such as:

P5   IF the goal is to move an object to a peg
       THEN set as subgoals
            1. To pick up the object
            2. Place it on a peg

Thus, the general character of problem solving in novel domains is that these general-strategy productions will break the task down into subgoals, and these into subgoals, and so on until subgoals are set that correspond to domain-specific rules at which point the domain-specific rules can take over. As we will see in the next chapter, one way to develop expertise in a problem-solving domain involves creating rules specific to that domain to replace domain-general rules.

Representation

The Importance of the Correct Representation

We have analyzed problem solution into problem states and operators for changing states. So far, we have discussed problem solving as if the only problem were operator selection. Difference reduction, means–ends analysis, working backward, and use of analogy all serve to help the problem solver select the right operator. However, the way in which states of the problem are represented also has significant effects.

A famous example illustrating the importance of representation is the *mutilated-checkerboard problem* (Kaplan, unpublished). Suppose we have a checkerboard in which the two diagonally opposite corner squares have been cut out. Figure 8-12 illustrates this mutilated checkerboard, on which 62 squares remain. Now suppose that we have 31 dominos, each of which covers exactly two squares of the board. Can we find some way of arranging these 31 dominos on the board so that they cover all 62 squares? If it can be done, explain how. If it cannot be done, prove that it cannot. Perhaps you would like to ponder this problem before reading on. Few people are able to solve this problem and very few see the answer quickly.

The answer is that the checkerboard cannot be covered by the dominos. The trick to seeing this is to include in your representation of the problem the fact that each domino must cover one black and one red square, not just any two squares. There is just no way to place a domino on two squares of the checkerboard without having it cover one black and one red square. This means that with 31 dominos we can cover 31 black squares and 31 red squares. But the mutilation has removed two red squares. Thus, there are 30 red squares and 32 black. It follows that the mutilated checkerboard cannot be covered by 31 dominos.

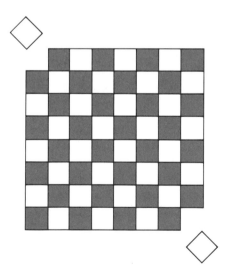

Figure 8-12. The mutilated checkerboard. (Adapted from W. A. Wickelgren, *How to solve problems.* W. H. Freeman and Company. Copyright 1974.)

Why is the mutilated-checkerboard problem easier to solve when we represent each domino as covering a red and a black space? The answer is that in so representing the problem we are encouraged to count and compare the number of red and black squares on the board. Thus, the effect of the problem representation is that it allows the critical operator to apply (i.e., counting red and black squares to check for parity).

Another problem that depends on correct representation is the *27 cubic apples problem*. Imagine 27 apples, each of which is shaped as a perfect cube. They are packed together in a crate 3 apples high, 3 apples wide, and 3 apples deep. A worm is in the center apple. Its life's ambition is to eat its way through all the apples in the crate, but it does not want to waste time by visiting any apple twice. the worm can move from apple to apple only by going from the side of one into the side of another. It cannot go from the corner of one apple to the corner of another or from the edge of one into the edge of another. Can you find some path by which the worm, starting from the center apple, can reach all the apples without going through any apple twice? If not, can you prove it is impossible? The solution is left to you. (*Hint:* The solution is based on a partial three-dimensional analogy to the solution for the mutilated-checkerboard problem; it is given at the end of the chapter.)

Functional Fixedness

Often, solutions to problems depend on the solver's ability to represent the objects in his or her environment in novel ways. This fact has been demonstrated in a series of studies by different experimenters. A typical experiment in the series is the two-string problem of Maier (1931), illustrated in Figure 8-13. Two strings hanging from the ceiling are to be tied together, but they are so far apart that the subject cannot grasp both at once. Among the objects in the room are a chair and a pair of pliers. Subjects try various solutions involving the chair but these do not work. The only solution is to tie the pliers to one string and set that string swinging like a pendulum, and then to get the second string, bring it to the center of the room, and wait for the first string to swing close enough to grasp. Only 39 percent of Maier's subjects were able to see this solution within 10 minutes. The difficulty is that subjects do not perceive the pliers as a weight that can be used as a pendulum. This phenomenon is called *functional fixedness*. It is so named because subjects are fixed on representing the object according to its conventional function and fail to represent its novel function.

Figure 8-13. The two-string problem used by Maier (1931).

Another demonstration of functional fixedness is an experiment by Duncker (1945). The task he posed to subjects is to support a candle on a door, ostensibly for an experiment on vision. The problem is illustrated in Figure 8-14. On the table are a box of tacks, some matches, and the candle. The correct solution is to tack the box to the door and use the box as a platform for the candle. This task is difficult for subjects because they see the box as a container, not as a platform. Subjects have greater difficulty with the task if the box is filled with tacks, reinforcing perception of the box as a container.

These demonstrations of functional fixedness are consistent with the interpretation that representation has its effect on operator selection. For instance, in Duncker's candle problem, subjects had to represent the tack box so that it could be used by the problem-solving operators that were looking for a support for the candle. When the box was conceived of as a container and not as a support, it was not available to the support-seeking operators.

247

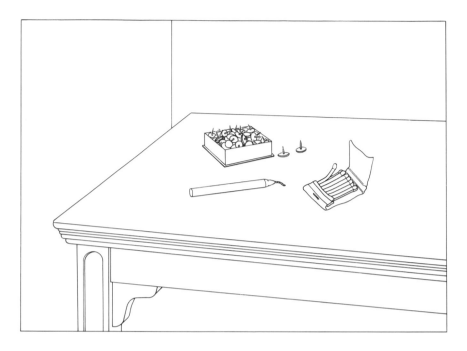

Figure 8-14. The candle problem used by Duncker. (Adapted from Glucksberg and Weisberg, 1966. Copyright 1966 by the American Psychological Association. Reprinted by permission.)

Set Effects

We have just discussed how problem representations can enable or block application of the operators that will lead to problem solution. It is also the case that problem solvers can become biased by their experiences to prefer certain problem-solving operators in solving a problem. Such biasing of the problem solution is referred to as a *set effect*. A good illustration involves the water-jug problem studied by Luchins (1942; Luchins & Luchins, 1959). In Luchins's water-jug experiments, a subject was given a set of jugs of various capacities and unlimited water supply. The subject's task was to measure out a specified quantity of water. Two examples are given below:

Problem	Capacity of Jug *A*	Capacity of Jug *B*	Capacity of Jug *C*	Desired quantity
1	5 cups	40 cups	18 cups	28 cups
2	21 cups	127 cups	3 cups	100 cups

Assume that subjects have a tap and a sink so that they can fill jugs and empty them. The jugs start out empty. Subjects are allowed only to fill the jugs, empty them, and pour water from one jug to another. In problem 1, subjects are told that they have three jugs—jug A, with a capacity of 5 cups; jug B, with a capacity of 40 cups; and jug C, with a capacity of 18 cups. To solve this problem, subjects would fill A and pour it into B, fill A again and pour it into B, and fill C and pour it into B. The solution to this problem is denoted by $2A + C$. The solution for the second problem is to first fill jug B with 127 cups; fill A from B so that 106 cups are left in B; fill C from B so that 103 cups are left in B; empty C; and fill C again from B so that the goal of 100 cups in B is achieved. The solution to this problem can be denoted by $B - A - 2C$. The first solution is called an *addition* solution because it involves adding the contents of the jugs together; the second solution is referred to as a *subtraction* solution because it involves subtracting the contents of one jug from another. Luchins studied the effect of giving subjects a series of problems, all of which could be solved by addition. This created an "addition set" such that subjects solved new addition problems faster than control subjects, who had no practice, and solved subtraction problems more slowly.

The set effect that Luchins is most famous for demonstrating is the *Einstellung effect*, or *mechanization of thought*, which is illustrated by the series of problems in Table 8-1. Subjects were given these problems in this order and were required to find solutions for each. Take time out from reading this text and try to solve each problem.

Table 8-1 *Luchin's 1942 Water-Jug Problems*

Problems	Capacity of Jug A	Capacity of Jug B	Capacity of Jug C	Desired Quantity
1	21	127	3	100
2	14	163	25	99
3	18	43	10	5
4	9	42	6	21
5	20	59	4	31
6	23	49	3	20
7	15	39	3	18
8	28	76	3	25
9	18	48	4	22
10	14	36	8	6

Note. All volumes are in cups.

All problems except 8 can be solved by using the $B - 2C - A$ method (i.e., filling B, twice pouring B into C, and once pouring B into A). For problems 1 through 5, this solution is the simplest, but for problems 7 and 9 the simpler solution of $A + C$ applies. Problem 8 cannot be solved by the $B - 2C - A$ method, but can be solved by the simpler solution of $A - C$. Problems 6 and 10 are also solved more simply as $A - C$ than $B - 2C - A$. Of Luchins's subjects who received the whole setup of 10 problems, 83 percent used the $B - 2C - A$ method on problems 6 and 7, 64 percent failed to solve problem 8, and 79 percent used the $B - 2C - A$ method for problems 9 and 10. The performance of subjects who worked on all 10 problems was compared with the performance of control subjects who saw only the last five problems. These control subjects did not see the biasing $B - 2C - A$ problems. Fewer than 1 percent of the control subjects used $B - 2C - A$ solutions, and only 5 percent failed to solve problem 8. Thus, the first five problems can create a powerful bias for a particular solution. This bias hurt solution of problems 6 through 10.

Note that the Einstellung effect does not involve creating a general bias for subtraction over addition. The critical problem, 8, involved subtraction too. Rather, subjects are remembering a particular sequence of operations, and it is memory for this sequence that is blinding them to other possibilities. While these effects are quite dramatic, they are relatively easy to reverse with the exercise of cognitive control. Luchins found that simply by warning subjects by saying, "Don't be blind," after problem 5, more than 50 percent of them overcame set for the $B - 2C - A$ solution.

Another kind of set effect in problem solving has to do with the influence of general semantic factors. This effect is nicely illustrated in the experiment of Safren (1962) on anagram solution. Safren presented subjects with lists such as the following in which each set of letters was to be unscrambled and made into a word:

| kmli | graus | teews |
| recma | foefce | ikrdn |

This is an example of an organized list, in that the individual words are all associated with drinking coffee. Safren compared solution times for organized lists such as this with those for unorganized lists. Median solution time was 12.2 seconds for anagrams from unorganized lists but 7.4 seconds for anagrams from organized lists. Presumably, the facilitation evident with the organized lists occurred because the earlier items in the list associatively primed, and so made more available, the later words.

Note that this anagram experiment contrasts with the water-jug experiment in that no particular procedure is being strengthened. Rather, what is being strengthened is part of the subject's factual (declarative) knowledge about spellings of associatively related words.

In general, set effects occur when some knowledge structures become more available at the expense of others. These knowledge structures can be either procedures, as in the water-jug problem, or declarative information, as in the anagram problem. If the available knowledge is what subjects need for solving the problem, their problem solving will be facilitated. If the available knowledge is not what is needed, problem solving will be inhibited. It is good to realize that set effects can sometimes be easily dissipated (as with Luchins's "Don't be blind" instruction). If you find yourself stuck on a problem and you keep generating similar unsuccessful approaches, it is often useful to force yourself to back off, change set, and try a different kind of solution.

Incubation Effects

Problem solvers frequently report that after trying and getting nowhere on a problem, they can put the problem aside for hours, days, or weeks and then, upon returning to it, can see the solution quickly. Numerous examples of this pattern were reported by the famous French mathematician Poincaré (1929), including for instance, the following:

> Then I turned my attention to the study of some arithmetical questions apparently without much success and without a suspicion of any connection with my preceding researches. Disgusted with my failure, I went to spend a few days at the seaside, and thought of something else. One morning, walking on the bluff, the idea came to me, with just the same characteristics of brevity, suddenness and immediate certainty, that the arithmetic transformations of indeterminate ternary quadratic forms were identical with those of non-Euclidean geometry. (p. 388)

Such phenomena are referred to as *incubation effects*. An incubation effect was nicely demonstrated in an experiment by Silveira (1971). The problem she posed to subjects, called the *cheap-necklace problem*, is illustrated in Figure 8-15. Subjects were given the following instructions:

> You are given four separate pieces of chain that are each three links in length. It costs 2¢ to open a link and 3¢ to close a link. All links

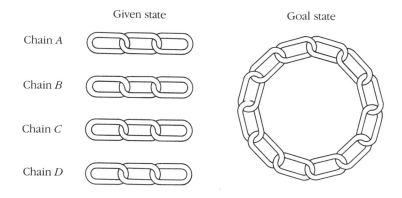

Given state   Goal state

Chain *A*

Chain *B*

Chain *C*

Chain *D*

Figure 8-15. The cheap-necklace problem. (Figure 4-5 from W. A. Wickelgren, *How to solve problems.* W. H. Freeman and Company. Copyright 1974.)

are closed at the beginning of the problem. Your goal is to join all 12 links of chain into a single circle at a cost of no more than 15¢.

Try to solve this problem yourself. (A solution is provided at the end of this chapter.) Silveira tested three groups. A control group worked on the problem for half an hour; 55 percent of these subjects solved the problem. For one experimental group, their half hour spent on the problem was interrupted by a half-hour break in which they performed other activities; 64 percent of these subjects solved the problem. A third group had a 4-hour break; and 85 percent of these subjects solved the problem. Silveira required her subjects to talk aloud as they solved the cheap-necklace problem. She found that subjects did not come back to the problems with solutions completely worked out. Rather, they started out trying to work out the problem much as before.

The best explanation for incubation effects relates them to set effects. During initial attempts on a problem, subjects set themselves to think about the problem in certain ways and bring to bear certain knowledge structures. If this initial set is appropriate, subjects will solve the problem. If the initial set is not appropriate, however, they will be stuck throughout the session with inappropriate procedures. By going away from the problem, the activation of the inappropriate knowledge structures will dissipate and subjects will be able to take a fresh approach to the problem.

Numerous other attempts have been made to display incubation effects by interrupting problem solving, only some of which have proven successful (for discussions see Dominowski & Jenrick, 1972; Murray &

Denny, 1969; Kaplan & Davidson, submitted). Sometimes worse performance is found with an interruption. A good example of a situation in which interruption is harmful is in the solving of a set of simultaneous equations. The only effect of interruption here would be subjects' losing their places in the solution. Incubation effects are most likely to be found in problems such as the cheap-necklace problem, which depend on a single key insight.

Metcalfe and Wiebe (1987) show that subjects have very different intuitions about insight and noninsight problems. The insight problems used by Metcalfe and Wiebe included ones like the cheap-necklace problem. Their noninsight problems required multistep solutions as in the Tower of Hanoi problem (see Figure 8-7). They asked subjects to judge every 15 seconds how close they felt they were to the solution. Fifteen seconds before they actually solved the problem subjects were fairly confident they were close to the solution on the noninsight problems. In contrast, on the insight problems subjects had little idea they were close to a solution 15 seconds before they actually solved the problem.

Remarks and Suggested Readings

A number of textbooks provide extensive reviews on problem solving. Many exhibit a certain tendency to equate the topic of thinking with problem solving. So, texts with the topic *thinking* in their title, such as Johnson (1972) or Vinacke (1974), include extensive discussions of the traditional problem-solving literature. Newell and Simon have been the most influential workers on problem solving in the modern era. Their work is extensively presented in their 1972 book. Newell's current conception of problem solving is best described in his new book (Newell, in press). A very detailed discussion of GPS is to be found in Ernst and Newell (1969). Recent work on the use of analogies in problem solving has been done by Carbonell (1985) and Gick and Holyoak (1983). A book edited by Vosniadou and Ortony (1989) is devoted to the topics of analogy and similarity. Holland, Holyoak, Nisbett, and Thagard (1986) contains a general view of the role of problem solving in cognition. Good reviews of the problem-solving literature are to be found in Greeno and Simon (1988) and VanLehn (in press).

A great deal of research in artificial intelligence could be classified under the topic of problem solving. This work has had particularly strong influence on the thinking of cognitive psychologists, partly because of the efforts of Newell and Simon. The texts by Hunt (1975), Nilsson

(1980), and Winston (1984) all provide discussions of the problem-solving techniques in artificial intelligence.

Appendix

A number of problems were presented in this chapter without solution. Figure 8-16 gives the minimum-path solution to the problem solved less efficiently in Figure 8-2.

With regard to the problem of the 27 cubic apples, the worm cannot succeed. To see that this is the case, imagine that the apples alternate in color, green and red, in a three-dimensional checkerboard pattern. If the center apple, from which the worm starts, is red, there are 13 red apples and 14 green apples in all. Every time the worm moves from one apple to another, he must change colors. Since the worm starts from the red, this

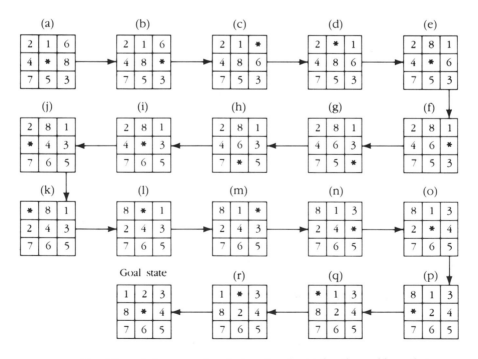

Figure 8-16. The minimum-path solution for the eight-tile problem that was solved less efficiently in Figure 8-2.

means that it cannot reach more green apples than red apples. Thus, it cannot visit all 14 green apples if it also visits each of the 13 red apples just once.

Solve the cheap-necklace problem in Figure 8-15 by opening all three links in one chain (at a cost of 6¢) and then using the three open links to connect together the remaining three chains (at a cost of 9¢).

CHAPTER

·9·

Development of Expertise

Summary

1. Skill learning occurs in three steps: (1) a cognitive stage, in which a description of the procedure is learned; (2) an associative stage, in which a method for performing the skill is worked out; and (3) an autonomous stage, in which the skill becomes more and more rapid and automatic.

2. Time to perform a task is a power function of the amount of practice on the task. Such a function implies that continued practice is of continued but ever diminishing benefit to the task performance.

3. There are a number of factors modulating the effects of practice: spacing of practice increases learning; skills can be learned better if independent parts are taught separately; subjects learn more rapidly if they are given immediate feedback.

4. *Proceduralization* refers to the process by which people convert their declarative, factual knowledge of a domain into a more efficient procedural representation.

5. *Tactical learning* refers to the improvement that comes about because people learn familiar subsequences of problem-solving steps that appear in multiple problems.

6. *Strategic learning* refers to the improvement that comes about because people learn the optimal way to organize their problem solving for a particular domain.

7. Problem solving also improves in a domain because people learn how to represent problems in the domain in terms of abstract (not surface-level) features that facilitate the problem solving.

8. As people become expert in a domain their memory for problems improves both because they learn the patterns that appear in these problems and because they can commit to memory more patterns in a problem.

9. Training in a particular skill transfers to another skill to the extent that the second skill involves use of the same facts, productions, and patterns. It is difficult to find any transfer between totally different cognitive skills and it is difficult to find any negative transfer between any cognitive skills.

It may sometimes seem that at every turn we are being faced with a novel problem, but generally we are achieving goals in domains that are highly familiar — speaking a language, driving a car, solving column addition, and the like. Here our behavior is often so automatic that it is difficult to even recognize that we are solving a problem. However, if we look at novices — someone trying to communicate in an unfamiliar language, a person behind the wheel of a car for the first time, a child learning addition — we can see that these can be difficult and quite novel problem domains. Through practice, however, we have become relatively expert. The skills just mentioned are ones at which a large fraction of the population becomes expert. There are other skills at which only a small fraction becomes expert — playing chess, doing science, hitting major league pitching, and so on. Nevertheless, it appears that development of expertise in these specialized areas is really no different than in the more general areas.

William G. Chase, late of Carnegie-Mellon University, was one of our local experts on expertise. He had two mottos that summarize much of the nature of expertise and its development:

No pain, no gain.

When the going gets tough, the tough get going.

The first motto reflects the fact that no one develops expertise without a great deal of hard work. Richard Hayes (1985), another CMU faculty member, has studied geniuses in fields varying from music to science to chess. He found that no one reached genius levels of performance without at least 10 years of practice.[1] Chase's second motto reflects the fact that the difference between relative novices and relative experts increases as we look at more difficult problems. For instance, there are many chess duffers who could play a credible, if losing, game against a master when they are given unlimited time to choose moves. However, they would lose embarrassingly if forced to play lightning chess, where they have only 5 s per move.

Chapter 8 reviewed some of the general principles governing problem solving, particularly in novel domains. This research has provided a framework for analyzing the development of expertise in problem solving. Research on expertise has been one of the major new developments in cognitive science. This is particularly exciting because it promises to have implications for education of technical or formal skill in areas such as mathematics, science, and engineering.

This chapter begins with a look at the general characteristics of the development of expertise in a skill. Then we will consider what factors might underlie the development of expertise. Finally, we will consider the vexing question of how skill might transfer from one domain of expertise to another.

Stages of Skill Acquisition

It is typical to distinguish among three stages in the development of a skill (Anderson, 1983; Fitts & Posner, 1967). Fitts and Posner call the first stage the *cognitive stage*. In this stage subjects develop a declarative

---

[1]Frequently cited as an exception to this generalization is Mozart, who wrote his first symphony when he was 8. However, his early works are not of genius caliber and are largely of historical value only. Schonberg (1970) claims that Mozart's great works were produced after the twentieth year of his career.

encoding (see the distinction between declarative and procedural representations at the beginning of Chapter 8) of the skill; that is, they commit to memory a set of facts relevant to the skill. Learners typically rehearse these facts as they first perform the skill. For instance, when I was first learning to shift gears in a standard transmission car, I memorized the location of the gears (e.g., "up, left") and the correct sequence of engaging the clutch and moving the stick shift. I rehearsed this information as I performed the skill.

In this stage the learners are using domain-general problem-solving procedures (see the distinction between domain-general and domain-specific procedures in Chapter 8) to perform and are using the facts they have learned about the domain to guide their problem solving. Thus, they might have a general means–ends production, such as:

IF the goal is to achieve a state X
and M is a method for achieving state X
THEN set as a subgoal to apply M

Applied to driving, if the goal is to go in reverse and if the learner knows that moving the stick shift to the upper left will put the car into reverse, then this production would set the subgoal of moving the gear to the upper left. The knowledge acquired in the cognitive stage is quite inadequate for skilled performance. There follows what is called the *associative stage*. Two main things happen in this second stage. First, errors in the initial understanding are gradually detected and eliminated. So, I slowly learned to coordinate the release of the clutch in first gear with the application of gas in order not to kill the engine. Second, the connections among the various elements required for successful performance are strengthened. Thus, I no longer had to sit for a few seconds trying to remember how to get to second gear from first. Basically, the outcome of the associative stage is a successful procedure for performing the skill. In this stage, the declarative information is transformed into a procedural form. However, it is not always the case that the procedural representation of the knowledge replaces the declarative. Sometimes the two forms of knowledge can coexist side by side, as when we can speak a foreign language fluently and still remember many rules of grammar. However, it is the procedural, not the declarative, knowledge that governs the skilled performance.

The output of the associative state is a set of procedures specific to the domain. So, for instance, rather than using the general means–ends production above in driving, the learner may develop a special production for moving into reverse:

```
   IF   the goal is to go in reverse
 THEN   set as subgoals
        1. To disengage the clutch
        2. Then to move the gear to the upper left
        3. Then to engage the clutch
        4. Then to push down on the gas
```

The third stage in the standard analysis of skill acquisition is the *autonomous stage*. In this stage, the procedure becomes more and more automated and rapid. No sharp distinction exists between the autonomous and associative stage. The autonomous might be considered an extension of the associative stage. Because facility in the skill increases, verbal mediation in the performance of the task often disappears at this point. In fact, the ability to verbalize knowledge of the skill can be lost altogether. This autonomous stage appears to extend indefinitely. Throughout it, the skill gradually improves.

Two of the dimensions of improvement with practice are speed and accuracy. The procedures come to apply more rapidly and more appropriately. Anderson (1982) and Rumelhart and Norman (1978) refer to the increasing appropriateness of the procedures as *tuning*. For instance, consider our production for moving into reverse. It is only applicable to an ordinary three-speed gear. The process of tuning would result in a production that had additional tests for the appropriateness of this operation. Such a production might be:

```
   IF   the goal is to go in reverse
        and there is a three-speed standard transmission
 THEN   set as subgoals
        1. To disengage the clutch
        2. Then to move the gear to the upper left
        3. Then to engage the clutch
        4. Then to push down on the gas
```

The Power Law of Practice

Figure 9-1 is a graph of some data from Blackburn (1936) showing the improvement in performance of mental addition as a function of practice. Blackburn had two subjects, S_1 and S_2, perform 10,000 addition problems! The data are plotted on a log–log scale. That is, the abscissa is the logarithm of practice (number of additions) and the ordinate is the logarithm of time per addition. On this log–log plot, the data for two

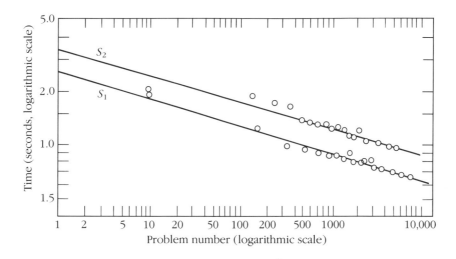

Figure 9-1. Improvement with practice in time taken to add two numbers. Data are given separately for two subjects. Both time and problem number are plotted on a logarithmic scale. (Plot by Crossman, 1959, of data from Blackburn, 1936.)

subjects approximate a straight line. Similar straight-line functions relating practice to performance time have been found over a wide range of tasks. In fact, virtually every study of skill acquisition has found a straight-line function on a log–log plot. There is usually some limit to how much improvement can be achieved, determined by the capability of musculature involved, age, level of motivation, and so on. There do not appear to be any cognitive limits on the speed with which a skill can be performed. In fact, one famous study followed the improvement of a woman whose job was to roll cigars in a factory. Her speed of cigar making followed this log–log relationship over a period of 10 years. When she finally stopped improving, it was discovered that she had reached the physical limit of the machinery with which she was working!

The linear relationship between time (T) and log practice (P) can be expressed as:

$$\log(T) = A - b \log(P)$$

which can be transformed into

$$T = aP^{-b}$$

where $a = 10^A$. In Chapter 6 we discussed such power functions in memory (see Figure 6-5). Basically, these are functions where the decrease in processing time with further practice becomes small very rapidly.

Effects of practice have also been studied in domains involving complex problem solving, such as giving justifications for geometrylike proofs (Neves & Anderson, 1981). Figure 9-2 shows a power function for that domain, in terms of both a normal scale and a log–log scale. Such

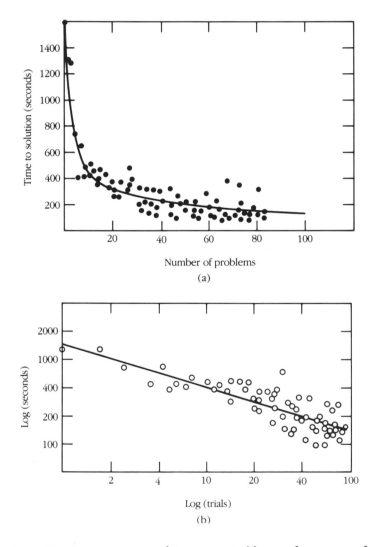

Figure 9-2. Time to generate proofs in a geometrylike proof system as a function of the number of proofs already done: (a) function on a normal scale, $RT = 1410P^{-55}$; (b) function on a log–log scale.

functions illustrate that the benefit of further practice rapidly diminishes, but that no matter how much practice we have had, further practice will help a little.

Kolers (1979) investigated the acquisition of reading skills using materials such as those illustrated in Figure 9-3. The first type of text (*N*) is normal, but the others have been transformed in various ways. In the *R* transformation, the whole line has been turned upside down; in the *I*

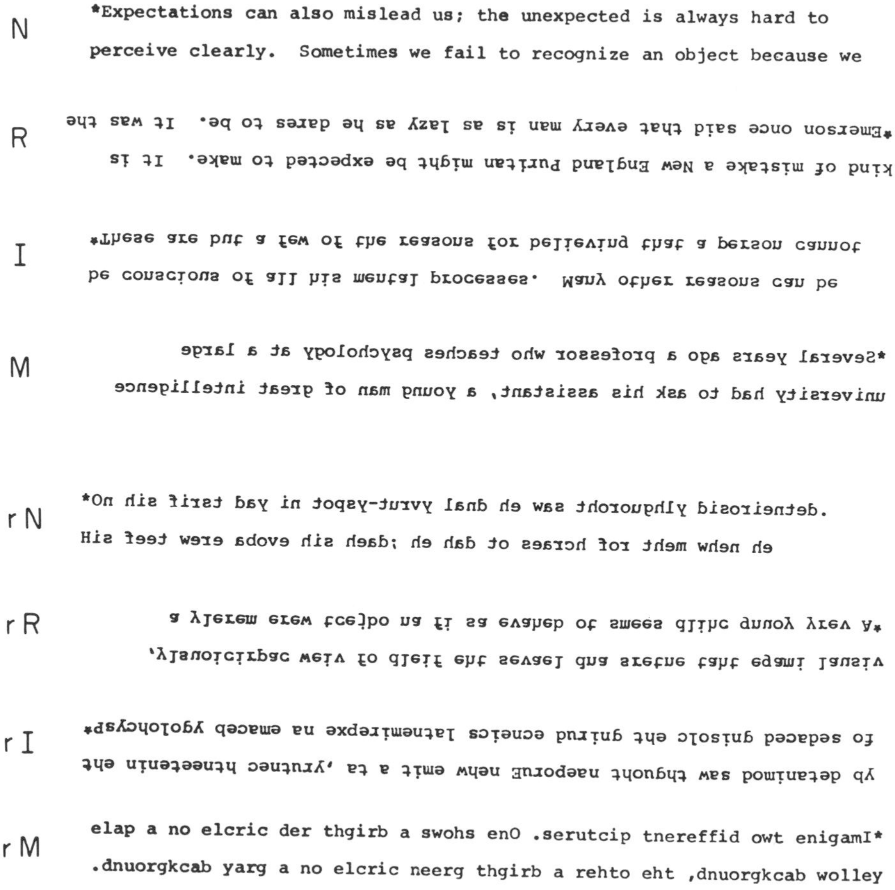

Factors Affecting Practice

N   *Expectations can also mislead us; the unexpected is always hard to perceive clearly. Sometimes we fail to recognize an object because we

R   [line printed upside down]

I   [line printed upside down]

M   [line printed upside down]

r N [line printed mirror-reversed]

r R [line printed mirror-reversed and inverted]

r I [line printed mirror-reversed and inverted]

r M elap a no elcric der thgirb a swohs enO .serutcip tnereffid owt enigamI* dnuorgkcab yarg a no elcric neerg thgirb a rehto eht ,dnuorgkcab wolley

Figure 9-3. Some examples of the spatially transformed texts used in Kolers's studies of the acquisition of reading skills. The asterisks indicate the starting point for reading. (From Kolers & Perkins, 1975.)

transformation, each letter has been inverted; in the *M* transformation, the sentence has been set as a mirror image of standard type. The rest are combinations of the several transformations. In one study, Kolers looked at the effect of massive practice on reading inverted (*I*) text. Subjects took more than 16 min to read their first page of inverted text as compared with 1.5 min for normal text. Following the initial test of reading speed, subjects practiced on 200 pages of inverted text. Figure 9-4 provides a log–log plot of reading time against amount of practice. In this figure, practice is measured in terms of number of pages read. The change in speed with practice is given by the curve labeled *Original training on inverted text*. Kolers interspersed a few tests on normal text; data for these are given by the curve labeled *Original tests on normal text*. We see the same kind of improvement for inverted text as in the Blackburn study (i.e., a straight-line function on a log–log plot). After reading 200 pages, Kolers's subjects were reading at the rate of 1.6 min per page, almost the same rate as subjects reading normal text.

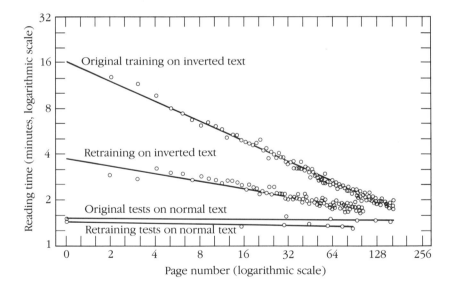

Figure 9-4. The results for readers in Kolers's reading-skills experiment (1976) on two tests more than a year apart. Subjects were trained with 200 pages of inverted text with occasional pages of normal text interspersed. A year later they were retrained with 100 pages of inverted text, again with normal text occasionally interspersed. The results show the effect of practice on the acquisition of the skill. Both reading time and number of pages practiced are plotted on a logarithmic scale. (From Kolers, 1976. Copyright by the American Psychological Association. Reprinted by permission.)

Kolers brought his subjects back a year later and had them read inverted text again. These data are given by the curve in Figure 9-4 labeled *Retraining on inverted text*. This time for the first page of the inverted text, subjects took about 3 min. Compared with their performance of 16 min on their first page a year earlier, subjects were displaying an enormous savings, but it was now taking them almost twice as long to read the text as it did after their 200 pages of training a year earlier. They had clearly forgotten something. As the figure illustrates, subjects' improvement on the retraining trials showed a log–log relationship between practice and performance, as had their original training. Subjects took 100 pages to reach the same level of performance that they had initially reached after 200 pages of training.

Factors Affecting Practice

Although practice is very important for the development of a skill, you should not think that this is all that is involved. The nature of the practice and the circumstances surrounding it can be very important. This is just the same as the effect of practice on the development of factual or declarative memories (Chapters 6 and 7). Practice was important there, too, but there were numerous modulating factors. In fact, it seems that some of the principles which apply to declarative memory also apply to memory for procedures. For instance, we discussed in Chapter 7 the powerful effects that spaced study can have on the learning of verbal materials. Spacing appears to have even more profound effects on skill learning. The inefficiency of massed practice was shown in one study involving intensive training in Morse code during World War II (reported in Bray, 1948). Students were found to learn as rapidly with 4 hours a day of practice as with 7 hours of practice. The 7-hour subjects were effectively wasting the 3 extra hours of practice crammed into the day. Similar advantages of spaced practice are found for the learning of more cognitive skills. For instance, Gay (1973) has shown that spaced practice of algebra rules results in better retention than massed practice.

Part Versus Whole Learning

Students working to acquire a skill frequently ask whether it is better to try to learn and practice the whole skill or to learn and practice parts of the skill, putting them together later. In the area of motor skills, the answer to this question depends on whether the parts to be practiced are independent. If they are, it is better to practice the parts separately. For instance, Koch (1923) taught subjects a rather bizarre skill — to type finger exercises using two typewriters simultaneously, one hand per typewriter. There were two groups of subjects — those who practiced each hand first and those who tried immediately to use both hands. The group that started by practicing with separate hands was better when they switched to both hands than the group that started with both hands, and they maintained this superiority with further practice. In contrast, experiments on tasks that require careful integration show superiority for whole learning over part learning. For example, in playing the piano it is better to try to learn the whole sequence rather than to try to integrate subsections of a sequence.

Much of education seems designed to decompose a complex skill into independent subcomponents, and to teach each separately. Gagne (1973) has argued that many skills in education can be decomposed into subskills and these into subsubskills, and so on. The lower-level skills are prerequisites to the higher skills. For instance, calculus assumes algebra as a subcomponent, which assumes arithmetic as a subcomponent, which assumes basic counting skills as a subcomponent. Gagne argued that the key to successful educational plans was to identify the correct hierarchy of subskills. The educational curriculum should be designed to teach separately each of the subskills in the hierarchy.

Knowledge of Results

Subjects learn a skill more rapidly if they receive feedback as to whether their skill attempts are correct and how they are in error (for a classic review of research on feedback see Bilodeau, 1969). The amount of time between the action and the feedback is important — an expected relationship, since for feedback to be useful, the action must be active in memory. After a delay, it may be hard to recall just what led to incorrect result.

Recently, Lewis and Anderson (1985) looked at this relationship in learning to play a maze game on the order of Dungeons and Dragons. In one condition, players received immediate feedback after making a wrong move. In a second condition, the consequences of a wrong move became apparent only after the next move, when players found themselves in a bad situation. As predicted, subjects learned to play the game better in the condition of immediate feedback.

On the other hand, there are a number of situations where immediate feedback or too much feedback can be harmful. Schmidt, Young, Swinnen, and Shapiro (1989) had subjects practice simple motor skills such as moving a shaft in a precise time. They contrasted giving subjects feedback about how much they were off the target time after every trial of practice or in a summary after 15 trials. Subjects appeared to learn more in the summary condition as measured by a final retention test. Schmidt et al. argue that subjects can become too dependent on feedback. It is also the case that processing the feedback can interfere with learning the task. Just how much feedback to present and when is a rather subtle issue. Private human tutors appear to be quite tuned to needs of students. Bloom (1984) compared the effectiveness of students learning with private tutors versus in a standard classroom. He found that the average student with a private tutor was doing better than 98 percent of the students in the standard classroom. Unfortunately, private tutors are very expensive and it is not possible to provide every student with a full-time private tutor.

One of the promises of computer-assisted instruction is that it would be an economical means of providing students with feedback that is tuned to their learning needs. Of course, it also requires a great deal of intelligence to provide such feedback. Endowing computers with sufficient intelligence has been a major stumbling block. However, there have been some successes (Anderson, Boyle, Farrell, & Reiser, 1984; Sleeman & Brown, 1982). These successes have relied heavily on cognitive psychology and artificial-intelligence research. We will be describing some of this research in the last chapter of this book.

The Nature of Expertise

We have discussed so far in this chapter some of the phenomena associated with skill acquisition. An understanding of the mechanisms behind these phenomena has come from examining the nature of expertise in various fields of endeavors. In the last decade or so there has been a great deal of research looking at expertise in such domains as mathematics, chess, computer programming, and physics. This research compares people at various levels of development of their expertise. Sometimes this research is truly longitudinal and will follow students from their introduction to a field to their development of some expertise. More typically such research samples people at different levels of expertise. For instance, research on medical expertise might look at students just beginning medical school, residents, and doctors with many years of medical practice. This research has begun to identify some of the ways that problem solving becomes more effective with experience. Below we will review some of these dimensions of the development of expertise.

Proceduralization

There are dramatic changes in the degree to which subjects rely on declarative versus procedural knowledge. This is illustrated in my own work on the development of expertise in geometry (Anderson, 1982). One student had just learned two postulates for proving triangles congruent—the side-side-side (SSS) postulate and the side-angle-side (SAS) postulate. The side-side-side postulate states that if three sides of one triangle are congruent to the corresponding sides of another triangle, the triangles are congruent. The side-angle-side postulate states that if two sides and the included angle of one triangle are congruent to the corresponding parts of another triangle, the triangles are congruent. Figure 9-5 illustrates the first problem the student had to solve. The first thing he did in trying to solve this problem was to decide which postulate to use. The following is a portion of his thinking-aloud protocol, during which he decided on the appropriate postulate:

"If you looked at the side-angle-side postulate (long pause) well *RK* and *RJ* could almost be (long pause) what the missing (long pause) the missing side. I think somehow the side-angle-side postulate works its way into here (long pause). Let's see what it says: 'Two sides and the included angle.' What would I have to have to have two sides. *JS* and *KS* are one of them. Then you could go back to *RS = RS*. So that would bring up the side-angle-side postulate (long pause). But where would Angle I and Angle 2 are right angles fit in (long pause) wait I see how they work (long pause). *JS* is congruent

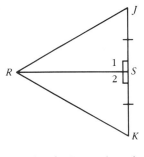

Given: ∠1 and ∠2 are right angles
$\overline{JS} \cong \overline{KS}$
Prove: $\triangle RSJ \cong \triangle RSK$

Figure 9-5. The first geometry proof problem encountered by a student after studying the side-side-side and side-angle-side postulates.

to *KS* (long pause) and with Angle 1 and Angle 2 are right angles that's a little problem (long pause). OK, what does it say—check it one more time: 'If two sides and the included angle of one triangle are congruent to the corresponding parts.' So I have got to find the two sides and the included angle. With the included angle you get Angle 1 and Angle 2. I suppose (long pause) they are both right angles, which means they are congruent to each other. My first side is *JS* is to *KS*. And the next time one is *RS* to *RS*. So these are the two sides. Yes, I think it is the side-angle-side postulate." (Anderson, 1982, pp. 381–382)

After reaching this point the student still went through a long process of actually writing out the proof, but this is the relevant portion in terms of assessing what goes into recognizing the relevance of the SAS postulate.

After a series of four more problems (two were solved by SAS and two by SSS), we came to the student's application of the SAS postulate for the problem illustrated in Figure 9-6. The method-recognition portion of the protocol follows:

"Right off the top of my head I am going to take a guess at what I am supposed to do: Angle *DCK* is congruent to Angle *ABK*. There is only one of two and the side-angle-side postulate is what they are getting to." (Anderson, 1982, p. 382)

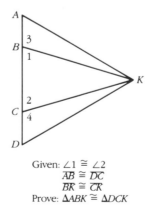

Given: ∠1 ≅ ∠2
$\overline{AB} \cong \overline{DC}$
$\overline{BK} \cong \overline{CK}$
Prove: △*ABK* ≅ △*DCK*

Figure 9-6. The sixth geometry proof problem encountered by a student after studying the side-side-side and side-angle-side postulates.

A number of things seem striking about the contrast between these two protocols. One is that there has been a clear speedup in the application of the postulate. A second is that there is no verbal rehearsal of the statement of the postulate in the second case. The student is no longer calling a declarative representation of the postulate into working memory. Note also in the first protocol that there are a number of failures of working memory—points where the student had to recover information that he had forgotten. The third feature of difference is that in the first protocol there is a piecemeal application of the postulate by which the student is separately identifying every element of the postulate. This is absent in the second protocol. It appears that the postulate is being matched in a single step.

These transitions are like the ones that Fitts and Posner characterized as belonging to the associative stage of skill acquisition. The student is no longer relying on a verbal recall of the postulate, but has advanced to the point where he can simply recognize the application of the postulate as a pattern. We can represent this ability by the following production rule:

> IF   the goal is to prove triangle 1 is congruent to triangle 2
> and triangle 1 has two sides and an included angle that
> appear congruent to two sides and an included angle of
> triangle 2
>
> THEN   set as subgoals to prove the corresponding sides and angles
> congruent
> and then to use the side-angle-side postulate to prove
> triangle 1 congruent to triangle 2

Thus, the student has converted the verbal or declarative knowledge of the postulate into a procedural knowledge as embodied in the production rule above.

A similar result is reported by Sweller, Mawer, and Ward (1983). They studied the development of expertise in solving simple kinematics problems and looked at how often subjects wrote down basic formulas involving velocity, distance, and acceleration such as $v = at$, where v is velocity, a is acceleration, and t is time. They found that initially subjects would write these formulas down to remind themselves of them but later on they would only write these equations with constants from the problem substituted for some of the variables—for example, $v = 2*10 = 20$. Thus, the formula was only implicit in their problem solving rather than being explicitly recalled.

Tactical Learning

As students practice problems they come to learn the sequences of moves required to solve the problem or portions of the problem. This is referred to as *tactical learning* in that a tactic refers to a method that accomplishes a particular goal. For instance, Greeno (1974) found that it took only about four repetitions of the hobbits and orcs problem (see discussion surrounding Figure 8-4 from the previous chapter) before subjects could solve the problem perfectly. Subjects were learning in this experiment the sequence of moves to get the creatures across the river. Once learned they could simply recall the sequence without further search.

In more complex domains problems do not repeat but components of problems do repeat and students remember the solutions to these components. For instance, consider the problem in Figure 9-7. As students gather expertise in geometry problem solving they learn to recognize that they should infer that the triangles *ACM* and *BDM* are congruent because they have two paris of congruent sides and the included angles are in a vertical angle (or opposite angle) configuration. This is a repeating sub-pattern that appears in multiple geometry problems. In effect they have learned the following production rule:

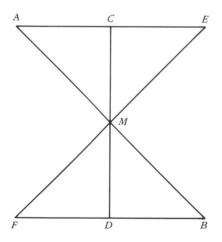

Given: *M* is the midpoint of $\overline{AB}$ and $\overline{CD}$
Prove: *M* is the midpoint of $\overline{EF}$

Figure 9-7. An advanced problem for high school geometry students.

IF   there are two triangles
     and they have two pairs of congruent sides
     and these sides combine to form a vertical-angle
     configuration

THEN   conclude the angles are congruent because of vertical
       angles and conclude the triangles are congruent because of
       the side-angle-side postulate

This rule will put in place one inference along the path to developing the full proof for this problem.

Strategic Learning

The discussion above was concerned with how students learn tactics that are sequences of moves to solve subproblems. There are also changes at the strategic level, which is concerned with how students organize their solution to the overall problem. Learning how to organize one's problem solving is referred to as *strategic learning*. The clearest demonstrations of such strategic changes have been in the domain of physics problem solving. Larkin (1981) compared novice and expert solutions on problems like the one in Figure 9-8. A block is sliding down an inclined plane of length l where θ is the angle between the plane and the horizontal. The coefficient of friction is μ. The subject's task is to find the velocity of the block when it reaches the bottom of the plane. Table 9-1 gives a typical novice solution to the problem and Table 9-2 gives a typical expert solution.

The novice solution typifies the method of *working backward*. It starts with the unknown, which is the velocity v. Then the novice finds an

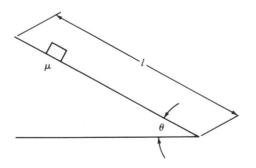

Figure 9-8. A sketch of a sample physics problem. (From Larkin, 1981.)

Table 9-1 *Typical Novice Solution to a Physics Problem*

To find the desired final speed v requires a principal with v in it, say

$v = v_0 + 2at$.

But both a and t are unknown, so that seems hopeless. Try instead

$v^2 - v_0^2 = 2ax$.

In that equation v_0 is zero and x is known, so it remains to find a. Therefore try

$F = ma$.

In that equation m is given, and only F is unknown, therefore use

$F = \Sigma\ F\text{'s}$.

which in this case means

$F = F_g'' - f$

where F_g'' and f can be found from

$F_g'' = mg \sin \Theta$,
$f = \mu N$.
$N = mg \cos \Theta$.

With a variety of substitutions, a correct expression for speed,

$v = \sqrt{2(g \sin \Theta - \mu g \cos \Theta)l}$,

can be found.

Adapted from Larkin, 1981.

equation to calculate v. However, to calculate v by this equation it is necessary to calculate a, the acceleration. So an equation is found involving a; and so the novice chains backward until a set of equations is found that enable solution of the problem.

The expert, on the other hand, uses similar equations but in the completely opposite order. The expert starts with quantities that can be directly computed, such as gravitational force, and works toward the desired velocity.

Larkin has shown that on such problems, experts and novices typically apply physics principles in just the opposite order. She developed a computer model that is able to simulate the development from a novice to expert with practice. This was done within a production-system framework. Novices start out with productions for working backward and slowly develop productions that make forward inferences.

Table 9-2 *Skilled Solution to a Physics Problem*

The motion of the block is accounted for by the gravitational force,

$$F_g'' = mg \sin \Theta$$

directed downward along the plane, and the frictional force,

$$f = \mu mg \cos \Theta$$

directed upward along the plane. The block's acceleration a is then related to the (signed) sum of these forces by

$$F = ma$$

or

$$mg \sin \Theta - \mu mg \cos \Theta = ma.$$

Knowing the acceleration a, it is then possible to find the block's final speed v from the relations

$$l = \tfrac{1}{2}at^2$$

and

$$v = at$$

Adapted from Larkin, 1981.

Novice students are simulated by means–ends productions such as:

IF   the goal is to calculate quantity x
and there is a physics principle that involves x
THEN   try to use that principle to calculate x

So, given the goal of calculating the acceleration, a, this production might invoke the use of the equation $v = v_0 + at$ (velocity equals initial velocity plus acceleration times time). With experience, however, her system developed productions that modeled expert students:

IF   the quantities v, v_0, and t are known
THEN   assert that the acceleration a is also known

A similar shift from backward reasoning to forward reasoning also occurs in geometry. There are real advantages to be had by forward reasoning in domains such as geometry and physics. Reasoning backward involves setting goals and subgoals and keeping track of them. For instance, the student must remember that he or she is calculating F so a can be calculated so *v* can be calculated. This puts a severe strain on working memory and can lead to errors. Reasoning forward eliminates the need to keep track of subgoals. However, to successfully reason forward one must know which of the many possible forward inferences are relevant to the final solution. This is what the expert learns with experience. The expert learns to associate various inferences with various patterns of features in the problem.

It is not the case that all domains see this shift from backward to forward problem solving. A good counterexample is computer programming (Anderson, Farrell, & Sauers, 1984; Jeffries, Turner, Polson, & Atwood, 1981). Both novice and expert programmers develop programs in what is called a *top-down* manner. That is, they work from the statement of the problem to subproblems to sub-subproblems, and so on, until they solve the problem. For instance. Figure 9-9 illustrates part of the development of a plan for a program to calculate the difference in mean

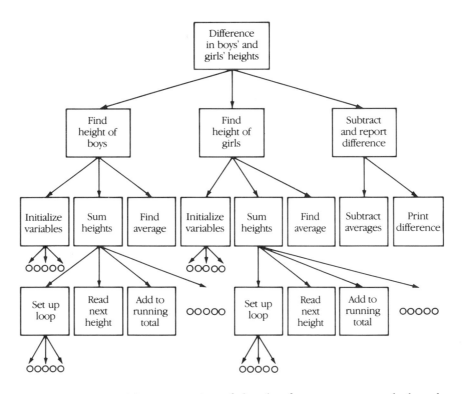

Figure 9-9. A partial representation of the plan for a program to calculate the difference in mean height between boys and girls in a classroom.

height between boys and girls in a classroom. First, the problem is developed into the subproblems of (1) calculating the mean height of the boys; (2) calculating the mean height of the girls; (3) subtracting the two. The problem of calculating the mean height of the boys is divided into the goals of adding up the heights and dividing by the number of boys. And so the program development continues until we get down to statements in the language such as:

$$AVERAGE = TOTAL/NUMBER$$

This top-down development is basically the same thing as what is called *working backward* in the context of geometry or physics. It is noteworthy that there is not a change to working forward as programmers become more expert. This is in sharp contrast to geometry and physics, where experts do change to working forward. This contrast can be understood by considering the differences in the problem domains. Physics and geometry problems have a rich set of givens that are more predictive of solutions than is the goal. In contrast, there is nothing in the typical statement of a programming problem that corresponds to the givens which would guide a working forward or bottom-up solution. The typical problem statement only describes the goal and often does so with information that will guide a top-down solution. Thus, we see that development of expertise does not follow the same course in all domains. Rather, experts adapt themselves to the characteristics of a particular domain.

Another difference has been noted between expert and novice development of computer programs (Anderson, 1983; Jeffries, Turner, Polson, & Atwood, 1981). Experts tend to develop problem solutions breadth first, whereas novices develop their solutions depth first. The differences are not striking with a simple problem like Figure 9-9, but can become quite dramatic with more complex programs that have more complex plans. The expert tends to expand a full level of the plan tree before going down to expand the next level, whereas the novice will expand the first problem down to its lowest levels. Thus, an expert will have decided on a basic plan of calculating both the boys' and the girls' heights in the figure before working out all the details of calculating the boys' heights, whereas the novice will completely work out the plan for the boys' heights before considering the plan for the girls' heights. The expert's approach is called breadth first because a whole layer of tree is created at a time. The novice's approach is called depth first because of the tendency to first complete the leftmost branch of the tree right to the bottom. There are good reasons for the expert's approach. Programming problems are typically nonindependent (see the discussion on p 238). Therefore, the solution of a later problem can often impact on the solution of an earlier problem. For instance, you might want to write a program to calculate the boys' heights in such a way that the same program could be used to calculate the girls' heights. Experts, because of breadth-first expansion, are likely to see these dependencies among subproblems.

In summary, it is not the case that the transition from novices to experts involves the same changes in strategy in all domains. Different problem domains have different structures that make different strategies optimal. What we see in the development of expertise in a domain is the discovery of those strategies which are optimal for that domain. Physics experts learn to reason forward while programming experts learn breadth-first expansion.

Problem Representation

Another dimension of expertise is that problem solvers learn to represent problems in ways that enable more effective problem-solving procedures to apply. This can be nicely demonstrated in the domain of physics. Physics, being an intellectually deep subject, has principles that are only implicit in the surface features of a physics problem. Experts learn to see these implicit principles and represent problems in terms of them.

Chi, Feltovich, and Glaser (1981) asked subjects to classify a large set of problems into similar categories. Figure 9-10 shows sets of problems that their novices thought were similar and the novices' explanations for the similarity groupings. As can be seen, the novices chose surface features, such as rotations or inclined planes, as their bases for classification. Being a physics novice myself, I have to admit these seem very intuitive bases for similarity. Contrast these classifications with pairs of problems that the expert subjects saw as similar in Figure 9-11. Problems that are completely different on the surface were seen as similar because they both involved conservation of energy or they both used Newton's second law. Thus, experts have the ability to map surface features of a problem onto these deeper principles. This is very useful because the deeper principles are more predictive of the method of solution. This shift in classification from reliance on surface features to deeper features has been found in a number of domains, including mathematics (Silver, 1979; Schoenfeld & Herrmann, 1982), computer programming (Weiser & Shertz, 1983), and medical diagnosis (Lesgold, Rubinson, Feltovich, Glaser, Klopfer, & Wang, 1988).

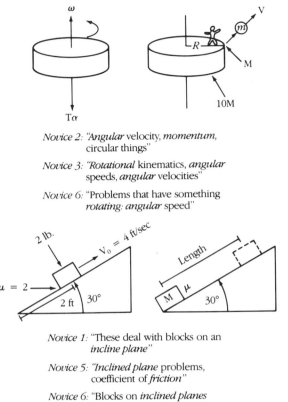

Novice 2: "*Angular* velocity, *momentum*,
circular things"

Novice 3: "*Rotational* kinematics, *angular*
speeds, *angular* velocities"

Novice 6: "Problems that have something
rotating: angular speed"

Novice 1: "These deal with blocks on an
incline plane"

Novice 5: "*Inclined plane* problems,
coefficient of *friction*"

Novice 6: "Blocks on *inclined planes*
with angles"

Figure 9-10. Diagrams depicting pairs of problems categorized by novices as similar and samples of their explanations for the similarity. (Adapted from Chi et al., 1981.)

An additional set of representational developments underlies the acquisition of expertise in computer programming. One aspect of acquiring programming expertise is the development of *language independence*. There are many programming languages that have different means of achieving the same final effect. For instance, most languages have multiple mechanisms for achieving *iteration*, which refers to the repetition of a sequence of instructions. Novices think of iteration in terms of the mechanisms of a particular language. Experts think of iteration in the abstract, independent of any particular language. This is much like the development observed in physics, where experts perceive problems in terms of abstract principles.

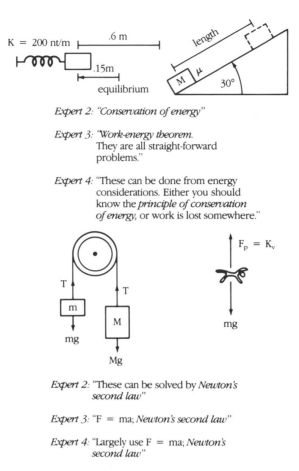

Expert 2: *"Conservation of energy"*

Expert 3: *"Work-energy theorem.*
They are all straight-forward
problems."

Expert 4: "These can be done from energy
considerations. Either you should
know the *principle of conservation
of energy,* or work is lost somewhere."

Expert 2: "These can be solved by *Newton's
second law*"

Expert 3: "F = ma; *Newton's second law*"

Expert 4: "Largely use F = ma; *Newton's
second law*"

Figure 9-11. Diagrams depicting pairs of problems categorized by experts as similar and samples of their explanations for the similarity. (Adapted from Chi et al., 1981.)

Another type of representational development is the appearance of a great deal of high-level vocabulary to describe a problem solution. Below I have reproduced an "expert" description of a computer program. Unless you are a good programmer, you should not feel that you should be able to understand it. However, note the high frequency of what might appear to be jargon. (I have italicized some of the more striking instances.) Actually, each of these instances of jargon is attached to an important programming construct and enables the programmer to more economically represent and think about the plan for the program:

BKT-DELETE is implemented as the *standard list deletion plan*. Inputs are a *key* and a *list of entries*. The plan is a *search loop* using two *pointers*: a pointer to the *current entry* which is *initialized* to the *input list*, and a *trailing pointer* which is initialized to *NIL*. On each *iteration*, it *tests the key* of the *first element* of the current list. If it is equal to the input key, it *splices the current element* out of the list by *RPLACD'ing* the *previous pointer*.

Thus, one important dimension of growing expertise is the development of a set of new constructs for representing the key aspects of a problem.

Problem Memory

One of the surprising discoveries about expertise is that experts seem to display a special enhanced memory for information about problems in their domain of expertise. This was first discovered in the research of de Groot (1965, 1966), who was attempting to determine what separated master chess players from weaker chess players. It turns out that chess masters are not particularly more intelligent in domains other than chess. de Groot found hardly any differences between expert players and weaker players — except, of course, that the expert players chose much better moves. For instance, chess masters consider about the same number of possible moves before selecting their move. In fact, if anything, masters consider fewer moves than chess duffers.

However, de Groot did find one intriguing difference between masters and weaker players. He presented chess masters with chess positions (i.e., chessboards with pieces in a configuration that occurred in a game) for just 5 seconds and then removed the chess positions. The chess masters were able to reconstruct the positions of more than 20 pieces after just 5 seconds of study. In contrast, the chess duffers could reconstruct only 4 or 5 pieces — an amount much more in line with the traditional capacity of working memory (see Chapter 6). It appears that chess masters build up patterns of 4 or 5 pieces that reflect common board configurations as a function of their massive amount of experience with the task. Thus, they remember not individual pieces but these patterns. In line with this analysis, if the players are presented with random chessboard positions rather than ones that are actually encountered in games, no difference is demonstrated between masters and duffers. Both types of subjects can reconstruct only a few chess positions. The masters also complain about being very uncomfortable and disturbed by such chaotic board positions.

This basic phenomenon of superior expert memory for meaningful problems has now been demonstrated in a large number of domains, including the game of Go (Reitman, 1976), electronic circuit diagrams (Egan & Schwartz, 1979), bridge hands (Engle & Bukstel, 1978; Charness, 1979), and computer programming (McKeithen, Reitman, Rueter, & Hirtle, 1981; Schneiderman, 1976). One might think that the memory advantage shown by experts is just a working memory advantage, but research has shown that their advantage extends to long-term memory. Charness (1976) compared experts' memory for chess positions immediately after they had viewed the positions or after a 30-second delay filled with an interfering task (like the Peterson and Peterson task discussed in Chapter 6). Class A chess players show no loss in recall over the 30-second interval, unlike other subjects, who show a great deal of forgetting. Thus, expert chess players, unlike duffers, have an increased capacity to store information about the domain. Interestingly, these subjects show the same poor memory for three-letter trigrams as ordinary subjects. Thus, their increased long-term memory is *only* for the domain expertise.

Chase and Simon (1973) examined the nature of the *patterns* or *chunks* used by masters. They used a chessboard-reproduction task, as illustrated in Figure 9-12. The subjects' task was simply to reproduce the positions of pieces of a target chessboard on a test chessboard. In this task, subjects glanced at the target board, placed some pieces on the test board, glanced back to the target board, placed some more pieces on the test board, and so on. Chase and Simon defined as a chunk those pieces that subjects moved following one glance. They found that these chunks tended to

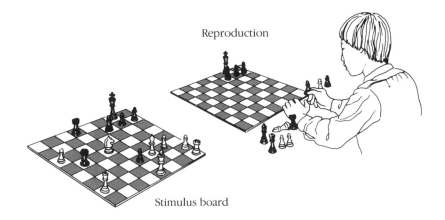

Reproduction

Stimulus board

Figure 9-12. The reproduction task in Chase and Simon (1973). Subjects were to reproduce the configuration of pieces on the reproduction board. (Adapted from Klatzky, 1979.)

define meaningful game relations among the pieces. For instance, more than half of the masters' chunks were pawn chains (configurations of pawns that occur frequently in chess).

Simon and Gilmartin (1973) estimate that masters have acquired on the order of 50,000 different chess patterns, that they can quickly recognize such patterns on a chessboard, and that this ability is what underlies their superior memory performance in chess. This 50,000 figure is not unreasonable when one considers the years of devoted study that becoming a chess master takes.

What might be the relationship between memory for so many chess patterns and superior performance in chess? Newell and Simon (1972) speculated that, in addition to learning many patterns, masters have also learned what to do in the presence of such patterns. Basically, they must have something on the order of 50,000 productions in which the condition (the IF part) of a production is a chess pattern and its action (the THEN part) is the appropriate response to that pattern. For instance, if the chunk pattern is symptomatic of a weak side, the response of the production might be to suggest an attack on the weak side. Thus, masters effectively "see" possibilities for moves; they do not have to think them out. This explains why chess masters do so well at lightning chess, in which they have only a few seconds to move.

So, to summarize, chess experts have stored the solutions to many problems that duffers must solve as novel problems. Duffers have to analyze different configurations, try to figure out their consequences, and act accordingly. Masters have all this information stored in memory, thereby claiming two advantages. First, they do not risk making errors in solving these problems, since they have stored the correct solution. Second, because they have stored the correct analysis of so many positions, they can focus their problem-solving efforts on more sophisticated aspects and strategies of chess.

Chess players become masters only after years of playing. They have to be able to store a great deal of information about chess to be experts. Native intelligence is no substitute for knowledge (there is more on this topic in Chapter 14).

It had been thought that better expert memory rested solely on possession of more and larger patterns with which to encode the problem. The advantage of the expert in chess was like the advantage of someone who knows English in remembering a sentence—in the latter case one can remember words and phrases and not individual letters. However, there is increasing reason to believe that the memory advantage goes beyond experts' ability to encode the problem in terms of familiar patterns.

Experts appear to be able to remember more patterns as well as larger patterns. Some of the evidence for this was in an experiment by Chase and Simon where they had subjects recall chess boards as did de Groot (in contrast to the reproduction task illustrated in Figure 9-12). They tried to identify the patterns that their subjects used to recall the chess boards. They found that subjects would tend to recall a pattern, pause, recall another pattern, pause, etc. They found that they could use a two-second pause to identify boundaries between patterns. With this objective definition of what a pattern is, they could then explore how many patterns were recalled. In comparing a master chess player with a beginner they found large differences in both measures. The pattern size of the master averaged 3.8 pieces while it was only 2.4 for the beginner. However, the master also recalled an average of 7.7 patterns per board while the beginner recalled only an average of 5.3. Thus, it seems that the experts memory advantage is based not only on larger patterns but also on the ability to recall more of them.

The strongest evidence that expertise involves the ability to remember more patterns as well as larger patterns comes Chase and Ericsson (1982), who studied the development of a simple but remarkable skill. They watched a subject, SF, increase his digit span, which is the number of digits that he could repeat back after one presentation. As discussed in Chapter 6, the normal digit span is about 7 or 8 items, just enough to accommodate a telephone number. After about 200 hours of practice, on Saturday, December 15, 1979, SF was presented with 81 random digits at the rate of 1 digit per second. He proceeded to reel off the 81 digits perfectly. Figure 9-13 illustrates how his memory span grew over 264 training trials.

What was behind this feat of superhuman memory? In part, SF was learning to chunk the digits into meaningful patterns. He was a long-distance runner, and part of his technique was to convert digits into running times. So, he would take four digits, like 3492, and convert them into "Three minutes, 49.2 seconds – near world-record mile time." Using such a strategy he could convert a memory span for 7 digits into a memory span for 7 digit patterns of length 3 or 4. This would get him to a digit span in the 20s, far short of his eventual performance. Gradually, he developed what Chase and Ericsson called a *retrieval structure*, which enabled him to recall 22 such patterns. This retrieval structure was very specific; it would not generalize to retrieving letters rather than digits. Chase and Ericsson hypothesize that part of what underlies development of expertise in other domains such as chess is development of retrieval structures, which allows superior recall for past patterns.

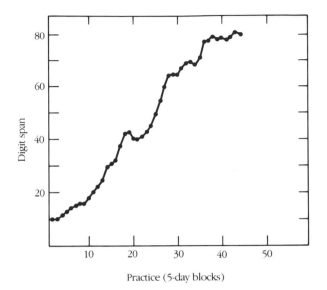

Figure 9-13. The growth in the memory span of the subject SF with practice. Notice how the number of digits he can recall increases gradually but continually with the number of practice sessions. (From Chase & Ericsson, 1982.)

Transfer of Skill

As noted, Chase and Ericsson's subject SF was unable to transfer memory span skill from digits to letters. This is an almost ridiculous extreme of what is becoming a depressing pattern in the development of cognitive skills. This is that these skills can be quite narrow and fail to transfer to other activities. Chess experts do not appear to be better thinkers for all their genius in chess. An amusing example of the narrowness of expertise is the study of Carraher, Carraher, and Schliemann (1985). They investigated the mathematical strategies used by Brazilian school children who also worked as street vendors. On the job, these children used quite sophisticated strategies for calculating the total cost of orders involving different numbers of different objects (e.g., the total cost of four coconuts and twelve lemons), and what's more, they could perform such calculations reliably in their heads. Carraher et al. actually went to the trouble of going to the streets and posing as customers for these children, making certain kinds of purchases and recording the percentage of correct calculations. The experimenters then asked the children to come with them to the laboratory, where they were given written mathematics tests that involved the same numbers and mathematical operations that had been manipulated successfully in the streets. For example, if a child had correctly calculated the total cost of five lemons at 35 cruzeiros a piece on the street, the child was given the following written problem:

$$5 \times 35 = ?$$

The results showed that, whereas children solved 98 percent of the problems presented in the situated context, they solved only 37 percent of the problems presented in the laboratory context. It needs to be stressed that these problems involved the exact same numbers and mathematical operations. Interestingly, if the problems were stated in the form of word problems in the laboratory, performance improved to 74 percent. This runs counter to the usual finding, which is that word problems are more difficult than equivalent "number" problems (Carpenter & Moser, 1982). Apparently, the additional context provided by the word problem allowed the children to make contact with their pragmatic strategies.

While the study of Carraher et al. showed a curious failure of expertise in real life to transfer to the classroom, the typical concern of educators is whether what is taught in one class will transfer to other classes and the real world. At the turn of the century educators were fairly optimistic on this issue. A number of educational psychologists subscribed to what has been called the Doctrine of Formal Discipline (Angell, 1908; Pillsbury, 1908; Woodrow, 1927), which held that studying such esoteric subjects as Latin and geometry was of significant value because it served to discipline the mind. Formal Discipline subscribed to the faculty view of mind, which extends back to Aristotle and was first formalized by Thomas Reid in the late eighteenth century (Boring, 1950). The faculty position held that the mind was composed of a collection of general faculties, such as observation, attention, discrimination, and reasoning, which were exercised in much the same way as a set of muscles. The content of the exercise made little difference; most important was the level of exertion (hence the fondness for Latin and geometry). Transfer in such a view is broad and takes place at a general level, sometimes spanning domains that share no content. For example, training in chess should transfer to computer programming since both skills involve the use of the general reasoning faculty.

At the beginning of this century Thorndike undertook a research program extending some 30 years to show that transfer was much narrower in scope than would be predicted by the Doctrine of Formal Discipline. According to Thorndike, the mind was not composed of general faculties but rather of specific habits and associations, which provided a person with a variety of narrow responses to very specific stimuli. In fact, the mind was regarded as just a convenient name for countless special operations or functions (Stratton, 1922). Thorndike's theory of transfer was the Theory of Identical Elements, which stated that training in one kind of activity would transfer to another only if the activities shared common situation-response elements:

> One mental function or activity improves others in so far as and because they are in part identical with it, because it contains elements common to them. Addition improves multiplication because multiplication is largely addition; knowledge of Latin gives increased ability to learn French because many of the facts learned in the one case are needed in the other. (Thorndike, 1906, p. 243)

Thus, Thorndike was happy to accept transfer between diverse skills as long as it could be shown that the transfer was mediated by identical elements. Generally, however, he concluded that:

> the mind is so specialized into a multitude of independent capacities that we alter human nature only in small spots, and any special school training has a much narrower influence upon the mind as a whole than has commonly been supposed. (p. 246)

In his first series of experiments (Thorndike & Woodworth, 1901), Thorndike subjected the strong version of the Doctrine of Formal Discipline to an empirical test. The strong version, as presented above, claims that transfer ranges across diverse tasks when those tasks involve the same general faculty. In one study, no correlation was found between memory for words and memory for numbers. In another, accuracy in spelling was not correlated with accuracy in arithmetic. Thorndike interpreted these results as evidence against the general faculties of memory and accuracy.

Thorndike formulated his Theory of Identical Elements in what proved to be an overly narrow manner. For instance, he argued that if you solved a geometry problem which involved one set of letters for points you would not be able to transfer to a geometry problem with a different set of letters. The research that we examined on analogy in the previous chapter indicated that this is not true. Transfer is not tied to identity of surface elements. There is in some cases very large positive transfer between two skills that have the same logical structure even if they have different surface elements (see Singley & Anderson, 1989, for a review). Thus, for instance, there is large positive transfer between different word processing systems, between different programming languages, and between using calculus to solve economic problems and using calculus to solve problems in solid geometry. However, all the available evidence is that there are very definite bounds on how far skills will transfer and that becoming an expert in one domain will have little positive benefit in becoming an expert in a very different area. There will be positive transfer only to the extent that the two domains involve use of the same facts, productions, and patterns — i.e., the same knowledge.

There is a positive side to this specificity in transfer of skill. This is that there seldom seems to be negative transfer, in which learning one skill makes a person worse at learning another skill. Interference, such as occurs in memory for facts (see Chapter 7), is almost nonexistent in skill acquisition. Polson, Muncher, & Kieras (in press) provide a good demonstration of lack of negative transfer in the domain of text editing. They had subjects learn one text editor and then learn a second, which was designed to be maximally confusing. Whereas the command to go down a line of text might be *n* and the command to delete a character might be *k* in one text editor, *n* would mean to delete a character in another text editor and *k* would mean to go down a line. However, subjects experienced overwhelming positive transfer in going from one text editor to the other because the two text editors worked in the same way, even though the surface commands had been scrambled.

There is only one clearly documented kind of negative transfer in the case of cognitive skills. This is like the Einstellung effect discussed in the previous chapter. Students can learn a way of solving a problem in one skill, which is no longer optimal for performing another skill. So, for instance, someone may learn tricks in algebra to avoid having to perform difficult arithmetic computations. These tricks may no longer be necessary when one goes to an environment where there are calculators to perform these calculations. Still students show a tendency to continue to perform these unnecessary simplifications in their algebraic manipulations. This is really not a case of failure to transfer. This is a case of transferring knowledge that is no longer useful.

Remarks and Suggested Readings

The work on the development of expertise in cognitive skills is a relatively recent phenomenon. The papers by Chase and Simon (1973) and Larkin, McDermott, Simon, and Simon (1980) are already considered classics. Lesgold (1984) reviews many of the concepts. The books edited by Anderson (1981) and Chi, Glazer, and Farr (1988) contain numerous recent papers on the topic. An issue of the 1985 *Canadian Journal of*

Psychology, edited by Charness, is devoted to the topic. Card, Moran, and Newell (1983) describe interaction with computer systems, especially text editors. Schneiderman (1976) reviews many aspects of computer programming. Soloway, Bonar, and Ehrlich (1983) have done some excellent research on programming in Pascal.

This chapter has focused mainly on the development of cognitive skills. However, considerable research has been done on the development of motor skills. Reviews can be found in Fitts and Posner (1967), Kelso (1982), Schmidt (1982), and Stelmach and Requin (1980). Rosenbloom and Newell (1983) have done a production-system analysis of practice and transfer in the domain of perceptual-motor skills. Singley and Anderson (1989) provide a review of research of transfer and a modern version of Thorndike's Theory of Identical Elements cast in terms of production systems.

Reasoning

Summary

1. Research on deductive reasoning has frequently compared human reasoning with the prescriptions of a logical system. A logical system consists of rules of inference that permit true conclusions to be derived from true premises.

2. Conditional reasoning is deduction involving statements of the form *If A then B*, where *A* and *B* are propositions. People make errors in conditional-reasoning tasks because they misinterpret the meaning of the connective *if*, and because they do not use the rule of inference known as *modus tollens*. Modus tollens allows a person to reason from the premises *If A then B* and *B is false* to the conclusion *A is false*.

3. *Categorical syllogisms* are reasoning problems involving the quantifiers *all, some, no,* and *some not*. People make many errors when dealing with categorical syllogisms, particularly errors that involve the acceptance of invalid conclusions. This pattern of errors is partially described by the *atmosphere hypothesis*, which asserts that people are inclined to accept conclusions similar to the premises.

4. For an argument to be inductively valid, the conclusion must be probable if the premises are true. This criterion contrasts with that for a deductively valid argument, in which the conclusion must be certain if the premises are true.

5. The components of the inductive-reasoning process are hypothesis formation and hypothesis evaluation.

6. Concept formation studies how people form hypotheses about the definition of a concept when given instances of the concept. A major limitation on human concept formation involves keeping track of all the relevant information and using that information correctly.

7. *Bayes's theorem* prescribes a way for evaluating a hypothesis. It updates the probability of a hypothesis in light of new evidence. In the terminology of Bayes's theorem, the original probability of a hypothesis is referred to as the *prior probability,* the updated probability as the *posterior probability,* and the probability of the evidence given the hypotheses as the *conditional probability.*

8. In evaluating hypotheses, human beings deviate from the norm prescribed by Bayes's theorem in that they do not adjust the posterior probabilities as radically as they should and they tend to ignore information about prior probabilities.

9. When people cannot directly observe the probability of a particular type of event, they try to estimate its probability by means of various *heuristics.* These heuristics are biased and can lead to serious distortions in probability estimates. It is the use of such heuristics that accounts for the deviations from the prescription of Bayes's theorem.

Logic and Reasoning

Reasoning refers to the processes by which people evaluate and generate logical arguments. *Logic* is a subdiscipline of philosophy and mathematics that tries to formally specify what it means for an argument to be logically correct. To understand the psychological research on reasoning, we have to understand the relationship of this research to logic. Until the twentieth century, logic and the psychology of thought were often considered one and the same. The famous Irish mathematician George Boole (1854) called his book on logical calculus *An Investigation of the Laws of Thought,* and designed it "in the first place, to investigate the fundamental laws of those operations of the mind by which reasoning is performed." Of course, humans did not always operate according to the prescriptions of logic, but such lapses were seen as the malfunctioning of mental machinery that was logical when it worked properly. In trying to improve the mind, people tried to train themselves to be logical. A hundred years ago, a section on "cognitive processes" in a psychology text would have been about "logical thinking." The fact that only one chapter in this book is on reasoning reflects the current understanding that a large portion of human thought is not logical reasoning in any useful sense.

Deductive Reasoning

Much of the research on deductive reasoning has been explicitly designed to compare human performance with the prescriptions of logic. In such experiments, the reasoning problems presented to subjects are analyzed in the terms used in logic. Therefore, it is essential to have some familiarity with the nature of systems of logic and the terminology of logic.

We will first consider research on deductive logic and deductive reasoning. In a deductive system, it is possible to reason with certainty from the premises of an argument to the conclusion. This is to be contrasted with inductive reasoning, where we go from the premises to the conclusions with a certain probability. We will discuss inductive reasoning later in the chapter.

In a logical system, *rules of inference* prescribe when it is possible to infer a conclusion from a set of premises. A particularly useful rule of inference is *modus ponens.* It states that given the proposition *A implies B* and given *A,* we can infer *B.* The statement *A implies B* is often rendered *If A then B.* So, suppose we are told the following:

1.   If it rains tomorrow, then the game will be canceled.

2.   If the game is canceled, then our team will surely lose the pennant.

3.   It will rain tomorrow.

From 1 and 3 we can infer 4 by modus ponens:

    4.   The game will be canceled.

From 2 and 4 we can infer 5:

    5.   Our team will surely lose the pennant.

This example is an instance of valid deduction. By *valid* we mean that if premises 1 through 3 are true, the conclusion 5 must be true. Of course, the premises might not be true, in which case the conclusion need not be true. Logic and deductive reasoning are not concerned with examining the truth of the premises in a logical argument. Rather, the concern is with whether the premises logically imply the conclusions.

    Another rule of inference is *modus tollens*. This rule states that if we are given the proposition *A implies B* and the fact that *B* is false, then we can infer that *A* is false. The following is an inference exercise that requires the use of modus tollens. Suppose we are given the following premises:

    6.   If it snows tomorrow, then we will go skiing.

    7.   If we go skiing, then we will be happy.

    8.   We are not going to be happy.

Then it follows from 7 and 8 by modus tollens that

    9.   We will not be going skiing.

And it follows from 6 and 9 by modus tollens that

    10.   It is not going to snow tomorrow.

    Most people find the operation of modus tollens much less intuitive than the operation of modus ponens.

Conditional Reasoning

Conditional reasoning refers to how people reason with implications or conditional statements; for example:

If the maid hid the gun, then the butler was not at the scene of the crime.

Such conditional statements are important in mathematics and science, and as this example suggests, they can be significant in the evaluation of evidence. Therefore, it is important to understand how people tend to reason about such statements and what errors they are prone to in their reasoning. A considerable amount of research has focused on reasoning with conditional syllogisms (e.g., Marcus & Rips, 1979; Rips & Marcus, 1977; Staudenmayer, 1975; Taplin, 1971; Taplin & Staudenmayer, 1973). Examples of conditional syllogisms (only one of which is valid) are:

1. If the ball rolls left, the green lamp comes on.
   The ball rolls left.
   Therefore, the green lamp comes on.

2. If God exists, life will be beautiful.
   God does not exist.
   Therefore, life is not beautiful.

Or, more abstractly, we may represent these syllogisms in the following way:

$$1.\ \frac{\begin{array}{l} P \supset Q \\ P \end{array}}{\therefore Q}$$

$$2.\ \frac{\begin{array}{l} P \supset Q \\ \sim P \end{array}}{\therefore \sim Q}$$

where the symbol $\supset$ stands for implication, and $\sim$ stands for negation. Conditional syllogisms involve such arguments as these, where one premise is an implication between two propositions, the second premise is one of these propositions or its negation, and the conclusion is the other proposition or its negation. Subjects are asked to determine whether these syllogisms are logically valid. In the above case, syllogism 1 is valid and 2 is not.

Consider a representative experiment by Rips and Marcus (1977) in which subjects from the University of Chicago were asked to evaluate eight types of syllogisms. Though the syllogisms are presented abstractly in Table 10-1, the subjects were actually tested with concrete propositions. An example would be:

Table 10-1 *Percentage of Total Responses for Eight Types of Conditional Syllogisms*

Syllogism	Always	Sometimes	Never
1. $P \supset Q$ P $\therefore Q$	100[a]	0	0
2. $P \supset Q$ P $\therefore \sim Q$	0	0	100[a]
3. $P \supset Q$ $\sim P$ $\therefore Q$	5	79[a]	16
4. $P \supset Q$ $\sim P$ $\therefore \sim Q$	21	77[a]	2
5. $P \supset Q$ Q $\therefore P$	23	77[a]	0
6. $P \supset Q$ Q $\therefore \sim P$	4	82[a]	14
7. $P \supset Q$ $\sim Q$ $\therefore P$	0	23	77[a]
8. $P \supset Q$ $\sim Q$ $\therefore \sim P$	57[a]	39	4

[a]The correct response.
Adapted from Rips and Marcus, 1977.

> If the ball rolls left, the green lamp comes on.
> The green lamp comes on.
> Therefore, the ball rolled left.

Subjects were asked to judge whether the conclusion was always true, sometimes true, or never true given the premises. The table gives the percentage of responses in each category for each type of syllogism.

Problems 1 and 2 in the table indicate that subjects could apply modus ponens quite successfully. However, they had much greater difficulty with the other form of the conditional syllogism permitting a valid conclusion. This is the form in problems 7 and 8, which required application of the rule of modus tollens. Here more than 30 percent of the subject population failed to realize that we can reason from the negation of the second term in a conditional to the negation of the first term. Syllogisms 3 and 4 display evidence for a fallacy in conditional reasoning known as *denial of the antecedent* (the first term in the conditional). Almost 20 percent of the subject population believed that we can conclude that Q is not true if we know that P *implies* Q and that P is not true. Problems 5 and 6 display a tendency for a fallacy known as *affirmation of the consequent* (the second term in the conditional). On these problems almost 20 percent of the subject population believed that we can conclude that P is true from knowing P *implies* Q and Q.

It seems that one source of the fallacies displayed in problems 3 through 6 is that subjects do not interpret conditionals in the same way that logicians do. This discrepancy has been demonstrated in a series of experiments by Taplin (1971), Taplin and Staudenmayer (1973), and Staudenmayer (1975). They showed that many subjects interpreted the conditional as being what logicians would call the *biconditional*. The biconditional is rendered in English unambiguously by the rather awkward construction *if and only if*. For instance:

Israel will use atomic weapons if and only if it is faced with annihilation.

With the biconditional, if either the first or second premise is true, the other will be true. Similarly, if either the first or second premise is false, the other will be false.

The Failure to Apply Modus Tollens

The hypothesis that subjects interpret the conditional as a biconditional explains why some subjects display the fallacies of affirming the consequent or denying the antecedent, but leaves unexplained the difficulty they have in applying modus tollens in problems 7 and 8 of Table 10-1. Modus tollens is a valid inference even if the conditional is interpreted as a biconditional. Table 10-1 actually is a rather mild case of failure to apply modus tollens. In other situations the failure can be much more grievous.

A very striking demonstration of failure to apply modus tollens comes from a series of experiments performed by Wason (for a review see Wason & Johnson-Laird, 1972, Chapters 13 and 14). In one of the principal experiments from this research, four cards showing the following symbols were placed in front of subjects:

Subjects were told that a letter appeared on one side of each card and a number on the other. The task was to judge the validity of the following rule, which referred only to these four cards:

> If a card has a vowel on one side, then it has an even number on the other side.

The subjects' task was to turn over only those cards that had to be turned over for the correctness of the rule to be judged. Forty-six percent of subjects elected to turn over both E and 4, which is a wrong combination of choices. The E had to be turned over, but the 4 did not have to be turned over, since neither a vowel nor a consonant on the other side would have falsified the rule. Only 4 percent elected to turn over E and 7, which are the correct choices. An odd number behind the E or a vowel behind the 7 would have falsified the rule. Another 33 percent of subjects incorrectly elected to turn over the E only. The remaining 17 percent made other incorrect choices.

So, subjects displayed two types of errors in the task. First, they often turned over the 4, another example of the fallacy of affirming the consequent. Again, this response might just have reflected an interpretation by subjects of the conditional as a biconditional. However, even more striking was the almost total failure to take the modus tollens step of disconfirming the consequent and determining whether the antecedent was also disconfirmed (in other words, turning over the 7).

The difficulty that students have with the Wason card task has been replicated numerous times. One of the interesting findings is that college-level training in logic has very little beneficial effect on performance in the task. In a study by Cheng, Holyoak, Nisbett, and Oliver (1986), college students who had just taken a semester course in logic did only 3 percent better on the card selection task than those who had no formal logic training. It was not that they did not know the rules of logic;

it was rather that they did not bring them to bear in this laboratory task outside the context of the classroom. This is another example of the depressing lack of transfer of training that we discussed in the previous chapter.

It turns out that subjects can do remarkably well on other problems that are formally equivalent to the Wason card task. Griggs and Cox (1982) presented students with the task of applying the following law, which was then in force in the state of Florida: "If a person is drinking beer, then the person must be over 19." Subjects were instructed to imagine that they were police officers responsible for ensuring that the regulation was followed. They were presented with four cards that represented people sitting around a table. On one side of each card was the age of the person and on the other side was the substance that the person was drinking. The cards were labeled "Drinking beer," "Drinking Coke," "16 years of age," and "22 years of age." The task was to select those people (cards to turn over) from whom further information was needed to determine whether the drinking law was being violated. In this situation 74 percent of subjects selected the right cards (namely, "Drinking beer" and "16 years of age").

Cheng and Holyoak (1985) argue that, while subjects do not know how to generalize their classroom logic training to the original Wason card task, they know how to reason about rules of permission such as the alcohol rule. An alternative hypothesis would be that what was at work was just the familiarity of the alcohol rule to Florida students and that they would not be able to reason about a similar unfamiliar law. To discriminate between these two possibilities, Cheng and Holyoak performed the following experiment. One group of subjects was asked to evaluate the following senseless rule against a set of instances: "If the form says 'entering' on one side, then the other side includes cholera among the list of diseases." Another group was given the same rule but also the rationale behind it, which made explicit contact with the idea of permission. The rationale was that, in order to satisfy immigration officials upon entering a particular country, one must have been vaccinated for cholera. The forms indicated on one side whether the passenger was entering the country or in transit, while the other side listed the names of diseases for which he or she was vaccinated. Subjects were presented with a set of forms that said "Transit," or "Entering," or "cholera, typhoid, hepatitis," or "typhoid, hepatitis." The performance of the group given the rationale was much better than that of the group given just the senseless rule—i.e., they knew to check the "Entering" form and the "typhoid, hepatitis" form.

Reasoning about Quantifiers

Much of human knowledge is cast with logical quantifiers such as *all* or *some*. Witness Lincoln's famous statement: "You may fool all the people some of the time; you can even fool some of the people all the time; but you can't fool all of the people all the time." Our scientific laws are cast with such quantifiers also. It is important to understand how people reason with such quantifiers.

The Categorical Syllogism

Modern logic is greatly concerned with analyzing the meaning of quantifiers such as *all* and *some*, as in, for example, the statement *All philosophers read some books*. At the turn of this century, the sophistication with which such quantified statements were analyzed increased considerably (see Church, 1956, for a historical discussion). This more advanced treatment of quantifiers is covered in most modern logic courses. However, most of the research on quantifiers in psychology has focused on a simpler and older kind of quantified deduction, called the *categorical syllogism*. Much of Aristotle's writing on reasoning concerned the categorical syllogism. Extensive discussion of categorical syllogisms can be found in older textbooks on logic such as Cohen and Nagel (1934).

Categorical syllogisms involve statements containing the quantifiers *some, all, no,* and *some not*. Examples of such categorical statements are:

1. All doctors are rich.
2. Some lawyers are dishonest.
3. No politician is trustworthy.
4. Some actors are not handsome.

In experiments, the categories (e.g., doctors, rich people, lawyers, dishonest people) in such statements are frequently represented by letters, say, *A*, *B*, *C*. This system serves as a handy shorthand for describing the material. In the traditional analysis of categorical statements, the foregoing sentences would be analyzed into *subject* and *predicate*, the first category (e.g., doctor) being the subject and the second category (rich people) the predicate. Thus, the statements might be rendered in this way:

1.' All *A*'s are *B*'s.
2.' Some *C*'s are *D*'s.

3.′ No *E*'s are *F*'s.
4.′ Some *G*'s are not *H*'s.

A categorical syllogism typically contains two premises and a conclusion. All three statements are of a categorical nature. The following is a simple example:

1. All *A*'s are *B*'s.
    All *B*'s are *C*'s.
    ∴All *A*'s are *C*'s

This syllogism, incidentally, is one that most people correctly recognize as valid. On the other hand, people accept with almost equal frequency the following invalid syllogism:

2. Some *A*'s are *B*'s.
    Some *B*'s are *C*'s.
    ∴ Some *A*'s are *C*'s.

(To see that this is invalid, consider replacing *A* with women, *B* with lawyers, and *C* with men.)

The Atmosphere Hypothesis

The general problem subjects seem to have with categorical syllogisms is that they are too willing to accept false conclusions. However, subjects are not completely indiscriminate in their acceptance of syllogisms. For instance, while they will accept example 2 above, they will not accept 3:

3. Some *A*'s are *B*'s.
    Some *B*'s are *C*'s.
    ∴ No *A*'s are *C*'s.

To account for this pattern of errors, Woodworth and Sells (1935) proposed the *atmosphere hypothesis*. This hypothesis states that the logical terms (*some, all, no, not*) used in the syllogism create an "atmosphere" that predisposes subjects to accept conclusions with the same terms. There are two parts to the atmosphere hypothesis. One part asserts that subjects would accept a positive conclusion to positive premises and a negative conclusion to negative premises. When the premises are mixed, subjects would prefer a negative conclusion. Thus, they would tend to accept the following syllogism:

> 4. No *A*'s are *B*'s.
>   All *B*'s are *C*'s.
>   ∴ No *A*'s are *C*'s.

(To see that this is invalid, consider replacing *A* with men, *B* with women, and *C* with humans.)

The other part of the atmosphere hypothesis concerns a subject's response to particular statements (*some,* or *some not*) versus universal statements (*all* or *no*). As example 4 above illustrates, subjects will accept a universal conclusion if the premises are universal. They will accept a particular conclusion if the premises are particular. This accounts for their acceptance of syllogism 2 given earlier. When one premise is particular and the other universal, subjects prefer a particular conclusion. So they will accept the following:

> 5. All *A*'s are *B*'s.
>   Some *B*'s are *C*'s.
>   ∴ Some *A*'s are *C*'s.

(To see that this is invalid, consider replacing *A* with men, *B* with humans, and *C* with women.)

Limitations of the Atmosphere Hypothesis

The atmosphere hypothesis has been quite successful in capturing many of the main trends in the data on syllogistic reasoning. However, it is becoming increasingly clear that this hypothesis does not describe what subjects are doing. For one thing, according to the atmosphere hypothesis, subjects would be just as likely to accept the atmosphere-favored conclusion when it was not valid as when it was valid. That is, it predicts that subjects would be just as likely to accept

> 6. All *A*'s are *B*'s.
>   Some *B*'s are *C*'s.
>   ∴ Some *A*'s are *C*'s.

which is not valid, as they would be to accept

> 7. Some *A*'s are *B*'s.
> All *B*'s are *C*'s.
> ∴ *Some A*'s are *C*'s.

which is valid. In fact, subjects are more likely to accept the conclusion in the valid case. Thus, subjects do display some ability to evaluate a syllogism accurately.

An even more serious limitation of the atmosphere hypothesis is that it fails to predict the effects that the form of a syllogism has on subjects' validity judgments. For instance, the hypothesis predicts that subjects would be no more likely to erroneously accept

> 8. Some *A*'s are *B*'s.
> Some *B*'s are *C*'s.
> ∴ *Some A*'s are *C*'s.

than they would be to erroneously accept

> 9. Some *B*'s are *A*'s.
> Some *C*'s are *B*'s.
> ∴ *Some A*'s are *C*'s.

In fact, it has been established (Johnson-Laird and Steedman, 1978) that subjects are more willing to erroneously accept the conclusion in the former case. In general, subjects are more willing to accept a conclusion from *A* to *C* (i.e., one that involves *A* as subject and *C* as predicate) if they can find a chain leading from *A* to *B* in one premise and from *B* to *C* in the second premise. Other effects of the form of the argument rather than the quantifiers have been shown by Dickstein (1978).

Thus, although the atmosphere hypothesis clearly describes many qualitative features of the data on syllogism evaluation, it cannot be describing all that subjects are doing. One explanation of subjects' reasoning behavior, developed by Johnson-Laird and Steedman (1978), is that the subject actually creates a little world that satisfies the premises. (A similar idea has been proposed by Guyote and Sternberg, 1981.) Consider these premises:

> All the artists are beekeepers.
> Some of the beekeepers are chemists.

A subject might imagine a group of artists who are beekeepers, perhaps add some additional beekeepers who are not artists, and then imagine that some of the beekeepers are chemists. To illustrate this possibility more specifically, let us suppose that for the premises above the subject imagines four individuals. Individuals 1, 2, and 3 are artists but 4 is not. All four are beekeepers. Individuals 2 and 4 are chemists. The subject inspects this group, notes that individual 2 is both an artist and a chemist, and concludes:

Some artists are chemists.

Thus, the subject is building a specific model for the premises and inspecting this to see what is true in that model. This kind of reasoning pattern is a fairly good heuristic but will lead to errors, as in this example. Johnson-Laird (1983) has developed a computer simulation of this theory which reproduces all the major errors that subjects make.

There are a number of other theories (e.g., Erickson, 1974; Chapman & Chapman, 1959; Henle, 1962; Ceraso & Provitera, 1971) of why subjects make errors in reasoning about categorical syllogisms. What all these theories have in common is the assumption that subjects do not treat the task as a logician would prescribe. Many, like Johnson-Laird, assume that subjects reason about a syllogism by applying a very specific and concrete interpretation to it. This research is often described as showing that subjects reason in terms of mental models (Gentner & Stevens, 1983). Rather than reasoning according to formal rules they build up a specific model of a situation and determine what is true of that specific situation.

It has been argued that non-Western cultures are even more concrete in their reasoning patterns. In one study (Cole & Scribner, 1974), a Kpelle tribal leader from Liberia was presented with the following syllogism:

Spider and black deer always eat together.
Spider is eating.
Is the black deer eating?

The following is the conversation that ensued between the tribal leader (S) and the experimenter (E):

S: Were they in the bush?
E: Yes.
S: Were they eating together?

E: Spider and black deer always eat together. Spider is eating. Is black deer eating?

S: But I was not there. How can I answer such a question?

E: Can't you answer it? Even if you were not there, you can answer it. (Repeats the question.)

S: Oh, oh, black deer is eating.

E: What is your reason for saying that black deer was eating?

S: The reason is that black deer always walks about all day eating leaves in the bush. Then he rests for a while and gets up again to eat.

The basic outcome was that the subject refused to reason from the abstract premises the experimenter provided him and instead reasoned from his own concrete experience.

As we saw in the case of the Wason card task, people find it hard to bring the prescriptions of logic to bear in their reasoning attempts; rather they choose to reason in terms of principles that appear in their daily lives. In the case of Cheng and Holyoak it was principles about permission and law and in the case of the Kpelle tribal leader, it was principles about black deer.

Inductive Reasoning

We now turn from considering deductive reasoning to considering inductive reasoning. To illustrate the difference between inductively valid and deductively valid conclusions, consider the following argument:

> The Abkhasian Republic of the USSR has 10 men over 160.
> No other place in the world has a man over 160.
> 1. The oldest man in the world today is in the USSR.
> 2. The oldest man in the world tomorrow will be in the USSR.

Conclusion 1 is deductively valid. If the premises are true (and I don't know if they are, but this is irrelevant), then the conclusion must be true. However, conclusion 2 is only inductively valid; that is, it is a highly likely conclusion if the premises are true, but it is conceivable that all 10 men could die before tomorrow.

Two major difficulties can be identified with respect to inductive reasoning. First, evaluating a particular inductive conclusion is often hard. Consider the predicament of Jane as she tries to evaluate the following argument:

> Often when Jane turns around in class, Dick is looking at her.
> Dick keeps asking Jane for suggestions on his homework.
> Dick has stopped seeing Janice.
> Therefore, Dick has a crush on Jane.

Many other possible explanations for Dick's behavior certainly exist, and evaluating the probability of the conclusion given the premises is extremely difficult for Jane.

The second difficulty in inductive reasoning occurs when only the premises are provided and we must come up with a conclusion. This is the process of hypothesis formation. As with deductive reasoning, deciding what conclusion, if any, should be drawn can be quite difficult. Consider the following premises:

> The first number in the series is 1.
> The second number in the series is 3.
> The third number in the series is 7.

What conclusions follows? One possible conclusion is that

1. The fourth number in the series is 15.

However, a better conclusion would probably be

2. The nth number in the series is $2^n - 1$.

This conclusion seems better because it is general and so describes the whole series. However, it might not be the correct conclusion. For instance, the series might actually obey the following rule:

3. The nth number is $2(n-1)$ larger than the $n-1$st.

Of course, this conclusion predicts that the fourth number in the series will be 13, whereas conclusion 2 predicts that the fourth number will be 15. However, the original three premises provide no means of selecting between the two extrapolations. This fact reflects the important feature of induction: We can never know for sure whether a conclusion is true or whether some other conclusion would be better. Thus, it is often hard to find an inductive conclusion; and once a set of possible conclusions has been found, it is often hard to decide which is the best of the set.

Research in cognitive psychology has tended to study separately each of these two aspects of inductive reasoning, *hypothesis formation* and *hypothesis evaluation*. The next two sections of this chapter will cover these major research domains.

Hypothesis Formation

Concept Identification

Our discussion of hypothesis formation will focus on a review of some of the significant results from the *concept-identification* or *concept-formation* literature. This material derives from one of the older research traditions in cognitive psychology. Historically, this domain is important not only because it studies hypothesis formation, but also because it was one area in which cognitive psychology first successfully broke from the predominant behaviorist traditions of the 1950s and early 1960s. It is generally regarded now as shedding light on how people do conscious hypothesis formation and not as relevant to how natural categories like *dog* are formed. (We discussed natural categories in Chapter 5 under the topic of Schemas.)

As an example of a concept-formation task, consider the following:

A dax can be large, bright, red, and square.
A dax can be large, dull, red, and square.
A dax cannot be small, dull, red, and square.
A dax cannot be large, bright, red, and triangular.
A dax can be large, dull, blue, and square.
What is a dax?

The best answer is probably that a dax is a large square. With carefully controlled material such as in this example, researchers have discovered a good deal about how people form inductive hypotheses.

A classic series of studies of concept identification was reported by Bruner, Goodnow, and Austin (1956). Figure 10-1 illustrates the kind of material that they used. The stimuli were all rectangular boxes containing various objects. The stimuli varied on four dimensions: number of objects (one, two, or three); number of borders around the boxes (one, two, or three); shape (cross, circle, or square); and color (green, black, and

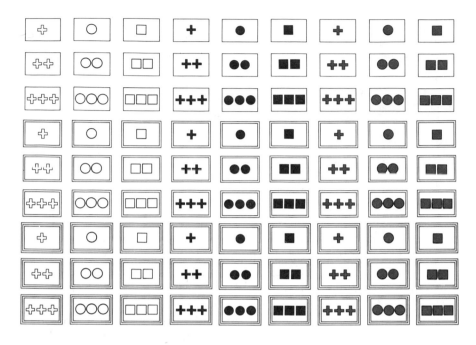

Figure 10-1. Material used by Bruner et al. in one of their studies of concept identification (1956). The array consists of instances formed by combinations of four attributes, each exhibiting three values. Open (white) shapes represent green figures, solid shapes represent black figures, and gray shapes represent red figures. (*A study of thinking.* Copyright 1956. Reprinted with permission of John Wiley & Sons, Inc.)

red, represented in the figure by white, black, and gray, respectively). Subjects were told that they were to discover some concept that described a particular subset of these instances. For instance, the concept might have been black crosses. Subjects were to discover the correct concept on the basis of information they were given about what were and what were not instances of the concept.

Figure 10-2 contains three illustrations (the three columns) of the information subjects might have been presented. Each column consists of a sequence of instances identified either as members of the concept (positive, +) or not (negative, −). Each column represents a different concept. Subjects would be presented with the instances in a column one at a time. From these instances subjects would determine what the concept was. Stop reading and try to determine the concept for each column.

The concept in the first example is *two crosses*. This concept is referred to as a *conjunctive concept,* since the conjunction of a number of features (in

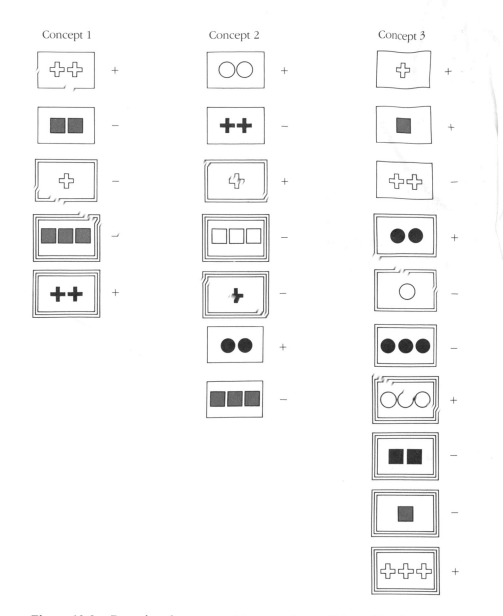

Figure 10-2. Examples of sequences of instances from which a subject is to identify concepts. Each column gives a sequence of instances and noninstances for a different concept. A plus (+) signals a positive instance and a minus (−) a negative instance.

this case the features are *two* and *cross*) must be present for the instance to be positive. Subjects typically find conjunctive concepts easiest to discover. In some sense conjunctive hypotheses seem to be the most "natural" kind of hypotheses and the type that has been researched most extensively. The solution to the second example is *two borders or circles.* This kind of concept is referred to as a *disjunctive concept,* since an instance is a member of the concept if either of the features is present. In the final example, the solution is that the number of objects must equal the number of borders. This example is a *relational concept,* since it specifies a relationship between two dimensions.

The problems in this series are particularly difficult, because to identify the concept a subject must both determine which features are relevant and discover the kind of rule that connects the features (e.g., conjunctive, disjunctive, or relational). Identifying what features are relevant is referred to as *attribute identification* and identifying the kind of rule as *rule learning* (Haygood & Bourne, 1965). In many experiments, either the form of the rule or the relevant attributes are identified for the subject. For instance, in the Bruner, Goodnow, and Austin (1956) experiments subjects had to identify only the correct attributes. They knew that they would be identifying conjunctive concepts.

Two Concept-Formation Strategies

Bruner et al. were interested in how subjects would go about identifying a concept. One of the experimental situations in which they studied concept formation is referred to as the *reception paradigm.* In this paradigm, subjects see instances one at a time and are asked to judge at presentation whether each is a member of the category. After making their classifications, subjects are given feedback as to whether their classifications were correct. Bruner et al. discovered that in this paradigm most of their subjects spontaneously adopted one or two strategies to identify the concept. The optimal strategy, called the *wholist strategy* and described in Table 10-2, was adopted to some degree by 65 percent of the subjects. Table 10-2 is a 2 × 2 matrix in which the situations are classified according to whether a positive or negative instance of the concept has been presented (columns) and whether the subject has correctly or incorrectly classified the instance (rows).

The table is a bit abstract and is best understood when applied to an example. Suppose, then, that the first stimulus subjects see is

one border, one green square

Table 10-2 *Wholist Strategy for Concept Identification*

Summary of strategy:
Take the set of all the features of the first positive instance as the initial hypothesis.
Then, as more instances are presented, eliminate any feature in this set that does
not occur with a positive instance.

Classifications	Positive Instance	Negative Instance
Correct	Maintain the hypothesis now in force.	Maintain the hypothesis now in force.
Incorrect	Take as the next hypothesis what the old hypothesis and the present instance have in common.	Impossible unless we have misreckoned.

and that this is a positive instance. The table specifies that all the features in this first positive instance be taken as the hypothesis. That is, subjects will hypothesize that the concept is defined by the conjunction of the features *one border, one object, green color,* and *square shape.* If subjects are then presented with

one border, two red circles

they would judge this instance not to be a member of the category because it does not match the hypothesis. Suppose this judgment is correct; this condition is described in the upper right cell of Table 10-2, and the hypothesis is kept. Then suppose subjects are presented with

two borders, one green square

They would also judge this instance not to be a member of the category. But suppose they are wrong and that this is a positive instance. This case is described in the lower left cell, and subjects take as their new hypothesis what the old hypothesis and the current instance have in common:

one green square

Suppose they are now presented with

three borders, one green square

309

They would classify this as an instance of the category and would be told that they are correct. They would then be in the condition described by the upper left cell, and would keep the hypothesis. Finally, assume that subjects are presented with

one border, two green crosses

They would say that this is not an instance of the category, but suppose it is. Again, the situation is that of the lower left cell of Table 10-2, and subjects would make a new hypothesis,

green

the feature that the old hypothesis and new instance have in common.

It is impossible, if subjects follow this wholist strategy faithfully, for them ever to make an error on a negative instance (lower right cell of the table). Note that subjects have to revise the hypothesis only when they fail to identify an instance (lower left cell). They never have to change the hypothesis when they are correct (upper cells). The wholist strategy is relatively easy to follow, for it requires that subjects remember only the current hypothesis, not past instances. Of the subjects who attempted to follow the wholist strategy in the Bruner et al. study, 47 percent were able to do so without ever deviating from the prescriptions of Table 10-2.

The other common subject strategy Bruner et al. detected they called the *partist strategy.* In this strategy, subjects started with a conjunctive hypothesis that was consistent with the first positive instance. It would involve some subset of the features contained in that instance. Thus, this strategy differs at the start from the wholist strategy, where subjects take as their first hypothesis *all* the features in the first positive instance. Table 10-3 describes the behavior of an "ideal" partist subject after the first trial (I use the word *ideal* because subjects often did not conform perfectly to this strategy). Subjects' behavior is presented in the same format as in Table 10-2 in order to facilitate comparison. When subjects are correct, they maintain the hypothesis. Here the partist strategy does not differ from the wholist strategy. When subjects are wrong, however, they try to select a new hypothesis consistent with the past items. This process requires memory for all the past items, and subjects often fail at this point because they are unable to remember past items. Bruner et al. classified 35 percent of their subjects as following a partist strategy. Of these, only 38 percent were able to behave in accord with Table 10-3 consistently over five trials.

Table 10-3 *Partist Strategy for Concept Identification*

Summary of strategy:
Begin with part of the first positive instance as a hypothesis (i.e., choose just a subset of the features in the instance). Then, as more instances are presented, retain the hypothesis or change it to be consistent with the instances.

Classifications	Positive Instance	Negative Instance
Correct	Maintain the hypothesis now in force.	Maintain the hypothesis now in force.
Incorrect	Change the hypothesis to make it consistent with past instances; in other words; choose a hypothesis not previously disconfirmed.	Change the hypothesis to make it consistent with past instances; in other words, choose a hypothesis not previously disconfirmed.

The reason that the partist strategy is less useful than the wholist strategy for identifying conjunctive concepts lies in the initially formed hypothesis. In the wholist strategy, all the potentially relevant information from the first instance is kept in the initial hypothesis, whereas in the partist strategy some potentially relevant features are dropped out. In the wholist strategy, a feature is dropped from the hypothesis only when it is proven irrelevant. The partist strategy can be seen as the outcome of an inappropriate application of a similarity heuristic (discussed in Chapter 8) to the task of hypothesis search. Subjects believe that the correct concept will involve a conjunction of one, two, or at most three of the features in the first instance. Therefore, they try to maximize the similarity between the first hypothesis and the eventual correct hypothesis by including only one, two, or three features in the initial hypothesis.

Actually, the Bruner et al. subjects (Harvard students) were relatively good at keeping track of the information required to form reasonable hypotheses. Other research (see Levine, 1975, for a review) has found that many subjects have even more difficulty keeping track of relevant information. In this, human concept formation compares rather unfavorably with computer programs (Mitchell, 1982), which can perform such tasks with flawless bookkeeping. Hypothesis formation, like deductive reasoning, does not seem to be a task for which most people are well prepared. This outcome should be rather comforting to scientists whose job is formulating scientific hypotheses. They need not fear being replaced by people who have to rely on their untrained abilities for hypothesis formation.

311

Hypothesis Evaluation

In our discussion of concept-identification and rule-induction tasks, the means of deciding if a hypothesis fit the facts and the degree to which it fit were fairly obvious. Consider, however, the following case. Suppose I come home and find the door to my house ajar. I am interested in the hypothesis that this might be the work of a burglar. How do I evaluate this hypothesis? The problem of hypothesis evaluation in this situation is more complicated than in a concept-formation experiment for two reasons. First, in concept-identification situations such as those discussed in the preceding section, each hypothesis (that is, a square, black, a triangle, and so on) is equally likely to be true from the beginning. This is not the case in the open-door mystery (where the two competing hypotheses are that the home has been burglarized and that it has not been burglarized). Before I noted that the door was open, I would have estimated the probability that my home had not been burglarized as high and the probability that it had been burglarized as correspondingly low. These unequal prior probabilities should have some influence on my hypothesis evaluation.

Second, the connection between hypotheses and observations is not absolute, as it is in a concept-identification experiment. In the latter, if the correct hypothesis is that the concept is black, then a large black triangle with two borders must be an instance of the concept. However, even if the hypothesis that my house has been burglarized is correct, it need not be the case that the door will be open. Perhaps the probability of this connection is only 80 percent.

Bayes's Theorem

Bayes's theorem provides a method for evaluating hypotheses in situations, such as that cited above, in which hypotheses vary in their prior probability and the connection between evidence and hypothesis is only probabilistic. The theorem is a mathematical prescription for estimating the posterior probability that a hypothesis is true from the prior probability that the hypothesis is true and the conditional probability of a piece of evidence given the hypothesis.

Prior probabilities are the probabilities that a hypothesis is true before evidence. Let us refer to the hypothesis that my house has been burglarized as H. Suppose that I know from police statistics that the probability (P) of a house in my neighborhood being burglarized on any particular day is 1 in 1000. This probability is expressed as

$$P(H) = .001$$

This equation expresses the prior probability of the hypothesis, or the probability of the hypothesis's being true before the evidence. We will refer to this hypothesis as H. The other prior probability needed is the probability that the house has not been burglarized. This alternate hypothesis is denoted $\bar{H}$. This value is 1 minus $P(H)$ and is

$$P(\bar{H}) = .999$$

A *conditional probability* is the probability that a particular type of evidence is true if a particular hypothesis is true. Let us consider what the conditional probabilities of the evidence (door ajar) would be under the two hypotheses. Suppose I believe that the probability of the door's being ajar is quite high if I have been burglarized; say, 4 out of 5. Let E denote the evidence, or the event of the door being ajar. Then we will denote this conditional probability by

$$P(E|H) = .8$$

which should be read *the probability of* E *given that* H *is true*. Second, we determine the probability of E if H is not true. Suppose I know that chances are only 1 out of 100 that the door would be ajar if no burglary had occurred (e.g., by accident, neighbors with a key). This we denote by

$$P(E|\bar{H}) = .01$$

the probability of E *given that* H *is not true.*

The *posterior probability* is the probability of a hypothesis's being true after some evidence. The notation $P(H \mid E)$ is the posterior probability of hypothesis H given evidence E. According to Bayes's theorem, we can calculate the posterior probability of H, that the house has been burglarized, in light of the evidence thus:

$$P(H|E) = \frac{P(E \mid H) \cdot P(H)}{P(E|H) \cdot P(H) + P(E|\bar{H}) \cdot P(\bar{H})} \tag{1}$$

Given our assumed values, we can solve for $P(H \mid E)$ by substituting into equation 1:

$$P(H \mid E) = \frac{(.8)(.001)}{(.8)(.001) + (.01)(.999)} = .074$$

Thus, the probability that my house has been burglarized is still less than 8 in 100. Note that this probability is true even though an open door is good evidence for a burglary and not for a normal state of affairs, $P(E \mid H) = .8$, and $P(E \mid \bar{H}) = .01$. The posterior probability is still quite low because the prior probability of $H - P(H) = .001$ was low to begin with. Relative to that low start, the posterior probability has been drastically revised upward.

Table 10-4 offers an informal explanation of Bayes's theorem as applied to the burglary example. There are four possible states of affairs, determined by whether the burglary hypothesis is true or not and by whether there is the evidence of an open door or not. The probability of each state of affairs is set forth in the four cells of the table. The probability of each state is the prior probability of that hypothesis times the conditional probability of the event given the hypothesis. For instance, consider the upper left cell. Since $P(H)$ is .001 and $P(E \mid H)$ is .8, the probability in that cell is .0008. The four probabilities in these cells must sum to 1. Given the evidence that the door is open, we can eliminate the two cells in the lower row of the table. Since one of the two remaining states of affairs must be the case, the posterior probabilities of the two remaining states must sum to 1. Bayes's theorem provides us with a means for recalculating the probabilities of the states in light of evidence that makes impossible one row of the matrix. What we have done in equation 1 in calculating the posterior probability is taken the probability of the upper left cell, where hypothesis H is true, and divided it by the sum of the probabilities in the two upper cells, which represent the only two possible states of affairs.

Table 10-4 *An Analysis of Bayes's Theorem*

Evidence	Burglarized (H)	Not Burglarized ($\bar{H}$)	Sum of Probabilities
Door open (E)	$P(E\mid H)P(H)$ = .00080	$P(E\mid\bar{H})P(\bar{H})$ = .00999	.01079
Door not open ($\bar{E}$)	$P(\bar{E}\mid H)P(H)$ = .00020	$P(\bar{E}\mid\bar{H})P(\bar{H})$ = .98901	.98921
Sum of probabilities	.00100	.99900	1.00000

Adapted from Hayes, 1984.

Bayes's theorem rests on a mathematical analysis of the nature of probability. The formula can be proven to evaluate hypotheses correctly; thus, it enables us to determine precisely the posterior probability of a hypothesis given the prior and conditional probabilities. The theorem serves as *prescriptive,* or *normative, model* specifying the means of evaluating the probability of a hypothesis. Such a model contrasts with a *descriptive model,* which specifies what people actually do.

Deviations from Bayes's Theorem

It should come as no surprise to learn that humans typically do not behave perfectly in accord with the Bayesian model. Ward Edwards (1968) extensively investigated how people use new information to adjust their estimates of the probabilities of various hypotheses. In one experiment, he presented subjects with two bags, each containing 100 poker chips. One of the bags contained 70 red chips and 30 blue and the other contained 70 blue chips and 30 red. The experimenter chose one of the bags at random and the subjects' task was to decide which bag had been chosen.

In the absence of any prior information, the probability that the chosen bag contained predominantly red chips was 50 percent. Thus,

$$P(H_R) = .50 \text{ and } P(H_B) = .50$$

where H_R is the hypothesis of a predominantly red bag and H_B is the hypothesis of a predominantly blue bag. To obtain further information, subjects sampled chips at random from the bag. Suppose the first chip drawn was red. The conditional probability of drawing a red chip if most of the chips in the bag are red is

$$P(R \mid H_R) = .70$$

Similarly, the conditional probability of drawing a red chip from a blue-majority bag is

$$P(R \mid H_B) = .30$$

Now, we can calculate the posterior probability of the bag's being predominantly red given the red chip by applying equation 1 to this situation:

$$P(H_R|R) = \frac{P(R|H_R) \cdot P(H_R)}{P(R|H_R) \cdot P(H_R) + P(R|H_B) \cdot P(H_B)}$$

$$= \frac{(.70) \cdot (.50)}{(.70) \cdot (.50) + (.30) \cdot (.50)} = .70$$

This result seems, to both naive and sophisticated observers, to be a rather sharp increase in probabilities. Typically, human subjects do not increase their probability of a red-majority bag to .70; rather, they make a more conservative revision to a value such as .60.

After this first drawing, the experiment continues: The poker chip is put back in the bag and a second chip is drawn at random. Suppose this chip too is red. Again, by applying Bayes's theorem, we can show that the posterior probability of a red bag is .84. Suppose our observations continued for 10 more trials and after all 12 we have observed 8 reds and 4 blues. By continuing the Bayesian analysis, we could show that the new posterior probability of the hypothesis of a red bag is .97. Subjects who see this sequence of 12 trials only estimate subjectively a posterior probability of .75 or less for the red bag. Edwards has used the term *conservative* to refer to subjects' tendency to underestimate the force of evidence. He estimates that they use between a half and a fifth of the available evidence from each chip.

Another problem is that subjects sometimes ignore prior probabilities. Kahneman and Tversky (1973) told one group of subjects that an individual had been chosen at random from a set of 100 individuals consisting of 70 engineers and 30 lawyers. This group of subjects was termed the engineer-high group. A second group, the engineer-low group, was told that the individual came from a set of 30 engineers and 70 lawyers. Both groups were asked to determine the probability that the individual chosen at random from the group would be an engineer given no information about the individual. Subjects were able to respond with the right prior probabilities: The engineer-high group estimated .70 and the engineer-low group estimated .30. Then subjects were told that another person was chosen from the population and they were given the following description:

Jack is a 45-year-old man. He is married and has four children. He is generally conservative, careful, and ambitious. He shows no interest in political and social issues and spends most of his free time on his many hobbies, which include home carpentry, sailing, and mathematical puzzles.

Subjects in both groups gave a .90 probability estimate to the hypothesis that this person was an engineer. No difference was displayed between the two groups, which had been given different prior probabilities for an engineer hypothesis. But Bayes's theorem prescribes that prior probability should have a strong effect, resulting in a higher posterior probability from the engineer-high group than the engineer-low group.

The following sample description was also used by Kahneman and Tversky:

> Dick is a 30-year-old man. He is married with no children. A man of high ability and high motivation, he promises to be quite successful in his field. He is well liked by his colleagues.

This example was designed to provide no diagnostic information either way with respect to Dick's profession. According to Bayes's theorem, the posterior probability of the engineer hypothesis should be the same as the prior probability, since this description is not informative. However, both the engineer-high and the engineer-low groups estimated that the probability was .50 that the individual described was an engineer. Thus, they allowed a completely uninformative event to change their probabilities. Again, subjects were shown to be completely unable to use prior probabilities in assessing the posterior probability of a hypothesis.

The failure to take prior probabilities into account can lead an individual to make some totally unwarranted conclusions. For instance, suppose you take a test for cancer. It is known that a particular type of cancer will result in a positive test 95 percent of the time. On the other hand, if a person does not have the cancer, there is only a 5 percent probability of a positive result. Suppose you are informed that your result is positive. If you are like most people, you will assume that your chances of having the cancer are 95 out of 100, and begin saying good-bye to your friends (Hammerton, 1973). You would be overreacting in assuming that the cancer would be fatal, but you would also be making a fundamental error in probability estimation. What is the error?

You would have failed to consider the base rate for the particular type of cancer in question. Suppose only 1 in 10,000 people have this cancer. This would be your prior probability. Now, with this information you would be able to determine the posterior probability of your having the cancer. Bringing out the Bayesian formula, you would express the problem this way:

$$P(H \mid E) = \frac{P(H)P(E|H)}{P(H)P(E|H) + P(\overline{H})P(E|\overline{H})}$$

317

where the prior probability of the cancer hypothesis is $P(H) = .0001$, and $P(\overline{H}) = .9999$, $P(E \mid H) = .95$, and $P(E|\overline{H}) = .05$. Thus,

$$P(H|E) = \frac{(.0001)(.95)}{(.0001)(.95) + (.9999)(.05)} = .0019$$

That is, the posterior probability of your having the cancer would still be less than 1 in 500.

Judgments of Probability

To understand why subjects do not operate according to Bayes's theorem in evaluating evidence, it is necessary to understand how they reason about probabilities. They certainly do not think about probabilities by performing mentally the kinds of arithmetic operations (additions, multiplications, and divisions) called for by Bayes's theorem. A number of experiments have asked subjects to make judgments of probabilities. In some circumstances they can do this quite accurately. Consider an experiment by Shuford (1961). He presented arrays such as that in Figure 10-3

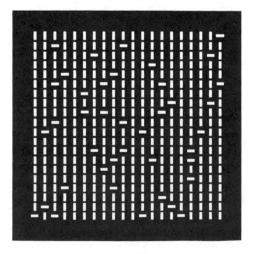

Figure 10-3. A random matrix composed of 90 percent vertical bars and 10 percent horizontal bars, presented to subjects to determine their accuracy in judging proportions. (From Shuford, 1961. Copyright 1961 by the American Psychological Association. Reprinted by permission.)

to subjects for 1 second. He then asked subjects to judge the proportion of vertical bars relative to horizontal bars. The numbers of vertical bars varied from 10 to 90 percent in different matrices. Shuford's results are shown in Figure 10-4. As can be seen, subjects' estimates are quite close to the true proportions.

Another experiment to assess judgments as to proportion was performed by Robinson (1964). He presented subjects with a sequence of flashes from a left light and a right light. The task was to estimate the proportion of left or right flashes in the sequence. Again, subjects were very accurate in making these estimates. Their estimates fell within .02 of the true proportions.

In both of these experiments, subjects were not actually estimating *probabilities:* rather, they were estimating the *proportions* of a type of event in a population. However, it seems that people think of probabilities in terms of proportion in a population—and, indeed, the mathematics of probability is based on a concept very close to this. In the two experiments cited, subjects were able to make an unbiased inspection of the population; thus, their estimates were unbiased. They could see all the

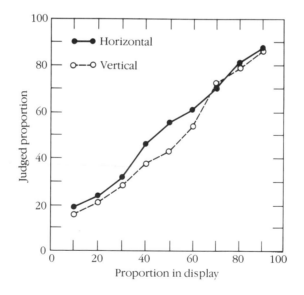

Figure 10-4. Mean estimated proportion as a function of the true proportion. Subjects exhibited a fairly accurate ability to estimate the proportions of vertical and horizontal bars i Figure 10-3. (From Shuford, 1961. Copyright 1961 by the American Psychological Association. Reprinted by permission.)

instances. However, as we will see, in many probability-estimation situations, we do not have total and unbiased access to the underlying population. It is in such situations that distortions in probability estimates occur.

Availability

Consider the following experiment reported by Tversky and Kahneman (1974), which demonstrates that probability judgments can be biased by differential availability of examples. They asked subjects to judge the proportion of words in the language that fit certain characteristics. For instance, they asked subjects to estimate the proportion of English words that begin with a *k* versus words with a *k* in third position. How might subjects perform this task? One obvious heuristic is to briefly try to think of words that satisfy the specification and words that do not and to estimate the relative proportion of target words. How many words can you think of that begin with *k*? How many words can you think of that don't? What is your estimate of their relative proportion? Now how many words can you think of that have *k* in the third position? How many words can you think of that don't? What is their relative proportion? Subjects estimated that more words begin with *k* than have *k* in the third position. In actual fact, three times as many words have *k* in the third position as begin with *k*.

As in this experiment, many real-life circumstances require that we estimate probabilities without having direct access to the population that these probabilities describe. In such cases, we must rely on memory as the source for our estimates. The memory factors we studied in Chapters 6 and 7 serve to explain how such estimates can be biased. Under the reasonable assumption that words are more strongly associated to their first letter than their third letter, the bias exhibited in the experimental results can be explained in terms of the spreading-activation theory (Chapter 6). In the case of these gross overestimates of words beginning with particular letters, with the focus of attention on, say, *k,* activation will spread from that letter to words beginning with it. This process will tend to make words beginning with *k* more available than other words. Thus, these words will be overrepresented in the sample that subjects take from memory to estimate the true proportion in the population. The same overestimation does not occur for words with *k* in the third position, since words are unlikely to be directly associated to the letters that occur in the third position. Therefore, it is not possible to associatively prime these words and make them more available.

Similarity

Other factors besides memory lead to biases in probability estimates. Consider another example from Tversky and Kahneman (1974). Which of the following sequences of six tosses from a fair coin is more likely (where H denotes *heads* and T *tails*): HTHTTH or HHHHHH? Many people think that the first sequence is more likely to occur, but the two sequences are actually equally probable. The probability of the first sequence is the probability of H on the first toss (which is .50) times the probability of T on the second toss (which is .50), times the probability of H on the third toss (which is .50), and so on. The probability of the whole sequence is $.50 \times .50 \times .50 \times .50 \times .50 \times .50 = .016$. Similarly, the probability of the second sequence is the product of the probabilities of each coin toss and the probability of a head on each coin toss is .50. Thus, the final probability again is also $.50 \times .50 \times .50 \times .50 \times .50 \times .50 = .016$. Why do some people have the illusion that the first sequence is more probable? It is because the first event seems similar to a lot of other events; for example, HTHTHT or HTTHTH. These similar events serve to bias upward a person's probability estimate of the target event. On the other hand, HHHHHH, straight heads, seems unlike any other event, and its probability will therefore not be biased upward by other similar sequences. In conclusion, a person's estimate of the probability of an event will be biased by other events that are similar to it.

Note that the effect of this fallacy is that subjects underestimate the frequency of runs of events, such as straight heads. This tendency to underestimate leads to a common phenomenon known as the *gambler's fallacy*. The fallacy is the belief that if an event has not occurred for a while, then it is more likely by the "law of averages" to occur in the near future. This phenomenon can be demonstrated in an experimental setting; for instance, where subjects see a sequence of coin tosses and must guess whether each toss will be a head or a tail. If they see a string of heads, they become more and more likely to guess that tails will come up on the next trial. Casino operators count on this fallacy to help them make money. Players who have had a string of losses at a table will keep playing, assuming that by the "law of averages" they will experience a compensating string of wins. However, the game is set in favor of the house. The dice do not know or care whether a gambler has had a string of losses. The consequence is that players tend to lose more as they try to recoup their losses. The "law of averages" is itself a fallacy.

The gambler's fallacy can be used to advantage in certain situations — for instance, at the racetrack. Most racetracks operate by a pari-mutuel system, in which the odds on a horse are determined by the number of people betting on the horse. By the end of the day, if favorites have won all the races, people tend to doubt that another favorite can win, and they switch their bets to the long shots. As a consequence, the betting odds on the favorite deviate from what they should be, and a person can sometimes make money by betting on the favorite.

Remarks and Suggested Readings

A good introduction to logic is Suppes (1957). A number of texts offer a more formal and technical development in logic, including Mendelson (1964), Church (1956), Kleene (1952), and Schoenfield (1967). Church's text is particularly significant as a standard in the field and provides discussions of many of the important conceptual issues. It is probably better to study mathematical logic as part of a formal course than just out of a textbook. Such courses are offered by many college departments, including philosophy, mathematics, and computer science.

There are basically three positions on how people engage in deductive reasoning. One position is that they use rational laws of deduction, which are somewhat like the logician's rules. For expositions of this viewpoint, read Braine (1978) and Rips (1983). The second, represented in Johnson-Laird (1983), is that people reason by reference to concrete situations. The third, represented in Cheng and Holyoak (1985) and Holland, Holyoak, Nisbett, and Thagard (1986), is that people reason by pragmatic inference schemas. Somewhat unreasonably, I think, no theorist has taken seriously the possibility that people may do all three at different times.

A good introduction to the philosophy of inductive logic is Skyrms (1966). A number of textbooks offer a thorough review of the concept-formation literature; these include Bourne (1966); Johnson (1972); Bourne, Ekstrand, and Dominowski (1971); and Kintsch (1970). Trabasso and Bower (1968) is an important book on concept formation. Levine (1975) provides a collection of papers spanning the history of research on concept formation. Bruner, Goodnow, and Austin (1956) remains a classic well worth reading. Simon and Lea (1974) provides a discussion of the similarity between inductive reasoning and problem solving. Tversky and Kahneman's (1974) *Science* article provides a good survey of their research on probabilistic judgment. A survey of research on probabilistic judgment is in the book edited by Kahneman, Slovic, and Tversky (1982). Nisbett and Ross (1980) is an extensive discussion of the failures of human inference. The Holland, Holyoak, Nisbett, and Thagard (1986) book is basically devoted to producing an information-processing model of induction.

CHAPTER
·11·

Language Structure

Summary

1. The linguist is concerned with characterizing our linguistic competence, which is our abstract knowledge about the structure of language. This concern contrasts with the psychologist's concern with language performance, which is how we actually use language.

2. The linguist wants to account for the productivity and regularity of language and the linguistic intuitions of language speakers. Productivity means that there are an infinite number of acceptable sentences. Regularity means that sentences have to satisfy a strict set of rules in order to be acceptable. Among the important linguistic intuitions are judgments of well-formedness, paraphrase, and ambiguity.

3. The phrase structure of a sentence is a hierarchical analysis of the sentence into phrases. Natural language also involves transformations of these phrase structures in which words are moved to new positions in the sentence.

4. It has long been debated whether language is dependent on thought, whether thought is dependent on language, or whether the two are independent of each other.

5. A current issue concerns whether language functions according to its own unique principles or whether it functions like other cognitive systems. Evidence about first language acquisition figures prominently in this debate.

6. Children's linguistic utterances slowly grow in size and complexity. Despite this slow growth, children eventually reach a mastery of their language not matched by adults learning a new language. Children also appear not to be much helped by direct linguistic instruction but rather learn language more implicitly.

7. It has been argued that children's acquisition of new language is guided by innate knowledge about the possible forms of natural language. While human languages do obey certain regularities called *universals,* it is unclear whether these universals reflect language-specific knowledge or constraints imposed by the nature of cognition generally.

Of all human beings' cognitive abilities, the use of language is the most impressive. The difference between human language and the natural communication systems of other species is enormous. More than anything else, language is responsible for the current advanced state of human civilization. It is the principal means by which knowledge is recorded and transmitted from one generation to the next.[1] Without language there would be little technology. Language is the principal medium for establishing religions, laws, and moral conventions. Therefore, without language no means would exist for establishing rules to govern groups ranging in size from tennis partners to nations. Language also provides people with the principal means of assessing what another person knows. So, without language human beings would experience countless more misunderstandings than they currently do. Language provides an important medium for art, a means of getting to know people, and a valuable aid to courtship. Therefore, without language much of the joy of living would be lost. In its written form, language enables humans to communicate over spatial distance and through time, as this book demonstrates.

This chapter will provide a general overview of the structure of language and its consequences for human cognition. We will review some of the basic ideas developed in linguistics about the structure of language and some evidence for their psychological reality. We will review research and speculation about the relationship between language and thought. One of the major issues concerns the claim that language is quite different from other cognitive faculties. Much of the evidence for and against this uniqueness claim comes from research on how children learn the structure of language. Therefore, we will conclude with a review of child language acquisition. This chapter will not contain detailed analyses of how language is processed. There has been considerable research on this topic and the whole next chapter of this book will be devoted to language processing.

The Field of Linguistics
Productivity and Regularity

The academic field of linguistics attempts to characterize the nature of language. It is distinct from psychology in that it studies the structure of natural languages rather than how people process natural languages. Despite this difference, the work from linguistics has been extremely influential in the psychology of language. As we will see, concepts from linguistics play an important role in theories of language processing. As noted in Chapter 1, the influence from linguistics was important in the decline of behaviorism and the rise of modern cognitive psychology. The linguist focuses on two aspects of language: its productivity and its regularity. The term *productivity* refers to the fact that an infinite number of utterances are possible in any language. *Regularity* refers to the fact that these utterances are systematic in many ways.

We need not seek far to convince ourselves of the highly productive and creative character of language. We have only to pick up a book and select a sentence from it at random. Suppose that, having chosen a sentence, an individual were instructed to go to the library and begin searching for a repetition of the sentence in another book! Obviously, no sensible person would take up this challenge. But, were a person to try, it is very unlikely that he or she would find the sentence repeated among the billions of sentences in the library. Still, it is important to realize that the components which make up sentences are quite small in number: In English, only 26 letters, 40 phonemes (see the discussion in the Speech Recognition section of Chapter 3), and 100,000 words are used. Nevertheless, with these components we can and do generate trillions of novel sentences.

A look at the structure of sentences makes clear why this productivity is possible. Natural language has facilities for endlessly embedding structure within structure and coordinating structure with structure. A mildly amusing party game is to start with a simple sentence and require participants to keep adding to the sentence:

The girl hit the boy.
The girl hit the boy and he cried.
The big girl hit the boy and he cried.
The big girl hit the boy and he cried loudly.
The big girl hit the boy who was misbehaving and he cried loudly.
The big girl with authoritarian instincts hit the boy who was misbehaving and he cried loudly.
The big girl with authoritarian instincts hit the boy who was misbehaving and he cried loudly and ran to his mother.
The big girl with authoritarian instincts hit the boy who was misbehaving and he cried loudly and ran to his mother who went to her husband.
The big girl with authoritarian instincts hit the boy who was misbehaving and he cried loudly and ran to his mother who went to her husband who called the police.

And so on until someone can no longer extend the sentence.

The fact that an infinite number of word strings can be generated would not be particularly interesting in itself. If we have 100,000 words for each position and if sentences can be of any length, it is not hard to see that a very large (in fact, an infinite) number of word strings is possible. However, if we just combine words at random we get "sentences" such as:

From runners physicians prescribing miss a states joy rests what thought most.

In fact, very few of the possible word combinations are acceptable sentences. The speculation is often jokingly made that, given enough monkeys working at typewriters during a long enough time, some monkey will type a best-selling book. It should be clear that it would take a lot of monkeys a long time to type just one acceptable *R@!#s.

So, balanced against the productivity of language is its highly regular character. One goal of linguistics is to discover a set of rules that will account for both the productivity and the regularity of natural language.

Such a set of rules is referred to as a *grammar.* A grammar should be able to prescribe or generate all the acceptable sentences of a language and be able to reject all the unacceptable sentences in the language. Besides rejecting such obvious nonsentences as the one given above, grammar must be able to reject such near misses as:

> The girls hits the boys.
> Did hit the girl the boys?
> The girl hit a boys.
> The boys were hit the girl.

The sentences above all contain *syntactic violations* (violations of sentence structure). That is, they are fairly meaningful but contain some mistakes in word combinations or word forms. Other nonsentences are possible in which the words are correct in form and syntactic position but their combination is nonsense. For instance:

> Colorless green ideas sleep furiously.
> Sincerity frightened the cat.

These constructions are called *anomalous sentences* and are said to contain *semantic violations* (violations of meaning). Still other sentences can be correct syntactically and semantically but be mispronounced. Such sentences are said to contain *phonological violations.* Consider this example:

> The Inspector opened his notebook.
> "Your name is Halcock, is't no?" he began.
> The butler corrected him.
> "H'alcock," he said, reprovingly.
> "H,a,double-l?" suggested the Inspector.
> "There is no h'aich in the name, young man. H'ay is the first letter, and there is h'only one h'ell." (Sayers, 1968, p. 73)

The butler, wanting to hide his Cockney dialect, which drops *h*'s, is systematically mispronouncing every word that begins with a vowel.

To account for the regularity of language, then, linguists need a grammar that will specify *phonology* (sound), *syntax* (structure), and *semantics* (meaning).

Linguistic Intuitions

Another feature that linguists want a grammar to explain is the *linguistic intuitions* of speakers of the language. Linguistic intuitions are judgments about the nature of linguistic utterances or about the relationships between linguistic utterances. Speakers of the language are often able to make these judgments without knowing how they do so. Among these linguistic intuitions are judgments about whether sentences are ill-formed and, if ill-formed, why. For instance, we can judge that some sentences are ill-formed because they have bad syntactic structure, and that other sentences are ill-formed because they lack meaning. Linguists require that a grammar capture this distinction and clearly express the reasons for it. Another kind of intuition is about *paraphrase.* A speaker of English will judge that the following two sentences are very similar in meaning, and hence are paraphrases:

> The girl hit the boy.
> The boy was hit by the girl.

Yet another kind of intuition is about *ambiguity.* The following sentence has two meanings:

> They are cooking apples.

This sentence can either mean that some people are cooking some apples or that the apples being referred to are for cooking. Moreover, speakers of the language can distinguish this type of ambiguity, which is called *structural ambiguity,* from *lexical ambiguity,* as in

> I am going to the bank.

where *bank* can refer either to a monetary institution or a riverbank. Lexical ambiguities arise when a word has two or more distinct meanings; structural ambiguities arise when an entire phrase or sentence has two or more meanings.

So, in summary, linguists strive to create grammars that (1) specify the nature of the well-formed sentence in a language; (2) specify which utterances are ill-formed and why; and (3) explain intuitions that speakers have about such things as paraphrase and ambiguity.

Competence versus Performance

Our everyday use of language does not always correspond to the prescriptions of linguistic theory. We generate sentences in conversation that, in a more reflective situation, we would judge to be ill-formed and unacceptable. We hesitate, repeat ourselves, stutter, and make slips of the tongue. We misunderstand the meaning of sentences. We hear sentences that are ambiguous but do not note their ambiguity.

Another complication is that linguistic intuitions are not always clear-cut. For instance, we find the linguist Lakoff (1971) telling us that the first sentence below is not acceptable but that the second is:

Tell John where the concert's this afternoon.
Tell John that the concert's this afternoon.

People are not always reliable in their judgments of such sentences and certainly do not always agree with Lakoff.

Considerations about the unreliability of human linguistic behavior and judgment led the linguist Noam Chomsky (1965) to make a distinction between *linguistic competence,* a person's abstract knowledge of the language, and *linguistic performance,* the actual application of that knowledge in speaking or listening. In Chomsky's view, the linguist's task is to develop a theory of competence; the psychologist's task is to develop a theory of performance.

The exact relationship between a theory of competence and a theory of performance is unclear and can be the subject of heated debates. Chomsky has argued that a theory of competence is central to performance — that our linguistic competence underlies our ability to use language, if indirectly. Others believe that the concept of linguistic competence is based on a rather unnatural activity (making linguistic judgments) and has very little to do with everyday language use.

Syntactic Formalisms

Phrase Structure

A great deal of emphasis in linguistics has been given to understanding the syntax of natural language. One central linguistic concept is *phrase structure.* Phrase-structure analysis is not only significant in linguistics, but is also very important to an understanding of language processing. Therefore, our coverage of this topic here is partially a preparation for material in the next chapter. Those of you who have had a certain kind of high school training in English will find the analysis of phrase structure to be similar to parsing exercises. For the rest of you, the analysis will be more novel.

The phrase structure of a sentence is the hierarchical division of the sentence into units called phrases. Consider this sentence:

The brave dog saved the drowning child.

If asked to divide this sentence into two major parts in the most natural way, most people would provide the following division:

(The brave dog)(saved the drowning child).

The parentheses distinguish the two separate parts. The two parts of the sentence correspond to what are traditionally called subject and predicate, or noun phrase and verb phrase. If asked to divide the second part, the verb phrase, further, most people would give

(The brave dog)(saved (the drowning child)).

Often analysis of a sentence is represented as an upside-down tree, as in Figure 11-1. In this phrase-structure tree, *sentence* points to its subunits, *noun phrase* and *verb phrase,* and each of these units points to its subunits.

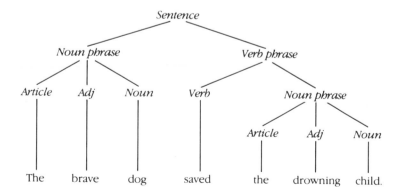

Figure 11-1. An example of the phrase structure of a sentence. The tree structure illustrates the hierarchical division of the sentence into phrases.

Eventually, the branches of the tree terminate in the individual words. Such tree-structure representations for surface structures are very common in linguistics. In fact, it is common to use the term *phrase structure* to refer to such tree structures.

An analysis of phrase structure can point up syntactic ambiguities. Consider again this sentence:

They are cooking apples.

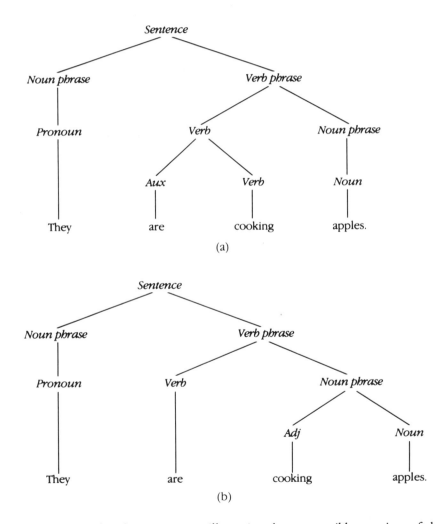

Figure 11-2. The phrase structures illustrating the two possible meanings of the ambiguous sentence *They are cooking apples:* (a) that those people (they) are cooking apples; (b) that those apples are for cooking.

Depending on the meaning, *cooking* is either part of the verb with *are* or part of the noun phrase with *apples*. Figure 11-2 illustrates the phrase structure for these two interpretations. In part (a) *cooking* is part of the verb, while in part (b) it is part of the noun phrase.

Rewrite Rules

Note that the various nodes in the trees showing phrase structure have meaningful labels, such as *sentence, noun phrase, verb phrase, verb, noun,* and *adj* (for *adjective*), which indicate the character of these sentence units, or constituents. Such labels can serve to form *rewrite rules* for actually generating sentences. Linguists formulate grammars for languages in terms of such rewrite rules. Table 11-1 consists of a set of rewrite rules indicating ways of rewriting these labels, or symbols. The symbol on the left can be rewritten as the symbols on the right. Thus, rule 1 says that *sentence* may be rewritten as *noun phrase* plus *verb phrase*. Rule 2A indicates that a noun phrase can be rewritten as an optional article, an optional adjective, and a noun. The parentheses indicate that the article and adjective are optional.

Table 11-1 *Rewrite Rules for Generating a Fragment of English*

	Symbol	Rewrite As
1.	Sentence	→ noun phrase + verb phrase
2A.	Noun phrase	→ (article) + (adj) + noun
2B.		→ pronoun
3A.	Verb phrase	→ verb + noun phrase
3B.		→ verb + prep phrase
4.	Prep phrase	→ preposition + noun phrase
5A.	Verb	→ aux + verb
5B.		→ hit, saved, cooking, danced
6.	Noun	→ dog, child, boy, girl, apples, river
7.	Article	→ the, a
8.	Adj	→ brave, drowning, cooking
9.	Pronoun	→ he, she, they
10.	Preposition	→ in, by
11.	Aux	→ was, were

Rule 2B indicates that another way to rewrite a noun phrase is as a pronoun. It is possible to derive a sentence through these rewrite rules. For instance, consider the following sequence:

$$Sentence \longrightarrow noun\ phrase + verb\ phrase \quad\quad (1)$$
$$\longrightarrow article + adj + noun + verb$$
$$+ prep\ phrase \quad\quad (2)$$
$$\longrightarrow article + adj + noun + verb$$
$$+ preposition + noun\ phrase \quad\quad (3)$$
$$\longrightarrow article + adj + noun + verb$$
$$+ preposition + article + noun \quad\quad (4)$$
$$\longrightarrow the + brave + boy + danced$$
$$+ in + the + river \quad\quad (5)$$

In line 1, we rewrote *sentence* as *noun phrase* plus *verb phrase* according to rewrite rule 1. In line 2, we rewrote *noun phrase* into *article* plus *adj* plus *noun* (according to rewrite rule 2A) and *verb phrase* into *verb* plus *prep phrase* (according to rule 3B). In line 3, we rewrote *prep phrase* into *preposition* plus *noun phrase* (according to rule 4). In line 4, we rewrote the *noun phrase* from line 3 into *article* plus *noun* (rule 2A). Finally, in line 5, we replaced each of the symbols with words according to rules 5B, 6, 7, 8, and 10.

The tree representation of the phrase structure of a sentence serves to illustrate derivation of the sentence through the rewrite rules. Figure 11-3 illustrates the phrase structure of the sentence derived in Table 11-1.

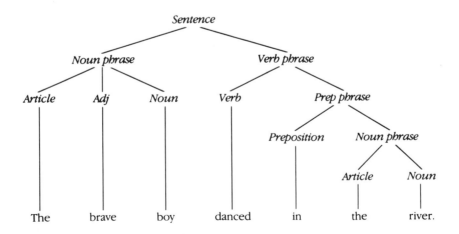

Figure 11-3. The phrase structure of the sentence *The brave boy danced in the river.* The branches in this tree derive from the rewrite rules in Table 11-1.

In such a tree structure, a symbol is connected below to the symbols that the rule rewrites into. For instance, the symbol *Verb phrase* is connected below to *Verb* and *Prep phrase,* which it rewrites into according to rule 3B.

A set of rewrite rules is referred to as a grammar. Such rules constitute one way of specifying the acceptable sentences of the language. As such they provide a means of achieving one important goal of linguistics, which is to devise a grammar that (1) generates all the acceptable sentences of the language, and (2) does not generate any unacceptable sentences. Can you find ways in which the simple set of rewrite rules in Table 11-1 fail to achieve these two criteria? Although linguists have come up with grammars that are much more complex and comprehensive than the one in Table 11-1, they have not yet come close to specifying a grammar that completely satisfies criteria 1 and 2 stated above. Many issues in the field remain unresolved, including whether these two goals are realistic.

Evidence for Phrase Structure in Speech.

There is abundant evidence that phrase structures play a key role in the processing of natural language. (In Chapter 12 we will examine the role phrase structures play in language comprehension.) When people produce a sentence they tend to generate it a phrase at a time. People tend to pause at the boundaries between large phrase units. For instance, although there were no tape recorders available in Lincoln's time one might guess he produced the first sentence of the Gettysburg Address with brief pauses at the end of each of the major phrases as indicated below:

> Four score and seven years ago (pause)
> our forefathers brought forth on this continent (pause)
> a new nation (pause)
> conceived in liberty (pause)
> and dedicated to the proposition (pause)
> that all men are created equal (pause)

Although Lincoln's speeches are not available for analysis, Boomer (1965) analyzed examples of spontaneous speech and found that pauses did occur more frequently at junctures between major phrases and that these pauses were longer than pauses at other locations. The average pause time at a grammatical juncture was 1.03 seconds, while the average within grammatical clauses was .75 seconds. This finding suggests that speakers tend to produce sentences a phrase at a time and often need to pause after one phrase to plan the next. Other researchers (Cooper & Paccia-Cooper, 1980; Grosjean, Grosjean, & Lane, 1979) have looked at subjects producing prepared sentences rather than spontaneous speech. The pauses of such subjects tend to be much shorter, around .2 seconds. Still the same pattern holds, with longer pauses at the major phrase boundaries.

As Figures 11-1 to 11-3 illustrate, there are multiple levels of phrases within phrases within phrases. What level do speakers choose for breaking up their sentence into pause units? Gee and Grosjean (1983) argue that speakers tend to choose the smallest level above the word that bundles together coherent semantic information. In English this tends to be noun phrases (e.g., *the young woman*), verbs plus pronouns (e.g., *will have been reading it*), and prepositional phrases (e.g., *in the house*).

Speech Errors

Other research has found evidence for phrase structure by looking at errors in speech. Maclay and Osgood (1959) analyzed spontaneous recordings of speech to determine whether speech is produced in phrase units. They found a number of speech errors which suggested that phrases do have a psychological reality. They found that when speakers repeated themselves or corrected themselves they tended to repeat or correct a whole phrase. For instance, the following is the kind of repeat that is found:

Turn on the heater/the heater switch.

And the pair below constitutes a common type of correction:

Turn on the stove/the heater switch.

In the preceding example, the noun phrase is repeated. In contrast, speakers do not provide repetitions in which part but not all of the verb phrase is repeated, such as:

Turn on the stove/on the heater switch.

Other kinds of speech errors also provide evidence for the psychological reality of constituents as major units of speech generation. For instance, some research has analyzed slips of the tongue in speech (Fromkin, 1971, 1973; Garrett, 1975). One kind of speech error is called a *spoonerism*, after the English clergyman William A. Spooner to whom are attributed some colossal and clever errors of speech. The following are among the errors of speech attributed to Spooner:

You have hissed all my mystery lectures.
I saw you fight a liar in the back quad; in fact, you have tasted the whole worm.
I assure you the insanitary spectre has seen all the bathrooms.
Easier for a camel to go through the knee of an idol.
The Lord is a shoving leopard to his flock.
Take the flea of my cat and heave it at the louse of my mother-in-law.

As illustrated above, spoonerisms involve exchanges of sound between words. There is every reason to suspect that the errors above were deliberate attempts at humor by Spooner. However, people do generate genuine spoonerisms, although they are seldom so funny.

By patient collecting, researchers have gathered a large set of errors made by friends and colleagues. Some of these involve simple sound anticipations and some involve sound exchanges as in spoonerisms:

> Take my bike → bake my bike [an anticipation]
> night life → nife lite [an exchange]
> beast of burden → burst of beaden [an exchange]

One that gives me particular difficulty is

> coin toss → toin coss

The first error listed above is an example of an anticipation, where an early phoneme is changed to a later phoneme. The others are examples of exchanges in which two phonemes switch. The interesting feature about these kinds of errors is that they tend to occur within a single phrase rather than across phrases. So, we are unlikely to find the following anticipation:

1. The dancer took my bike. → The bancer took my bike.

where an anticipation occurs between subject and object noun phrases. Also unlikely are sound exchanges where an exchange occurs between the initial prepositional phrase and the final noun phrase, as in

2. At night John lost his life. → At nife John lost his lite.

Another kind of speech error consistent with the phrase model is called the *stranded morpheme*. (A morpheme is a minimum unit of meaning, such as *trunk,* which indicates an object, or –*ed,* which indicates past tense.) Some examples are:

> I'm not in the read for mooding.
> She's already trunked two packs.
> Fancy getting your model renosed.

This type of error exhibits two interesting features. First, like the other errors, this type tends to occur within a phrase boundary. Second, the content morphemes, such as *trunk* and *pack,* are always the ones that are switched. The functional morphemes, such as *ing, ed,* and *s,* stay put. Thus, we do not find such errors as:

> I'm not in the mooding for read.

The phenomenon of the stranded morpheme seems to suggest that speakers first decide on the pattern they want to produce; for example, a phrase such as:

> noun for verb + ing

In the process of filling in the specific words of the pattern, however, the speaker switches the noun and verb.

Transformations

A phrase structure describes a sentence hierarchically as pieces within larger pieces. There are certain types of linguistic constructions that some linguists think violate this strictly hierarchical structure. Consider the following pair of sentences:

1. The dog is chasing Bill down the street.

2. Whom is the dog chasing down the street?

In sentence 1, *Bill,* the object of the chasing, occurs as part of the verb phrase. On the other hand, in sentence 2, *whom,* the object of the verb phrase, occurs at the beginning of the sentence. The object is no longer part of the verb phrase structure to which it would seem to belong. Linguists propose that, formally, such questions are generated by starting with a phrase structure which has the object *whom* in the verb phrase, as in:

> 3. The dog is chasing whom down the street?

This is a somewhat strange sentence but with the right questioning intonation of the *whom* it can be made to sound reasonable. In some languages, such as Japanese, it is normal to leave the interrogative pronoun in the verb phrase as in sentence 3. However, in English the proposal is that there is a movement transformation which moves the *whom* into its more normal position. Note that this is a linguistic proposal as to the formal structure of language and may not describe the actual process of producing the question.

Such a transformation can also operate on more complicated sentences. For instance, we can apply it to sentences of the form:

> 4. John believes that the dog is chasing Bill down the road.

The corresponding question forms are:

> 5. John believes that the dog is chasing whom down the street?
>
> 6. Whom does John believe that the dog is chasing down the street?

Sentence 5 is strange even with a questioning intonation for *whom* but still linguists believe that sentence 6 is transformationally derived from it, even though we would never produce sentence 5.

One of the intriguing issues to linguists is that there seem to be real limitations on just what things can be moved by transformations. For instance, consider the following set of sentences:

> 7. John believes the fact that the dog is chasing Bill down the road.
>
> 8. John believes the fact that the dog is chasing whom down the road?
>
> 9. Whom does John believes the fact that the dog is chasing down the road?

As sentence 7 illustrates, the basic sentence form is acceptable, but one cannot move *whom* from question form 8 to produce question form 9. Sentence 9 just sounds very bizarre. We will return later to the issue of what restrictions there are on movement transformations.

In contrast to the abundant evidence for phrase structure in language processing, the evidence is very poor that people actually compute anything analogous to transformations in understanding or producing sentences. It remains very much an open question how people process such transformationally derived sentences.

The Relationship Between Language and Thought

The Behaviorist Proposal

We have now reviewed the structure of language as it is seen by the linguist. The question that naturally arises is what effect does the structure of language have on cognition. A wide variety of proposals have been put forth as to the connection between language and thought. The strongest was advanced by John B. Watson, the father of behaviorism. It was one of the tenets of Watson's behaviorism (Watson, 1930) that no such thing as internal mental activity existed.

All humans did, Watson argued, was to emit responses that had been conditioned to stimuli. This radical proposal, which, as noted in Chapter 1, held sway in America for some time, seemed to fly in the face of the abundant evidence that humans can engage in thinking behavior (e.g., do mental arithmetic) which involves no response emission. To deal with this obvious counter, Watson proposed that thinking was just subvocal speech, that when people were engaged in such "mental" activities they were really talking to themselves. Hence, Watson's proposal was that a very important component of thought was simply subvocal speech. (The philosopher Herbert Feigl once said that Watson "made up his windpipe that he had no mind.")

This proposal was a stimulus for a research program that engaged itself in taking recordings to see if evidence could be found for subvocal activity of the speech apparatus during thinking. Indeed, often when a subject is engaged in thought it is possible to get recordings of subvocal speech activity. However, the more important observation is that in some situations people engage in various silent thinking tasks with no detectable vocal activity. However, this finding did not upset Watson. He claimed that we think with our whole bodies—for instance, with our arms. He cited the fascinating evidence that deaf mutes actually make signs while asleep. (Speaking people who have done a lot of communication in sign language also sign while asleep.)

The decisive experiment addressing Watson's hypothesis was performed by Smith, Brown, Toman, and Goodman (1947). They used a curare derivative that paralyzed the entire human musculature. Smith was the subject for the experiment and had to be kept alive by means of an artificial respirator. Because his entire musculature was completely paralyzed, it was impossible for him to engage in subvocal speech or any other body movement. Nonetheless, under curare, Smith was able to observe what was going on around him, comprehend speech, remember these events, and think about them. Thus, it seems clear that thinking can proceed in the absence of any muscle activity. For our current purposes, the relevant additional observation is that thought is not just implicit speech but is truly an internal, nonmotor activity.

Additional evidence that thought is not to be equated with language comes from the research on propositional memories that was reviewed in Chapter 5. There we discussed that people tend to retain not the exact words of a linguistic communication, but rather some more abstract representation of the meaning of the communication. Thought should be identified, at least in part, with this abstract, nonverbal propositional code.

Still more information comes from the occasional cases of individuals who have no apparent language at all but who certainly give evidence of being able to think. Also, it seems hard to claim that nonverbal animals such as apes are unable to think. Recall, for instance, the problem-solving exploits of Sultan in Chapter 8. It is always hard to determine the exact character of the "thought processes" of nonverbal subjects and how these differ from the thought processes of verbal subjects, since there is no language with which subjects can be interrogated. Thus, the apparent dependence of thought on language may be an illusion which derives from the fact that it is hard to obtain evidence about thought without using language.

The Whorfian Hypothesis of Linguistic Determinism

Linguistic determinism is the claim that language determines or strongly influences the way a person thinks or perceives the world. This proposal is much weaker than Watson's position, because it does not claim that language and thought are identical. The hypothesis has been advanced by a good many linguists but has been most strongly associated with Whorf (1956). Whorf was quite an unusual character himself. He was trained as a chemical engineer at MIT, spent his life working for the Hartford Fire Insurance Company, and studied North American Indian languages as a hobby. He was very impressed by the fact that different languages emphasize in their structure rather different aspects of the world. He believed that these emphases must have a great influence on the way language speakers think about the world. For instance, he claimed that Eskimos have many different words for snow, each of which refers to snow in a different state (wind-driven, packed, slushy, and so on), whereas English speakers have only a single word for snow.[1] Many other examples exist at the vocabulary level: The Hanunoo people in the Philippines supposedly have 92 names for different varieties of rice. The Arabic language has many different ways of naming camels. Whorf felt that such a rich variety of terms would cause the speaker of the language to perceive the world differently from a person who had only a single word for a particular category.

Deciding how to evaluate the Whorfian hypothesis is very tricky. Nobody would be surprised to learn that Eskimos know more about snow than average English speakers. After all, snow is a more important part of their life experience. The question is whether their language has any effect on the Eskimos' perception of snow over and above the effect of experience. If speakers of English went through the Eskimo life experience, would their perception of snow be any different than that of the Eskimo-language speakers? (Indeed, ski bums have a life experience that involves a great deal of exposure to snow and have a great deal of knowledge about snow.)

One fairly well researched test of the issue involves color words. English has 11 *basic color words*—black, white, red, green, yellow, blue, brown, purple, pink, orange, and gray—a relatively large number. These words are called basic color words because they are short and are used frequently, in contrast to such terms as saffron, turquoise, or magenta. At the other extreme is the language of the Dani, a Stone Age agricultural people of Indonesian New Guinea. This language has just two basic color terms: *mili* for dark, cold hues and *mola* for bright, warm hues. If the categories in language determine perception, the Dani should perceive

---

[1]Recently there have been challenges to Whorf's claims about the richness of Eskimo vocabulary for snow (Martin, 1986; Pullman, 1989). In general, there is a feeling that Whorf exaggerated the variety of words in various languages.

color in a less refined manner than English speakers do. The relevant question is whether this speculation is true.

Speakers of English, at least, judge a certain color within the range referred to by each basic color term to be the best — for instance, the best red, the best blue, and so on (see Berlin and Kay, 1969). Each of the 11 basic color terms in English appears to have one generally agreed upon best color, called a *focal color*. English speakers find it easier to process and remember focal colors than nonfocal colors (e.g., Brown & Lenneberg, 1954). The interesting question is whether the special cognitive capacity for identifying focal colors evolved because English speakers have special words for these colors. If so, this would be a clear case of language influencing thought.

To test whether the special processing of focal colors was an instance of language influencing thought, Rosch (she has published some of this work under her former name, Heider) performed an important series of experiments on the Dani. The point was to see whether the Dani processed focal colors differently than English speakers. One experiment (Rosch, 1973) compared the ability of the Dani to learn nonsense names for focal versus nonfocal colors. English speakers find it easier to learn arbitrary names for focal colors. Dani subjects also found it easier to learn arbitrary names for focal colors than for nonfocal colors even though they have no names for these colors. In another experiment (Heider, 1972), subjects were shown a color chip for 5 seconds; 30 seconds after the presentation ended they were required to select the color from among 160 color chips. English speakers perform better at this task when the chip they are to remember is a focal color rather than a nonfocal color. The Dani also perform better at this task for focal colors.

Thus, it appears that despite the differences in their linguistic terminology for colors, the Dani and English speakers see colors in much the same way. It appears that the 11 focal colors are processed specially by all people regardless of language. In fact, some facts about the physiology of color vision suggest that these focal colors are specially processed by the visual system (de Valois & Jacobs, 1968). The fact that many languages develop basic color terms for just these 11 colors can be seen as an instance of thought determining language.

Another test of the Whorfian hypothesis was performed by Carroll and Casagrande (1958). The Navaho language requires different verb forms depending on the nature of the thing being acted upon, particularly regarding its shape, rigidity, and material. Carroll and Casagrande presented Navaho-speaking children with three objects, such as a yellow stick, a piece of blue rope, and a yellow rope. The children had to say which of the two objects went with the third. Since Navaho requires that a different verb form be used for sticks (rigid) than ropes (flexible), the experimenters predicted that the Navaho-speaking subjects would tend to match the ropes and not match on color. They found that Navaho-speaking children preferred shape and that English-speaking Navaho children preferred color. However, in another study they found that English-speaking Boston children exhibited an even greater tendency to match on the basis of form. It seems that the Boston children's experience with toys (for which shape and rigidity are critical) was more important than the Navaho-language experience, although the language experience may have had some effect.

To conclude, the evidence tends not to support the hypothesis that language has any significant effect on the way we think or on the way we perceive the world. It is certainly true that language can influence us (or else there would be little point in writing this book), but its effect is to communicate ideas, not to determine the kinds of ideas we can think about.

Does Language Depend on Thought?

The alternative possibility is that the structure of language is influenced by thought. Aristotle argued 2500 year ago that the categories of thought determined the categories of language. There are some reasons for believing that he was correct, but most of these reasons were not available to Aristotle. So, although the hypothesis has been around for 2500 years, we have better reasons for holding it today.

There are numerous reasons to suppose that humans' ability to think (i.e., to engage in nonlinguistic cognitive activity such as remembering and problem solving) appeared earlier evolutionarily and occurs sooner developmentally than the ability to use language. Many species of animals without language appear to be capable of a complex cognition. Children, before they are effective at using their language, give clear evidence of relatively complex cognition. If we accept that thought occurred before language, it seems natural to suppose that language is a tool whose function is to communicate thought. It is generally true that tools are shaped to fit the objects on which they must operate. Analogously, it seems reasonable to suppose that language has been shaped to fit the thoughts it must communicate. In addition to general arguments for the view that language depends on thought, a number of pieces of evidence to support the notion have been generated in cognitive psychology and related fields. I will review a few of the lines of evidence.

We saw in Chapter 5 that propositional structures constituted a very important type of knowledge structure in representing information both derived from language and derived from pictures. Every language has a phrase structure. The basic phrase units of a language tend to convey propositions. For instance, *the tall boy* conveys the proposition that the boy is tall. This phenomenon itself—the existence of a linguistic structure, the *phrase,* designed to accommodate a thought structure, the *proposition*—seems to be a clear example of the dependence of language on thought.

Another example of the way in which thought shapes language comes from Rosch's research on focal colors. As stated earlier, the human visual system is maximally sensitive to certain colors. As a consequence, languages have special, short, high-frequency words with which to designate these colors. We noted that in English these basic color words are black, white, red, yellow, green, blue, brown, purple, pink, orange, and gray. Thus, the visual system has determined how the English language divides up the color space.

We find additional evidence for the influence of thought on language when we consider word order. Every language has a preferred word order for expressing subject (S), verb (V), and object (O). Consider this sentence, which exhibits the preferred word order in English:

Lynne petted the Labrador.

English is referred to as SVO language. In a study of a diverse sample of the world's languages, Greenberg (1963) found that only four of the six possible orders of S, V, and O are used in natural languages, and one of these four orders is rare. Below are the six possible word orders and the frequency with which each order occurs in the world's languages (the percentages are from Ultan, 1969):

SOV	44 percent	VOS	2 percent
SVO	35 percent	OVS	0 percent
VSO	19 percent	OSV	0 percent

The important feature is that the subject almost always precedes the object. This order makes good sense when we think about cognition. An action starts with the agent and then affects the object. Therefore, it is natural that the subject of a sentence, when it reflects its agency, occurs first.

The Uniqueness of Language

We have considered the possibility that thought might depend on language and the possibility that language might depend on thought. There is a third logical possibility, which is that language and thought might be independent. Chomsky (1980) has advanced this position and more recently it has been given a very articulate development by the philosopher and psychologist Fodor (1983). This is known as the *modularity position* for it holds that language is a module which functions independent of the rest of cognition. The modularity hypothesis has turned out to be a major dividing issue in the field with different researchers lining up in support or in opposition. Two domains of research are relevant to evaluating the modularity proposal. One concerns language acquisition. Here the issue is whether language is acquired according to unique learning principles or whether it is acquired like other cognitive skills. The second domain is language comprehension. Here the issue is whether major aspects of language processing occur without utilization of any general cognitive processes. We will discuss some of the issues with respect to comprehension in the next chapter. In this chapter we will look at what is known about language acquisition. We will first overview the general course of language acquisition by young children and then turn to the implications for the uniqueness of language.

Child Language Acquisition

Having watched my two children acquire a language, I understand how easy it is to lose sight of what a remarkable feat it is. Days and weeks go by with little apparent change in their linguistic abilities. Progress seems slow. However, something remarkable is happening. With very little and often no deliberate instruction, children by the time they reach age 10 have accomplished what generations of Ph.D. linguists have not. They have internalized all the major rules of a natural language, and there appear to be thousands of such rules with subtle interactions. No linguist in a lifetime has been able to formulate a grammar for any language that will identify all and only the grammatical sentences. However, we as children internalize such a grammar. Unfortunately, our knowledge of the grammar of our language is not something that we can articulate. It is procedural knowledge (see Chapter 8), which we can only display in using the language.

The process by which children acquire a language has some characteristic features that seem to hold no matter what their native language is (and languages around the world differ in marked ways): Children are notoriously noisy creatures from birth. At first, the variety in their sounds is quite impoverished. Their vocalizations consist almost totally of an "ah" sound. In the months following birth, children's vocal apparatus matures and by the end of the first year they have articulated a great variety of speech sounds, including some that may not be part of the language spoken by their linguistic community. At about 6 months a change takes place in children's utterances. They begin to engage in what is called babbling. Babbling consists of generating a rich variety of speech sounds with interesting intonation patterns. However, the sounds are totally meaningless.

It is at about a year that the first words appear, always a point of great excitement to the parents. The very first words are there only to the ears of very sympathetic parents and caretakers but soon the child develops a considerable repertoire of words recognizable to the untrained ear and which the child uses effectively to make requests and to describe what is happening. The early words are concrete and refer to the here and now. Among my children's first words were Mommy, Daddy, Rogers (for Mister Rogers), cheese, puter (for computer), eat, hi, bye, go, and hot. One remarkable feature of this stage is that the utterances are all one-word utterances. Even though children know many words, they never put them together to make multiple-word utterances. Children's use of single words is quite complex. They often use a single word to communicate a whole thought. This kind of speech is called *holophrastic*. Children will also overextend their words. Thus, the word *dog* might be used to refer to any furry four-legged animal.

The one-word stage, which lasts about 6 months, is followed by a stage in which children will put two words together. I can still remember our excitement as parents when our son said his first two-word utterance at 18 months — "more gee," which meant for him "more brie" — he was a connoisseur of cheese. Table 11-2 illustrates some of the typical two-

Table 11-2 *Two-word Utterances*

Kendall swim	pillow fell
doggie bark	Kendall book
see Kendall	Papa door
writing book	Kendall turn
sit pool	towel bed
shoe off	there cow

From Bowerman, 1973.

word utterances generated by children at this stage. All their utterances are one or two words. There are no three-word utterances, and this is interesting because there is no corresponding three-word stage. Once their utterances extend beyond two words one can find many different lengths of utterances. The two-word utterances reflect about a dozen or so semantic relationships, including agent-action, agent-object, action-object, object-location, object-attribute, possessor-object, negation-object, and negation-event. The order in which they place these words usually corresponds to one of the orders that would be correct in adult speech in the children's linguistic community.

Even when children leave the two-word stage and speak in sentences ranging from three to eight words, their speech retains a peculiar quality, which is sometimes referred to as telegraphic. Table 11-3 contains some of these longer multiword utterances. They speak somewhat like one would in a telegraph, omitting unimportant function words like *the* and *is*. In fact, it is rare to find in early child speech any utterance that would be considered to be a well-formed sentence. Yet it is out of this beginning that grammatical sentences eventually appear. One might have expected to see children learn to speak some kinds of sentences perfectly, then learn to speak other kinds of sentences perfectly, and so on. However, it seems that children start out speaking all kinds of sentences and all of them imperfectly. Their language development is not characterized by learning more kinds of sentences but by their sentences becoming gradually better approximations to adult sentences.

Besides the missing words, there are other dimensions in which children's early speech is incomplete. A classic example of this concerns the rules for pluralization in English. Initially, children do not distinguish in their speech between singular and plural, using a singular form for both. Then they will learn the add *s* rule for pluralization but overextend it, producing "foots" or even "feets." Gradually, they learn the pluraliza-

Table 11-3 *Multiword Utterances*

Put truck window	My balloon pop
Want more grape juice	Doggie bit me mine boot
Sit Adam chair	That Mommy nose right there
Mommy put sock	She's wear that hat
No I see truck	I like pick dirt up firetruck
Adam fall toy	No pictures in there

From Brown, 1973.

tion rules for the irregular words. This goes on into adulthood. Cognitive scientists had to learn that the plural of schema was schemata (a fact I saved the reader from having to deal with when schemas were discussed in Chapter 5).

Another dimension in which children have to perfect their language concerns word order. They have particular difficulties with those aspects of language that involve transformational movements of terms from their natural position in the phrase structure (see the discussion on pp. 338–340). So, for instance, there is a point where children form questions without moving the verb auxiliary from the verb phrase:

What me think?

What the doggie have?

Even later when children's spontaneous speech seems to be well formed, they will display errors in comprehension that reveal they have not yet captured all the subtleties in their language. For instance, Chomsky (1970) found that children had difficulty comprehending sentences such as "John promised Bill to leave," interpreting Bill as the one who leaves. The verb *promise* is unusual in this respect—for instance, compare "John told Bill to leave," which children will properly interpret.

By the time children are 6, they have mastered most of their language although they continue picking up details at least until 10. In that time they have learned tens of thousands of special case rules and tens of thousands of words. Studies of the rate of word acquisition by children estimate that they are learning more than five words a day (Carey, 1978; Clark, 1983). A natural language requires more knowledge to be acquired for mastery than any of the domains of expertise we considered in Chapter 9. Of course, children also put an enormous amount of time into the language acquisition process—easily 10,000 hours must have been spent practicing speaking before a child is 6.

An important difference between children's first language acquisition and acquisition of many skills (including typical second language acquisition) is that a child receives little if any instruction. Thus, the child's task is one of *inducing* (see the discussion in Chapter 10) the structure of natural language from listening to parents, caretakers, and older children. In addition to not receiving any direct instruction, the child does not get much information about what are not correct forms in natural language. Many parents do not correct their children's speech at all and those that do correct their children's speech appear to do so without any effect. This lack of negative information is puzzling to theorists of natural language acquisition. We have seen that children's early speech is full of errors. If they are never told that about their errors, why do children ever abandon these incorrect ways of speaking and adopt the correct forms?

The very fact that young children accomplish such a difficult task so successfully has been used to argue that the way we learn language must in some way be different than the way we learn other cognitive skills. It is pointed out that children learn their first language successfully at a point in development when their general intellectual abilities are still weak.

A Critical Period for Language Acquisition

A related argument has to do with the claim that young children appear to acquire a second language much faster than older children or adults. It is claimed that there is a certain critical period, from 2 to about 11 years of age, when it is easiest to learn a language. Until recently, the claim that children learn second languages more readily was based on informal observations of children of various ages and of adults in new linguistic communities; for example, when families are moved to a foreign country in response to a corporate assignment or when immigrants come to a country permanently. Young children are said to acquire a facility to get along in the new language more quickly than older children or adults. However, there are a great many differences among adults versus the older children versus younger children in terms of amount of linguistic exposure, type of exposure (e.g., whether stocks, history, or marbles are being discussed), and willingness to try to learn (McLaughlin, 1978; Nida, 1971). In careful studies in which situations have been selected that controlled for these factors, a positive relationship is exhibited between children's ages and language development (Ervin-Tripp, 1974). That is, older children (greater than 11 years) learn faster than younger children.

While older children and adults may learn a new language more rapidly than younger children initially, they seem not to acquire the same level of final mastery of the fine points of language, such as the phonology and morphology (Lieberman, 1984; Newport, 1986). For instance, the ability to speak a second language without an accent severely deteriorates with age. An interesting study of first language acquisition has been performed by Newport and Supalla (1987). They looked at the acquisition of American sign language, one of the few languages that is acquired as a first language in adolescence or adulthood. Deaf children of speaking parents are sometimes not exposed to sign language until late in life and consequently acquire no language in their early years. Adults who acquire sign language have a poorer mastery of it than children. In summary, while it is not true that language learning is best for the youngest, it is true that the greatest eventual mastery of the fine points of language will be achieved by those who start youngest.

Lenneberg's (1967) observations about recovery from traumatic aphasias (aphasia is a loss of language function) offer other evidence that an early critical period does exist for language acquisition. Damage to the left hemisphere of the brain often results in aphasia. Children who suffer such damage before the age of 11 appear to have a 100 percent chance of recovering language function. For older aphasics recovery is 60 percent at best.

As we reviewed in Chapter 2, considerable evidence (e.g., Gazzaniga, 1967) suggests that the left hemisphere is specialized in the adult for language function and other symbolic, analytic functions, while the right hemisphere is specialized for nonanalytic, wholistic functions such as art appreciation. This process of the specialization of the hemispheres is referred to *lateralization.* Much of it takes place after birth. Lenneberg argued for a causal connection between lateralization and loss of ability to recover from aphasias. He claimed that this lateralization was complete by about puberty. Thus, he argued, before puberty the brain had not specialized, and in aphasics the right hemisphere could take over the language functions of the left hemisphere. After puberty and lateralization it was much harder for the now specialized right hemisphere to take over language function. This line of evidence appeared to indicate that the ability to acquire language is especially programmed as a phase of our neural development, a suggestion that is certainly consistent with the view that language is a unique cognitive ability.

It appears, however, that Lenneberg considerably overestimated the period during which lateralization of the brain takes place. More recent evidence (e.g., Kinsbourne & Smith, 1974; Krashen & Harshman, 1972) has indicated that lateralization is complete somewhere between ages 2 and 5. Children show 100 percent recovery from aphasias after age 5. Thus, loss of ability to recover from aphasias does not seem to be related to lateralization.

Language Universals

Chomsky (1965) has argued that special mechanisms underlie the acquisition of language. Specifically, his claim is that the number of formal possibilities for a natural language is so great that learning the language would simply be impossible unless we possessed some innate information about the possible forms of natural human languages. It is possible to prove formally that Chomsky is correct in his claim. While the formal analysis is beyond the scope of this book, an analogy might help. In Chomsky's view, the problem that child-learners face is to discover the grammar of their language when given instances of utterances of the language. The task can be compared to trying to find a matching sock from a pile of socks. One can use various features of the sock in hand to determine if any particular sock in the pile was the matching one. If the pile of socks was big enough and the socks were similar enough, this would prove an impossible task. Likewise, enough formally possible grammars are similar enough to each other to make language learning impossible. Thus, since language learning obviously occurs, according to Chomsky we must have special, innate knowledge that allows us to powerfully restrict the number of possible grammars we have to consider. In the sock analogy, the effect would be knowing ahead of time which part of the pile to inspect.

Chomsky proposes that *language universals* exist which limit the possible characteristics of a natural language and a natural grammar. He assumes that children can learn a natural language because they possess innate knowledge of these language universals. A language that violated these universals would simply be unlearnable. This means that there are hypothetical languages which no humans could learn. Languages that humans can learn are referred to as *natural languages.*

As noted above, we can prove formally that Chomsky's assertion is correct — that is, that constraints on the possible form of a natural language exist. However, the critical issue is whether these constraints reflect any linguistic-specific knowledge on children's part, or whether they simply reflect general cognitive constraints on learning mechanisms. Chomsky would argue that the constraints are language specific. It is this claim that is open to serious question. Stated as a question the issue is: Are the constraints on the form of natural languages universals of language or universals of cognition?

In speaking of language universals, Chomsky is concerned with a competence grammar. Recall that a competence analysis is concerned with an abstract specification of what a speaker knows about a language; in contrast, a performance analysis is concerned with the way a speaker uses language. Thus, Chomsky is claiming that children possess innate constraints about the types of phrase structures and transformations that might be found in a natural language. Because of the abstract, non-performance-based-character of these purported universals, evaluating Chomsky's claims about their existence has proven very difficult.

Although languages can be quite different from one another, some clear uniformities, or near-uniformities, exist. For instance, as we saw earlier, virtually no language favors the word order subject-after-object. However, as we noted, this constraint (and many other limits on language form) appears to have a cognitive explanation.

Often, the uniformities among languages seem so natural that we do not realize that other possibilities might exist. One such language universal is that adjectives occur near the nouns they modify. Thus, we translate *The brave woman hit the cruel man* into French as

> La femme brave a frappé l'homme cruel

and not as

> La femme cruel a frappé l'homme brave

although a language in which the adjective beside the subject noun modified the object noun and vice versa would be logically possible. However, it is clear that such a language design would be absurd in terms of its cognitive demands. It would require that listeners hold the adjectives from the beginning of the sentence until the noun at the end. No natural language has this perverse structure. If it really needed showing, I have shown with artificial languages that adult subjects were unable to learn such a language (Anderson, 1978b).

The A-over-A Constraint

There are a set of peculiar constraints on movement transformations that have been used to argue for the existence of linguistic universals. One of the more extensively discussed of these is the *A-over-A constraint*. Compare sentence 1 with sentence 2:

1. Which woman did John meet who knows the senator?

2. Which senator did John meet the woman who knows?

Linguists would consider sentence 1 to be acceptable but not sentence 2. Sentence 1 can be derived by a transformation from sentence 3 below. This transformation moves *which woman* forward.

3. John met which woman who knows the senator?

4. John met the woman who knows which senator?

Sentence 2 can be derived by a similar transformation operating on *which senator* in sentence 4, but apparently such a transformation cannot move a noun phrase like *which senator* if it is embedded within another noun phrase (in this case, *which senator* is part of the clause modifying *the woman* and so is part of the noun phrase associated with *the woman*). Transformations can move deeply embedded nouns if these nouns are not in clauses modifying other nouns. So, for instance, sentence 5, which is acceptable, is derived transformationally from sentence 6:

5. Which senator does Mary believe that Bill said that John likes?

6. Mary believes that Bill said that John likes which senator.

Thus, we see that there is a very arbitrary constraint on the transformation that forms which-questions. It can apply to any embedded noun unless that noun is part of another noun phrase. The arbitrariness of this constraint makes it hard to imagine how a child would ever figure it out—unless the child already knew it as a universal of language. Certainly the child is never explicitly told this fact about language.

The existence of such constraints on the form of language certainly offers a challenge to any theory of language acquisition. They are so peculiar that it is hard to imagine how they could be learned unless the child were especially prepared to deal with them.

Parameter Setting

With all this discussion about language universals, one might get the impression that all languages are basically alike. Far from it. On many dimensions the languages of the world are radically different. There are some abstract properties, such as the A-over-A constraint, they might have in common but there are many properties on which they differ. We have already mentioned how different languages prefer different orders for subject, verb, and object. Languages also differ in how strict they are about word order. English is very strict but other languages, such as Finnish, allow people to say their sentences with almost any word order they choose. There are languages that do not mark verbs for tense and languages that do mark verbs for the flexibility of the thing being acted upon.

Another example of a difference which proves to be interesting is that some languages, such as Italian or Spanish, are what are called "pro-drop" languages: they allow one to optionally drop the pronoun when it appears in the subject position. Thus, while in English we would say, "I go to the cinema tonight," Italians can say, "Vado al cinema stasera" and Spaniards "Voy al cine esta noche"—in both cases just starting with the verb and omitting the first-person pronoun. It has been argued that "pro-drop" is a parameter on which natural languages vary and, while children cannot be born knowing whether their language is pro-drop or not, they can be born knowing it is one way or the other. Thus, knowledge that the pro-drop parameter exists is one of the universals of natural language.

Knowledge of a parameter like pro-drop is useful because a number of features are determined by it. For instance, if a language is not pro-drop it requires what are called expletive pronouns. In English, a non-pro-drop language, the expletive pronouns are *it* and *there* when they are used in sentences such as "It is raining" or "There is no money." English requires these rather semantically empty pronouns since by definition it cannot have empty slots in the subject position. Pro-drop languages such as Spanish and Italian lack such empty pronouns because they are not needed.

Hyams (1986) has argued that children starting to learn any language, including English, will treat it as a pro-drop language and optionally drop pronouns even though this may not be correct in the adult language. They will also not use expletive pronouns even when they are part of the adult language. When children in a non-pro-drop language start using expletive pronouns they simultaneously stop optionally dropping pronouns in the subject position. Hyams argues that this is the point at which they learn that their language is not a pro-drop language.

It is argued that much of the variability among natural languages can be accommodated by setting a hundred or so parameters such as the pro-drop parameter and that a major part of learning a language is learning the setting of these parameters (of course, there is a lot more to be learned than just this—for instance, an enormous vocabulary). This parameter setting view of language acquisition is new, poorly worked out, and controversial. Nonetheless, it provides us with the clearest picture to date of how a child may be prepared to learn a language with innate, language-specific knowledge.

The Uniqueness of Language: A Summary

With respect to the issue of whether language is really a system different from other human cognitive systems, it is a fair summary to say that the jury is still out. In my opinion, the status of language is shaping up to be a major issue for cognitive psychology. The issue will be resolved by empirical and theoretical efforts more detailed than those reviewed in this chapter. The ideas here have served to define the context for the investigation. The next chapter will review the current state of our knowledge about the details of language comprehension. Careful experimental research on such topics will finally resolve the question of the uniqueness of language.

Remarks and Suggested Readings

A number of introductions to linguistics are available. These include Akmajian, Demers, and Harnish (1984), Radford (1988), and Sells (1985). The recent work of the linguist Noam Chomsky can be found in his 1980, 1981, and 1986 books. For a description of an alternative linguistic theory read the book edited by Bresnan (1981), which contains a series of papers putting forth the lexicalist position.

There are a number of textbooks on the psychology of language, sometimes called psycholinguistics. These include Cairns and Cairns (1976); Clark and Clark (1977); Fodor, Bever, and Garrett (1974); Foss and Hakes (1978); and Glucksberg and Danks (1975). A great deal of research on language has been performed in artificial intelligence. Charniak and Wilks (1976) provide an introduction to some of this work. A more recent book is Winograd (1983).

Roger Brown has done a great deal of research on child language acquisition; much of it is reviewed in his 1973 book. Other reviews of first language acquisition include deVilliers and deVilliers (1978) and Maratsos (1983). McLaughlin (1978) provides a review of research on second language acquisition. MacWhinney (1987) has edited a book describing a range of views on the nature of language acquisition. Wexler and Culicover (1980) is one effort to develop a theory of language acquisition that depends on a set of language-specific assumptions. Pinker (1984) contains a different language-specific theory of language acquisition. Roeper and Williams (1987) contains a series of articles on the parameter setting approach to language acquisition. Anderson (1983) develops a language-learning model based on general learning principles. Rumelhart and McClelland (1986) provide a model of language learning based on neural, connectionist principles, as described in Chapter 2. Pinker and Prince (1988) have written a critique of this work.

Language Use: Comprehension

Summary

1. Comprehension can be analyzed into three stages: perception, parsing, and utilization. *Perception* concerns translation from sound to a word representation. *Parsing* concerns translation from the word representation to a meaning representation. *Utilization* concerns the use to which the comprehender puts the meaning of the message.

2. The comprehender parses a sentence by analyzing it into phrases, or constituents, and interpreting the meaning of each constituent. This process can be described by productions whose conditions describe constituent patterns and whose actions place meaning interpretations in memory.

3. As each word is processed comprehenders try to extract as much as they can from that word. They do not wait until the end of a phrase before trying to understand it.

4. Comprehenders combine cues from the syntax of the sentence, the meaning of words, and the context to interpret a sentence.

5. Comprehenders tend to select just one meaning for ambiguous words and phrases. Consequently, they have to reanalyze the clause if later information indicates that the original choice was wrong.

6. Important parts of the utilization process involve embellishing what is asserted with information that can be inferred and identifying the reference of noun phrases and pronouns.

7. Linguistic units larger than sentences, such as paragraphs and texts, are structured hierarchically according to certain relations. Narrative structures are also organized according to causal relationships. Information higher in a text structure tends to be better recalled than information lower in the structure. Comprehension of a text depends critically on the perceiver's ability to identify the hierarchical and causal structures that organize it.

8. The output of the comprehension process is represented as a set of propositions that encode the information in the text and inferences made from the text. A major limitation on comprehension is that only a few propositions can be held active in working memory at one time.

A favorite device in science fiction is the computer or robot that can understand and speak language—whether evil, like HAL in *2001,* or beneficial, like C3PO in *Star Wars.* Workers in artificial intelligence have been trying to develop computers that understand and generate language. Some progress is being made, but it is clear from current research on language that actually inventing a language-processing machine will be a monumental achievement. An enormous amount of knowledge and intelligence underlies the successful use of language. This chapter will look at language use and, in particular, language comprehension in distinction to language production. In choosing this focus we are choosing to look where the light is—a great deal more is known about language comprehension than language production.

In discussing language comprehension, we will be treating comprehension as it is involved in both listening and reading. It is often thought that of the two, the listening process is the more basic. However, it seems that much the same factors are involved in both listening and reading.

Researchers' choice of whether to use written or spoken material is determined by considerations of experimental tractability. More often than not, this has meant studying reading.

Comprehension can be analyzed into three stages. The first stage comprises the *perceptual processes* by which the acoustic or written message is originally encoded. The second stage is termed the parsing stage. *Parsing* is the process by which the words in the message are transformed into a mental representation of the combined meaning of the words. The third stage is the *utilization* stage, in which comprehenders actually use the mental representation of the sentence's meaning. If the sentence is an assertion, the listeners may simply store the meaning in memory; if it is a question, they may answer; if it is an instruction, they may obey. However, listeners are not always so compliant. They may use an assertion about the weather to make an inference about the speaker's personality, they may answer a question with a question, or they may do just the opposite of what the speaker asks. These three stages — perception, parsing, and utilization — are by necessity partially ordered in time; however, they also partly overlap. Listeners can be making inferences from the first part of a sentence while they are perceiving a later part.

This chapter will focus on the two higher-level processes — parsing and utilization. The perceptual stage was already discussed in Chapter 3.

Parsing

Sentence Patterns

Language is structured according to a set of rules that tell us how to go from a particular string of words to an interpretation of that string's meaning. For instance, in English we know that if we hear a sequence of the form *A noun verb a noun,* the speaker means that an instance of the first noun has the specified relation (verb) to an instance of the second noun. In contrast, if the sentence is of the form *A noun was verbed by a noun,* the speaker means that an instance of the second noun has the specified relation to the first noun. Thus, our knowledge of the structure of English allows us to appreciate the difference between *A doctor shot a lawyer* and *A doctor was shot by a lawyer.* One way to represent our knowledge of such rules is as a series of production rules, in which the condition of each production specifies the word pattern and the action builds into memory the meaning conveyed by that pattern. Such constructs are called *parsing productions.* We might represent our knowledge of the two English structures cited above with the following pair of productions:

> IF the sentence is of the form *A noun-1 verb a noun-2*
> THEN the meaning is that an instance of *noun-1* has the relation *verb* to an instance of *noun-2*

> IF the sentence is of the form *A noun-1 was verbed by a noun-2*
> THEN the meaning is that an instance of *noun-2* has the relation *verbed* to an instance of *noun-1*

In these productions, *noun-1, verb,* and *noun-2* serve to indicate whether the words should be nouns or verbs. The first production would apply if the sentence was *A sailor loved a maiden,* and its action would be to build a representation of the sentence's meaning: that an instance of *sailor* had the relation of *loving* to an instance of *maiden.* (For simplicity we are ignoring the distinction between words and the concepts they refer to.) The effect of these productions can be represented as building propositional networks in active memory (see Chapter 5). So, for instance, the first production above applied to the sentence *A sailor loved a maiden* would build the network illustrated in Figure 12-1.

In learning to comprehend a language we acquire a great many rules that encode the various linguistic patterns in the language and relate these patterns to meaning interpretations. However, production rules that process whole sentences are not always possible because of the productivity of language discussed in the last chapter. Sentences can be very long and complex. A very large (probably infinite) number of patterns would be required to encode all possible sentence forms. Consider this example:

> There is a tendency in the average citizen, even if he has a high standing in his profession, to consider the decisions relating to the

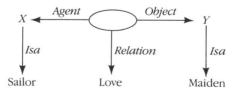

Figure 12-1. The network representation of the meaning corresponding to the sentence *A sailor loved a maiden.* The letter *X* represents an instance of a sailor and *Y* an instance of a maiden.

life of the society to which he belongs as matters of fate on which he
has no influence.

A single pattern constructed to process this sentence might take the
following form:

There is a *noun preposition* the *adjective noun,* even if *pronoun verb* a
adjective noun preposition adjective noun, to *verb* the *noun participle preposition* the *noun preposition* the *noun preposition relative-pronoun pronoun
verb* as *noun preposition noun preposition relative-pronoun pronoun verb
adjective noun.*

Note that most words in the sentence are replaced by classes such as noun,
verb, and preposition. Thus, this pattern could characterize a large number of sentences; for instance:

There is an inclination in the adult female, even if she practices a
great deal of personal independence, to regard the officials partici-
pating in the government of the community in which she lives as
men of character to whom she owes absolute allegiance.

While many potential sentences would satisfy this pattern, it is unlikely that we have encountered any of them until reading these two
sentences. To see that this is so, let us calculate the number of different
patterns 43 words long. We can do this by considering how many
variations there are on the pattern above. At almost any point, this pattern
could be continued in a variety of ways. For instance, consider the
possible ways of continuing the sentence after the first three words, *There
is a:*

1. with a noun, as in the original example

2. with an adjective, as in *There is a funny story* . . .

3. with an adverb, as in *There is a very funny story* . . .

Having chosen a noun for this position, consider the number of options
we have for continuing *There is a noun:*

1. with a preposition, as in the original example

2. with the infinitive *to,* as in *There is a tendency to
believe* . . .

3. with a relative pronoun, as in *There is a tendency that is hard to resist . . .*

4. with an article, as in *There is a tendency, a desire, and a compulsion . . .*

5. with a participle, as in *There is a tendency growing in our society . . .*

6. with an adverb, as in *There is a tendency, unfortunately, to construct . . .*

A conservative assumption might be that each fragment can be continued in three possible ways. Since there are 43 positions in the sentence, this assumption would mean that $3^{43} \cong 328,260,000,000,000,000,000$ different 43-word patterns are possible in the English language. This number, a great deal larger than the number of seconds in a human life, is another testament to the productivity of natural language. It is by this reasoning that we can be certain that learned patterns do not exist in any language for every possible sentence structure within that language.

The Concatenation of Constituents

Although we have not learned to process full sentence patterns such as the one above, we have learned to process subpatterns, or phrases, of these sentences and to combine, or *concatenate,* these subpatterns. These subpatterns correspond to basic phrases, or units, in a sentence's surface structure. These units are referred to as *constituents.*

Table 12-1 displays three productions capable of analyzing a variety of sentences by concatenating analyses of the sentence constituents. This production set uses the term *string* to refer to sequences of words that occur in the sentence. The productions look for various string patterns. Production NP will recognize some simple noun phrases; RELATIVE will recognize some relative clause patterns (i.e., noun-modifying clauses such as *who ate the cheese, who loved a sailor*); and MAIN will recognize some simple subject-verb-object sentences. This set of productions can handle sentences composed from indefinite articles, nouns, verbs, and relative clauses. An example of such a sentence is

A princess, who loved a sailor, bought a ship.

Table 12-1 *Production for Parsing Various Sentence Constituents*

Name of Production		Form of Production
NP	IF	the string is of the form *A noun*
	THEN	the meaning is an instance of *noun*
RELATIVE	IF	the string is of the form *person who verb object*
	THEN	the meaning is that *person* has the relation *verb* to *object*
MAIN	IF	the string is of the form *person verb object*
	THEN	the meaning is that *person* has the relation *verb* to *object*

The whole sentence can be regarded as a string of words; the productions in Table 12-1 enable the perceiver to pick out various constituents in the string. Figure 12-2 illustrates the application of these productions to the analysis of this sentence. Part (a) shows the range over which each production would apply, and part (b) shows the resulting meaning representation.

It is worthwhile to emphasize the important features of this example:

1.   Language-processing productions look for typically oc-curring sentence patterns or constituents, such as *a noun* or *person verb object.*

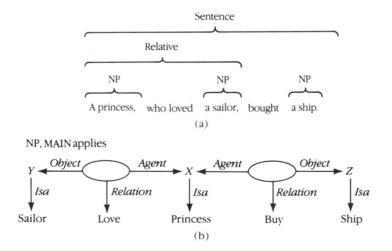

(a)

(b)

Figure 12-2. (a) Range of the example sentence over which the productions in Table 12-1 apply; (b) meaning representation built as a result of their application.

2. The productions build in memory the semantic interpretation of these patterns.

3. A total sentence is processed through the concatenation of a number of pattern-recognizing productions.

Pattern-recognizing production systems are a means of implementing the idea that people have a set of strategies and rules for dividing a sentence up into constituents, identifying the character of each constituent, and applying a semantic interpretation to each constituent. Each production embodies one such rule. The productions rely for their success on the fact that sentences contain various clues (word order; key words, such as *who;* inflections) that allow the constituents to be identified. This conception of parsing has been proposed by many researchers (e.g., Bever, 1970; Fodor & Garrett, 1967; Kimball, 1973; Watt, 1970).

A similarity exists between pattern-recognizing productions and the rewrite rules that generate the surface structure of a sentence, discussed in Chapter 11. The three rewrite rules that correspond to the productions in Table 12-1 are:

SENTENCE → NP verb NP	(MAIN)
NP → NP who verb NP	(RELATIVE)
NP → a noun	(NP)

In applying these rewrite rules,[1] we would generate the example sentence — *A princess, who loved a sailor, bought a ship* — in the following steps:

SENTENCE → NP *bought* NP	(apply MAIN)
SENTENCE → NP *bought a ship*	(apply NP)
SENTENCE → NP, *who loved* NP, *bought a ship*	(apply RELATIVE)
SENTENCE → *A princess, who loved a sailor, bought a ship.*	(apply NP twice)

Thus, parsing productions analyze a sentence by reversing the process of deriving a sentence through rewrite rules, interpreting the meaning of each phrase as they do so.

---

[1]In Chapter 11 we followed the traditional linguistic practice of analyzing SENTENCE into subject + predicate, subject into NP, and predicate into verb + NP. The subject-predicate distinction has been glossed over here for the sake of simplicity.

The Psychological Reality of Constituent Structure

The production systems examined in the preceding subsection process a sentence in terms of constituents, or phrases. If this analysis accurately models language comprehension, we would expect that the more clearly identifiable the constituent structure of a sentence is, the more easily understandable the sentence would be. Graf and Torrey (1966) presented sentences to subjects a line at a time. The passages could be presented in form A, in which each line corresponded with a major constituent boundary, or in form B, in which this was not the case. Examples of the two types of passages follow:

Form A	Form B
During World War II,	During World War
even fantastic schemes	II, even fantastic
received consideration	schemes received
if they gave promise	consideration if they gave
of shortening the conflict.	promise of shortening the
	conflict.

Subjects showed better comprehension of passages in form A. This finding demonstrates that the identification of constituent structure is important to the parsing of a sentence.

When people read such passages they naturally pause at boundaries between clauses. Aaronson and Scarborough (1977) had subjects read sentences word by word displayed on a computer display screen. Subjects would press the key each time they wanted to read another word. Figure 12-3 illustrates the pattern of reading times for a sentence subjects were reading for later recall. Notice the U-shaped patterns with prolonged pauses at the phrase boundaries. It appears that with the completion of each major phrase subjects need time to process it.

Another feature of the parsing process is that after a production has applied to interpret a constituent, the exact words in the constituent are no longer needed. Thus, we would predict that subjects will show poorer memory for the exact wording of a constituent after it has been parsed and parsing on another constituent has begun. An experiment by Jarvella (1971) confirms this prediction. He read subjects passages that were interrupted at various points. At the points of interruption, subjects were instructed to write down as much of the passage as they could remember. Of interest were passages that ended with 20 words, such as the following:

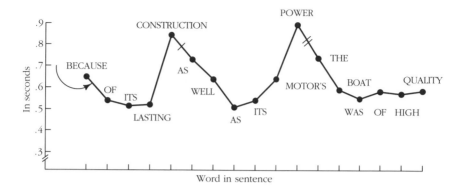

Figure 12-3. Word-by-word reading times for a sample sentence. The short-line markers on the graphs indicate breaks between phrase structures. (From Aaronson & Scarborough, 1977.)

```
1    2    3    4      5       6        7
The tone of the document was threatening.

 8      9    10    11    12     13
Having failed to disprove the charges,

14    15    16    17  18  19     20
Taylor was later fired by the president
```

Subjects were prompted, after hearing the last word, to recall the entire passage. Each passage ended with a seven-word sentence followed by a sentence composed of a six-word subordinate clause followed by a seven-word main clause. The two clauses are the two major constituents of the second sentence. Because the production-system model outlined earlier retains a verbatim representation of only the last constituent in the sentence it is currently processing, that model would predict that a subject would have better memory for the second constituent of the second sentence than for its first constituent.

Figure 12-4 plots probability of recall for each of the 20 words in a passage of the form shown above. Note that sharp rises in the function occur at two points—once at word 8, the beginning of the second sentence, and once at word 14, the beginning of the main clause. The graph indicates that subjects have the poorest memory for the first sentence, that a jump occurs to better memory for the first clause of the

367

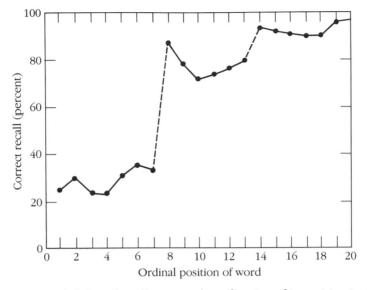

Figure 12-4. Probability of recalling a word as a function of its position in the last 20 words in a passage. The broken lines show jumps in recall at constituent boundaries. (Adapted from Jarvella, 1971.)

second sentence, and that another jump occurs to best memory for the most recent clause. Thus, these data reflect two effects. First, as expected, subjects show best memory for the last major constituent, a result consistent with the hypothesis that they retain a verbatim representation of the last constituent only. The second effect, the sharp dropoff at the sentence boundary, requires a different explanation. It may occur because subjects work on a different meaning structure for each sentence. After finishing a sentence, they lose their access to that sentence's meaning representation. This effect would make reconstruction of the previous sentence quite difficult.

An experiment by Caplan (1972) also presents evidence for use of constituent structure, but this study uses a reaction-time methodology. Subjects were presented aurally first with a sentence and then with a probe word; they then had to indicate as quickly as possible whether the probe word was in the sentence. Caplan contrasted pairs of sentences such as the following:

1. Now that artists are working fewer hours oil prints are rare.

2. Now that artists are working in oil prints are rare.

Interest focused on how quickly subjects would recognize *oil* in these two sentences when probed at the ends of the sentences. The sentences were cleverly constructed so that in both sentences the word *oil* was fourth from the end and was followed by the same words. In fact, by splicing tape, Caplan arranged the presentation so that subjects heard the same recording of these last four words whichever full sentence they heard. However, in sentence 1 *oil* is part of the last constituent, *oil prints are rare,* whereas in sentence 2 it is part of the first constituent, *now that artists are working in oil.* Caplan predicted that subjects would recognize *oil* more quickly in sentence 1 because they would still have active in memory a representation of this constituent. As he predicted, the probe word was recognized more rapidly if it occurred in the last constituent.

Immediacy of Interpretation

While the production rule representation of parsing given earlier is good for representing the importance of constituent structure, it is misleading in that it implies one does not process a phrase until one has completed it. People are not nearly so patient; they try to extract as much as they can out of each word as they take that word in. Just and Carpenter (1980) studied the eye movements of subjects as they read a sentence. While reading a sentence subjects will typically fixate on almost every word. Just and Carpenter find that the time subjects spend fixating on a word is basically proportional to the amount of information provided by the word. Thus, if a sentence contains a relatively unfamiliar or a surprising word, they pause on that word. They also pause longer at the end of the phrase involving that word. Figure 12-5 illustrates the eye fixations of one of their college students reading a scientific passage. Gazes within each sentence are indicated by circles above the point where the gaze occurred. The order of the gazes is left to right except for the three gazes above *engine contains,* where the order of gazes is indicated. Note that unimportant function words like *the* and *to* may be skipped and if not skipped receive relatively little processing. Note the amount of time spent on the word *flywheels.* The subject is not waiting until the end of the sentence to process this word. Again look at the amount of time spent on the highly informative adjective *mechanical*—the subject is not waiting until the end of the noun phrase to process it.

Just and Carpenter (1987) propose that a more accurate production rule model would be one which had a separate production rule for each word. These production rules would be organized according to phrase structure principle but would enable one to get as much as possible from

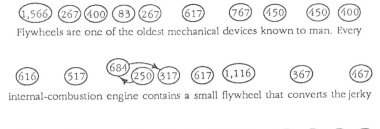

Figure 12-5. The time a college reader spent on the words in the opening two sentences of a technical article about flywheels. The times, indicated above the fixated word, are in milliseconds. This reader read the sentences from left to right with one regressive fixation to an earlier part. (Adapted from Just & Carpenter, 1980.)

the sentence immediately. Thus, our earlier production rule MAIN from Table 12-1 for main sentences would be broken down into three separate rules such as:

> IF   the sentence begins with a description of a person
> THEN   create a fact in which the person participates and set a subgoal to process the fact

> IF   the sentence contains an action verb and the goal is to process a fact about a person
> THEN   make the person the agent of the fact and make the verb the relation of the fact and set a subgoal to process the object of the fact

> IF   the sentence contains a description of a thing and the goal is to process the object of the fact
> THEN   make the thing the object of the fact

This immediacy of processing implies that we will begin to attribute an interpretation to the sentence even before we encounter the main verb. This certainly is the experience of speakers of languages such as German, which tend to have the verb in the final position. It is also the experience in English in those rare constructions that put the verb last. Consider what happens as we process the following sentence:

It was the president whom the terrorist from the Middle East shot.

Before we get to *shot* we have already built up a partial model of what might be happening between the president and the terrorist.

If people do process a sentence as each word comes in then it might seem strange that there is all the evidence that we reviewed for the importance of phrase structure boundaries. This evidence just reflects the fact that the meaning of a sentence is defined in terms of the phrase and even if listeners try to extract all they can from each word there will be some things that they are only able to put into place at the end of a phrase. Thus, people will pause at a phrase boundary because some of the information cannot be processed until the phrase is complete. People have to maintain a representation of the current phrase in memory because their interpretation of it may be wrong and they may have to reinterpret the beginning of the phrase. Manipulations like those of Graf and Torrey are important because they signal the end of the phrase perceptually to the reader.

The Use of Syntactic Cues

So far we have mainly focused on how subjects process the content words in a sentence. Function words, such as *a* and *who,* are important to parsing because they signal the various types of constituents, such as noun phrase or relative clause. Consider the following set of sentences:

1. The boy whom the girl liked was sick.

2. The boy the girl liked was sick.

3. The boy the girl and the dog were sick.

Sentences 1 and 2 are equivalent except that in 2 *whom* is deleted. Sentence 2 is a shorter sentence, but the cost of shortening is the loss of a cue as to how the sentence should be analyzed. At the point of *The boy the girl* it is ambiguous whether we have a relative clause, as in sentence 2, or a conjunction, as in sentence 3. If it is true that function words such as *whom* are used to indicate which parsing patterns are relevant, then constructions such as sentence 2 should be more difficult to parse than those similar to sentence 1.

Hakes and Foss (1970; Hakes, 1972) tested this prediction using what has been called the *phoneme-monitoring task.* They used double embedded sentences such as the following:

4. The zebra which the lion that the gorilla chased killed was running.

5. The zebra the lion the gorilla chased killed was running.

Sentence 5 lacks relative pronouns and so is easily confused with sentences having a noun-conjunction structure. Subjects were required to perform two simultaneous tasks. One task was to comprehend and paraphrase the sentence. The second task was to listen for a particular phoneme—in this case a [g] (in gorilla). Hakes and Foss predicted that the more difficult a sentence was to comprehend, the more time subjects would take to detect the target phoneme, since they would have less attention left over from the comprehension task with which to perform the monitoring. In fact, the prediction was borne out; subjects did take longer to indicate hearing [g] when presented with sentences such as sentence 5, which lacked relative pronouns.

The dominant syntactic cue in English is word order. For instance, a person appearing before an action verb is usually the agent. Other languages rely less on word order and instead use inflections of words to indicate semantic role. There is a small remnant of such an inflectional system in some English pronouns. For instance, *he* versus *him*, *I* versus *me*, etc., signal agent versus object. McDonald (1984) compared English with German, which has a richer inflectional system. She asked her English subjects to interpret sentences such as:

6. Him kicked the girl.

7. The girl kicked he.

The word order cue suggests one interpretation while the inflection cue suggests an alternative interpretation. English speakers use the word order cue, interpreting sentence 6 with *him* as the agent and *girl* as the object. German speakers, judging comparable sentences in German, do just the opposite. Interestingly, German-English bilinguals tend to interpret the English sentences more like German sentences—i.e., assigning *him* in sentence 6 to object and *girl* to agent roles.

Semantic Considerations

While it is clear that people use syntactic patterns, such as those illustrated above, for understanding sentences, they can also make use of the meanings of the words involved. An individual can determine the meaning of a string of words simply by considering how they can be put together in order to make sense. Thus, when Tarzan says, "Jane fruit eat," we know what he means even though this sentence does not correspond to the syntax of English. We realize that a relationship is being asserted between something edible and someone capable of eating.

Considerable evidence suggests that people use such semantic strategies in language comprehension. Strohner and Nelson (1974) had 2- and 3-year-old children act out with animal dolls the following two sentences:

> The cat chased the mouse.
>
> The mouse chased the cat.

In both cases, the children interpreted the sentence as indicating that the cat chased the mouse, a meaning that corresponded to their prior knowledge about cats and mice. Thus, these young children were relying more heavily on semantic patterns than on syntactic patterns.

Fillenbaum (1971, 1974) had adults paraphrase sentences among which were "perverse" items such as:

> John was buried and died.

More than 60 percent of the subjects paraphrased the sentences in a way that gave them a more conventional meaning; for example, here indicating that John died first and then was buried. However, the normal syntactic interpretation of such constructions would be that the first activity occurred before the second, as in

> John had a drink and went to the party.

as opposed to

> John went to the party and had a drink.

So it seems that when a semantic principle is placed in conflict with a syntactic principle the semantic principle sometimes (but not always) will determine the interpretation of the sentence.

Integration of Syntax and Semantics

It appears that a listener combines both syntactic and semantic information in comprehending a sentence. Tyler and Marslen-Wilson (1977) had subjects try to continue fragments such as:

1. If you walk too near the runway, landing planes are

2. If you've been trained as a pilot, landing planes are

The phrase *landing planes,* by itself, is ambiguous. It can mean either "planes that are landing" or "to land planes." Followed by the plural verb *are,* however, it must have the first meaning. Thus, the syntactic constraints determine a meaning for the ambiguous phrase. The prior context in fragment 1 is consistent with this meaning, whereas the prior context in fragment 2 is not. Subjects took longer to continue 1, which suggests that they were using both the semantics of the prior context and the syntax of the current phrase to disambiguate *landing planes.* When these factors are in conflict, the subject's comprehension is hurt.[2]

Bates, McNew, MacWhinney, Devesocvi, and Smith (1982) looked at the issue of combining syntax and semantics in a different paradigm. They had subjects interpret word strings such as:

Chased the dog the eraser

If you were forced to, what meaning would you assign to this word string? The syntactic fact that objects follow verbs seems to imply that it was the eraser that did the chasing and the dog who was being chased. The semantics, however, suggest the opposite. In fact, American speakers prefer to go with the syntax, but sometimes will adopt the semantic interpretation — that is, most say *The eraser chased the dog,* but some say *The dog chased the eraser.* On the other hand, if the word string is

Chased the eraser the dog

listeners all agree on the interpretation — that is, that the dog chased the eraser.

Another interesting part of the Bates et al. study concerned comparing Americans with Italians. When syntactic cues were put in conflict with semantic cues, Italians tended to go with the semantic cues, whereas Americans preferred the syntax. The most critical case concerned sentences such as:

---

[2]The original Tyler and Marslen-Wilson experiment has drawn methodological criticisms from Townsend and Bever (1982) and Cowart (1983). For a response read Marslen-Wilson and Tyler (1987).

The eraser bites the dog

or its Italian translation:

La gomma morde il cane

Americans almost always followed the syntax and interpreted this sentence to mean that the eraser is doing the biting. In contrast, Italians preferred to use the semantics and interpret that the dog is doing the biting. Like English, however, Italian has a subject-verb-object syntax. Thus, we see that listeners combine both syntactic and semantic cues in interpreting the sentence. Moreover, the weighting of these two types of cues can vary from language to language. This and other evidence indicates that speakers of Italian weight semantic cues more heavily than do speakers of English.

Recently, there has been some controversy as to whether semantics are involved in the initial analyses of a sentence. The experiments we have just reviewed by Tyler and Marslen-Wilson and by Bates et al. show that semantic considerations play an important role in interpretation, but they leave open the question of how soon such semantic considerations come into play. One theory holds that subjects first do an analysis of sentences using only syntactic factors and then use semantic factors. It has been argued that one can use word-by-word reading data to show this. For instance, Ferreira and Clifton (1986) had subjects read sentences such as:

1. The woman painted by the artist was very attractive to look at.

2. The woman that was painted by the artist was very attractive to look at.

3. The sign painted by the artist was very attractive to look at.

4. The sign that was painted by the artist was very attractive to look at.

Ferreira and Clifton note that people have a natural tendency to encode noun-verb combinations like *The woman painted* as agent-action combinations. Evidence for this is that subjects take longer to read *by the artist* in the first sentence than the second. The reason is that they discover their agent-action interpretation is wrong in the first sentence and have to recover while the syntactic cues *that was* in the second sentence prevent them from ever making this misinterpretation.

The real interest in the Ferreira and Clifton experiments is in sentences 3 and 4. Semantic factors should rule out the agent-action interpretation of sentence 3 since a sign cannot be an animate agent and engage in painting. Nonetheless, subjects took just as long to read, *by the artist in 3* as in 1 and longer than in 2 or 4. Thus, argue Ferreira and Clifton, subjects first use only syntactic factors and so misinterpret the phrase *The sign painted* and use the syntactic cues in the phrase *by the artist* to correct that misinterpretation. Thus, while semantic factors could have done the job and avoided the misinterpretation it seems that subjects are doing all their initial processing using syntactic cues.

Experiments of this sort (see also Rayner, Carlson, & Frazier, 1983) have been used to support the position described in the previous chapter about the uniqueness or modularity of language. The argument is that our initial processing of language makes use of something specific to language, namely syntax, and ignores other general, nonlinguistic knowledge we have of the world, such as that signs cannot paint. However, others (e.g., McClelland, 1987) have argued that this result just reflects what happens when one places what is a very strong syntactic cue in English (the tendency to interpret noun-verb sequences as agent-action) against a weaker semantic cue. Taraban and McClelland (1988) report an experiment where semantic cues do have an effect when the syntactic cues are weaker.

Ambiguity

As the study of Ferreira and Clifton illustrates, one of the problems a language comprehender must deal with is ambiguity. There are sentences that are capable of two or more interpretations, either because of ambiguous words or ambiguous syntactic constructions. Examples of such sentences are the following:

> John went to the bank.

> Flying planes can be dangerous.

It is also useful to distinguish between *transient ambiguity* and *permanent ambiguity*. The examples above are permanent ambiguity. That is, the ambiguity remains to the end of the sentence. Transient ambiguity refers to sentences that are temporarily ambiguous but that are no longer ambiguous by the end of the sentence. An instance is:

> The old train the young.

Following the word *train,* it is unclear whether *old* is a noun or an adjective. The sentence could have continued to yield a sentence in which *train* was a noun:

The old train left the station.

This ambiguity is resolved by the end of the sentence.

Transient ambiguity is quite prevalent in language. Consider this sentence:

The model snapped the picture.

After *The model,* it is ambiguous whether the sentence refers to a person or an inanimate object, or an adjective, or a theory. After *snapped,* a great many interpretations are still possible. Consider the following alternative continuations:

The model snapped at the photographer.

The model snapped at by the photographer cried.

The model snapped on a dress.

The model snapped open and the parts spewed over the table.

Each of these continuations represents a different interpretation of the phrase *The model snapped.* Partly because of the ambiguity of natural language, efforts to develop computer programs that will understand natural languages have not yet been fully successful. Because a sentence can be interpreted in many ways at many points, it is difficult to program a computer to choose the intended meaning for a whole sentence. Often, programs must compute a large number of different meanings for sentences. As this number of meanings grows, so does the cost of computation time.

We do not fully understand how humans deal with ambiguity in order to comprehend natural language, although some of the mechanisms are clear. Humans make heavy use of contextual constraints in their efforts to select a single meaning for each pattern to be interpreted. However, it appears that they select only one interpretation (their best guess) for a pattern and carry it through to the end of the sentence. If the best guess turns out to be wrong, their comprehension suffers and they have to backtrack and try another interpretation. Consider this example:

I know more beautiful women than Miss America

although she knows quite a few.

Such instances indicate that we can be misled in our initial interpretation of a sentence. It is sometimes said that the listener has been "led down a garden path."

The immediacy of processing principle that we described earlier implies that we will commit to one interpretation of an ambiguous sentence at the earliest possible moment and backtrack should that prove wrong. We have already reviewed the Ferreira and Clifton experiment that made this point. They found that presented with the following sentence:

The woman painted by the artist was very attractive to look at.

subjects committed to the agent-action interpretation of *The woman painted,* which they had to retract when reading *by the artist.* Unlike the Miss America example above, most people reading *The woman painted* sentence are not even aware that they have changed their interpretation. Nonetheless, their reading times do indicate a double take. This phenomenon of immediate commitment to one interpretation and subsequent reinterpretation if necessary has shown up in a number of reading time studies (e.g., Frazier & Rayner, 1982; Rayner, Carlson, & Frazier, 1983; Taraban & McClelland, 1988).

Lexical Ambiguity

A series of experiments by Swinney (e.g., Swinney, 1979) has been useful in revealing how ambiguous words are disambiguated. He had subjects listen to sentences such as the following:

Rumor had it that, for years, the government building had been plagued with problems. The man was not surprised when he found several spiders, roaches, and other bugs in the corner of the room.

Swinney was concerned with the ambiguous word *bugs.* Just after hearing the word, subjects would be presented with a string of letters on the screen, and their task was to judge whether that string made a correct word or not. Thus, if they saw *sew* they would say *yes;* but if they saw *siw,* they would say *no,* it was not a word. This is the lexical decision task that we described in Chapter 6 in discussing the mechanisms of spreading activation.

The critical contrasts involved having subjects judge words such as *spy*, *ant*, or *sew*, following *bugs*. The word *ant* is related to the primed meaning of *bugs*, while *spy* is related to the unprimed meaning. The word *sew* defines a neutral control condition. If the to-be-judged word is presented within 400 milliseconds of the prime, *bugs*, Swinney found that recognition of both *spy* and *ant* was speeded. Thus, the presentation of *bugs* immediately activates both of its meanings and their associations. If Swinney waited more than 700 milliseconds, however, there was facilitation only for the related word *ant*. It appears that a correct meaning is selected in this time and the other meaning is deactivated. Thus, two meanings of an ambiguous word are momentarily active, but context operates very rapidly to select the appropriate meaning.

Propositional Representation

So far we have mainly focused on the processes by which a comprehender goes from a string of words to a meaningful interpretation of that string. We have shown that factors which affect the complexity of this interpretation (ambiguity, presence of syntactic cues) affect the comprehension process. However, it should also be the case that comprehension will be affected by the complexity of the resulting interpretation. One way to measure this is in terms of the number of propositions in the meaning interpretation. For instance, Kintsch and Keenan (1973) compared the comprehension of the following two sentences:

1. Romulus, the legendary founder of Rome, took the women of the Sabine by force.

2. Cleopatra's downfall lay in her foolish trust in the fickle political figures of the human world.

According to Kintsch's propositional analysis (see Chapter 5), sentence 1 consists of four propositions:

> (took, Romulus, women, by force)
> (found, Romulus, Rome)
> (legendary, Romulus)
> (Sabine, women)

Sentence 2 consists of eight propositions:

(because, α, β)[3]
(fell down, Cleopatra) = α
(trust, Cleopatra, figures) = β
(foolish, trust)
(fickle, figures)
(political, figures)
(part-of, figures, world)
(Roman, world)

While these two sentences differ in terms of number of propositions, they are similar in terms of length and other factors. Kintsch and Keenan found that subjects took longer to read the second sentence, reflecting the fact that there were more propositions to extract from it.

Utilization

Once a sentence has been parsed and mapped into a meaning representation, what then? A listener seldom simply passively records the meaning. If the sentence is a question or imperative, the speaker expects the listener to take some action in response. However, even for declarative sentences there is usually more to be done than simply to register the sentence. Consider this sentence:

The General Assembly condemned Israeli occupation of Arab lands.

Figure 12-6 (part a) illustrates the propositional-network representation that might be assigned to this sentence by a set of parsing productions. However, a number of connections are necessary in order to relate this sentence to the listener's other knowledge. Part (b) shows the memory structure after these connections have been made to integrate this new knowledge with existing knowledge. The dotted lines indicate additional connections. The listener will probably recognize the lands in the sentence as an entity already known—the lands captured by Israel in the 1967 war. Thus, a link will be established between node X, which stands for the lands mentioned in the sentence, and node Z, representing the concept of the captured land, already in memory. Another connection

---

[3]The α and β indicates that the second and third proposition occur as arguments to the first. See the discussion of the hierarchical organization of propositions on p. 128.

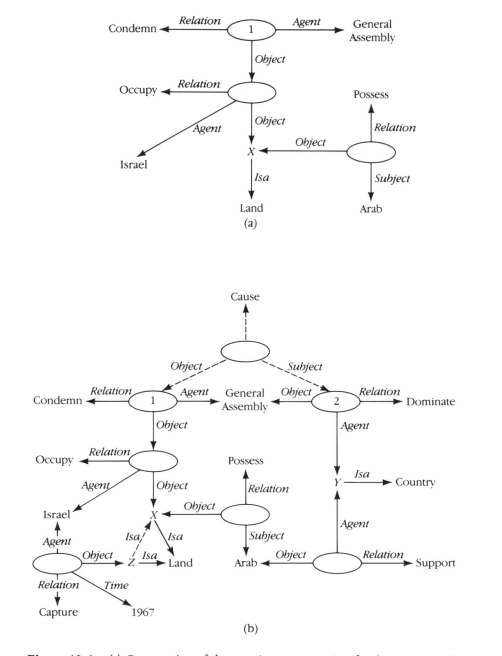

Figure 12-6. (a) Construction of the meaning representation for the sentence. *The General Assembly condemned Israeli occupation of Arab lands;* (b) integration of this structure with past knowledge. The dotted lines indicate new links added in order to achieve this integration.

relates the condemnation (proposition node 1) to the knowledge (proposition node 2) that the United Nations is dominated by countries supportive of the Arabs. Thus, at the very least, listeners try to relate the information in sentences to knowledge they have about the world. Basically, this task involves relating new information to old. Most sentences in a comprehensible communication contain both new and old information. This is because the speaker, in trying to assert new information, must relate it to old information that the listener knows. The speaker is said to *suppose* the old information in order to *assert* the new information. In the example given, the old information is that Israel occupied Arab lands and the new information is that the General Assembly voted to condemn this.

Inference of the Unstated

Linguistic messages leave a lot unsaid and part of the task of a comprehender is to fill in this missing information. For instance, consider this sentence:

Alice pounded in the nail until the board was safely secured.

Do readers infer that Alice used a hammer although it is not explicitly stated? When people are later asked to recall the sentence they will often recall *with a hammer*. This result leaves open the issue of whether the inference was made on initial reading or only at the time of final recall (see the discussion in Chapter 7). McKoon and Ratcliff (1981) found evidence that, under some circumstances, subjects do make such inferences while reading the text. They had subjects read a sequence of five sentences that began:

1. Bobby got a saw, hammer, screwdriver, and a square from the toolbox.

Subjects read three more sentences and then the final, critical sentence:

2. Then Bobby pounded the boards together with nails.

Immediately after reading the last sentences subjects were presented with a test word and asked if it occurred anywhere in the paragraph. Subjects were faster to recognize that they had seen *hammer* given this sentence than when the control sentence was the following:

3. Then Bobby stuck the boards together with glue.

Thus, McKoon and Ratcliff concluded that subjects had inferred *hammer* in the "pounding" sentence. However, if sentence 1 had not established the existence of *hammer,* subjects do not infer this instrument when they read sentence 2.

Just and Carpenter (1987) used another methodology to show that people will fill in unstated parts of a sentence. They presented their subjects with two-sentence sequences such as the following:

3a. The maid diligently swept the floor until it was spotless.

3b. The broom had been worn down by her excessive zeal.

Their interest was in whether subjects inferred the instrument *broom* before reading it in the second sentence. To determine this they compared such sequences with two-sentence sequences such as the following:

4a. The maid diligently cleaned the floor until it was spotless.

4b. The broom had been worn down by her excessive zeal.

The second sentence is identical in both sequences. Just and Carpenter looked at the time to read the second sentence. Subjects were 500 milliseconds faster on 3b than 4b, indicating that they had already inferred the instrument *broom* in the prior sentence (3a).

Inference of Reference

Another aspect of language processing involves resolving reference. Certain expressions in a linguistic communication refer to the same thing and it is critical that the comprehender identify these common references. For instance, consider the following classic exchange between Abbott and Costello:

Abbott:	Strange as it may seem they give ball players nowadays very peculiar names.
Costello:	Funny names?
Abbott:	Nicknames, nicknames. Now on the St. Louis team we have Who's on first, What's on second, I Don't Know is on third—

Costello:	That's what I want to find out. I want you to tell me the names of the fellows on the St. Louis team.
Abbott:	I'm telling you. Who's on first, What's on second, I Don't Know is on third—
Costello:	You know the fellows' names?
Abbott:	Yes.
Costello:	Well, then who's playing first?
Abbott:	Yes.
Costello:	I mean the fellow's name on first base.
Abbott:	Who.
Costello:	The fellow playin' first base.
Abbott:	Who.
Costello:	The guy on first base.
Abbott:	Who is on first.
Costello:	Well, what are you askin' me for?
Abbott:	I'm not asking you—I'm telling you. Who is on first.
Costello:	I'm asking you—who's on first?
Abbott:	That's the man's name.
Costello:	That's who's name?
Abbott:	Yes.

Of course, the humor in the exchange lies in the fact that Costello does not realize that the expressions *who* and *the guy on first* have the same reference. Normally, we have little difficulty in recognizing reference of expressions (and consequently miss the opportunity for humor).

Some of the principles that are used to help resolve reference are becoming understood. One linguistic cue in English turns on the difference between the definite article *the* and the indefinite article *a*. The definite article *the* tends to be used to signal that the comprehender should know the reference of the noun phrase while *a* tends to be used to introduce a new object. Compare the difference between the meaning of these sentences:

1. Last night I saw the moon.

2. Last night I saw a moon.

Sentence 1 indicates a rather uneventful fact about seeing the same old moon as always but 2 carries the clear implication of having seen a new moon. There is considerable evidence that language comprehenders are quite sensitive to the meaning communicated by this small difference in the sentences.

Haviland and Clark (1974) report an experiment directed at this issue. They compared subjects' comprehension time for two sentence pairs such as the following:

3. Ed was given an alligator for his birthday. The alligator was his favorite present.

4. Ed wanted an alligator for his birthday. The alligator was his favorite present.

Both pairs have the same second sentence. Pair 3 introduces in its first sentence a specific antecedent for the *alligator*. On the other hand, although in pair 4 *alligator* is mentioned in the first sentence, a specific alligator is not posited. Thus, no antecedent occurs in the first sentence of pair 4 for *the alligator*. The definite article *the* in the second sentence of the pair supposes a specific antecedent. Therefore, we would expect that subjects would have difficulty with the second sentence in pair 4 but not in pair 3. In the Haviland and Clark experiment subjects saw pairs of such sentences one at a time. After they comprehended each sentence they pressed a button. The time was measured from the presentation of the second sentence until subjects pressed a button indicating that they understood that sentence. Subjects took an average of 1031 milliseconds to comprehend the second sentence in pairs such as 3 above, in which an antecedent was given, but they took an average of 1168 milliseconds to comprehend the second sentence in pairs such as 4 above, in which no antecedent for the definite noun phrase occurred. Thus, comprehension took more than a tenth of a second longer when no antecedent occurred.

Loftus and Zanni (1975) did an experiment which showed that choice of articles could impact on listeners' beliefs. These experimenters showed subjects a film of an automobile accident and asked them a series of questions. Some subjects were asked:

5. Did you see a broken headlight?

Other subjects were asked:

6. Did you see the broken headlight?

In fact, there was no broken headlight in the film, but question 6 uses a definite article, which supposes the existence of a broken headlight.

Subjects were more likely to respond *yes* when asked the question in form 6. As Loftus and Zanni note, this finding has important implications for the interrogation of eyewitnesses.

Pronominal Reference

Another aspect of processing reference concerns the interpretation of pronouns. When one hears a pronoun such as *she* it is critical to decide who is being referred to. There can be a number of people already mentioned and they are all candidates for the reference of the pronoun. As Just and Carpenter (1987) discuss, there are a number of bases for resolving the reference of pronouns:

1. One of the most straightforward is to use number or gender cues. Consider:

Melvin, Susan, and their children left when (he, she, they) became sleepy.

Each possible pronoun would have a unique referent.

2. A syntactic cue to pronominal reference is that pronouns tend to refer to objects in the same grammatical role (e.g., subject versus object). Consider:

Floyd punched Bert and then he kicked him.

Most people would agree that the subject *he* refers to Floyd and the object *him* refers to Bert.

3. There is also a strong recency effect such that the most recent candidate referent is preferred. Consider:

Dorothea ate the pie; Ethel ate cake; later she had coffee.

Most people would agree that *she* probably refers to Ethel.

4. Finally, people can use their knowledge of the world to determine reference. Compare:

Tom shouted at Bill because he spilled the coffee
Tom shouted at Bill because he had a headache.

Most people would agree that *he* in the first sentence refers to Bill because you tend to scold people who make mistakes, while *he* in the second sentence refers to Tom because people tend to be cranky when they have headaches.

In keeping with the immediacy of interpretation principle articulated earlier, people tend to try to assign a referent to a pronoun immediately upon encountering it. For instance, in studies of eye fixations (Carpenter & Just, 1977; Ehrlich & Rayner, 1983; Just & Carpenter, 1987) researchers find that people pause while the pronoun is being fixated. Moreover, the pause is longer if the antecedent occurred farther back in the text.

Corbett and Chang (1983) have found evidence that subjects consider multiple candidates for a referent. They had subjects read sentences such as:

Scott stole the basketball from Warren and he sank a jumpshot.

After reading the sentence subjects saw a probe word and had to decide whether the word occurred in the sentence. Cheng and Corbett found that time to recognize either Scott or Warren was decreased after reading such a sentence. They also had subjects read the following control sentence, which did not require the referent of a pronoun to be determined:

Scott stole the basketball from Warren and Scott sank a jumpshot.

In this case only recognition of Scott was facilitated. (Warren was facilitated only in the first sentence because in that sentence subjects had to consider it as the referent of *he*.)

Negatives

Negative sentences appear to suppose a positive sentence and then assert the opposite. For instance, the sentence *John is not a crook* supposes that it is reasonable to assume *John is a crook* but asserts that this is false. As another example, imagine the following four replies from a normally healthy friend to the question *How are you feeling?*

1. I am well.

2. I am sick.

3. I am not well.

4. I am not sick.

Replies 1 through 3 would not be regarded as unusual linguistically, but reply 4 does seem peculiar. By using the negative it is supposing that thinking of our friend as sick is reasonable. In contrast, the negative in reply 3 is quite acceptable, since supposing that the friend is normally well is reasonable.

Clark and Chase (e.g., Chase & Clark, 1972; Clark & Chase, 1972; Clark, 1974) conducted a series of experiments on the verification of negatives (see also Trabasso, Rollins, & Shaughnessy, 1971; Carpenter & Just, 1975). In a typical experiment, they presented subjects with a card like that shown in Figure 12-7 and asked them to verify one of four sentences about this card:

1. The star is above the plus — true affirmative.

2. The plus is above the star — false affirmative.

3. The plus is not above the star — true negative.

4. The star is not above the plus — false negative.

The terms *true* and *false* refer to whether the sentence is true of the picture; the terms *affirmative* and *negative* refer to whether the sentence

Figure 12-7. A card such as that presented to subjects in sentence-verification experiments of Clark and Chase. Subjects were to say whether simple affirmative and negative sentences correctly described these pictures.

structure has a negative element. Sentences 1 and 2 involve a simple assertion, but sentences 3 and 4 involve a supposition plus an assertion. Sentence 3 supposes that the plus is above the star and asserts that this supposition is false; sentence 4 supposes that the star is above the plus and asserts that this supposition is false. Clark and Chase assume that subjects will check the supposition first and the assertion next. In sentence 3, the supposition does not match the picture, but in sentence 4 the supposition does match the picture. Assuming that mismatches will take longer to process, Clark and Chase predict that subjects will take longer to respond to sentence 3, a true negative, than to sentence 4, a false negative. In contrast, subjects should take longer to process sentence 2, the false affirmative, than sentence 1, the true affirmative, because sentence 2's assertion mismatches the picture. In fact, the difference between sentences 2 and 1 should be identical to the difference between sentences 3 and 4 because both differences reflect the extra time due to a mismatch to the picture.

Clark and Chase developed a simple and elegant mathematical model for such data. They assumed that processing sentences 3 and 4 took N time units longer than processing 1 and 2 because of the more complex supposition-plus-negation structure of 3 and 4. They also assumed that processing sentence 2 took M time units longer than processing 1 because of the mismatch between picture and assertion, and similarly that processing 3 took M time units longer than processing 4 because of the mismatch between picture and supposition. Finally, they assumed that processing a true affirmative such as sentence 1 took T time units. The time T reflects the time used in processes not involving the negation-and-supposition mismatch. Let us consider the total time subjects should spend processing a sentence such as 3. This sentence has a complex supposition-and-negation structure, which costs N time units, and a supposition mismatch, which costs M time units. Therefore, total processing time should be $T + M + N$. Table 12-2 shows both the observed data and the reac-

Table 12-2 *Observed and Predicted Reaction Times in Experiment Verification*

Condition	Observed Time	Equation	Predicted Time
True affirmative	1463 ms	T	1469 ms
False affirmative	1722 ms	$T + M$	1715 ms
True negative	2028 ms	$T + M + N$	2035 ms
False negative	1796 ms	$T + N$	1789 ms

tion-time predictions that can be derived for the Clark and Chase experiment. The best predicting values for T, M, and N for this experiment can be estimated from the data as $T = 1469$ milliseconds, $M = 246$ milliseconds, and $N = 320$ milliseconds. As you can confirm, the predictions match the observed time remarkably well. In particular, the difference between true negatives and false negatives is close to the difference between false affirmatives and true affirmatives. This finding supports the hypothesis that subjects do extract the suppositions of negative sentences and match these to the picture.

Text Processing

So far we have focused on the comprehension of single sentences in isolation. Sentences are more frequently processed in larger contexts; for example, in the reading of a textbook. We consider now the effects on the utilization process of the structure of larger portions of text.

Texts, like sentences, are structured according to certain patterns, although these patterns are perhaps more flexible than those associated with sentences. Much research has been conducted on the ways in which texts tend to be structured (e.g., Grimes, 1975; Kintsch, 1977; Kintsch & van Dijk, 1976; Mandler & Johnson, 1977; Meyer, 1974; Rumelhart, 1975; Thorndyke, 1977; van Dijk, 1977; van Dijk & Kintsch, 1976). Researchers have noted that a number of recurring relationships serve to organize sentences into larger portions of a text. Some of the relations that have been identified are listed in Table 12-3. These structural relations provide cues as to how a sentence should be utilized. For instance, the first text structure (response) in the table directs the reader to relate one set of sentences as part of the solution to problems posed by other sentences. These relations can occur at any level of a text. That is, the main relation organizing a paragraph might be any of the eight in the table. Subpoints in a paragraph may also be organized according to any of these relations.

To see how the relations in Table 12-3 might be used, consider Meyer's (1974) analysis of the following paragraph:

Parakeet Paragraph
The wide variety in color of parakeets that are available on the market today resulted from careful breeding of the color mutant offspring of green-bodied and yellow-faced parakeets. The light green body and yellow face color combination is the color of the parakeets in their natural habitat, Australia. The first living parakeets

Table 12-3 *Some Possible Types of Relationships Among Sentences in a Text*

Type of Relationship	Description
1. Response	A question is presented and an answer follows, or a problem is presented and a solution follows.
2. Specific	Some specific information is given following a more general point.
3. Explanation	An explanation is given for a point.
4. Evidence	Evidence is given to support a point.
5. Sequence	Points are presented in their temporal sequence as a set.
6. Cause	An event is presented as the cause of another event.
7. Goal	An event is presented as the goal of another event.
8. Collection	A loose structure of points is presented. (This is perhaps a case where there is no real organizing relation.)

were brought to Europe from Australia by John Gould, a naturalist, in 1840. The first color mutation appeared in 1872 in Belgium; these birds were completely yellow. The most popular color of parakeets in the United States is sky-blue. These birds have sky-blue bodies and white faces; this color mutation occurred in 1878 in Europe. There are over 66 different colors of parakeets listed by the Color and Technical Committee of the Budgerigar Society. In addition to the original green-bodied and yellow-faced birds, colors of parakeets include varying shades of violets, blues, grays, greens, yellows, and whites. (p. 61)

Her analysis of this paragraph is approximately reproduced in Table 12-4. Note that this analysis tends to organize various facts as more or less major points. The highest level organizing relationship in this paragraph is explanation (see item 3, Table 12-3). Specifically, the major points in this explanation are that (A) there has been careful breeding of color mutants and (B) there is a wide variety of parakeet color, and point A is given as an explanation of point B. Organized under A are some events from the history of parakeet breeding. This organization is an example of a sequence relationship. Organized under these events are specific details. So, for instance, organized under A2 is the fact that John Gould was a naturalist. Organized under point B is evidence supporting the assertion about the wide variety and some details about the variation in color available.

Table 12-4 *Analysis of the Parakeet Paragraph*

1. A explains B.
   A. There was careful breeding of color mutants of green-bodied and yellow-faced parakeets. The historical sequence is
      1. Their natural habitat was Australia. Specific detail:
         a. Their color here is light-green body and yellow-face combination.
      2. The first living parakeets were brought to Europe from Australia by John Gould in 1840. Specific detail:
         a. John Gould was a naturalist.
      3. The first color mutation appeared in 1872 in Belgium. Specific detail:
         a. These birds were completely yellow.
      4. The sky-blue mutation occurred in 1878 in Europe. Specific details:
         a. These birds have sky-blue bodies and white faces.
         b. This is the most popular color in America.

   B. There is a wide variety in color of parakeets that are on the market today. Evidence for this is
      1. There are over 66 different colors of parakeets listed by the Color and Technical Committee of the Budgerigar Society.
      2. There are many available colors. A collection of these is
         a. The original green-bodies and yellow-faced birds
         b. Violets
         c. Blues
         d. Grays
         e. Greens
         f. Yellows
         g. Whites

From Meyer, 1974.

Text Structure and Memory

A great deal of research has demonstrated the psychological significance of text structure. Considerable disagreement prevails in the field as to exactly what system of relations should be used in the analysis of texts, and uncertainty exists as to how such systems should be applied to a text. However, memory experiments have yielded evidence that subjects do, to some degree, respond to the structure of a text.

The kind of hierarchical structure exemplified in Meyer's analysis is reminiscent of the hierarchical structures we studied in Chapter 7 on memory. From the data cited in that chapter we would expect such hierarchies to have large effects on memory—if the subjects use these hierarchies in comprehension. Meyer has shown that subjects do display better memory for the major points in such a structure. For instance, subjects are more likely to remember that there was careful breeding of color mutants (point A) than that John Gould was a naturalist (point A2a).

Meyer, Brandt, and Bluth (1978) studied students' perception of the high-level structure of a text—that is, the structural relations at the higher levels of hierarchies like that in Table 12-4. They found considerable variation in subjects' ability to recognize the high-level structure that organized a text. Moreover, they found that subjects' ability to identify the top-level structure of a text as an important predictor of their memory for the text. In another study, on ninth graders, Bartlett (1978) found that only 11 percent of subjects consciously identified and used high-level structure to remember text material. This select group did twice as well as other students on their recall scores. Bartlett also showed that training students to identify and use top-level structure more than doubled recall performance.

In addition to its hierarchical structure, a text tends to be held together by causal and logical structures. This is clearest in narratives where there are sequences of events in which one event in the sequence caused the next. The scripts we discussed in Chapter 5 are one kind of knowledge structure that is designed to encode such causal relationships. Often the causal links are not explicitly stated but rather have to be inferred. For instance, we might hear on a newscast:

> There is an accident on the Parkway East. Traffic is being rerouted through Wilkinsburg.

It is left to the listener to infer that the first fact is the cause of the second fact. Keenan, Baillet, and Brown (1984) did a study of the effect of the probability of the causal relationship connecting two sentences on the processing of the second sentence. They had subjects read pairs of sentences of which the first might be one of the following:

1a. Joey's big brother punched him again and again.

1b. Racing down the hill, Joey fell off his bike.

1c. Joey's crazy mother became furiously angry with him.

1d. Joey went to a neighbor's house to play.

Keenan et al. were interested in the effect of the first sentence on time to read a second sentence such as:

2. The next day, his body was covered with bruises.

Sentences 1a through 1d are ordered in decreasing probability of a causal connection to the second sentence. Correspondingly, Keenan et al. found that subjects' reading times for sentence 2 increased from 2.6 seconds when preceded by high probable causes like 1a to 3.3 seconds when preceded by low probable causes like 1d. It takes longer to create a more distant causal relationship.

There are also effects of causal relatedness on recall. Those parts of a story that are more central to its causal structure are more likely to be recalled (Black & Bern, 1981; Trabasso, Secco, & van den Broek, 1984). For instance, Black and Bern had subjects study stories that included pairs of sentences such as:

> The cat leapt up on the kitchen table.
> Fred picked up the cat and put it outside.

which are causally related. They contrasted these with pairs of sentences such as the following:

> The cat rubbed against the kitchen table.
> Fred picked up the cat and put it outside.

which are only temporally related. Although the second sentence is identical in both cases, subjects displayed better memories for the sentence in the case of a causally related pair.

Thorndyke (1977) has also shown that memory for text is poorer if the organization of the text conflicts with what would be considered its "natural" structure. This is clearly what we would expect given the results of Chapter 7 (consider, for instance, the experiment of Bower et al., 1969, in that chapter). Some subjects studied the original story while other subjects studied the story with its sentences presented in a scrambled order. Subjects were able to recall 85 percent of the facts in the original story but only 32 percent of the facts in the scrambled story.

Mandler and Johnson (1977) showed that children are much poorer than adults at recalling the causal structure of a story. Adults recall events and the outcomes of those events together, whereas children recall the outcomes but tend to forget how they were achieved. For instance, children might recall from a particular story that the butter melted but forget that this occurred because the butter was out in the sun. Adults do not have trouble with such simple causal structures, but they may have difficulty perceiving the more complex relationships connecting portions of a text. For instance, how easy is it for you to specify the relationship that connects this paragraph to the preceding text?

Kintsch and van Dijk's Text Comprehension Model

Kintsch and van Dijk (1978) have brought many of the ideas we have discussed into an overall information-processing model of how one comprehends and remembers a text. Their model assumes that parsing processes have been applied to analyze the text into a set of propositions and their analysis focuses on the further processing of the text after the initial set of propositions has been identified. As a simple example, consider this short text from Kintsch (1979):

> The Swazi tribe was at war with a neighboring tribe because of a dispute over cattle. Among the warriors were two unmarried men, Kakra and his younger brother Gum. Kakra was killed in battle. (p. 6)

This would be analyzed into the following propositions:

1. (name tribe1 Swazi)
2. (neighbor tribe2 tribe1)
3. (at-war tribe1 tribe2) = α
4. (cause α β)
5. (dispute tribe1 tribe2 cattle) = β
6. (among warriors men)
7. (number men two)
8. (unmarried men)
9. (name men [Kakra Gum])
10. (younger-brother-of Kakra Gum)
11. (killed Kakra battle)

According to the Kintsch and van Dijk model, as the propositions are processed the comprehender must relate new propositions to previous ones. This is done by overlap of terms. Thus, proposition 2 above can be easily related to proposition 1 because they overlap in the term *tribe1*. It is usually easy to relate the propositions within a sentence. Difficulties frequently arise when one must relate propositions across sentence boundaries. In the example above, there is a difficulty relating proposition 6 to the preceding. To relate the proposition, comprehenders have to make what is called a *bridging inference* (Haviland & Clark, 1974). In this case the bridging inference is that the warriors in proposition 6 were the people from the Swazi tribe. According to Kintsch and van Dijk, one of the things that makes comprehension difficult is the need to make such bridging inferences.

According to Kintsch and van Dijk, there is a capacity limit (which they estimate to be four, on average) on the number of propositions one can keep active in working memory (see Chapter 6). There are two important consequences of this capacity limit. One is that the comprehender may fail to relate a new proposition to the previous text because the previous proposition with the shared term is no longer active. We noted earlier in our discussion of reference that subjects need more time to process a referring expression the farther back in the text that referring expression occurred. According to Kintsch and van Dijk, this is because of a reinstatement search in which comprehenders reactivate past propositions from long-term memory looking for a proposition that overlaps in terms with the current proposition.

The second consequence of this limitation on the number of active propositions involves recall. Referring to previous research on memory (see Chapter 6), Kintsch and van Dijk argue that the longer a proposition is held active the greater the strength of its long-term encoding and the higher the probability of its eventual recall. Since there is a limitation on the number of propositions a person can keep active in working memory, one has to pick propositions to stay in working memory and propositions to go. Depending on what one picks, different propositions will enjoy different levels of recall.

According to Kintsch and van Dijk, comprehenders use some combination of recency and importance to select which propositions to keep active. They propose what has been called the *leading edge* strategy, in which subjects keep active the most recent proposition that has been processed and propositions which are superior to it in a hierarchical representation of a text (e.g., see Table 12-4). Thus, upon reading proposition 5 about the cattle dispute, they would keep it active; they would do the same with proposition 4, which relates it to the war proposition. More recently, Fletcher (1986) has found that subjects not only keep active those propositions which are high in the hierarchy, but those propositions which are causally important. This is consistent with the earlier evidence that both position in the text structure and causal centrality are important in text processing. One consequence of such strategies for keeping the more central propositions active is that the Kintsch and van Dijk model produces the phenomenon noted earlier—that the hierarchically and causally central facts from a text are the better recalled.

Kintsch and van Dijk propose that there are two kinds of elaborations a reader makes to embellish on the propositions in the text. The first are the bridging inferences that we have already discussed, in which the comprehender adds inferences to relate otherwise unrelated terms. The other is the formation of what Kintsch and van Dijk called *macropropositions,* which are summaries of the gist of the text. So, for instance, one summary proposition for the text we just read is "A soldier is killed in war." The formation of these macropropositions also leads to the observed phenomenon of better recall for the main points of a text in contrast to the details.

Kintsch and Vipond (1979) describe an interesting application of this analysis to the speeches of Eisenhower and Stevenson from the presidential campaign of 1952. It has been argued that Stevenson lost the election because his speeches were hard to understand. However, if one does a comparison of the speeches using standard readability measures that consider features such as word length, word frequency, and sentence length, the speeches of Eisenhower are rated as more complex. On the other hand, if one applies the Kintsch and van Dijk comprehension model to Stevenson's speeches one finds that they required a number of bridging inferences and reinstatement searches to determine reference, whereas Eisenhower's speeches did not. The implication is that listeners found it too taxing to try to integrate the references in Stevenson's speeches.

Conclusion

The number and diversity of topics covered in this chapter give witness to the impressive cumulative progress that has been made in the area of language comprehension. It is fair to say we knew almost nothing about language processing when cognitive psychology emerged from the collapse of behaviorism 30 years ago. Now we have a rather articulate picture of what is happening in scales that range from 100 milliseconds after a word is heard to the integration of large stretches of complex text. The field of language processing turns out to have a number of theoretical controversies and some of those controversies have been discussed in our review of the field (e.g., whether early language processing is separate from the rest of cognition). Such controversies should not blind us to the impressive progress that has been made. The heat in the field has also generated much light.

Remarks and Suggested Readings

The research on language comprehension is extensively reviewed in Clark and Clark (1977). Just and Carpenter (1987) provide a more recent review of the literature on language comprehension with an emphasis on reading. Garfield (1987) contains a set of articles relevant to the issue of modularity in language comprehension. A number of schemes have been proposed in computational linguistics for the processing of natural language. Good references include Schank (1975), Marcus (1980), Berwick and Weinberg (1984), Kaplan and Bresnan (1982), and Dowty, Kartunnen, and Zwicky (1985).

Black (1984) provides a review of research on story comprehension. Kintsch and van Dijk (1978) and van Dijk and Kintsch (1983) describe their theory. Applications of such text structures have been criticized (Black and Wilensky, 1979) for being too syntactic, formally ill defined, and not incorporating enough world knowledge. The book edited by Spiro, Bruce, and Brewer (1980) contains articles on text processing.

CHAPTER

·13·

Cognitive Development

Summary

1. According to Piaget, an infant enters the world lacking most basic cognitive competencies and passes through a series of stages in which the child develops more and more adequate bases for representing the world and reasoning about it.

2. Piaget demonstrated a large number of changes that occur in child cognition around the age of 6 in tasks which require reasoning about numbers, abstract relationships, and the world. These changes appear related to children's ability to more fully encode the information in these tasks.

3. A major factor in cognitive development before the age of 2 is maturation of the nervous system; a major factor after 2 is accumulation of knowledge and the strengthening of knowledge representations.

4. It is also argued that children's cognition improves because of increased processing resources. Children's rate of information processing and effective working memory capacity can be shown to increase with age.

5. Children's memory improves because they can better elaborate on to-be-recalled information and because they have better strategies for learning material and monitoring their memory.

6. As children get older they encode material in less concrete ways that are more effective for many cognitive tasks.

7. Children's problem solving improves because they can represent problems in ways that are more effective. Young children's deficits in problem representation show up as inability to set appropriate subgoals.

8. Children's arithmetic skills are organized hierarchically such that simple addition and subtraction are built out of counting skills and algorithmic calculations are built from simple addition and subtraction. When children are forced to attempt arithmetic problems for which they are not ready, systematic errors can develop.

Part of the uniqueness of the human species concerns the way children are brought into the world and develop to become adults. Humans have very large brains in relation to their body size, which eventuated in a major evolutionary problem: How was the birth of such large-brained babies to be effected? One way was through progressive enlargement of the birth canal, which is now as large as is considered possible given the constraints of mammalian skeletons (Geschwind, 1980). In addition, children are born with a skull that is sufficiently pliable for it to be compressed into a cone shape in order to fit through the birth canal. Still, the human birth process is particularly difficult compared to that of most other mammals.

Not even the evolutionary modifications just mentioned would suffice, however, if humans were born with fully developed brains. Compared with many other mammals, human infants are born with particularly immature brains. At birth a human brain occupies a volume of about 350 cm³. During the first year it doubles to 700 cm³; and before a human being reaches puberty, the size of its brain doubles again. Most other mammals do not have as much growth in brain size after birth (Gould, 1977). Since the human birth canal has been expanded to its limits, much of our neural development has been postponed until after birth.

Even though they spend nine months developing in the womb, human infants are quite helpless at birth and spend an extraordinarily long time growing to adult stature—around 15 years, which is about a fifth of our life span. Contrast this with a puppy: After a gestation period of just nine weeks, it is born more capable than an infant. In less than a year, less than a tenth of its life span, it has reached full size and reproductive capability.

Childhood is prolonged more than would be needed to develop large brains. Indeed, most neural development is complete by age 2 and almost all by age 5. Humans are kept children by the slowness of their physical development. It has been speculated (deBeer, 1959) that the function of this slow physical development has been to keep children in a dependency relationship to adults. There is much that has to be learned in order to become a competent adult, and staying a child so long gives the human time enough to acquire that knowledge. Childhood is an apprenticeship for adulthood.

Modern society is so complex that we cannot learn all that is needed by simply associating with our parents for 15 years. To provide the needed training, society has created social institutions such as high schools, colleges, and post-college professional schools. It is not unusual for people to spend more than 25 years, almost as long as their professional life, preparing for their role in society.

Viewed from this perspective, we should expect a study of cognitive development to provide major insights into the nature of human intelligence. However, the study of child cognition is more difficult than the study of adult cognition. It is very hard to get children to follow instructions before the age of 3, and children younger than 6 months are capable of only a few motor movements, such as sucking, swinging their hands, and kicking. However, many of the most interesting cognitive changes are occurring in these early years. Developmental psychologists have had to be very clever in finding methodologies to determine what children know.

In their research, developmental psychologists have been influenced by the Swiss psychologist Jean Piaget, who studied and theorized about child development for more than half a century. Recent information-processing work in cognitive development has largely been concerned with correcting and restructuring Piaget's theory of cognitive development. Despite these revisions, his research has organized a large set of qualitative observations about cognitive development spanning the period from birth to adulthood. Modern cognitive psychology research has been concerned with identifying the mechanisms that account for these developments. Thus, in this chapter, we will first describe Piaget's view of cognitive development and then turn to the more recent research.

Piaget's Stages of Development

According to Piaget, a child enters the world lacking virtually all the basic cognitive competencies of the adult, and gradually develops these competencies by passing through a series of *stages* of development. Piaget distinguishes four major stages: the *sensory-motor stage* occupies the first two years. During this stage, children develop schemes for thinking about the physical world — for instance, they develop the notion of an object as a permanent thing in the world. The second stage is the *preoperational stage,* which is characterized as spanning the period from 2 to 7 years. Unlike the younger child, a child in this period can engage in internal thought about the world, but these mental processes are intuitive and lack systematicity. For instance, a 4-year-old asked to describe his painting of a farm and some animals said, "First over here is a house where the animals live. I live in a house. So do my mommy and daddy. This is a horse. I saw horses on TV. Do you have a TV?"

The next stage is the *concrete-operational stage,* which spans the period from 7 to 11 years. In this period children develop a set of mental operations that allow them to treat the physical world in a systematic way. However, children still have major limitations on their capacity to reason formally about the world. The capacity for formal reasoning emerges during Piaget's fourth period, the *formal-operational stage,* spanning the years from 11 to 15. After emerging from this period, the child has become an adult conceptually and is capable of scientific reasoning — which Piaget takes as the paradigm case of mature intellectual functioning.

Piaget's concept of a stage has always been a sore point in developmental psychology. Obviously a child does not suddenly change on an eleventh birthday from the stage of concrete operations to the stage of formal operations. There are large differences among children and cultures, and the ages given are just rough figures. However, careful analysis of the development within a single child also fails to find abrupt changes at any age. One response to this gradualness has been to break down the stages into smaller substages. Another response has been to interpret stages as simply ways of characterizing what is inherently a gradual and continuous process.[1]

Just as important as Piaget's stage analysis is his analysis of children's performance in specific tasks within these stages. These task analyses

---

[1] Indeed, Piaget himself never said there were abrupt changes between stages although he is frequently so interpreted.

provide the empirical substance to back up his broad and abstract characterization of the stages. Below we describe some of the tasks that Piaget used to trace out intellectual development in his four stages. The intellectual development exposed by each task nicely illustrates Piaget's concept of that stage.

Hidden Objects

As adults we would be surprised if objects started to magically appear and disappear in our environment. A question that interested Piaget is whether newborn children would be similarly surprised. That is, do children come into the world thinking of objects as having separate existences that continue over transformations in time and space? Piaget concluded from his experiments that children do not, and that they develop a concept of object permanence during the first year. If a cloth is placed over a toy that a 6-month-old is reaching for, the infant stops reaching and appears to lose interest in the toy (see Figure 13-1). It is as if the object ceases to exist for the child when no longer in view.

According to Piaget, the concept of object permanence develops slowly and is one of the major intellectual developments in the sensory-motor stage. An older infant will search for an object that has been hidden, but more demanding tests reveal failings in the older infant's understanding of a permanent object. In one experiment, an object is put under cover A and then, in front of the child, is removed and put under cover B. The child will often look for the object under cover A. It is only after the age of 12 months that the child can succeed consistently at this task.

Recently, researchers (Bjork & Cummings, 1984; Sophian, 1984a) have provided evidence that the behavior Piaget documented on the hidden objects task may really reflect a memory or encoding failure rather than the lack of the concept of an enduring object. It seems that the infant simply forgets the move from A to B. Sophian has produced evidence for this conclusion in two ways. First she showed that if an infant was practiced on the move from A to B (by moving the object from A to B multiple times in front of the child), he or she was much more likely to correctly look under B. Thus, by increasing the probability that the child would remember the A-to-B move, Sophian increased the probability of correct performance on the task. The second paradigm involved three locations — A, B, and C — for hidden objects. As before, the object would be moved from A to B, but now it was possible to determine how often children made incorrect searches at C as well as at A. If the infant simply forgot everything, he or she would be just as likely to search at A as C. In

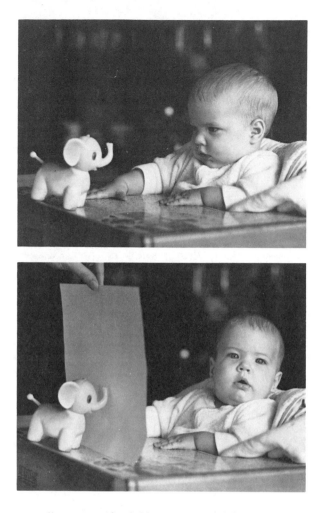

Figure 13-1. An illustration of a child's apparent inability to understand the permanence of an object. (Monkmeyer Press Photo Service, Inc. From John W. Santrock and Steven R. Yussen, *Child Development: An Introduction,* 4th ed. Copyright © 1989 Wm. C. Brown Publishers, Dubuque, IA. All Rights Reserved. Reprinted by permission.)

fact, this is just what was found. Thus, much of what Piaget thought of as fundamental conceptual changes in understanding the nature of the world may be just improvements in memory.

Conservation

A number of important cognitive developments occur around the age of 6, which, according to Piaget, is the transition between the preoperational and concrete operational stages. Before this age children can be shown to have some glaring errors in their reasoning. These errors start to correct themselves at this point in time. There has been considerable controversy about the cause of this change, with different theorists pointing to language (Bruner, 1964) and the advent of schooling (Cole & D'Andrade, 1982), among other possible causes. Here we will content ourselves with describing the changes. Perhaps the most famous cognitive shift concerns something Piaget referred to as conservation of quantity.

As adults we can almost instantaneously recognize that there are four apples in a bag and can confidently know that these apples will remain four when dumped into a bowl. Piaget was interested in how a child develops the concept of quantity and learns that quantity is something that is preserved under various transformations, such as moving the objects from a bag to a bowl. His research on this topic is referred to as research on *conservation* because he was interested in how children come to know that quantity is conserved under some transformations.

Figure 13-2 illustrates a typical conservation problem that has been posed by psychologists in many variations to countless preschool children. A child is presented with two rows of objects, such as checkers. The two rows contain the same number of objects and have been lined up so as to correspond. The child is asked whether the two rows have the same amount, and says that they do. The child can be asked to count the objects in the two rows to confirm that conclusion. Now, before the child's eyes, one row is compressed so that it is shorter than the other row, but the number is not changed. Again asked which row has more objects, the child now says the longer row has. The child appears not to know that quantity is something which is preserved under transformations such as compression of space. If asked to count the two rows, the child expresses great surprise that they have the same number.

The general feature of lack of conservation is that children are distracted by irrelevant physical features of a display. Figure 13-3 illustrates the liquid conservation task. A child is shown two identical beakers containing identical amounts of water, and an empty, tall, thin beaker. He is asked whether the two identical beakers hold the same amount of water, and agrees that they do. Now the water from one beaker is poured into the tall, thin beaker, and when asked whether the amount of water in the two containers is the same, the child now says that the tall beaker holds more. Children are distracted by physical appearance and do not relate their having seen the water go from one beaker into the other to the quantity of liquid. Bruner (1964) demonstrated that a child is less likely to make this error if the tall beaker is hidden from sight while it is

Figure 13-2. A typical experimental situation to test for conservation of number. (Monkmeyer Press Photo Service. From John W. Santrock and Steven R. Yussen, *Child Development: An Introduction,* 4th ed. Copyright © 1989 Wm. C. Brown Publishers, Dubuque, IA. All Rights Reserved. Reprinted by permission.)

filled so that the child cannot see the physical appearance. So, it is a case of being overwhelmed by physical appearance, not that the child does not know that water preserves its quantity after being poured.

Failure of conservation has also been shown with weight and volume of solid objects (for a discussion of studies of conservation see Brainerd, 1978; Flavell, 1985; Ginsburg & Opper, 1980). It was once thought that

Figure 13-3. A typical experimental situation to test for conservation of liquid. (Monkmeyer Press Photo Service. From John W. Santrock and Steven R. Yussen, *Child Development: An Introduction,* 4th ed. Copyright © 1989 Wm. C. Brown Publishers, Dubuque, IA. All Rights Reserved. Reprinted by permission.)

failure of conservation was a more or less unitary problem. Now, however, it is clear that successful conservation appears earlier on some tasks than on others. For instance, conservation of number usually appears before conservation of liquid. Also, children in transition will show conservation of number in one experimental situation but not another.

Transitive Inference

One of the fundamental abilities of adults is to reason about transitive relationships. For instance, if we are told that *Fred is taller than Bill* (Fred > Bill) and *George is taller than Fred,* (George > Fred) we have no difficulty in concluding that *George is tallest.* In contrast, children in the preoperational stage have great difficulty in ordering objects serially. Given the problem just stated, they will often conclude that *Fred is tallest* because he alone is mentioned in two *tall* sentences. As another example, a child given a set of wooden sticks and asked to order them will produce

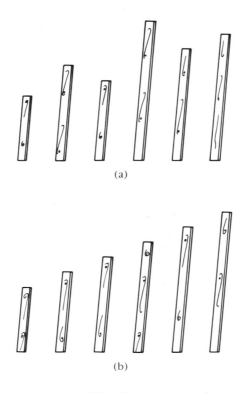

(a)

(b)

Figure 13-4. A preoperational child will produce an ordering of sticks like that in (a) rather than the correct ordering in (b).

an order like the one in Figure 13-4 (part a) rather than the correct order (part b). Piaget felt that these problems in transitive inference were important because they reflected fundamental problems in logical reasoning during the preoperational period.

Trabasso and his coworkers speculated that children's difficulties occur because they have not memorized and properly represented the pairwise relationships (e.g., A > B). Bryant and Trabasso (1971) taught preschoolers the pairwise orderings among five colored sticks (e.g., the red stick is longer than the blue stick). Unlike the typical procedure, they drilled the children on the four pairwise relations A > B, B > C, C > D, D > E until the children were able to recall with a high level of accuracy. Having been forced to achieve this memory criterion, the children were able to make the transitive inferences (e.g., B > D) with a high degree of accuracy. Thus, it appears that part of the children's difficulty was their failure to keep the pairwise relations in mind.

Riley and Trabasso (1974) compared two training procedures for getting children to memorize the pairwise relations. In one condition they had subjects answer questions of both the form *Which is shorter, A or B?* and the form *Which is longer, A or B?* In the other condition they had children answer questions of just one form or the other. Of the 4-year-olds trained with both forms, 87 percent were able to learn the relations, whereas only 35 percent were successful when trained with just one form. Riley and Trabasso propose that children trained just that *Stick A is longer than B* simply encoded *Stick A is long* and *Stick B is long.* Such absolute encoding did not enable them to answer the questions. The effect of using both *longer* and *shorter,* Trabasso and Riley claimed, was to force the children to encode the sticks in a relative form such that they could answer the transitive questions. Thus, we find that a major factor in children's success on a problem is the way they represent the information in the task. For further discussion of transitive inference read Halford (1984), who argues that preschool children show deficits on complex transitive reasoning tasks which cannot be explained in terms of failures of memory or failures of problem encoding.

Balance-Scale Task

Inhelder and Piaget (1958) have also looked at children's reasoning on a wide variety of elementary physics tasks: balance scales, projections of shadows, pendulums, falling bodies, and the like.On all these tasks they tend to find the same developmental trends: 5-year-olds (preoperational) have little or no systematic understanding; 10-year-olds (concrete operations) understand the qualitative but not the quantitative relations; 15-

year-olds (formal operations) understand both the qualitative and quantitative relations and have some understanding of the relevant theoretical constructs. Thus, these tasks are particularly interesting because they allow us to trace a child's development across three stages.

Figure 13-5 illustrates the balance-scale task. Piaget collected protocols of children solving various problems involving the balance scale. The problems involved two sets of various weights placed at various distances from the fulcrum. Children around the age of 5 predict that the side with more weights will go down: they do not consider distance from the fulcrum. Children around the age of 10 engage in crude attempts to trade off distance and weight. Children at 15 reason quite accurately about the problems, often bringing to bear the correct mathematical formula.

Siegler (1980) provided a rule-based analysis of the balance-scale problems. He proposes that children operate according to one of the four rule sets in Table 13-1 when working with the balance scales.

Rule set 1 represents a child completely dominated by the dimension of weight. If the weights are different, the child chooses the greater weight (rule A); otherwise the child believes the scale will balance (rule B). Siegler found that this rule set characterized 5-year-olds. As children get older, rule B is replaced by rules C and D, which enable the child to respond to the distance from the fulcrum if the weights are equal. This defines rule set 2. Rule set 2 still has rule A, and so the child erroneously decides that the side with more weights will go down even when distance from the fulcrum invalidates this decision. Rule set 3 is derived by replacing rule A with rule E, which decides that the side with more weights will go down if the distances from the fulcrum are consistent. Siegler found that children in the 8- to 12-year range could be characterized as following either rule set 2 or rule set 3. Rule set 2 has children incorrectly responding when a distance difference compensates a weight difference. Rule set 3 does not provide the child with a basis for deciding when weight and distance are in conflict, and children using this rule set

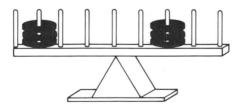

Figure 13-5. The balance-scale problem used by Inhelder and Piaget.

Table 13-1 *Siegler's Four Rule Sets*

Rule set 1:

A   IF   the number of weights is greater on side 1
       THEN   side 1 will go down.

B   IF   the number of weights on the two sides are equal
       THEN   the two sides will stay in balance.

Rule set 2:   Rule A from rule set 1 plus

C   IF   the number of weights on the two sides are equal
            and the weights are farther from the fulcrum on side 1
       THEN   side 1 will go down.

D   IF   the number of weights on both sides are equal
            and the distances from the fulcrum are equal
       THEN   the weights will balance.

Rule set 3:   Rules C and D from rule set 2 plus

E   IF   the number of weights is greater on side 1
            and the weights are as far or farther from the fulcrum on side 1
       THEN   side 1 will go down.

Rule set 4:   Rules C, D, and E from rule set 3 plus

F   IF   the number of weights on side 1 is greater
            and the weights are as far or farther from the fulcrum on side 2
       THEN   multiply weight and distance for each side and compare the
                  products.

Adapted from Siegler, 1980.

respond randomly. Only rule set 4 prescribes the correct multiplicative combination of weight and distance. Siegler found a few 12-year-olds who used the multiplicative rule and a few more college students. However, even a majority of the college students did not know the multiplicative rule.

Siegler (1976) shows that these rule sets are very accurate in modeling the behavior of individual children. He has argued that development can be modeled by adding better rules and deleting poorer ones. Klahr and Siegler (1978) also showed that very young children do not even notice the differences in distance. If these children are instructed to attend to these differences in distance and encode them, they will benefit from experience with the balance scale. So 5-year-olds behaving according to rule set 1 can be trained to behave according to rule set 3 if they attend to the distance dimension. Thus, once again we see that adopting the correct representation is critical to cognitive development.

What Develops?

Clearly, as Piaget has documented, major intellectual changes occur during childhood. However, there are serious questions concerning what underlies these changes. There are two basic classes of explanation for why children perform better on various intellectual tasks as they get older: One is that they think better and the other is that they know better. The *think-better* option holds that children's basic cognitive processes are better. Perhaps they can hold more information in working memory, retrieve information faster, apply productions faster. The *know-better* option holds that children have learned more and more facts and methods as they get older. I refer to this as *know-better* not *know-more* because it is not just a matter of adding knowledge but also a matter of eliminating erroneous facts and inappropriate methods. Perhaps this superior knowledge enables them to perform the tasks more efficiently. Once again, the computer metaphor is apt. A computer system (e.g., for doing deduction) can be made to perform better by running the same program on a faster machine that has more memory or by running a better program on the same machine. Which is it in the child's case — better machine or better program?

Of course this is not an either-or situation. The child's improvement is due to both factors, but this leaves open the relative contributions of the two. It is tempting to emphasize the improvement in processing capacity. After all, consider the physical difference between a 2-year-old and an adult. When my son was 2, he had difficulty mastering the unsnapping of his pajama buttons. If his muscles and coordination had so much maturation ahead, why not his brain? This analogy, however, does not hold: A 2-year-old has reached only 20 percent of his adult body weight, whereas the brain has already reached 80 percent of its final size. We might argue that cognitive development after age 2 will, to an approximation, depend on the knowledge an individual puts in the brain rather than on physical improvement in the capacities of the brain.

Siegler (in press) argues that much of the developmental changes that take place over the first two years are to be understood in terms of neural changes. Huttenlocher (1979) noted that the density of synapses (that is, the number of synapses from one neuron to another — see Chapter 2) in the brain increases until age 2 when it reaches levels higher than adult levels, after which it gradually decreases. Goldman-Rakic (1987) has argued that performance in the hidden objects task, for instance, depends on achieving a certain level of synaptic density. It turns out that children first start succeeding at this task at age 6 months and monkeys at age 2 months—in both species this is the time when synaptic density reaches adult levels.

Increased Knowledge

Beyond the first couple of years development may depend mainly on the acquisition of knowledge. Chi (1978) has demonstrated that developmental differences may be knowledge related. Her domain of demonstration was memory. Not surprisingly, children do worse than adults on almost every memory task. Is this because their memories have less capacity, or is it because they know less about what they are being asked to remember? To address this question, she compared memory performance of 10-year-olds to that of adults on two tasks—a standard digit-span task and a chess memory task (see the discussion of these tasks in Chapters 6 and 9). The 10-year-olds were skilled chess players, whereas the adults were novices at chess. The chess task was the one illustrated earlier in Figure 9-12—a chessboard was presented for 10 seconds and then withdrawn, and subjects were asked to reproduce the chess pattern.

Figure 13-6 illustrates the number of chess pieces recalled by children and adults. The figure also contrasts these results with the number of digits recalled in the digit-span task. As Chi predicted, the adults were better on the digit-span task but the children were better on the chess

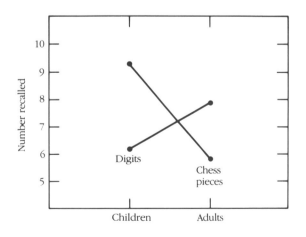

Figure 13-6. Number of chess pieces and number of digits recalled by children versus adults. (From Chi, 1978.)

task. The children's superior chess performance was attributed to their greater knowledge of chess. The adults' superior digit performance was due to their greater familiarity with digits—the dramatic digit-span performance of SF in Chapter 9 shows just how much digit knowledge can lead to improved memory performance.

The novice-expert contrasts from Chapter 9 are often used to explain developmental phenomena. We saw that a great deal of experience in a domain is required if a person is to become an expert. Chi's argument is that children, because of their lack of knowledge, are universal novices and can become as expert as adults only through experience.

The Chi experiment contrasted child experts with adult novices. Recently, Schneider, Körkel, and Weinert (1988) looked at the effect of expertise at various age levels. They categorized German school children as either experts or novices with respect to soccer. They did this separately for grade levels 3, 5, and 7. The students at each grade level were asked to recall a story about soccer. Table 13-2 illustrates the amount of recall displayed as a function of grade level and expertise. There is a much larger effect of expertise than grade level. On a recognition test there was no effect of grade level and only an effect of expertise. They also classified each group of subjects into high-ability and low-ability subjects on the basis of their performance on intelligence tests. Although such tests generally predict memory for stories they found no effect of general ability level but only of knowledge for soccer. Schneider et al. argue that high-ability students are just those who know a lot about a lot of domains and consequently generally do well on memory tests. However, when tested for a soccer story, a high-ability student who knows nothing about soccer will do worse than a low-ability student who knows a lot about soccer.

Another perspective on the nature of developmental changes is provided by Kail (1988). He looked at a number of cognitive tasks, including the mental rotation task we examined in Chapter 4. He presented subjects

Table 13-2 *Mean Percentages of Idea Units Recalled as a Function of Grade and Expertise*

Grade	Soccer Experts	Soccer Novices
3	54	32
5	52	33
7	61	42

From Körkel, 1987.

414

with pairs of letters in different orientations and asked them to judge whether the letters were the same or were mirror images of one another. As we discussed in Chapter 4, subjects tend to mentally rotate an image of one object into congruence with the other in order to make this judgment. Kail observed people from the ages of 8 to 22 performing this task and found that they got systematically faster with age. He was interested in rotation rate, which he measured as number of seconds to rotate one degree of angle. Figure 13-7 shows this data, plotting rate of rotation as a function of age. It turns out that the time to rotate a degree of angle decreases as a power function of age. The reader will recall from Chapters 6 and 9 that such power functions are typical of skill acquisition. One possible implication is that mental rotation is a skill which improves with the practice that age brings. This is a conclusion that Kail seems to be coming to in his more recent publications (Kail & Park, in press).

Increased Mental Capacity

A number of recent developmental theories have argued that an important component of development is the trend of increasing mental capacity that continues through the teenage years (Case, 1985; Fischer, 1980; Halford, 1982; Pascal-Leone, 1980). These are often called neo-Piagetian theories of development. I will review here the memory-space approach of Case, whose key proposal is that a growing working-memory capacity is the key to the developmental sequence. The basic idea is that more advanced cognitive performance requires that more information be held in working memory.

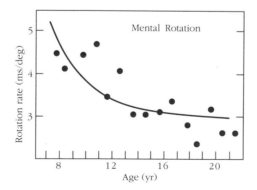

Figure 13-7. Rates of mental rotation, estimated from the slope of the function relating response time to the orientation of the stimulus. (Kail, 1988.)

415

As an example of this analysis, consider Case's (1978) description of how children solve Noelting's (1975) juice problems. The child is given two empty pitchers, A and B, and is told that several tumblers of orange juice and water will be poured into each. The child's task is to predict which pitcher will taste most strongly of orange juice. Figure 13-8 illustrates the problems that children can solve at various ages. At the youngest age, children can reliably solve only problems where all orange juice goes into one pitcher and all water into another. At ages 4–5, they can count the number of tumblers of orange juice going into a pitcher and choose the pitcher with the larger number—not considering the number of tumblers of water. At ages 7–8, they notice whether there is more orange juice or more water going into a pitcher. If pitcher A has more orange juice than water and pitcher B has more water than orange juice, they will choose pitcher A even if the absolute number of orange juice glasses is less. Finally, at ages 9–10, children compute the difference between the amount of orange juice and the amount of water (still not a perfect solution).

Case argues that the working-memory requirements differ for the various types of problems represented in Figure 13-8. For the simplest problems the child has to keep only one fact in memory—which set of tumblers has the orange juice. Children at ages 3–4 can keep only one such fact in mind. If both sets of tumblers have orange juice, the child cannot solve the problem. For the second type of problem the child needs

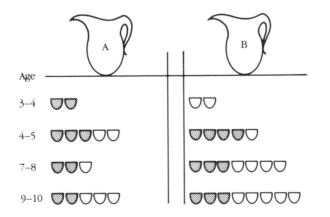

Figure 13-8. The Noelting juice problem that children can solve at various ages. The problem is to tell which pitcher will taste more strongly of orange juice after observing the tumblers of water and juice that will be poured into each.

to keep two things in memory—the number of orange juice tumblers in each array. In the third type of problem the child needs to keep additional partial products in mind to determine which side has more orange juice. To solve the fourth type of problem, the child needs four facts to make a judgment:

1. the absolute difference in tumblers going into pitcher A

2. the sign of the difference for pitcher A (i.e., whether there is more water or more orange juice going into pitcher A)

3. the absolute difference in tumblers going into pitcher B

4. the sign of the difference for pitcher B

Case argues that children's developmental sequences are controlled by their working-memory capacity for the problem. Only when they can keep four facts in memory will they achieve the fourth stage in the developmental sequence. Case's theory has been criticized (e.g., Flavell, 1978) because it is hard to decide how to count the working-memory requirements.

Another question concerns what controls the growth in working memory. Case believes it is somewhat experience-based. We noted in Chapter 9 that effective working memory increases with experience. However, Case argues that the major factor in the increase of working memory is increased speed of neural function. He cites evidence that the degree of myelination increases with age, with spurts approximately at those points where he postulates major changes in working memory. Recall from Chapter 2 that the degree of myelination of axons determines the rate of neural transmission of information.

Development of Cognitive Processes

Having now reviewed the Piagetian theory and some alternative views of cognitive development, it would be useful to examine some of the recent research on the development of various aspects of cognition. The previous chapters have looked at these processes as they are manifested in adults. Here I would like to review what has been learned about how these cognitive processes reach their adult form.

Memory

Despite Chi's demonstration in Figure 13-6, adults and older children typically outperform younger children on memory tasks. One point of view is that this is not due to greater capacity but rather to the use of better strategies for encoding and retrieving information. When we look at simple recognition memory, something that typically does not involve an important strategic component, there is little change through the span of childhood (Brown, 1975; Perlmutter, 1980).

Young children appear to lack some of the most basic strategies of memory performance. The clearest case concerns rehearsal. If you were asked to dial a novel seven-digit number, I would hope you would rehearse it to yourself until you were confident you had it memorized or until you had dialed the number. It would not occur to young children that they should rehearse the number. In one study comparing 5-year-olds with 10-year-olds, Keeney, Cannizzo, and Flavell (1967) found that 10-year-olds almost always verbally rehearsed a set of objects to be remembered, whereas 5-year-olds seldom did. Young children's performance often improves if they are instructed to follow a verbal rehearsal strategy, although very young children are simply unable to execute such a strategy.

Part of the reason children do not spontaneously use verbal rehearsal may be their inaccurate knowledge about how their memories work. Flavell, Friedrichs, and Hoyt (1970) presented children with 10 pictures and asked them how many they could remember. Most nursery-schoolers and kindergartners thought they could remember all 10. Older children had more realistic estimates. In another study, Kreutzer, Leonard, and Flavell (1975) asked children what they would do if they were told a new phone number to dial and also wanted a drink of water. Almost all (95 percent) of the third and fifth graders said they would phone first before getting a drink of water, but only 40 percent of the kindergartners thought that to be a wise strategy. In addition, almost all of the older children thought they would adopt some measure like writing the number down or rehearsing it. In contrast, only 60 percent of the kindergartners thought that any special measures were required.

Chapter 7 emphasized the importance of elaborative strategies for good memory performance. Particularly for long-term retention, elaboration appears to be much more effective than rote rehearsal. There also appear to be sharp developmental trends with respect to the use of elaborative encoding strategies. For instance, Paris and Lindauer (1976) looked at the elaborations that children use to relate two paired-associate nouns such as *lady* and *broom.* Older children are more likely to generate interactive sentences such as *The lady flew on the broom* than static sentences such as *The lady had a broom.* Such interactive sentences will lead to better memory performance. Children are also poorer at drawing the inferences that improve memory for a story (Stein & Trabasso, 1981).

Another difficulty young children have is that they often are not aware of when they are not learning something. Brown and her colleagues (Campione & Brown, 1978; Brown, Smiley, & Lawton, 1978) looked at how students from the fifth grade through college studied texts. Students were allowed to read the texts multiple times. Older students shifted their attention on later readings to focus on material that they did not pick up in the first reading. In contrast, younger students kept focusing on the same material (typically the main points) on reading after reading long after they had mastered this material.

Young children often are not even aware of when they have not understood a passage they have read. Markman (1979) studied children's memory for the following description of how to make Baked Alaska:

> To make it they put the ice cream in a very hot oven. The ice cream in Baked Alaska melts when it gets very hot. Then they take the ice cream out of the oven and serve it right away. When they make Baked Alaska, the ice cream stays firm and does not melt. (p. 656)

Many children in the third through sixth grades were not able to detect the inconsistency in this passage.

Palinscar and Brown (1984) attempted to help poor-performing seventh graders (at the 20th percentile in their classes) by instruction on how to monitor their comprehension of a text. This was done by a reciprocal modeling procedure in which the teacher would model how to monitor comprehension by summarizing one paragraph and noting points that need clarification and then the student would do this for the next. Students given this training advanced from the 20th to the 56th percentile in reading performance.

In summary, memory improves as children get older for the following reasons:

1. Children learn the proper strategies for memorization and practice these strategies until they become effective at applying them.

2. They learn to monitor their memory and comprehension and to focus on the places where they are having difficulty.

3. As they get older they acquire more knowledge, which enables more effective encoding and elaboration.

Knowledge Representation

A frequent key to developmental improvement is the representation of knowledge in such a way that efficient and effective mental processes can apply to that knowledge. Earlier in the book (Chapters 4 and 5) we contrasted perceptually based representations with meaning-based representations. There we noted that meaning-based representations were often more effective. A recurring hypothesis in developmental psychology is that young children rely more on perceptually based representations, whereas adults depend on meaning-based representations (Bruner, Oliver, & Greenfield, 1966; Kosslyn, 1980; Piaget & Inhelder, 1971). Although this conjecture is appealing, it has proven remarkably resistant to experimental exploration.

An experiment reported by Kosslyn (1980) represents one attempt to get at this issue. He had first graders and adults verify statements such as *A cat has claws.* He reasoned that for adults, the efficient way to verify this assertion was to retrieve an abstract proposition. In contrast, he thought children would have to inspect an image of a cat and notice the claws. This was a less efficient strategy but the only one the children had, given their representational abilities. Of course, he found adults faster to respond. However, he also manipulated how the adults decided on their responses. Some he explicitly asked to inspect an image, whereas others were free to respond as fast as they could. He used a similar instructional manipulation with children. Figure 13-9 presents his results. Adults are very much slower with the imagery strategy, suggesting that it is more efficient to inspect abstract propositions. In contrast, first graders are almost as slow given no instructions as they are given imagery instructions, suggesting that the imagery strategy is their default strategy even when they are not instructed to use it.

Although the results of this study support the hypothesis that children are more inclined to use imagery representations than abstract representations, the study leaves open the cause of their different representational usage. Is it that children are unable to form abstract representations? Or, given their young ages, do they just have less information encoded abstractly? Perhaps it is not that they are unable to encode a propositional representation of the fact that *A cat has claws,* but that they simply have not yet had the opportunity to do so.

It is also the case that some developments do not involve going from

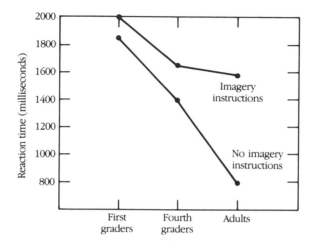

Figure 13-9. Time to verify a statement for adults and for children. Subjects were instructed to verify the assertion by imagery or were given no instruction as to method of verification. (From Kosslyn, 1980.)

abstract representations to concrete representations, but rather from less adequate to more adequate abstract representations. For instance, in solving problems such as the balance-scale problem, it is important that the child be able to think in terms of ratios rather than differences. Both ratios and differences are abstract concepts; however, ratios are a more complex abstract concept that takes more experience (schooling) to acquire.

Another shift in children's knowledge representation concerns their representation of categories. Initially, their representation of a category seems to be tied to the surface features of members of the category. Later they begin to develop a more definitional conception of the categories. Keil and Batterman (1984) demonstrated this transition in children's understanding of category membership by presenting them with contrasting problems such as the following pair:

> 1. This smelly, mean old man with a gun in his pocket came to your house one day and took your colored television set because your parents didn't want it anymore and told him that he could have it. Could he be a robber?

> 2. This very friendly and cheerful woman came up to you and gave you a hug, but then she disconnected your toilet bowl and took it away without permission and never returned it. Could she be a robber?

The first individual has many of the features we associate with robbers — male, unpleasant, has a gun, and takes colored TVs. But since he has permission he lacks the critical feature of a robber. However, many kindergarteners judged the first and not the second as a robber. By the fourth grade most children confidently rated the second and not the first to be a robber.

Gelman (1988) showed that children begin to learn which features might be associated with which categories. In her experiment, children are shown a red apple and told the apple has two properties these children have never heard of. First, they are told it "has pectin inside" and second that "you can repast with it." Preschool children show very little difference in their willingness to say that these predicates might be true for a green apple while second graders are much more willing to attribute "has pectin" to the green apple. In another example, they are shown a teacup and told it is "made out of ceramic" and "used for imbibing." Preschoolers show little difference in their willingness to attribute such predicates to a plastic cup while second graders are much more willing to extend the "used for imbibing" predicate. Gelman argues that by the second grade children learn the difference between natural objects such as apples and artifacts such as teacups. All members of a natural category tend to be constituted the same way (e.g., has pectin) while all members of an artifact category tend to have the same function (e.g., used for imbibing).

Carey (1985) has studied the relationship between children's conception of humans and other animals. Initially she notes a considerable asymmetry. Four-year-olds will generalize properties learned to be true of people to animals but not vice versa. For instance, told that a person has a spleen, 4-year-olds will conclude a dog has a spleen. However, if told a dog has a spleen, they will not conclude a human has. By age 10 this asymmetry in generalization disappears. Carey argues that young children see people as the prototypical animal and other animals are thought of as humanlike with additional features (e.g., fur and tail). Thus, if told a dog has a spleen, the child thinks it may be one of the things that you add to a human to get a dog. By age 10 their conception of animals and people has evolved to the point where people are just one animal among many.

Problem Solving

A series of studies by Klahr (Klahr, 1978; Klahr & Robinson, 1981) provides an interesting vantage point on the problem-solving abilities of children. He looked at the ability of children to solve the Tower of Hanoi problem (discussed in Chapter 8). However, to make the problem more interesting and sensible to young children, he used the setup illustrated in Figure 13-10. The three cans were colored and described as monkeys — a big yellow daddy, a medium-sized blue mommy, and a little red baby. These monkeys jumped from tree to tree with the constraint that big cans (monkeys) could fit only on little cans. Children were shown one configuration of cans (monkeys) and were asked to arrange a second configuration of copycat monkeys (cans) into the same configuration.

The child's task was to make a tower, as in the regular Tower of Hanoi task, but the problem was started at varying numbers of moves from the goal, or final tower state. Problems were classified according to the number of moves required for successful solution. The original three-disk problem in Chapter 8 involved seven moves. Figure 13-11 illustrates configurations that require (a) two moves, (b) three moves, and (c) six moves from the goal state in order to have all the cans on peg 3. On average, 4-year-olds were able to solve problems requiring 2.5 moves; 5-year-olds, 3.8 moves; and 6-year-olds, 5.6 moves. There is clearly a very strong developmental progression with age. It is interesting, however, that only one 6-year-old was able to solve the full seven-move Tower of Hanoi problem.

What underlies the developmental improvement in problem-solving ability? Klahr and Robinson note that children gradually pick up the strategic features needed to solve the problem. Critical to solving

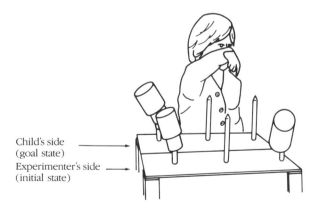

Child's side (goal state)

Experimenter's side (initial state)

Figure 13-10. Children's version of the Tower of Hanoi problem.

the problem is the ability to move an obstructing can out of the way. The youngest children do not have this ability, and can solve only problems such as Figure 13-11 (part a), where there are no obstructing cans. Next, if an obstructing can is to be moved, as in part b, it is important to choose the right peg to move it to. We would not want to move the can from peg 2 to peg 3 because this would obstruct the move of the bottom can on peg 2 to peg 3. Children who are capable of solving such a problem are capable of solving a subgoal. They set the subgoal of moving one can out of the way so that they can correctly place another can. Klahr and Robinson found that children are reliably able to achieve such subgoals only after the age of 5. The next level of problem solving involves handling more than one level of subgoals, as required in part c. The evidence from Klahr's work is that children are only beginning to handle this level of complexity by age 6.

The simple conclusion might be that over this period children are developing a general ability to handle subgoals. However, Klahr and Robinson note that even at 18 months a child can set the subgoal of removing one object to get at another. When my son was 3, he was capable of getting a parent so that the parent would open a door so that he

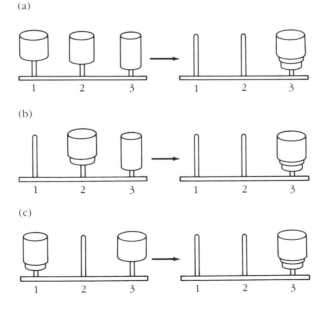

Figure 13-11. Tower of Hanoi problems that are (a) two, (b) three, and (c) six moves from the goal state.

could go upstairs so he could play with Daddy's computer terminal. Thus, it seems that children have the ability to deal with subgoals at a very early age. Klahr and Robinson suggest that young children fail to represent the problem in such a way that they can apply their subgoaling ability. For instance, children may perceive one can as simply on top of another can rather than more abstractly as blocking the move of the can. Thus, the major developmental trend may not be in problem-solving ability per se, but rather in representational ability.

Development of Basic Cognitive Abilities: A Summary

In general, it seems that the improvement in children's intellectual abilities depends on increased knowledge of what to do rather than increased ability to do it. Development of memory and development of problem solving seem related to appropriate encoding strategies. Also, children seem to develop more effective representational abilities over time.

Development of Mathematics

The understanding of mathematics is subject to a developmental progression that starts with the preverbal child and continues well into college. It is perhaps the most sustained developmental process that members of our society engage in. It is also characterized by a considerable range in the end points reached—some can barely count reliably, whereas others become professional mathematicians. Therefore, understanding the development of mathematical knowledge has enormous potential benefits to society. Recent research in developmental psychology has focused on the approximately eight-year span of development from initial conceptions of number to addition and subtraction skills.

Initial Conceptions of Number

There is some evidence that children younger than 1 can discriminate one object from two and two objects from three (Antell & Keating, 1983; Starkey & Cooper, 1980; Strauss & Curtis, 1981). Basically, this research involves presenting infants with displays of varying numbers of objects and observing how long they look at the display. If they are shown a new display they will look at the new display longer if that display involves a

425

different number of objects. These effects are only found for small numbers of objects. For instance, while infants will discriminate between two and three objects, they do not appear to discriminate between five and six objects.

By the time they are 4 years old most children have learned to count. Counting might appear to be a rather primitive skill but it involves a good deal more than just memorizing the digit sequence. Gelman and Gallistel (1978) show that children who can count objects have mastered five rather abstract skills:

1. *The one-to-one principle.* Each item to be counted must get one and only one number assigned to it. Very young children who have not mastered this will skip objects and double count objects.

2. *The stable order principle.* The numbers must be assigned in a fixed order. Again very young children will pretend to count but assign numbers randomly.

3. *The cardinal principle.* The final number counted out is the measure of set of objects counted. Children tend to say the last digit with a special emphasis indicating that they appreciate it is the measure of the set.

4. *The abstraction principle.* The same principles apply to any set of objects. Thus, children when they have mastered counting will apply it to toys, sets of apples and oranges, or to steps they take across the room.

5. *The order irrelevance principle.* It does not matter what order you count objects in; they will always have the same number. One way to test this is to require children to count objects in a nonconventional way—for instance, starting in the middle of the row. Children find this novel task rather difficult but by the time they are 4 most children can adjust their counting to count the middle object first and still count all objects once and just once.

Given the richness of understanding of counting that a 4-year-old can display one might wonder about the number of conservation tasks cited earlier where children failed to recognize that two arrays of objects had the same number after one was transformed by decreasing the space among objects (see Figure 14-2). It now appears that children simply have not learned to connect their ability to count to this task. Gelman (1982) showed that when children are taught to count the objects in these arrays they are able to make correct judgments at the age of 4 and 5.

Addition

Thanks to enrichment programs such as "Sesame Street" and "The Electric Company," many preschoolers now know how to solve addition problems with sums under 10. Siegler and Shrager (1984) videotaped 4- and 5-year-olds as they solved such problems. Sometimes they counted on their fingers, sometimes they counted aloud without use of fingers, and sometimes they just said the answer. Children tended to be more accurate when they counted but it of course took a good bit longer to come up with the answer. The interesting observation is that children were very judicious with respect to the choice of which strategy to use. Almost no children counted to add $1 + 1$ while 50 percent would count to add $4 + 5$. Siegler and Shrager argue that children have solved the smaller addition problems many times and have memorized the solutions to these problems while they have encountered the larger problems less often and still must resort to counting in order to answer them.

Siegler (1986) questions the educational practice that discourages finger counting because it is a less efficient method. He argues that this policy is forcing children to try to retrieve answers that they have not learned well, with the consequent risk of error. These errors can start to compete with correct answers. He argues that it is better to let children use the reliable finger counting method until they have learned the answers well. The evidence is that children will spontaneously switch to direct retrieval and abandon finger counting.

Subtraction

About the second year of school addition and subtraction education no longer focuses on the direct retrieval of facts. Children are now introduced to multi-digit numbers and algorithms for mastering their addition and subtraction. Children executing these algorithms make many errors that are not errors of number facts but errors of algorithm execution. These error patterns, particularly in the case of subtraction, have attracted a lot of attention. For instance, Brown and Burton (1978) observed a middle school student produce the following two errors:

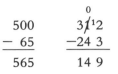

$$
\begin{array}{r}
500 \\
-65 \\
\hline
565
\end{array}
\qquad
\begin{array}{r}
{}^{0}\\
3\cancel{1}{}^{1}2 \\
-24\ 3 \\
\hline
14\ 9
\end{array}
$$

The response of most people, including some schoolteachers, to such errors is to conclude that the child is extremely careless, is responding randomly, or knows nothing. It turns out that this child is following faithfully a procedure for subtraction that has only one error, or "bug," as Brown and Burton call it. The child believes that $0 - N = N$; that is, the student thinks that if a digit is subtracted from 0, the result is that digit.

Brown and Burton found no less than 110 such bugs that can adversely affect the subtraction procedures of young children. Although children are sometimes careless or respond randomly, the important discovery is that many of their mistakes are caused by systematic errors in the subtraction procedures they are using. Thus, the appropriate remedial action is not just drill and practice, which will only ingrain these errors, but specific instruction to correct the errors. One of the important contributions of Brown and Burton (1978) and Burton (1982) is that they have produced a diagnostic computer program that can look at a child's behavior and identify the bug(s) that child has. This can be a considerable aid to the mathematics teacher.

Thus, students' development of subtraction skills is much like their development of conservation or their development on the balance-scale problem. They have procedures for solving these problems that can be more or less accurate. Indeed, Brown and Van Lehn (1980) have shown that subtraction skills can be modeled by production systems, and improvement or development can occur by replacing less adequate productions with more adequate productions. Young and O'Shea (1981) have argued for a similar conclusion.

Origins of Subtraction Bugs

How are these bugs in the subtraction skill generated in the first place? Certainly, the teacher did not tell the student that when subtracting N from 0 to write N. Brown and Van Lehn (1980) have addressed this issue, and their answer may indicate how erroneous procedures arise in other domains. They suppose that children sometimes fail to learn the complete procedure, and consequently that certain critical steps are missing. This means that, when solving a problem, children will reach an impasse when they come to the point where a missing rule should be applied. Brown and Van Lehn assume that the child creates a solution to bridge this impasse, and that this solution becomes encoded as a new rule. If the rule is incorrect, the child has, in effect, taught himself or herself a bug.

Let us consider an example: One rule of subtraction is that if the digit in the upper row is smaller than the digit in the bottom row, the student should borrow from the preceding digit in the upper row. Suppose the student has not learned that rule and comes upon the following problem:

$$413$$
$$-242$$

When it comes to subtracting 4 from 1, the child hits an impasse. What is the child to do? One thing might be to simply leave the 10's column of the answer blank, but the child knows answers don't have holes in them and therefore this repair is rejected. Another possibility is to subtract the 1 from the 4. This leaves an answer that looks right even if it is nonsense. Some children do this and develop this as a systematic bug. Another possibility is to write 0, the smallest digit available. Other children do this and develop that as a systematic bug.

Thus, errors in procedures occur as a result of the child's attempt to fill in the missing steps of a procedure. Note that the child is not totally uncritical in producing repairs. For instance, repairs are not generated that leave holes in the answer. Van Lehn and Brown (1981) have argued that mathematics education would be improved if children were given a deeper understanding of domains like subtraction so that they would be able to recognize the nonsense in other repairs they make.

There is a level at which Brown and Van Lehn's analysis of errors in algorithmic subtraction is similar to Siegler's analysis of basic addition errors. In both cases the errors arise because children are asked to do something they cannot do yet (retrieve an answer without finger counting or solve a subtraction problem for which they do not know the appropriate algorithm). In both cases there is the danger that a child may make an error and remember the error as the answer. This argues that early mathematics teachers should be careful that a child has mastered the prerequisites before promoting the child to a more advanced skill. This corresponds to the recommendation of Gagne (1973) for hierarchical learning.

Remarks and Suggested Readings

Piaget and his coauthors have written a great many books on child development that have been translated from the original French. These include *The origins of intelligence in children* (1952a), *The child's conception of number* (1952b), and by Inhelder and Piaget, *The growth of logical thinking from childhood to adolescence* (1958). Brainerd (1978) and Gruber and Voneche (1977) are secondary books written about Piaget's theory. More general texts on cognitive development include those by Flavell (1985) and Siegler (1986). Mussen's (1983) handbook contains a thorough overview of the whole field of developmental psychology. Three recent Carnegie Symposia on Cognition (Siegler, 1978; Sophian, 1984b; Granrud, in press) contain a large number of papers presenting information-processing approaches to cognition. Klahr and Wallace (1976) present a theory of development heavily influenced by production systems.

CHAPTER

·14·

The Nature of Intelligence

Summary

1. Human intelligence is a result of an interaction of accumulated knowledge with special capabilities for processing certain kinds of information.

2. Intelligence tests measure intellectual abilities that are predictive of future academic success. By design these tests emphasize knowledge and abilities that are general rather than knowledge and abilities that are specialized to a field of expertise.

3. Performance on intelligence tests tends to cluster into abilities such as verbal, spatial, and reasoning. People with high abilities of a particular type appear to process material of that type more rapidly.

4. There is no scientific basis for a unitary concept of intelligence such that we can judge one person as more intelligent than another in the same way we can judge one person taller than another.

5. Work on expert systems in artificial intelligence has shown that intelligence can be achieved for a specialized task if one codifies enough knowledge about that task.

6. The concept of intelligence is too much tied to our humanness and to our culture for us to be able to judge whether computers are more or less intelligent than humans. Rather, we can judge them as intelligent in different ways.

7. Work on intelligent tutors has shown that computers can convey their codified knowledge to human students in a highly effective manner.

The first chapter of this book introduced the discussion of cognitive psychology by noting that intelligence is considered to be the most distinguishing feature of our species, homo sapiens. Now that we have completed our survey of cognitive psychology it is appropriate to ask, "What is the nature of human intelligence?" The basic outline of the answer to this centuries-old question has been identified in previous chapters. The answer consists of two parts, which define a creative tension within the field of cognitive science. First, we are blessed with a very powerful brain. We have reviewed the statistics about its size and complexity but even more important are its powerful subspecializations. It consists of extremely powerful systems for processing incoming visual and auditory messages. These are not unique to the human species. However, it also consists of a number of uniquely human information-processing capabilities such as those for language processing.

Second, human intelligence depends on the accumulation of a great deal of knowledge. As we determined when we examined what it takes to read a word, what it takes to be an expert in a field, what it takes to learn a language, and what it takes to be an adult, there is a lot of acquired knowledge that is required for intelligence. The heart of this book (Chapters 4–9) was devoted to discussing how that knowledge is represented, stored, and deployed to solve problems. This is the contribution of our experience to intelligence.

Perhaps the greatest controversy in psychology is the nature versus nurture controversy—whether human intelligence is principally a result of innate capacity or of experience. If the reader has abstracted anything from this book, I would hope it is the perspective to realize that this question cannot have a sensible answer. It is like asking which is more critical to enjoying a record—a good stereo system or a good musical piece. The motto should not be nature versus nurture. It should be nature plus nurture.

The previous chapters nearly completed our sketch of human intelligence. There is one important issue we have not addressed: Intelligence is a comparative as well as an absolute term. We speak of one person as being *more intelligent* than another. People will claim that one artificial intelligence system is *more intelligent* than another or *as intelligent as* a human. The previous chapters have focused on what are the components of human intelligence. This chapter will focus on the issue of differences in intelligence. We will present what has been learned about this issue both from the study of individual differences in human intelligence and from the study of artificial intelligence.

Individual Differences in Cognition
Intelligence Tests

Research on the study of individual differences in intelligence (often characterized as intelligence testing) has had a much longer sustained intellectual history than cognitive psychology. In 1904 the Minister of Public Instruction in Paris named a commission charged with identifying children in need of remedial education. Alfred Binet set about developing a test that would objectively identify students having intellectual difficulty. Terman adapted Binet's test for use with American students. His efforts led to the development of the Stanford-Binet, which is one of the major general intelligence tests in use today in America (Terman & Merrill, 1973). The other major intelligence test used in America is the Wechsler, which has separate scales for children and adults. These tests include measures of digit span, vocabulary, analogical reasoning, spatial judgments, and arithmetic. A typical question for adults on the Stanford-Binet is "Which direction would you have to face so your right hand would be to the north?" A great deal of effort goes into selecting test items that will predict scholastic performance.

Both of these tests produce measures that are called *intelligence quotients* or IQs. The original definition of IQ involved relating mental ages and chronological ages. The test establishes one's mental age. If a child can solve problems on the test that the average 8-year-old can, then the child has a mental age of 8 independent of his chronological age. IQ is defined as the ratio of mental age to chronological age times 100 or

$$IQ = 100 \times MA/CA$$

where MA is mental age and CA is chronological age. Thus, if the child's mental age were 8 and chronological age were 6, the IQ would be $100 \times 8/6 = 133$.

This definition of IQ proved unsuitable for a number of reasons. It cannot extend to measurement of adult intelligence since performance on intelligence tests starts to level off in the late teens. To deal with such difficulties, the common way of defining IQ now is in terms of what are called *deviation scores*. One subtracts the score of a person from the mean score for that age group and then transforms this difference score into a measure that will vary around 100 roughly as the earlier IQ scores would. The precise definition is:

$$IQ = 100 + 15 \times \frac{(\text{score} - \text{mean})}{\text{standard deviation}}$$

where standard deviation is a measure of the variance of the scores. IQs so measured tend to be distributed according to a normal distribution. Figure 14-1 shows such a normal distribution of intelligence scores and the percentage of people who have scores in various ranges.

While the Stanford-Binet and the Weschler are two general intelligence tests, there are many others, some of which were developed to test specialized abilities such as spatial ability. Both the general and the specialized tests are sometimes referred to as *psychometric tests*. These tests partly owe their continued use in our society to the fact that they do predict with some accuracy performance in school, which was one of

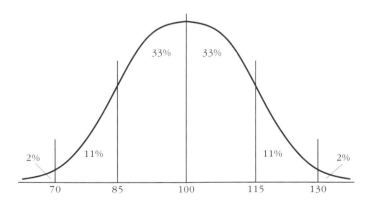

Figure 14-1. A normal distribution of IQ measures.

Binet's original goals. There is, however, considerable controversy about their use for this purpose. In particular, since such tests can be used to determine who can have access to what educational opportunities, there is a great deal of concern that they not be constructed to be biased against certain groups.

The very concept of intelligence is culturally relative. What one culture values as intelligent another culture will not. For instance, the Kpelle (discussed in Chapter 10) think the way Westerners sort instances into categories (a basis for some items in intelligence tests) is foolish (Cole, Gay, Glick, & Sharp, 1971). Still the fact remains that intelligence tests do predict performance in our (Western) schools. It is an extremely subtle question as to when they are doing a valuable service in assessing students for schools and when they are simply enforcing arbitrary cultural beliefs about what is to be valued.

Related to the issue of the fairness of intelligence tests is whether they reflect innate endowment or acquired ability. Potentially definitive data would seem to come from studies of identical twins reared apart. Usually these involve cases in which twins are adopted into different families. Such twins are people who have identical genetic endowment and yet very different experiences. The research on this topic is controversial (Kamin, 1974) but recent analyses (Bouchard, 1983; Bouchard & McGue, 1981) indicate that identical twins raised apart have IQs much more similar to each other than nonidentical fraternal twins raised in the same family. This certainly seems to be evidence that there is a strong innate component to IQ. One of the most pernicious mistakes in our society is to generalize this to the conclusion that intelligence is largely innate. Intelligence and IQ are by no means the same thing. Because of the goals of intelligence tests, they must predict success across a broad range of environments, particularly academic. This means that they must discount the contributions of specific experiences to intelligence. We noted in Chapter 9, for instance, that chess masters tend not to have particularly high IQs. This is more a comment on the IQ test than on chess masters. If an IQ test focused on chess experience, it would have little success in predicting academic success generally. Thus, intelligence tests measure raw abilities and general knowledge that it is reasonable to expect of everyone in a culture. However, as we saw in Chapter 9, excellence in any specific domain depends on knowledge and experience that are not general in the culture.

An interesting demonstration of this lack of correlation between expertise and IQ was performed by Ceci and Liker (1986). They looked at the ability of avid horse race fans to handicap races. They found that handicapping ability was related to developing a complex interactive model of horse racing but that there was no relationship between this ability and IQ.

While specific experience is clearly important to success in any field, the remarkable fact is that these intelligence tests are able to predict success in certain endeavors. They predict with modest accuracy performance in school and general success in life (or at least in Western societies). What is it about the mind that they are measuring? Much of the theoretical work in the field has been concerned with trying to find an answer to this question. To understand how this question has been pursued, one must understand a little about a major method of the field, factor analysis.

Factor Analysis

The general intelligence tests contain a number of subtests that measure individual abilities. Also, as noted, there are many specialized tests available for particular abilities. The basic observation is that people who do well on one test or subtest tend to do well on another test or subtest. The degree to which people perform comparably on two subtests is measured by a correlation coefficient. If all the same people who did well on one test did just as well on another, the correlation between the two tests would be 1. If all the people who did well on one test did proportionately badly on another, the correlation coefficient would be -1. If there was no relationship between how people did on one test and how they did on another test, the correlation coefficient would be 0. Typical correlations between tests are positive but not 1, indicating a less than perfect relationship between performance on one test and another.

As an example of this Hunt (1985) looked at the relationship among the seven tests described in Table 14-1. Table 14-2 shows the intercorrelations among these test scores. As can be seen, some pairs of tests are more correlated than others. For instance, there is a relatively high .67 correlation between reading comprehension and vocabulary but a relatively low .14 correlation between reading comprehension and spatial reasoning. Factor analysis is a way of trying to make sense of these correlational patterns. The basic idea is to try to place these tests into some dimensional space such that the distance among the tests reflects the correlation. Items close together will have high correlations. Figure 14-2 shows an attempt to organize the tests in Table 14-1 into a two-dimensional space. The reader may confirm that the closer items are in this space the higher the correlation they have in Table 14-2.

The interesting question is how to make sense of this space. As we go from the bottom to the top we get more and more symbolic and linguis-

Table 14-1 *Description of Some of the Tests on the Washington Pre-College Test Battery*

Test Name	Description
1. Reading comprehension	Answer questions about paragraph
2. Vocabulary	Choose synonyms for a word
3. Grammar	Identify correct and poor usage
4. Quantitative skills	Read word problems and decide whether problem can be solved
5. Mechanical reasoning	Examine a diagram and answer questions about it; requires knowledge of physical and mechanical principles
6. Spatial reasoning	Indicate how two-dimensional figures will appear if they are folded through a third dimension
7. Mathematics achievement	A test of high school algebra

From Hunt, 1985.

tic. One might refer to this dimension as a linguistic factor. Second, one might argue that as we go from the left to the right the tests become more computational in character. We might consider this a reasoning factor. High correlations are now to be explained in terms of students having similar values of these factors. Thus, there is a high correlation between quantitative skills and mathematics achievement because they both have an intermediate degree of linguistic involvement and require

Table 14-2 *Intercorrelations Between Results of the Tests Listed in Table 14-1*

Test No.	1	2	3	4	5	6	7
1	1.00	.67	.63	.40	.33	.14	.34
2		1.00	.59	.29	.46	.19	.31
3			1.00	.41	.34	.20	.46
4				1.00	.39	.46	.62
5					1.00	.47	.39
6						1.00	.46
7							1.00

From Hunt, 1985.

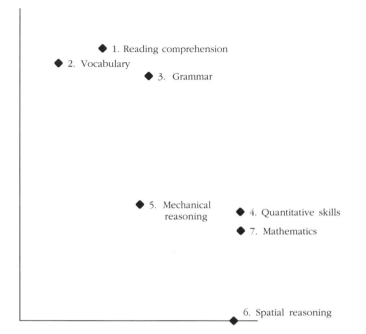

Figure 14-2. A representation of the tests in Table 14-1 in a two-dimensional space such that distance between points decreases with increases in the intercorrelations from Table 14-2.

substantial reasoning. People who are high on reasoning ability and not too low on verbal ability will do well on these tests.

Factor analysis is basically an effort to go from a set of intercorrelations like those in Table 14-2 to a small set of factors that explain those intercorrelations. Unfortunately, there has been considerable controversy about what the underlying factors are. Perhaps you can see other ways to explain the correlations in Table 14-1. For instance, one might argue that there is a linguistic factor linking tests 1 through 3, a reasoning factor linking tests 4, 5, and 7, and a separate spatial factor for test 6. Indeed, we will see that there have been many proposals for separate linguistic, reasoning, and spatial factors although, as in the data of Table 14-2, it is a little difficult to separate the spatial and reasoning factors.

The difficulty of interpreting such data is reflected in the wide variety of positions that have been taken as to what the underlying factors of human intelligence are. Spearman (1904) argued that there was only one general factor which underlay performance across tests. He called his factor *g*. In contrast, Thurstone (1938) argued that there were a number of separate factors, including the verbal, spatial, and mathematical we mentioned above. Guilford (1982) proposed no less than 120 distinct intellectual abilities. Cattell (1963) proposed a distinction between fluid and crystallized intelligence; crystallized intelligence referred to acquired knowledge while fluid intelligence referred to ability to reason or problem solve in novel domains. Horn (1968), elaborating on Cattell's theory, argued that there is a spatial intelligence which can be separated from fluid intelligence. Table 14-2 can be interpreted in terms of the Horn-Cattell theory, where crystallized intelligence maps into the linguistic factor (tests 1-3), fluid intelligence into the reasoning factor (tests 4, 5, and 7), and visual intelligence into the spatial factor (test 6). Fluid intellignce tends to be tapped strongly in mathematical tests but it is probably better referred to as a reasoning ability than a mathematical ability per se. As we noted with respect to Figure 14-2 and as is generally true, it is a bit difficult to separate out the fluid and spatial intelligences in factor analytic studies, but it appears possible (Horn & Stankov, 1982).

It is hard to come away from this debate with any very firm conclusions but it seems clear that in fact there is some differentiation in human intelligence as it appears on intelligence tests. Probably, the Horn-Cattell theory or the Thurstone theory offer the best analyses, producing what we will call a verbal factor, a spatial factor, and a reasoning factor. The rest of this chapter will provide further evidence for the division of the human intellect into various abilities. This is a significant conclusion because it indicates that there is some specialization in achieving human cognitive function.

Individual Differences and Information Processing

Recently, there has been considerable interest in how these measures of individual differences relate to the kinds of theories of information processing that are found in cognitive psychology. For instance, how do high and low spatial subjects differ in terms of the processes involved in spatial imagery discussed in Chapter 4? Makers of intelligence tests have tended to ignore such questions because their major goal is to predict scholastic performance. We will look at some recent information-processing studies that try to understand the reasoning factor, the verbal factor, and the spatial factor.

Reasoning Ability

Typical tests that are used to measure reasoning include mathematical problems, analogy problems, series extrapolation problems, deductive syllogisms, and problem-solving tasks. These are the kinds of tasks that we analyzed in great detail in Chapters 8 to 10 of this book. Most of the research in psychometric tests has only been concerned with whether a person gets a question right or not. In contrast, information-processing analysis tries to examine the steps by which a person comes to an answer to such a question and the time to perform each step.

The research of Robert Sternberg (1977; Sternberg & Gardner, 1983) is an attempt to connect the psychometric research tradition with the information-processing tradition. He has analyzed how people process a wide variety of reasoning problems. Figure 14-3 illustrates one of his analogy problems. Subjects are asked to solve the analogy A is to B as C is to D_1 or D_2? Sternberg analyzes the process of making such analogies into a number of stages. Two critical stages in his analysis are called reasoning and comparison. Reasoning involves finding each feature change between A and B and applying it to C. Thus, A and B differ in the figure by a change in costume from spotted to striped. Thus, one predicts that C

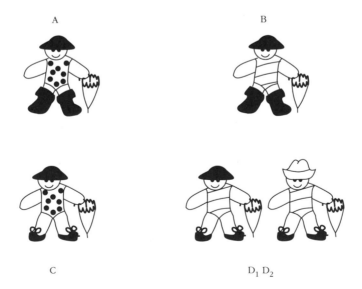

Figure 14-3. An example of an analogy problem used by Sternberg and Gardner, 1983. (Copyright 1983 by the American Psychological Association. Adapted by permission.)

440

will change from spotted to striped to yield D. Comparison involves comparing the predicted version of D to the two choices, D_1 and D_2. Each feature is compared until one is found that enables a choice. Thus, the subject may first check that both D_1 and D_2 have an umbrella (which they do), then that they have a striped suit (which they do), and then that they have a dark hat (which only D_1 has). The dark hat feature will allow the subjects to reject D_2 and so accept D_1.

Sternberg was interested in the time subjects took to make these judgments. He theorized that they would take a certain amount longer for each feature that A differed from B because this feature would have to be changed to derive D from C. Sternberg and Gardner (1983) estimated a time of about .28 seconds for each such feature. This is the *reasoning parameter*. They also estimated .60 seconds to compare a feature predicted of D with the features of D_1 and D_2. This is the *comparison parameter*. The values .28 and .60 are just averages; the actual values of these reasoning and comparison times varied across subjects. They looked at the correlations between the values of these parameters for individual subjects and psychometric measures of subjects' reasoning abilities. They found correlations of .79 for the reasoning parameter and .75 for the comparison parameter. This means that subjects who are slow in reasoning or comparison do poorly in psychometric tests. Thus, they were able to show that components identified in an information-processing analysis are critical to psychometric measures of intelligence.

Verbal Ability

Probably the most robust factor to emerge from intelligence tests is the verbal factor. There has been considerable interest in determining what processes distinguish people with strong verbal abilities. Goldberg, Schwartz, and Stewart (1977) compared high- and low-verbal people with respect to their ability to make various kinds of word judgments. One kind of word judgment was simply whether pairs of words were identical. Thus, they would say yes to a pair such as:

bear, bear

Other subjects were asked to judge whether pairs of words sounded alike. Thus, they would say yes to a pair such as:

bare, bear

441

A third group of subjects were asked to judge whether pairs of words were in the same category. Thus, they would say yes to a pair such as:

lion, bear

Figure 14-4 shows the difference between high-verbal and low-verbal subjects in terms of their time to make these three kinds of judgments. As can be seen, the high-verbal subjects enjoy a small advantage on the physical match judgments but show much larger advantages on the sound and category matches. This and other studies (e.g., Hunt, Davidson, & Lansman, 1981) have convinced researchers that a major advantage of high-verbal subjects is the speed with which they can go from a linguistic stimulus to information about it — in the case of the study above, subjects

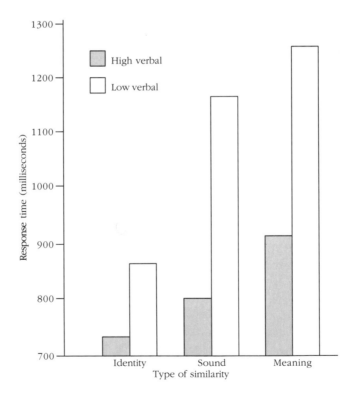

Figure 14-4. Response time to judge similarity of pairs of words for high- and low-verbal subjects and three types of similarity. (From Goldberg, Schwartz, & Stewart, 1977.)

were going from the visual word to information about its sound and meaning.

There is also evidence of a fairly strong relationship between working memory capacity for linguistic material and for verbal ability. Daneman and Carpenter (1980) developed the following test of individual differences. Subjects would read or hear a number of unrelated sentences such as:

> When at last his eyes opened, there was no gleam of triumph, no shade of anger.
> The taxi turned up Michigan Avenue where they had a clear view of the lake.

After reading or hearing these sentences subjects had to recall the last word of each sentence. They were tested with groups of sentences ranging from two to seven. The largest group of sentences for which they could recall the last words was defined as the reading span or listening span. College students had spans from 2 to 5.5. It turns out that these spans are very strongly related to their comprehension scores and to tests of verbal ability. These reading and listening spans are much more strongly related than are measures of simple digit span. Daneman and Carpenter argue that a larger reading and listening span indicates the ability to store a larger portion of the text during comprehension. The Kintsch and van Dijk model, reviewed in Chapter 12, illustrated how holding a larger portion of the text in working memory might enhance comprehension.

Spatial Ability

There have also been efforts to relate measures of spatial ability to research on mental rotation such as that discussed in Chapter 4. Just and Carpenter (1985) compared low-spatial-ability and high-spatial-ability subjects performing the Shepard and Metzler mental rotation tasks (see Figure 4-4). Figure 14-5 plots the speed with which these two types of subjects rotate figures of differing angular disparity. As can be seen, the low-spatial subjects were not only performing the task more slowly but also are more affected by angle of disparity. This means that the rate of mental rotation is slower for the low-spatial subjects.

Spatial ability has often been set in contrast with verbal ability. While there are people who are high on both abilities or low on both, interest often focuses on people who have a relative imbalance of the abilities.

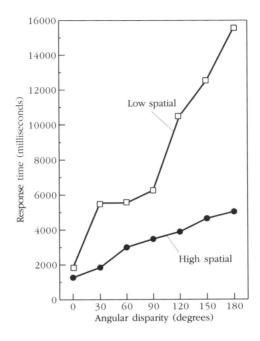

Figure 14-5. Mean time to determine that two objects have the same three-dimensional shape as a function of the angular difference in their portrayed orientations. Separate functions are plotted for high- and low-spatial subjects. (From Just & Carpenter, 1985. Copyright 1985 by the American Psychological Association. Adapted by permission.)

MacLeod, Hunt, and Matthews (1978) found evidence that these different types of people will solve a cognitive task differently. They looked at performance on the Clark and Chase sentence verification task that we considered in Chapter 12. Recall that this task involves presenting subjects with sentences such as "The plus is above the star" or "The star is not above the plus" and asking subjects to determine whether the sentence accurately describes the picture. Typically, it is found that subjects are slower when there is a negative like *not* in the sentence and when the supposition of the sentences mismatches the picture.

MacLeod et al. speculated, however, that there were really two groups of subjects—those who took a representation of the sentence and matched it against a picture and those who first converted the sentence to an image of a picture and then matched that against the picture. They speculated that the first group would be high in verbal ability while the second group would be high in spatial ability. In fact, they did find two groups of subjects. Figure 14-6 shows the judgment times of these two

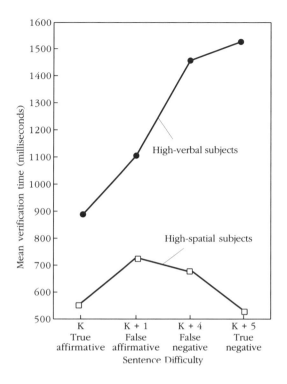

Figure 14-6. Mean time to judge a sentence as a function of sentence type for high-verbal subjects and high-spatial subjects. (From MacLeod, Hunt, & Matthews, 1978.)

groups as a function of whether the sentence was true or not and whether it involved a negative. As can be seen, one group of subjects showed no effect of whether the sentence involved a negative while the other group showed a very substantial effect. The group of subjects not showing the effect of a negative had higher scores on tests of spatial ability than the other group. This was the group of subjects that were comparing an image formed from the sentence against the picture. Such an image would not have a negative in it.

Conclusions from Information-Processing Studies

One of the major outcomes of the research relating psychometric measures to cognitive tasks has been to reinforce the distinction between verbal and spatial ability. The reader will recall from Chapters 2 and 4 that there is considerable nonpsychometric evidence for this distinction as well. A second outcome of this research is to locate the effects of ability on rate of processing and strategy selection. Good illustrations of this are Figures 14-5 and 14-6. In Figure 14-5 we saw that high-spatial subjects can rotate images more rapidly — a rate difference. In Figure 14-6 we saw that they adopt a different strategy for solving a sentence verification task. Some people have argued that the strategy differences are derivative from the rate differences. That is, high-ability subjects will adopt a particular strategy for solving a problem because they can effectively perform that strategy given their higher rates of processing.

Gardner's Multiple Intelligences

In his 1983 book, Howard Gardner argued for the existence of at least six domain-specific types of intelligence — linguistic, musical, logical-mathematical, spatial, bodily-kinesthic, and personal. The real contribution of his book is the juxtaposition of a wide variety of existing evidence on these issues. He supplements the traditional psychometric evidence for such traits with a large number of other criteria. He uses evidence that there are separate neural centers underlying these various intelligences, that people can be found who are exceptionally talented in just one of these dimensions, that information-processing research has found evidence for such abilities, that there are separate developmental histories for each intelligence, that there are cross-cultural universals in the display of such abilities, and that distinct symbol systems have emerged for each of these intelligences. He cannot apply each of his criteria to produce convincing evidence for each of his intelligences but enough criteria apply to each of the intelligences to present a rather convincing picture.

Clearly the strongest case exists for linguistic intelligence. As we noted in Chapters 2, 4, and 11 there is good evidence for separate neural centers. Gardner regards the great poets and writers as people with truly exceptional linguistic talent. We have already discussed in this chapter and in Chapters 11 and 12 the rather distinctive cognitive processes that underlie language. In Chapter 11 we also discussed the cross-linguistic universals of language and the rather distinctive developmental history of language. Finally, language does have a distinctive symbol system, which is its written form.

There is also a fairly strong case for a separate spatial intelligence. Again we noted in Chapters 2 and 4 the evidence for separate neural centers for spatial processing both in perception and imagery. We have reviewed the psychometric and experimental data pointing to a separate ability for spatial processing. Gardner takes the ubiquity of visual art across cultures to be further evidence for the existence of a special spatial intelligence.

Psychometrically, measures of mathematical ability tend to be strongly correlated with spatial ability. Gardner's case in general for a separate mathematical ability is somewhat weak. Part of the problem is definitional. All cultures have counting systems but much of what psychometric tests measure under mathematical abilities is unique to modern societies. It is hard to make the case that there are universals of modern algebra in the way that there are universals of natural language. There may be universals of simpler number abilities such as counting. Gardner points to a syndrome called Gerstmann's syndrome, which is associated with damage to the left parietal lobes and the temporal and occipital association areas contiguous to them. People with damage to these neural centers will suffer problems in arithmetic calculation, left-right orientation, and in identifying their fingers. However, there is not much consensus about the nature of this problem. Probably it would be wise to read Gardner's mathematical ability as not specific to mathematics but rather as a more general reasoning factor, as discussed earlier.

The other three intelligences Gardner mentions are not typically thought of as cognitive and many researchers sharply question Gardner's use of the term *intelligence* to describe them. Nonetheless, his discussion makes the point that individual differences go beyond the purely cognitive. The case for a musical ability would seem to be quite good. There are indeed striking individual differences in musical ability, with the existence of such remarkably precocious children as Mozart. Music is certainly a cultural universal. Gardner argues that musical ability is localized in the right hemisphere in contrast to language, which is localized in the left hemisphere.

By bodily-kinesthic intelligence he refers to skilled use of the body and regards a mime like Marcel Marceau as someone who is especially skilled in this way. We reviewed in Chapter 2 the evidence for special neural centers for body movement. Gardner views the universality of tool-building and dance as evidence for a universal human-specific ability involving body movement.

Gardner distinguishes between two types of personal intelligence, one concerned with self-understanding and one associated with the ability for social success. He argues that humans around the world reflect a very distinctive and universal developmental history in the unfolding of their personalities, starting with the strong infant attachments to mothers and progressing through the rebellious teenage years during which independence is established.

One of the implications of Gardner's view of multiple intelligences is that it does not make sense to talk about one person as more intelligent than another. Intelligence is not a unitary concept like height. As Horn, a well-known psychometrician, has put it: "Although the word intelligence (as a unitary concept) continues to be useful in everyday life, this does not represent a good scientific concept" (Horn, 1986, p. 69).

Artificial Intelligence: The Power of Knowledge

Artificial intelligence is a very broad field that might be best defined as concerned with creating intelligent machines. There are strong research efforts associated with problem solving, reasoning, language processing, spatial reasoning, perception, and learning, which involve many of the themes we discussed in earlier chapters. Indeed there has been a strong cross-fertilization of ideas between artificial intelligence and cognitive psychology and I have freely borrowed from artificial intelligence in earlier chapters. Part of the impact of work in artificial intelligence is to support the specialized capacity view of human intelligence that was articulated above. For instance, artificial intelligence research on vision and research on language use largely independent principles.

Many aspects of work in artificial intelligence have already been discussed in other chapters, in which the relevant aspects of human cognition were the focus. Here I am exclusively concerned with drawing the insights that artificial intelligence research offers about the nature of intelligence. Specifically in this section, however, I would like to discuss another development in artificial intelligence that emphasizes the other aspect of intelligence—that it is very knowledge intensive. During the past fifteen years there has grown up a field of research called *expert systems*. Expert systems are computer programs that are built to match human expertise in some domain—be that medical diagnosis, deciding where to drill oil wells, or deciding how to configure computers. The basic mode of operation in building expert systems is to sit down with a human expert and extract the knowledge that expert has of a particular field, codify that knowledge, and put it into a computer system capable of applying the knowledge. Such systems are now a substantial commercial enterprise, and almost every major company finds it profitable to have expert systems built to replace or supplement some of their own human experts. Unlike humans, such systems do not quit or retire (these will be serious problems particularly in the future with anticipated shortages of skilled workers). Without a doubt these expert systems have been the greatest practical contribution of artificial intelligence to date.

The MYCIN System

The lesson of expert systems is clear and reinforces the other theme throughout this book: intelligent behavior in any domain requires that a lot of knowledge be acquired about that domain. Raw capacity does not get one very far by itself. Rather than simply assert that lesson I think it would be useful to examine some of the detail of one of the classical expert systems. MYCIN, created by Shortliffe (Shortliffe, 1976; Buchanan & Shortliffe, 1984) at Stanford University, gives consultative advice on diagnosis and therapy for infectious diseases. MYCIN tries to identify what bacterium is causing an infectious disease, and from that knowledge it prescribes an antibiotic to give a patient to kill the bacteria. In the course of doing its diagnosis MYCIN can request information and tests to determine the identity of the bug. The tests include taking cultures in which bacteria are grown and studied. Table 14-3 illustrates a short dialogue between MYCIN and a physician.

Table 14-3 *Excerpts from a MYCIN Consultation*

---

1) Patient's name: (first-name)
**FRED BRAUN
2) Sex: *(Questions 1–3 request*
**M   *background patient data.)*
3) Age:
**55
4) Are there any cultures for Fred Braun which may be related to the present illness, and from which organisms have been grown successfully in the microbiology laboratory?
**Y

-------- CULTURE-1 --------
5) From what site was the specimen for
   CULTURE-1 taken?
**BLOD
= BLOOD   *(System corrects typing error.)*
6) Please give the date and time when
   CULTURE-1 was obtained. (mo/da/yr time)
**JUN 20, 1977
The first organism isolated from the blood culture of 20-JUN-77 (CULTURE-1) will be referred to as:

-------- ORGANISM-1 --------

Table 14-3 *Excerpts from a MYCIN Consultation (Continued)*

7) Enter the laboratory-reported identity of
ORGANISM-1:
**UNKNOWN   *(Typically identity is not yet known.)*
8) The stain (gram or Ziehl-Neelsen
acid-fast) of ORGANISM-1:
**NEG   *(Preliminary lab results give some clues.)*
9) Is ORGANISM-1 rod or coccus (etc.):
**ROD
10) What is the form of the individual
organisms (e.g., lancet-shaped for cocci,
fusiform for rods, etc.)?
**FUSIFORM

> *(. . . more questions follow in order to gather sufficient*
> *information to infer the identity and*
> *significance of the infecting organisms . . .)*

23) What is the suspected portal of entry of the
gramneg rod from the blood culture of
20-JUN-77 (ORGANISM-1) into this sterile
site?
**GI (6)   *(User indicates the uncertainty of his response.)*
24) Is Fred Braun a burn patient?
**N
25 Is Fred Braun a compromised host (e.g.
alcoholic, sickle-cell-disease,
immunosuppressed)?
**N
26) Is Fred Braun febrile?
**Y

> *(. . . after about 50–60 questions, MYCIN prints the diagnostic*
> *hypotheses on which therapy will be based . . .)*

My therapy recommendations will be designed to treat for organisms that are
either very likely or, although less likely, would have a significant effect on
therapy selection if they were present. It is important to cover for the following
probable infection(s) and associated organism(s):

INFECTION-1 is BACTEREMIA

  <ITEM-1> E.COLI [ORGANISM-1]
  <ITEM-2> KLEBSIELLA [ORGANISM-1]
  <ITEM-3> ENTEROBACTER [ORGANISM-1]
  <ITEM-4> KLEBSIELLA-PNEUMONIAE [ORGANISM-1]

Comments in italics are not part of the actual interaction.
From van Melle (1984).

To build MYCIN, Shortliffe and Buchanan interviewed expert physicians to determine how they went about doing these diagnoses. This involved presenting various cases to the experts, observing how they diagnosed these test cases, asking them why they made their judgments, trying to implement the experts' knowledge within MYCIN, asking the experts to comment on the MYCIN process, and revising MYCIN in response. They found they had to build some 500 production rules to represent the various pieces of knowledge these experts possessed in this area of medicine. The following is one of the rules that encode information about how to interpret the organism found in a culture:

> IF the result of a gram stain of the organism is negative
> and the organism is shaped like a rod
> and the organism grows without air
> THEN there is suggestive evidence (.6) that the organism is
> bacteroides

Note that these rules do not encode a certain inference. Rather they encode the fact that the information increases the likelihood of the diagnosis of bacteroides. (The .6 in the rule measures the strength of the evidence.) It is characteristic of medical diagnosis that the information is not certain in its implications and a major problem is to combine this uncertain information in coming up with a diagnosis.

MYCIN's overall flow of control is determined by what is called a *backwards reasoning strategy*. It starts with the following general rule:

> IF there is an organism which requires therapy
> THEN compile a list of possible therapies which may be effective
> and determine the best therapy

The problem with applying this rule is that MYCIN does not know whether there is an organism which requires therapy. Therefore, it looks in its rule set to see if there are any rules that would enable it to determine that an organism needs therapy. It may have a rule that says that if the organism is bacteroides it requires therapy. Unfortunately, it does not know whether the organism is bacteroides. Therefore, it searches for rules like the one given earlier which allow one to conclude bacteroides. However, this rule requires that one have the results of a stain. Again one may not have this knowledge, which initiates a request for laboratory data. Thus, what MYCIN does is chain backwards from the rules that it wants to apply, through rules that establish these rules, until it finally gets to rules whose conditions can be satisfied by such things as laboratory tests. The reader will recognize this backwards problem-solving strategy from Chapter 8.

MYCIN proved to be a fairly successful system. Independent medical experts rated the recommendations made by MYCIN as good as those made by experts on Stanford's infectious disease faculty. This is perhaps not surprising since MYCIN was designed to incorporate the knowledge of that faculty. However, it makes the point that the expertise of the faculty lay in its knowledge and if that knowledge was codified and transferred to a computer program, the computer program could be as intelligent as the human experts in this special domain.

Can Computers be Truly Intelligent?

There is a perennial debate on the issue of whether computers are capable of true humanlike intelligence or, put more categorically, whether computers can think. The example of MYCIN might seem to make the point that they are intelligent. However, MYCIN's intelligence is so narrow that it is not convincing to many. Even if its diagnoses were as good as those of Stanford faculty, these Stanford faculty were widely knowledgeable about medicine and life in a way MYCIN was not. Many years went into codifying the 500 rules in the knowledge base that was MYCIN. It is just not reasonable to imagine coding all the knowledge that a human possesses. An active area of research in artificial intelligence involves learning systems that will automatically acquire such knowledge (Marcus, 1988). However, it seems basically impossible to give a machine the same experiences as a child from which to acquire human knowledge. This makes the point that our notion of human intelligence is perhaps inextricably tied to the knowledge that a person has. A system with a radically different knowledge base cannot be intelligent in the same sense. We noted earlier in our discussion of human intelligence that it is relative to a culture. Computers just cannot participate in a culture the way humans can.

Some forty years ago the famous British mathematician, Alan Turing, proposed a test to determine if a computer could think. His proposal is an imitation game described below:

> The new form of the problem can be described in terms of a game which we call the "imitation game." It is played with three people, a man (A), a woman (B), and an interrogator (C) who may be of either sex. The interrogator stays in a room apart from the other two. The object of the game for the interrogator is to determine which of the

two is the man and which is the woman. He knows them by labels X and Y, and at the end of the game he says either "X is A and Y is B" or "X is B and Y is A." The interrogator is allowed to put questions to A and B thus:

C: Will X please tell me the length of his or her hair?

Now suppose X is actually A, then A must answer. It is A's object in the game to try and cause C to make the wrong identification. His answer might therefore be:

"My hair is shingled, and the longest strands are about nine inches long."

In order that tones of voice may not help the interrogator the answers should be written, or better still, typewritten. The ideal arrangement is to have a teleprinter communication between the two rooms. Alternatively the question and answers can be repeated by an intermediary. The object of the game for the third player (B) is to help the interrogator. The best strategy for her is probably to give truthful answers. She can add such things as "I am the woman, don't listen to him!" to her answers, but it will avail nothing as the man can make similar remarks.

We now ask the question, "What will happen when a machine takes the part of A in this game?" Will the interrogator decide wrongly as often when the game is played like this as he does when the game is played between a man and a woman? These questions replace our original, "Can machines think?" (Turing, 1950; p. 433–434)

The second-order nature of this imitation game has always struck many as peculiar. A more direct test would seem to be to judge which is the computer and which is the human rather than to judge which is the woman and which is the man (played by a computer) pretending to be a woman. The point of the second-order test is to focus the tester away from tests of human versus computer. Thus, we would not ask of the computer unfair questions such as, "How many creases are there on the knuckle of your left index finger?" Rather the computer is left just to make up information on a second-hand basis even as the man must make up his answers about a woman on a second-hand basis. However, to judge a computer intelligent just because it can do as good a job imitating a woman as a man leaves something to be desired. It is as narrow a definition as being able to diagnose infectious diseases.

Ultimately, I think we have to conclude that our notion of human intelligence is inextricably tied to being human. Human intelligence depends on having the knowledge of a human, which in turn depends on having a human body and a human experience.

The research on computer chess is a good point in case. For thirty years now, humans have programmed computers to play chess. Early enthusiasm led Herbert Simon in 1957 to predict "that within 10 years a digital computer will be the world's chess champion, unless the rules bar it from competition." This proved overly optimistic but computers have steadily improved in the level of performance to the point where the best computer programs (for example, a program built at Carnegie Mellon called Deep Thought) have been rated at the master level. It turns out that the way computers achieve their intelligence at chess is quite different than humans. Humans engage in relatively little search in choosing a move. They will consider less than 100 sequences of moves. Computers, on the other hand, will consider millions of sequences. While this is a great number, it is still only a small fraction of the number of sequences possible in chess. (At a typical point in the game there are about 30 possible next moves, 30×30 sequences of move and opponent's response, $30 \times 30 \times 30$ sequences of move, opponent's response, and player's next move, etc.) What a chess program will do is, for instance, to consider all legal sequences of 8 moves (4 by the player and 4 by the opponent) and choose the move that is in what seems to be the best sequence.

For a long time this placed a premium on programs that ran on very fast computers or computers with special chess hardware for making fast moves. In tournament chess there is only so much time one can spend in selecting a move. The faster the program ran, the more sequences and the longer the sequences it could consider in a fixed time and the more judicious it would be in selecting moves. The early programs brought very little knowledge of chess to bear but rather counted on their ability to search millions of positions. Later programs like Deep Thought brought more knowledge to help guide this search process. There was also a lot of special hardware built to help Deep Thought compute its decisions. Thus, we see computers are achieving intelligence in chess by combining extensive knowledge with powerful special-purpose computation. It is probably also true of human performance in chess, although the way humans approach chess is different than computers. As discussed in Chapter 9, humans appear to bring together extensive knowledge with the brain's facility for efficient pattern matching (in contrast to search).

Deep Thought is the best of the chess-playing programs and can play better chess than most humans. On October 22, 1989, it became the first program to play a world chess champion (Gary Kasparov). It lost. However, even if it had won, it would not convince us to consider computers as more intelligent than humans any more than the fact that computers have always been able to perform arithmetic calculations better than humans. They are achieving their successes in a very nonhuman way. The concept of intelligence is a fleeting one too much bound up in our concept of a human and our own culture.

Intelligent Tutoring

One of the developments in artificial intelligence that I find personally most appealing is the development of intelligent computer systems which offer students tutoring in various educational subjects. It changes the question of "Are computers intelligent?" to "Can computers transfer intelligence to humans?" It is a research area that forces us to become precise about the nature of human intelligence and how it can be acquired. One example of such a tutor is the LISP tutor (Anderson, Conrad, & Corbett, in press; Corbett & Anderson, in press; Anderson & Reiser, 1985), which teaches the programming language LISP. LISP is the main programming language used in artificial intelligence. The LISP tutor has been continuously teaching LISP to students at Carnegie-Mellon University since the fall of 1984. It has also been used at a number of other universities, in government, and in industry. It has been shown that people learn faster using it than they learn in standard university classrooms.

One of the motivations for research on intelligent tutoring is the evidence showing that private human tutoring is very effective. Studies have shown that 98 percent of students with private human tutors do better than the student in a standard classroom (Bloom, 1984). An ideal private tutor is one who is with you at all times while studying a subject matter. It is particularly important to have the tutor present while one solving problems in a domain like LISP, which requires complex problem-solving skills. In LISP, problem solving takes the form of writing computer programs or functions as they are often called in LISP. Therefore, in developing the LISP tutor we chose to focus on providing students with tutoring while they are writing computer programs.

Table 14-4 presents a short dialogue between a student and the LISP tutor on an early problem in the curriculum. Note how carefully the tutor monitors the student's performance in solving the problem. The tutor can do this because it knows how to write LISP functions, and as the student is writing the function, the tutor is simultaneously trying to solve

Table 14-4 *An Interaction Between the LISP Tutor and the Student*

The student is working on writing a piece of code to satisfy the problem description below. Before each point where the tutor and student interact, the partial code that the student has written is printed out.

The Problem Description

Define a function called ctof that takes a degree reading in Celsius degrees and converts it to Fahrenheit degrees. First, you need to change the scale by multiplying the argument by 1.8. Then you need to translate the scale by adding 32, since 0 Celsius = 32 Fahrenheit. For example, (ctof 20) returns 68.

Cycles in which the tutor communicates with the student

Code: *(defun ctof (cdeg)*
          ((*)

Tutor: Yes, you will need to call "*" to get the degree on the enlarged scale, but you are ultimately trying to get the fahrenheit equivalent of the celsius degree. So you need to code a different function here that takes a call to "*" as an argument.

Code: *(defun ftoc (cdeg)*
          (+ <NUM> <NUM2>))

Student: Help

Tutor: You need to multiply together the celsius degree reading and the size of fahrenheit degrees using the function *. When you multiply these numbers you will get the degree on the enlarged scale, which is 36 in our example.

Code: *(defun ctof (cdeg)*
          (+ (1.8 cdge) <NUM2>))*

Tutor: Did you mean cdeg?

Student: Yes

Code: *(defun ctof (cdeg)*
          (+ (1.8 cdeg) 32))*

Tutor: You are done. Type next to go on after testing the function you have defined.

the same problem the student is working on. As soon as the tutor sees the student making a mistake the tutor can intervene with some remedial instruction.

Underlying the tutor's ability to solve problems and monitor the student's problem solving is an expert model of what is required to solve such LISP programming problems. As in the case with MYCIN, this knowledge is encoded as production rules. In all there are some 500 production rules that encode the knowledge about LISP. A typical production rule in the LISP tutor is:

IF the goal is to multiply one number by another.
THEN use * and set subgoals to code the two numbers.

The basic goal of the LISP tutor is to communicate these 500 production rules to the student, monitor the performance to see if he or she possesses these rules in correct form, and provide the student practice on these rules. The success of the LISP tutor is one piece of evidence that these 500 rules are indeed what underlie coding skill in LISP.

Besides providing an instructional tool, the LISP tutor is a research tool for studying the course of skill acquisition. The tutor can monitor how well the student is doing on each of the 500 production rules, recording statistics such as the number of errors a student is making and the time it takes a student to type the code corresponding to each of these production rules. These data have indicated that students acquire the skill of LISP by independently acquiring each of the 500 rules. Figure 14-7 displays the learning curves for these rules. The two dependent measures in the figure are the number of errors made on a production rule and the time to write the code corresponding to a rule (when that rule is correctly coded). These statistics are plotted as a function of learning opportunity. A learning opportunity occurs each time the student comes to a point in a problem where that rule can be applied. As can be seen, performance on these rules dramatically improves from first to second learning opportunity and more gradually improves thereafter. These learning curves are similar to those we identified in Chapter 6 for the learning of simple associations.

We have also pursued the issue of individual differences in the learning of these rules. Students who have learned a prior programming language are at a considerable advantage compared to students for whom this is their first programming language. This advantage can be accounted for in terms of the identical elements model of transfer (see the discussion in Chapter 9) in which rules for programming in one language transfer to programming in another language.

We also did factor analyses of student performance in the LISP tutor and found evidence for two factors. One factor concerned how rapidly they learned productions that were new in a particular lesson. The other factor was how well they retained the productions from earlier lessons. These acquisition and retention factors were both strongly related to math SATs but not verbal SATs. Thus, reinforcing the conclusions of the early part of the chapter, we see in the LISP tutor performance evidence

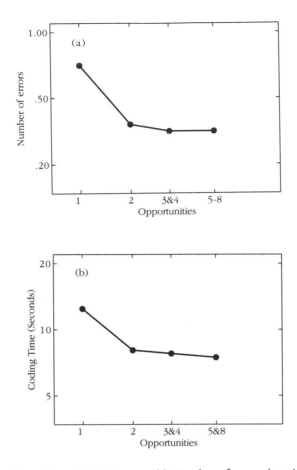

Figure 14-7. Data from the LISP tutor: (a) Number of errors (maximum is 3) per production as a function of number of opportunities for practice; (b) time to correctly code productions as a function of amount of practice.

for the specific ability view of intelligence as well as the importance of accumulated knowledge.

Students emerge from their interactions with the LISP tutor having acquired a complex and sophisticated skill. Their enhanced programming abilities make them appear more intelligent among their peers. However, when we examine what underlies that newfound intelligence, we find that it is the methodical acquisition of some 500 rules of programming. Some students can acquire these rules more easily because of past experience and specific abilities. However, when they graduate from the LISP course they all have learned the 500 new production rules. Having acquired these rules, there are no remaining differences among the students with respect to ability to program in LISP. Thus, we can see why expertise in areas such as programming, chess, or racehorse handicapping can be unrelated to measures of IQ. At high levels of expertise what matters is what specifically you have learned and not your general abilities.

Conclusions

We have now reviewed two bodies of research. The research on individual differences has emphasized that there are specific capacities in which humans vary. The research in artificial intelligence has emphasized how critical domain-specific knowledge is to intelligence. We find that computers are intelligent to the extent that they possess knowledge, that they fall short of humans to the extent they lack knowledge, and that they can educate humans to the extent they can transfer knowledge. As we reviewed in earlier chapters, language is one of the important human abilities. Over and above its direct contribution to intelligence, it has opened a communication channel among humans that allows knowledge to be transferred and accumulated.

Remarks and Suggested Readings

The books by Kail and Pellegrino (1985) and Sternberg (1985a) provide two good reviews of psychometric and information-processing research in the area of individual differences in intelligence. Sternberg (1985b) describes his own very influential theory and research in the area. Gardner (1983) is a very readable and literate discussion of the issue of individual differences.

There are a good number of textbooks in the area of artificial intelligence, including Charniak and McDermott (1985), Winston (1984), and Rich (1983). Hayes-Roth, Waterman, and Lenat (1983) provide a good introduction to expert systems. Buchanan and Shortliffe (1984) provide a good review of the research on MYCIN. Reviews of work on intelligent tutoring include Sleeman and Brown (1982), Polson and Richardson

(1988), and Wenger (1987). Clancey (1987) discusses the history of his research with the GUIDON program, which was an attempt to build an intelligent tutor around the MYCIN program. Pylyshyn (1986) contains a thoughtful development of the relationship between artificial intelligence and cognitive psychology. For an influential critique of machine intelligence read Searle (1980).

References

Aaronson, D., & Scarborough, H. S. (1977). Performance theories for sentence coding: some quantitative models. *Journal of Verbal Learning and Verbal Behavior, 16,* 277–304.

Abelson, R. P. (1981). Psychological status of the script concept. *American Psychologist, 36,* 715–729.

Akmajian, A., Demers, R. A., & Harnish, R. M. (1984). *Linguistics: An introduction to language and communication,* 2nd Ed. Cambridge, MA: MIT Press.

Alba, J. W. & Hasher, L. (1983). Is memory schematic? *Psychological Bulletin, 93,* 203–231.

Anderson, J. A. (1973). A theory for the recognition of items from short memorized lists. *Psychological Review, 80,* 417–438.

Anderson, J. R. (1972). Recognition confusions in sentence memory. Unpublished manuscript.

Anderson, J. R. (1974a). Retrieval of propositional information from long-term memory. *Cognitive Psychology, 6,* 451–474.

Anderson, J. R. (1974b). Verbatim and propositional representation of sentences in immediate and long-term memory. *Journal of Verbal Learning and Verbal Behavior, 13,* 149–162.

Anderson, J. R. (1976). *Language, memory, and thought.* Hillsdale, NJ: Erlbaum.

Anderson, J. R. (1978a). Arguments concerning representations for mental imagery. *Psychological Review, 85,* 249–277.

Anderson, J. R. (1978b). Computer simulation of a language acquisition system: A second report. In D. LaBerge & S. J. Samuels (Eds.), *Perception and comprehension*. Hillsdale, NJ: Erlbaum.

Anderson, J. R. (Ed.) (1981). *Cognitive skills and their acquisition*. Hillsdale, NJ: Erlbaum.

Anderson, J. R. (1982). Acquisition of cognitive skill. *Psychological Review, 89*, 369–406.

Anderson, J. R. (1983). *The architecture of cognition*. Cambridge, MA: Harvard University Press.

Anderson, J. R. (1984). Spreading activation. In J. R. Anderson & S. M. Kosslyn (Eds.), *Essays in learning and memory*. New York: W. H. Freeman and Company.

Anderson, J. R., & Bower, G. H. (1973). *Human associative memory*. Washington, DC: Winston.

Anderson, J. R., Boyle, C. F., Corbett, A. T., & Lewis, M. W. (In press). Cognitive modelling and intelligent tutoring. *Artificial intelligence*.

Anderson, J. R., Boyle, C. F., Farrell, R., & Reiser, B. (1984). Cognitive principles in the design of computer tutors. *Proceedings of the Cognitive Science Program, 2–11*.

Anderson, J. R., Conrad, F. G., & Corbett, A. T. (In press). Skill acquisition and the LISP tutor. *Cognitive Science*.

Anderson, J. R., Farrell, R., & Sauers, R. (1984). Learning to program in LISP. *Cognitive Science, 8*, 87–129.

Anderson, J. R., & Kosslyn, S. M. (Eds.) (1984). *Tutorials in learning and memory*. New York: W. H. Freeman and Company.

Anderson, J. R., & Reder, L. M. (1979). An elaborative processing explanation of depth of processing. In L. S. Cermak and F. I. M. Craik (Eds.), *Levels of processing in human memory*. Hillsdale, NJ: Erlbaum.

Anderson, J. R., & Reiser, B. J. (1985). The LISP tutor. *Byte, 10*, 159–175.

Anderson, R. C., & Biddle, W. B. (1975). On asking people questions about what they are reading. In G. H. Bower (Ed.), *The psychology of learning and motivation*, Vol. 9. New York: Academic Press.

Anderson, T. H. (1978). Another look at the self-questioning study technique. Technical Education Report No. 6. Champaign: University of Illinois, Center for the Study of Reading.

Angell, J. R. (1908). The doctrine of formal discipline in the light of the principles of general psychology. *Educational Review, 36*, 1–14.

Angiolillo-Bent, J. S., & Rips, L. J. (1982). Order information in multiple element comparison. *Journal of Experimental Psychology: Human Perception and Performance, 8*, 392–406.

Corbett, A. T., & Chang, F. R. (1983). Pronoun disambiguation: Accessing potential antecedents. *Memory & Cognition, 11*, 283–294.

Cowart, W. (1983). Reference relations and syntactic processing: Evidence of pronoun's influence on a syntactic decision that affects naming. Indiana University Linguistics Club.

Craik, F. I. M., & Lockhart, R. S. (1972). Levels of processing: A framework for memory research. *Journal of Verbal Learning and Verbal Behavior, 11*, 671–684.

Crick, F. H. C., & Asanuma, C. (1986). Certain aspects of the anatomy and physiology of the cerebral cortex. In J. L. McClelland & D. E. Rumelhart (Eds.), *Parallel distributed processing: Explorations in the microstructure of cognition*, Vol. 2. Cambridge, MA: MIT Press/Bradford Books.

Crossman, E. R. F. W. (1959). A theory of the acquisition of speed-skill. *Ergonomics, 2*, 153–166.

Crowder, R. G. (1976). *Principles of learning and memory*. Hillsdale, NJ: Erlbaum.

Crowder, R. G. (1982). The demise of short-term memory. *Acta Psychologica, 50*, 291–323.

Daneman, M., & Carpenter, P. A. (1980). Individual differences in working memory and reading. *Journal of Verbal Learning and Verbal Behavior, 19*, 450–466.

Darwin, C. J., Turvey, M. T., & Crowder, R. G. (1972). The auditory analogue of the Sperling partial report procedure: Evidence for brief auditory storage. *Cognitive Psychology, 3*, 255–267.

de Beer, G. R. (1959). Paedomorphesis. *Proceedings of the 15th International Congress of Zoology*, 927–930.

de Groot, A. D. (1965). *Thought and choice in chess*. The Hague: Mouton.

de Groot, A. D. (1966). Perception and memory versus thought. In B. Kleinmuntz (Ed.), *Problem-solving*. New York: Wiley.

Desimone, R., Albright, T. D., Gross, C. G., & Bruce, C. (1984). Stimulus-selective properties of inferior temporal neurons in the macaque. *Neuroscience, 4*, 1051–2062.

de Valois, R. L., & Jacobs, G. H. (1968). Primate color vision. *Science, 162*, 533–540.

deVilliers, J. G., & deVilliers, P. A. (1978). *Language acquisition*. Cambridge, MA: Harvard University Press.

Dickstein, L. S. (1978). The effect of figure on syllogistic reasoning. *Memory & Cognition, 6*, 76–83.

Dominowski, R. L., & Jenrick, R. (1972). Effects of hints and interpolated activity on solution of an insight problem. *Psychonomic Science, 26*, 335–338.

Dooling, D. J., & Christiaansen, R. E. (1977). Episodic and semantic aspects of memory for prose. *Journal of Experimental Psychology: Human Learning and Memory, 3*, 428–436.

471

Downs, R. M., & Stea, M. (1977). *Maps in minds: Reflections in cognitive mapping.* New York: Harper & Row.

Dowty, D., Kartunnen, L., & Zwicky, A. M. (1985). *Natural language parsing: Psycholinguistic, computational, and theoretical perspectives.* Cambridge, MA: Cambridge University Press.

Duncker, K. (1945). On problem-solving (translated by L. S. Lees). *Psychological Monographs, 58,* No. 270.

Ebbinghaus, H. (1885). Memory: A Contribution to Experimental Psychology (translated by H. A. Ruger & C. E. Bussenues, 1913). New York: Teachers College, Columbia University.

Eccles, J. C. (1979). Synaptic plasticity. *Naturwissenchaften, 66,* 147–153.

Edwards, W. (1968). Conservatism in human information processing. In B. Kleinmuntz (Ed.), *Formal representations of human judgment.* New York: Wiley.

Egan, D. E., & Schwartz, B. J. (1979). Chunking in recall of symbolic drawings. *Memory and Cognition, 7,* 149–158.

Ehrlich, K., & Rayner, K. (1983). Pronoun assignment and semantic integration during reading: Eye movements and immediacy of processing. *Journal of Verbal Learning and Verbal Behavior, 22,* 75–87.

Eich, E. (1985). Context, memory, and integrated item/context imagery. *Journal of Experimental Psychology: Learning, Memory, and Cognition, 11,* 764–770.

Eich, J., Weingartner, H., Stillman, R. C., & Gillin, J. C. (1975). State-dependent accessibility of retrieval cues in the retention of a categorized list. *Journal of Verbal Learning and Verbal Behavior, 14,* 408–417.

Eich, J. M. (1982). A composite holographic associative recall model. *Psychological Review, 89,* 627–661.

Eimas, P. D., & Corbit, J. (1973). Selective adaptation of linguistic feature detectors. *Cognitive Psychology, 4,* 99–109.

Engle, R. W., & Bukstel, L. (1978). Memory processes among bridge players of differing expertise. *American Journal of Psychology, 91,* 673–689.

Erickson, J. R. A. (1974). A set analysis theory of behavior in formal syllogistic reasoning tasks. In R. L. Solso (Ed.), *Theories in cognitive psychology: The Loyola Symposium.* Hillsdale, NJ: Erlbaum.

Ernst, G., & Newell, A. (1969). *GPS: A case study in generality and problem solving.* New York: Academic Press.

Ervin-Tripp, S. M. (1974). Is second language learning like the first? *TESOL Quarterly, 8,* 111–127.

Farah, M. J. (1988). Is visual imagery really visual? Overlooked evidence from neuropsychology. *Psychological Review, 95,* 307–317.

Farah, M. J., Hammond, K. M., Levine, D. N., & Calvanio, R. (1988). Visual and spatial mental imagery: Dissociable systems of representation. *Cognitive Psychology, 20,* 439–462.

Fernandez, A., & Glenberg, A. M. (1985). Changing environmental context does not reliably affect memory. *Memory and Cognition, 13,* 333–345.

Ferreira, F., & Clifton, C. (1986). The independence of syntactic processing. *Journal of Memory and Language, 25,* 348–368.

Fillenbaum, S. (1971). On coping with ordered and unordered conjunctive sentences. *Journal of Experimental Psychology, 87,* 93–98.

Fillenbaum, S. (1974). Pragmatic normalization: Further results for some conjunctive and disjunctive sentences. *Journal of Experimental Psychology, 103,* 913–921.

Finke, R. A. (1985). Theories relating mental imagery to perception. *Psychological Bulletin, 98,* 235–259.

Fischer, K. W. (1980). A theory of cognitive development: The control and construction of hierarchies of skills. *Psychological Review, 87,* 477–531.

Fitts, P. M., & Posner, M. I. (1967). *Human performance.* Belmont, CA: Brooks Cole.

Flavell, J. H. (1985). *Cognitive development.* Englewood Cliffs, NJ: Prentice-Hall.

Flavell, J. H. (1978). Comment. In R. S. Siegler (Ed.), *Children's thinking: What develops?* Hillsdale, NJ: Erlbaum.

Flavell, J. H., Friedrichs, A. G., & Hoyt, J. D. (1970). Developmental changes in memorization processes. *Cognitive Psychology, 1,* 324–340.

Fletcher. C. R. (1986). Strategies for the allocation of short-term memory during comprehension. *Journal of Memory and Language, 25,* 43–58.

Flexser, A. J., & Tulving, E. (1978). Retrieval independence in recognition and recall. *Psychological Review, 85,* 153–172.

Fodor, J. A. (1975). *The language of thought.* New York: Thomas Y. Crowell.

Fodor, J. A. (1983). *The modularity of mind.* Cambridge, MA: MIT/Bradford Books.

Fodor, J. A., Bever, T. G., & Garrett, M. F. (1974). *The psychology of language.* New York: McGraw-Hill.

Fodor, J. A., & Garrett, M. F. (1967). Some syntactic determinants of sentential complexity. *Perception and Psychophysics, 2,* 289–296.

Fodor, J. A., & Pylyshyn, Z. W. (1988). Connectionism and cognitive architecture: A critical analysis. *Cognition, 28,* 3–71.

Foss, D. J., & Hakes, D. T. (1978). *Psycholinguistics.* Englewood Cliffs, NJ: Prentice-Hall.

Frase, L. T. (1975). Prose processing. In G. H. Bower (Ed.), *The psychology of learning and motivation,* Vol. 9. New York: Academic Press.

Frazier, L., & Rayner, K. (1982). Making and correcting errors during sentence comprehension: Eye movements in the analysis of structurally ambiguous sentences. *Cognitive Psychology, 14,* 178–210.

Frederiksen, C. H. (1975). Representing logical and semantic structure of knowledge acquired from discourse. *Cognitive Psychology, 7,* 371–458.

Fromkin, V. (1971). The non-anomalous nature of anomalous utterances. *Languages, 47,* 27–52.

Fromkin, V. (1973). *Speech errors as linguistic evidence.* The Hague: Mouton.

Gagne, E. D. (1985). *The cognitive psychology of school learning.* Boston, MA: Little, Brown.

Gagne, R. M. (1973). Learning and instructional sequence. *Review of Research in Education, 1,* 3–33.

Gardner, H. (1975). *The shattered mind: The person after brain damage.* New York: Knopf.

Gardner, H. (1983). *Frames of mind: The theory of multiple intelligences.* New York: Basic Books.

Gardner, H. (1985). *The mind's new science: A history of the cognitive revolution.* New York: Basic Books.

Garfield, J. L. (1987). *Modularity in knowledge representation and natural-language understanding.* Cambridge, MA: MIT Press.

Garrett, M. F. (1975). The analysis of sentence production. In G. H. Bower (Ed.), *The psychology of learning and motivation,* Vol. 9. New York: Academic Press.

Gay, I. R. (1973). Temporal position of reviews and its effect on the retention of mathematical rules. *Journal of Educational Psychology, 64,* 171–182.

Gazzaniga, M. S. (1967). The split brain in man. *Scientific American, 217,* 24–29.

Gazzaniga, M. S. (1983). Right hemisphere language following brain bisection: A 20-year perspective. *American Psychologist, 38,* 525–537.

Gee, J. P., & Grosjean, F. (1983). Performance structures: A psycholinguistic and linguistic appraisal. *Cognitive Psychology, 15,* 411–458.

Gelman, R. (1982). Basic numerical abilities. In R. J. Sternberg, (Ed.), *Advances in the psychology of human intelligence,* Vol. 1. Hillsdale, NJ: Erlbaum.

Gelman, R., & Gallistel, C. R. (1978). *The child's understanding of numbers.* Cambridge, MA: Harvard University Press.

Gelman, S. A. (1988). The development of induction within natural kind and artifact categories. *Cognitive Psychology, 20,* 65–95.

Gentner, D., & Stevens, A. L. (1983). *Mental models.* Hillsdale, NJ: Erlbaum.

Gernsbacher, M. A. (1985). Surface information loss in comprehension. *Cognitive Psychology, 17,* 324–363.

Geschwind, N. (1980). Neurological knowledge and complex behaviors. *Cognitive Science, 4,* 185–194.

Gibson, E. J., & Levin, H. (1975). *The psychology of reading.* Cambridge, MA: MIT Press.

Gibson, J. J. (1950). *Perception of the visual world.* Boston: Houghton.

Gibson, J. J. (1966). *The senses considered as perceptual systems.* Boston: Houghton.

Gibson, J. J. (1979). *The ecological approach to visual perception.* Boston: Houghton Mifflin.

Gick, M. L., & Holyoak, K. J. (1980). Analogical problem solving. *Cognitive Psychology, 12,* 306–355.

Gick, M. L., & Holyoak, K. J. (1983). Schema induction and analogical transfer. *Cognitive Psychology, 15* 1–38.

Gillund, G., & Shiffrin, R. M. (1984). A retrieval model for both recognition and recall. *Psychological Review, 91,* 1–67.

Ginsburg, H. J., & Opper, S. (1980). *Piaget's theory of intellectual development.* Englewood Cliffs, NJ: Prentice-Hall.

Glucksberg, S., & Danks, J. H. (1968). Effects of discriminative labels and of nonsense labels upon availability of novel function. *Journal of Verbal Learning and Verbal Behavior, 7,* 72–76.

Glucksberg, S., & Danks, J. H. (1975). *Experimental psycholinguistics.* New York: Halsted Press.

Glucksberg, S., & Weisberg, R. W. (1966). Verbal behavior and problem solving: Some effects of labeling in a functional fixedness problem. *Journal of Experimental Psychology, 71,* 659–664.

Godden, D. R., & Baddeley, A. D. (1975). Context-dependent memory in two natural environments: On land and under water. *British Journal of Psychology, 66,* 325–331.

Goldberg, R. A., Schwartz, S., & Stewart, M. (1977). Individual differences in cognitive processes. *Journal of Educational Psychology, 69,* 9–14.

Goldman-Rakic, P. S. (1987). Development of cortical circuitry and cognitive function. *Child Development, 58,* 601–622.

Goldstein, E. B. (1989). *Sensation and perception,* 3rd Ed. Belmont, CA: Wadsworth.

Gould, S. J. (1977). *Ontogeny and phylogeny.* Cambridge, MA: Belknap.

Graesser, A. C. (1981). *Prose comprehension beyond the word.* New York: Springer-Verlag.

Graf, P., Squire, L. R., & Mandler, G. (1984). The information that amnesic patients do not forget. *Journal of Experimental Psychology: Learning Memory and Cognition, 10,* 164–178.

Graf, P., & Torrey, J. W. (1966). Perception of phrase structure in written language. *American Psychological Association Convention Proceedings, 83–88.*

Granrud, C. (In press). *Visual perception and cognition in infancy.* Hillsdale, NJ: Erlbaum.

Gray, G. W. (1948). The great ravelled knot. *Scientific American, 179,* 26–38.

Gray, J. A., & Wedderburn, A. A. I. (1960). Grouping strategies with simultaneous stimuli. *Quarterly Journal of Experimental Psychology, 12,* 180–184.

Greenberg, J. H. (1963). Some universals of grammar with particular reference to the order of meaningful elements. In J. H. Greenberg (Ed.), *Universals of language.* Cambridge, MA: MIT Press.

Greeno, J. G. (1974). Hobbits and orcs: Acquisition of a sequential concept. *Cognitive Psychology, 6,* 270–292.

Greeno, J. G. (1976). Cognitive objectives of instruction: Theory of knowledge for solving problems and answering questions. In D. Klahr (Ed.), *Cognition and instruction.* Hillsdale, NJ: Erlbaum.

Greeno, J. G., & Simon, H. A. (1988). Problem-solving and reasoning. In R. C. Atkinson, H. Hernstein, G. Lindzey, & R. D. Luce (Eds.), *Steven's handbook of experimental psychology.* New York: Wiley.

Griggs, R. A., & Cox, J. R. (1982). The elusive thematic-materials effect in Wason's selection task. *British Journal of Psychology, 73,* 407–420.

Grimes, L. (1975). *The thread of discourse.* The Hague: Mouton.

Grosjean, F., Grosjean, L., & Lane, H. (1979). The patterns of silence: Performance structures in sentence production. *Cognitive Psychology, 11,* 58–81.

Grossberg, S. (1987). *The adaptive brain, I: Cognition learning, reinforcement and rhythm.* Amsterdam: North-Holland, Elsevier.

Gruber, H. E., & Voneche, J. J. (Eds.) (1977). *The essential Piaget: An interpretative reference and guide.* London: Routledge & Kegan Paul.

Guilford, J. P. (1982). Cognitive psychology's ambiguities: Some suggested remedies. *Psychological Review, 89,* 48–59.

Guyote, M. J., & Sternberg, R. S. (1981). A transitive-chain theory of syllogistic reasoning. *Cognitive Psychology, 13,* 461–525.

Hakes, D. T. (1972). Effects of reducing complement constructions on sentence comprehension. *Journal of Verbal Learning and Verbal Behavior, 11,* 278–286.

Hakes, D. T., & Foss, D. J. (1970). Decision processes during sentence comprehension: Effects of surface structure reconsidered. *Perception and Psychophysics, 8,* 413–416.

Halford, G. S. (1982). *The development of thought.* Hillsdale, NJ: Erlbaum.

Halford, G. S. (1984). Can young children integrate premises in transitivity and serial order tasks? *Cognitive Psychology, 16,* 65–93.

Hammerton, M. (1973). A case of radical probability estimation. *Journal of Experimental Psychology, 101,* 252–254.

Harris, R. J. (1977). Comprehension of pragmatic implications in advertising. *Journal of Applied Psychology, 62,* 603–608.

Haviland, S. E., & Clark, H. H. (1974). What's new? Acquiring new information as a process in comprehension. *Journal of Verbal Learning and Verbal Behavior, 13,* 512–521.

Hayes, J. R. (1984). *Problem solving techniques.* Philadelphia: Franklin Institute Press.

Hayes, J. R. (1985). Three problems in teaching general skills. In J. Segal, S. Chipman, & R. Glaser (Eds.), *Thinking and learning,* Vol. 2. Hillsdale, NJ: Erlbaum.

Hayes-Roth, F., Waterman, D. A., & Lenat, D. B. (1983). *Building expert systems.* Reading, MA: Addison-Wesley.

Haygood, R. C., & Bourne, L. E. (1965). Attribute- and rule-learning aspects of conceptual behavior. *Psychological Review, 72,* 175–195.

Heider, E. (1972). Universals of color naming and memory. *Journal of Experimental Psychology, 93,* 10–20.

Henle, M. (1962). On the relation between logic and thinking. *Psychological Review, 69,* 366–378.

Higbee, K. L. (1988). *Your memory: How it works and how to improve it.* Englewood Cliffs, NJ: Prentice-Hall.

Hilgard, E. R. (1968). *The experience of hypnosis.* New York: Harcourt Brace Jovanovich.

Hintzman, D. L. (1974). Theoretical implications of the spacing effect. In R. L. Solso (Ed.), *Theories in cognitive psychology: The Loyola symposium.* Potomac, MD: Erlbaum.

Hintzman, D. L. (1986). "Schema abstraction" in a multiple-trace memory model. *Psychological Review, 93,* 411–428.

Hintzman, D. L., O'Dell, C. S., & Arndt, D. R. (1981). Orientation in cognitive maps. *Cognitive Psychology, 13,* 149–206.

Hoffman, D. D., & Richards, W. (1985). Parts of recognition. *Cognition, 18,* 65–96.

Holland, J. H., Holyoak, K., Nisbett, R. E., & Thagard, P. R. (1986). *Induction: Processes of inference, learning, and discovery.* Cambridge, MA: MIT Press.

Horn, J. L. (1968). Organization of abilities and the development of intelligence. *Psychological Review, 75,* 242–259.

Horn, J. L. (1986). Intellectual ability concepts. In R. J. Sternberg (Ed.), *Advances in the psychology of human abilities,* Vol. 1. Hillsdale, NJ: Erlbaum.

Horn, J. L., & Stankov, L. (1982). Auditory and visual intelligence. *Intelligence, 6,* 165–185.

Hubel, D. H., & Wiesel, T. N. (1962). Receptive fields, binocular interaction, and functional architecture in the cat's visual cortex. *Journal of Physiology, 166,* 106–154.

Hunt, E. B. (1975). *Artificial intelligence.* New York: Academic Press.

Hunt, E. B. (1985). Verbal ability. In R. J. Sternberg (Ed.), *Human abilities: An information-processing approach.* New York: W. H. Freeman and Company.

Hunt, E. B., Davidson, J., & Lansman, M. (1981). Individual differences in long-term memory access. *Memory and Cognition, 9,* 599–608.

Hunt, M. (1982). *The universe within.* New York: Simon & Schuster.

Huttenlocher, P. R. (1979). Synaptic density in human frontal cortex — developmental changes and effects of aging. *Brain Research, 163,* 195–205.

Hyams, N. M. (1986). *Language acquisition and the theory of parameters.* Dordrecht: D. Reidel.

Hyde, T. S., & Jenkins, J. J. (1973). Recall for words as a function of semantic, graphic, and syntactic orienting tasks. *Journal of Verbal Learning and Verbal Behavior, 12,* 471–480.

Inhelder, B., & Piaget, J. (1958). *The growth of logical thinking from childhood to adolescence.* New York: Basic Books.

Jacoby, L. L. (1978). On interpreting the effects of repetition: Solving a problem versus remembering a solution. *Journal of Verbal Learning and Verbal Behavior, 17,* 649–667.

Jacoby, L. L. (1983). Remembering the data: Analyzing interactive processes in reading. *Journal of Verbal Learning and Verbal Behavior, 22,* 485–508.

James, W. (1890). *The principles of psychology,* Vols. 1 and 2. New York: Holt.

Jarvella, R. J. (1971). Syntactic processing of connected speech. *Journal of Verbal Learning and Verbal Behavior, 10,* 409–416.

Jeffries, R. P., Turner, A. A., Polson, P. G., & Atwood, M. E. (1981). The processes involved in designing software. In J. R. Anderson (Ed.), *Cognitive skills and their acquisition.* Hillsdale, NJ: Erlbaum.

Jeffries, R. P., Polson, P. G., Razran, L., & Atwood, M. (1977). A process model for missionaries-cannibals and other river-crossing problems. *Cognitive Psychology, 9,* 412–440.

Johnson, D. M. (1939). Confidence and speed in the two-category judgment. *Archives of Psychology, 241,* 1–52.

478

Johnson, D. M. (1972). *A systematic introduction to the psychology of thinking.* New York: Harper & Row.

Johnson, M. K., & Raye, C. L. (1981). Reality monitoring. *Psychological Review, 88,* 67–85.

Johnson, N. F. (1970). The role of chunking and organization in process of recall. In G. H. Bower (Ed.), *Psychology of language and motivation,* Vol. 4. New York: Academic Press.

Johnson-Laird, P. N. (1983). *Mental models.* Cambridge, MA: Harvard University Press.

Johnson-Laird, P. N., & Steedman, M. (1978). The psychology of syllogisms. *Cognitive Psychology, 10,* 64–99.

Just, M. A., & Carpenter, P. A. (1978). Inference processes during reading: Reflections from eye fixations. In J. W. Sanders, D. F. Fisher, & R. A. Monty (Eds.), *Eye movement and the higher psychological functions.* Hillsdale, NJ: Erlbaum.

Just, M. A., & Carpenter, P. A. (1980). A theory of reading: From eye fixations to comprehension. *Psychological Review, 87,* 329–354.

Just, M. A., & Carpenter, P. A. (1985). Cognitive coordinate systems: Accounts of mental rotation and individual differences in spatial ability. *Psychological Review, 92,* 137–172.

Just, M. A., & Carpenter, P. A. (1987). *The psychology of reading and language comprehension.* Boston, MA: Allyn and Bacon.

Kahneman, D. (1973). *Attention and effort.* Englewood Cliffs, NJ: Prentice-Hall.

Kahneman, D., Slovic, P., & Tversky, A. (Eds.) (1982). *Judgment under uncertainty: Heuristics and biases.* New York: Cambridge University Press.

Kahneman, D., & Tversky, A. (1972). Subjective probability: A judgment of representiveness. *Cognitive Psychology, 3,* 430–454.

Kahneman, D., & Tversky, A. (1973). On the psychology of prediction. *Psychological Review, 80,* 237–251.

Kail, R. (1988). Developmental functions for speeds of cognitive processes. *Journal of Experimental Child Psychology, 45,* 339–364.

Kail, R., & Park, Y. (In press). Impact of practice on speed of mental rotation. *Journal of Experimental Child Psychology.*

Kail, R., & Pellegrino, J. W. (1985). *Human intelligence.* New York: W. H. Freeman and Company.

Kamin, L. J. (1974). *The science and politics of IQ.* Potomac, MD: Erlbaum.

Kandel, E., & Schwartz, J. (1984). *Principles of neural science.* 2nd Ed. New York: Elsevier.

Kaplan, C. A., & Davidson, J. (Submitted). Incubation effects in problem solving.

Kaplan, C. A., & Simon, H. A. (1988). *In search of insight* (Technical Report AIP 55). Carnegie-Mellon University, Computer Science Department.

Kaplan, R. M., & Bresnan, J. W. (1982). Lexical-functional grammar: A formal system for grammatical representation. In J. W. Bresnan (Ed.), *The mental representation of grammatical relations.* Cambridge, MA: MIT Press.

Katz, B. (1952). The nerve impulse. *Scientific American, 187,* 55–64.

Keenan, J. M., Baillet, S. D., & Brown, P. (1984). The effects of causal cohesion on comprehension and memory. *Journal of Verbal Learning and Verbal Behavior, 23,* 115–126.

Keeney, T. J., Cannizzo, S. R., & Flavell, J. H. (1967). Spontaneous and induced verbal rehearsal in a recall task. *Child Development, 38,* 953–966.

Keeton, W. T. (1980). *Biological science.* New York: Norton.

Keil, F. C., & Batterman, N. (1984). A characteristic-to-defining shift in the development of word meaning. *Journal of Verbal Learning and Verbal Behavior, 23,* 221–236.

Kelso, J. A. S. (Ed.) (1982). *Human motor behavior: An introduction.* Hillsdale, NJ: Erlbaum.

Keppel, G., & Underwood, B. J. (1962). Proactive inhibition in short-term retention of single items. *Journal of Verbal Learning and Verbal Behavior, 1,* 153–161.

Kimball, J. P. (1973). Seven principles of surface structure parsing in natural language. *Cognition, 2,* 15–47.

Kinney, G. C., Marsetta, M., & Showman, D. J. (1966). Studies in display symbol legibility, part XXI. The legibility of alphanumeric symbols for digitized television (ESD-TR-66-117). Bedford, MA: The Mitre Corporation.

Kinsbourne, M., & Smith, W. L. (1974). *Hemispheric disconnection and cerebral function.* Springfield, IL: Charles C Thomas.

Kintsch, W. (1970). *Learning memory and conceptual processes.* New York: Wiley.

Kintsch, W. (1974). *The representation of meaning in memory.* Hillsdale, NJ: Erlbaum.

Kintsch, W. (1977). On comprehending stories. In M. A. Just & P. A. Carpenter (Eds.), *Cognitive processes in comprehension.* Hillsdale, NJ: Erlbaum.

Kintsch, W. (1979). On modeling comprehension. *Educational Psychologist, 14,* 3–14.

Kintsch, W., & Keenan, J. (1973). Reading rate and retention as a function of the number of propositions in the base structure of sentences. *Cognitive Psychology, 5,* 257–274.

Kintsch, W., & van Dijk, T. A. (1976). Recalling and summarizing stories (*Comment on se rappelle et on résume des histoires*). *Languages, 40,* 98–116.

Kintsch, W., & van Dijk, T. A. (1978). Toward a model of text comprehension and reproduction. *Psychological Review, 85,* 363–394.

Kintsch, W., & Vipond, P. (1979). Reading comprehension and readability in educational practice and psychological theory. In L. G. Nilsson (Ed.), *Perspectives on memory research.* Hillsdale, NJ: Erlbaum.

Klahr, D. (1978). Goal formation, planning, and learning by pre-school problem solvers, or: My socks are in the dryer. In Siegler, R. S. (Ed.), *Children's thinking: What develops?* Hillsdale, NJ: Erlbaum.

Klahr, D., Chase, W. G., & Lovelace, E. A. (1983). Structure and process in alphabetic retrieval. *Journal of Experimental Psychology: Learning, Memory, and Cognition, 9,* 462–477.

Klahr, D., & Robinson, M. (1981). Formal assessment of problem-solving and planning processes in preschool children. *Cognitive Psychology, 13,* 113–148.

Klahr, D., & Siegler, R. S. (1978). The representations of children's knowledge. In H. Reese & L. P. Lipsitt (Eds.), *Advances in child development,* Vol. 12. New York: Academic Press.

Klahr, D., & Wallace, J. G. (1976). *Cognitive development: An information processing view.* Hillsdale, NJ: Erlbaum.

Klatzky, R. L. (1975). *Human memory,* 1st Ed. New York: W. H. Freeman and Company.

Klatzky, R. L. (1979). *Human memory.* New York: W. H. Freeman and Company.

Kleene, S. C. (1952). *Introduction to metamathematics.* Princeton, NJ: Van Nostrand.

Koch, H. L. (1923). A neglected phase of a part/whole problem. *Journal of Experimental Psychology, 6,* 366–376.

Köhler, W. (1927). *The mentality of apes.* New York: Harcourt, Brace.

Köhler, W. (1956). *The mentality of apes.* London: Routledge & Kegan Paul.

Kolers, P. A. (1976). Reading a year later. *Journal of Experimental Psychology: Human Learning and Memory, 2,* 554–565.

Kolers, P. A. (1979). A pattern analyzing basis of recognition. In L. S. Cermak & F. I. M. Craik (Eds.), *Levels of processing in human memory.* Hillsdale, NJ: Erlbaum.

Kolers, P. A., & Perkins, P. N. (1975). Spatial and ordinal components of form perception and literacy. *Cognitive Psychology, 7,* 228–267.

Korkel, J. (1987). *Die Entwicklung von Gedachtnis- und Metagedachtnisleistungen in Abhagigkeit von bereichsspezifischen Vorkenntnissen.* Frankfurt: Lang.

Kosslyn, S. M. (1980). *Image and mind.* Cambridge, MA: Harvard University Press.

Kosslyn, S. M. (1983). *Ghosts in the mind's machine.* New York: Norton.

Kosslyn, S. M., Ball, T. M., & Reiser, B. J. (1978). Visual images preserve metric spatial information: Evidence from studies of image scanning. *Journal of Experimental Psychology: Human Perception and Performance, 4,* 47–60.

Kosslyn, S. M., & Pomerantz, J. P. (1977). Imagery, propositions, and the form of internal representations. *Cognitive Psychology, 9,* 52–76.

Kotovsky, K., Hayes, J. R., & Simon, H. A. (1985). Why are some problems hard? Evidence from Tower of Hanoi. *Cognitive Psychology, 17,* 248–294.

Krashen, S., & Harshman, R. (1972). Lateralization and the critical period. *Working Papers in Phonetics, 23,* 13–21.

Kreutzer, M. A., Leonard, C., & Flavell, J. H. (1975). An interview study of children's knowledge about memory. *Monographs of the Society for Research in Child Development, 40,* 1, Series No. 159.

Kuffler, S. W. (1953). Discharge pattern and functional organization of mammalian retina. *Journal of Neurophysiology, 16,* 37–68.

LaBerge, D., & Samuels, S. J. (1974). Toward a theory of automatic information processing in reading. *Cognitive Psychology, 6,* 293–323.

Labov, W. (1973). The boundaries of words and their meanings. In C.-J. N. Bailey & R. W. Shuy (Eds.), *New ways of analyzing variations in English.* Washington, DC: Georgetown University Press.

Lachter, J., & Bever, T. G. (1988). The relation between linguistic structure and associative theories of language learning—A constructive critique of some connectionist learning models. *Cognition, 28,* 195–247.

Lakoff, G. (1971). On generative semantics. In D. Steinberg & L. Jakobovits (Eds.), *Semantics—An interdisciplinary reader in philosophy, linguistics, anthropology, and psychology.* London: Cambridge University Press.

Langley, P. W., Simon, H. A., Bradshaw, G. L., & Zytkow, J. (1987). *Scientific discovery: Computational explorations of the cognitive processes.* Cambridge, MA: MIT Press.

Larkin, J. (1981). Enriching formal knowledge: A model for learning to solve textbook physics problems. In J. R. Anderson (Ed.), *Cognitive skills and their acquisition.* Hillsdale, NJ: Erlbaum.

Larkin, J. H., McDermott, J., Simon, D. P., & Simon, H. A. (1980). Expert and novice performance in solving physics problems. *Science, 208,* 1335–1342.

Lee, C. L., & Estes, W. K. (1981). Item and order information in short-term memory: Evidence for multilevel perturbation processes. *Journal of Experimental Psychology: Human Learning and Memory, 7,* 149–169.

Lenneberg, E. H. (1967). *Biological foundations of language.* New York: Wiley.

Lenneberg, E. H., Nichols, I. A., & Rosenberger, E. F. (1969). Primitive stages of language development in mongolism. In *Disorders of communication,* Vol. 42. Baltimore, MD: Williams & Wilkins.

Lesgold, A. M. (1984). Acquiring expertise. In J. R. Anderson & S. M. Kosslyn (Eds.), *Tutorials in learning and memory.* New York: W. H. Freeman and Company.

Lesgold, A., Rubinson, H., Feltovich, P., Glaser, R., Klopfer, D., & Wang, Y. (1988). Expertise in a complex skill: Diagnosing X-ray pictures. In M. T. H. Chi, R. Glaser, & M. J. Farr (Eds.), *The nature of expertise*. Hillsdale, NJ: Erlbaum.

Levine, M. (1975). *A cognitive theory of learning*. Hillsdale, NJ: Erlbaum.

Lewis, C. H., & Anderson, J. R. (1976). Interference with real world knowledge. *Cognitive Psychology, 7*, 311–335.

Lewis, M. W., & Anderson, J. R. (1985). Discrimination of operator schemata in problem solving. Learning from examples. *Cognitive Psychology, 17*, 26–65.

Lieberman, P. (1984). *The biology and evolution of language*. Cambridge, MA: Harvard University Press.

Lindsay, P. H., & Norman, D. A. (1977). *Human information processing*. New York: Academic Press.

Lisker, L., & Abramson, A. (1970). The voicing dimension: Some experiments in comparative phonetics. *Proceedings of Sixth International Congress of Phonetic Sciences, Prague, 1967*. Prague: Academia.

Loftus, E. F. (1974). Activation of semantic memory. *American Journal of Psychology, 86*, 331–337.

Loftus, E. F. (1979). *Eyewitness testimony*. Cambridge, MA: Harvard University Press.

Loftus, E. F., & Zanni, G. (1975). Eyewitness testimony: The influence of the wording of a question. *Bulletin of the Psychonomic Society, 5*, 86–88.

Loftus, G. R., & Loftus, E. F. (1976). *Human memory*. Hillsdale, NJ: Erlbaum.

Lorayne, H., & Lucas, J. (1974). *The memory book*. New York: Stein & Day.

Luchins, A. S. (1942). Mechanization in problem solving, *Psychological Monographs, 54*, No. 248.

Luchins, A. S., & Luchins, E. H. (1959). *Rigidity of behavior: A variational approach to the effects of Einstellung*. Eugene, OR: University of Oregon Books.

Lynch, G., & Baudry, M. (1984). The biochemistry of memory: A new and specific hypothesis. *Science, 224*, 1057–1063.

Maclay, H., & Osgood, C. E. (1959). Heistation phenomena in spontaneous speech. *Word, 15*, 19–44.

MacLeod, C. M., Hunt, E. B., & Matthews, N. N. (1978). Individual differences in the verification of sentence-picture relationships. *Journal of Verbal Learning and Verbal Behavior, 17*, 493–507.

MacWhinney, B. (1987). *Mechanisms of language acquisition*. Hillsdale, NJ: Erlbaum.

Madigan, S. A. (1969). Intraserial repetition and coding processes in free recall. *Journal of Verbal Learning and Verbal Behavior, 8*, 828–835.

Maier, N. R. F. (1931). Reasoning in humans: II. The solution of a problem and its appearance in consciousness. *Journal of Comparative Psychology, 12*, 181–194.

Mandler, G. (1967). Organization and memory. In K. W. Spence & J. A. Spence (Eds.), *The psychology of learning and motivation*, Vol. 1. New York: Academic Press.

Mandler, G. (1972). Organization and recognition. In E. Tulving & W. Donaldson (Eds.), *Organization and memory*. New York: Academic Press.

Mandler, J. M., & Johnson, N. S. (1977). Remembrance of things parsed: Story structure and recall. *Cognitive Psychology, 9,* 111–151.

Mandler, J. M., & Ritchey, G. H. (1977). Long-term memory for pictures. *Journal of Experimental Psychology: Human Learning and Memory, 3,* 386–396.

Maratsos, M. P. (1983). Some current issues in the study of the acquisition of grammar. In P. Mussen (Ed.), *Carmichael's manual of child psychology*, 4th Ed. New York: Wiley.

Marcus, M. P. (1980). *A theory of syntactic recognition for natural language.* Cambridge, MA: MIT Press.

Marcus, S. (1988). *Automating knowledge acquisition for expert systems.* Boston, MA: Klaver.

Marcus, S. L., & Rips, L. J. (1979). Conditional reasoning. *Journal of Verbal Learning and Verbal Behavior, 18,* 199–223.

Markman, E. M. (1979). Realizing that you don't understand: Elementary school children's awareness of inconsistencies. *Child Development, 49,* 168–177.

Marr, D. (1976). Early processing of visual information. *Philosophical Transactions of the Royal Society, London, Series B, 275,* 483–524.

Marr, D. (1982). *Vision.* San Francisco: W. H. Freeman and Company.

Marr, D., & Hildreth, E. (1980). Theory of edge detection. *Proceedings of the Royal Society, London, Series B, 207,* 187–217.

Marr, D., & Nishihara, H. K. (1978). Representation and recognition of the spatial organization of three-dimensional shapes. In *Proceedings of the Royal Society, London, B, 200,* 269–294.

Marslen-Wilson, W., & Tyler, L. K. (1987). Against Modularity. In J. L. Garfield (Ed.), *Modularity in knowledge representation and natural-language understanding.* Cambridge, MA: MIT Press.

Martin, L. (1986). Eskimo words for snow: A case study on the genesis and decay of an anthropological example. *American Anthropologist, 88,* 418–423.

Massaro, D. W. (1975). *Experimental psychology and information processing.* Chicago: Rand McNally.

Mayer, A., & Orth, I. (1901). Zur qualitativen utersuchung der Association. *Zeitschaft für Psychologie, 26,* 1–13.

McClelland, J. L. (1981). Retrieving general and specific knowledge from stored knowledge of specifics. In *Proceedings of the Third Annual Conference of the Cognitive Science Society.* Berkeley, CA.

McClelland, J. L. (1987). The case for interactionism in language processing. In M. Coltheart (Ed.), *Attention and Performance XII.* London: Erlbaum.

McClelland, J. L., & Rumelhart, D. E. (1981). An interactive model of context effects in letter perception: I. An account of basic findings. *Psychological Review, 88,* 375–407.

McClelland, J. L., & Rumelhart, D. E. (Eds.) (1986). *Parallel distributed processing: Explorations in the microstructure of cognition,* Vol. 2. Cambridge, MA: MIT Press/Bradford Books.

McClelland, J. L., Rumelhart, D. E., & Hinton, G. E. (1986). The appeal of parallel distributed processing. In D. E. Rumelhart & J. L. McClelland (Eds.), *Parallel distributed processing: Explorations in the microstructure of cognition,* Vol. 1. Cambridge, MA: MIT Press/Bradford Books.

McCloskey, M. E., & Glucksberg, S. (1978). Natural categories. Well-defined or fuzzy sets? *Memory & Cognition, 6,* 462–472.

McDonald, J. L. (1984). The mapping of semantic and syntactic processing cues by first and second language learners of English, Dutch, and German. Unpublished doctoral dissertation, Carnegie-Mellon University.

McKeithen, K. B., Reitman, J. S., Rueter, H. H., & Hirtle, S. C. (1981). Knowledge organization and skill differences in computer programmers. *Cognitive Psychology, 13,* 307–325.

McKoon, G., & Ratcliff, R. (1981). The comprehension processes and memory structures involved in instrumental inference. *Journal of Verbal Learning and Verbal Behavior, 20,* 671–682.

McLaughlin, B. (1978). *Second-language acquisition in childhood.* Hillsdale, NJ: Erlbaum.

McNamara, T. P. (1986). Mental representations of spatial relations. *Cognitive Psychology, 18,* 87–121.

Mendelson, E. (1964). *Introduction to mathematical logic.* New York: Van Nostrand.

Metcalfe, J., & Wiebe, D. (1987). Intuition in insight and non-insight problem solving. *Memory and Cognition, 15,* 238–246.

Metzler, J., & Shepard, R. N. (1974). Transformational studies of the internal representations of three dimensional objects. In R. L. Solso (Ed.), *Theories of cognitive psychology: The Loyola Symposium.* Hillsdale, NJ: Erlbaum.

Meyer, B. J. F. (1974). The organization of prose and its effect on recall. Unpublished doctoral dissertation, Cornell University.

Meyer, B. J. F., Brandt, D. M., & Bluth, G. J. (1978). Use of author's textual schema: Key for ninth-grader's comprehension. Paper presented at the annual conference of the American Educational Research Association, Toronto.

Meyer, D. E., & Schvaneveldt, R. W. (1971). Facilitation in recognizing pairs of words: Evidence of a dependence between retrieval operations. *Journal of Experimental Psychology, 90,* 227–234.

Miller, G. A. (1956). The magical number seven, plus or minus two: Some limits on our capacity for processing information. *Psychological Review, 63,* 81–97.

Miller, G. A., & Nicely, P. (1955). An analysis of perceptual confusions among some English consonants. *Journal of the Acoustical Society of America, 27,* 338–352.

Milner, B. (1962). Les troubles de la memoire accompagnant des lesions hippocampiques bilaterales. In P. Passonant (Ed.), *Physiologie de l'hippocampe.* Paris: Centre National de la Recherche Scientifique.

Minsky, M. (1975). A framework for representing knowledge. In P. H. Winston (Ed.), *The psychology of computer vision.* New York: McGraw-Hill.

Mitchell, T. M. (1982). Generalization as search. *Artificial Intelligence, 18,* 203–226.

Moray, N. (1959). Attention in dichotic listening: Affective cues and the influence of instruction. *Quarterly Journal of Experimental Psychology, 11,* 56–60.

Moray, N., Bates, A., & Barnett, T. (1965). Experiments on the four-eared man. *Journal of the Acoustical Society of America, 38,* 196–201.

Moyer, R. S. (1973). Comparing objects in memory: Evidence suggesting an internal psychophysics. *Perception and Psychophysics, 13,* 180–184.

Murdock, B. B., Jr. (1961). The retention of individual items. *Journal of Experimental Psychology, 62,* 618–625.

Murdock, B. B., Jr. (1982). A theory for the storage and retrieval of item and associative information. *Psychological Review, 89,* 609–626.

Murray, H. G., & Denny, J. P. (1969). Interaction of ability level and interpolated activity (opportunity for incubation) in human problem solving. *Psychological Reports, 24,* 271–276.

Mussen, P. H. (Ed.) (1983). *Handbook of child psychology.* New York: Wiley.

Neisser, U. (1967). *Cognitive psychology.* New York: Appleton.

Neisser, U. (1976). *Cognition and reality: Principles and implications of cognitive psychology.* New York: W. H. Freeman and Company.

Nelson, D. L. (1979). Remembering pictures and words: Appearance, significance, and name. In L. S. Cermak & F. I. M. Craik (Eds.), *Levels of processing in human memory.* Hillsdale, NJ: Erlbaum.

Nelson, T. O. (1971). Savings and forgetting from long-term memory. *Journal of Verbal Learning and Verbal Behavior, 10,* 568–576.

Nelson, T. O. (1976). Reinforcement and human memory. In W. K. Estes (Ed.), *Handbook of learning and cognitive processes,* Vol. 3. Hillsdale, NJ: Erlbaum.

Nelson, T. O. (1978). Detecting small amounts of information in memory: Savings

Shepard, R. N. (1967). Recognition memory for words, sentences, and pictures. *Journal of Verbal Learning and Verbal Behavior, 6,* 156–163.

Shepard, R. N., & Cooper, L. A. (1983). *Mental images and their transformations.* Cambridge, MA: MIT Press.

Shepard, R. N., & Metzler, J. (1971). Mental rotation of three-dimensional objects. *Science, 171,* 701–703.

Shiffrin, R. M., & Dumais, S. T. (1981). The development of automatism. In J. R. Anderson (Ed.), *Cognitive skills and their acquisition.* Hillsdale, NJ: Erlbaum.

Shiffrin, R. M., & Schneider, W. (1977). Controlled and automatic human information processing: II. Perceptual learning, automatic attending, and a general theory. *Psychological Review, 84,* 127–190.

Shneiderman, B. (1980). *Software psychology.* Cambridge, MA: Winthrop.

Shortliffe, E. H. (1976). *Computer-based consultation: MYCIN.* New York: American Elsevier.

Shuford, E. H. (1961). Percentage estimation of proportion as a function of element type, exposure time, and task. *Journal of Experimental Psychology, 61,* 430–436.

Siegler, R. S. (1976). Three aspects of cognitive development. *Cognitive Psychology, 8,* 481–520.

Siegler, R. S. (Ed.) (1978). *Children's thinking: What develops?* Hillsdale, NJ: Erlbaum.

Siegler, R. S. (1980). Developmental sequences within and between concepts. *Monographs of the Society for Research in Child Development.*

Siegler, R. S. (1986). *Children's thinking: An information processing approach.* Englewood Cliffs, NJ: Prentice-Hall.

Siegler, R. S. (In press). Mechanisms of cognitive development. *Annual Review of Psychology.*

Siegler, R. S., & Shrager, J. (1984). Strategy choices in addition: How do children know what to do? In C. Sophian (Ed.), *Origins of cognitive skills.* Hillsdale, NJ: Erlbaum.

Silveira, J. (1971). Incubation: The effect of interruption timing and length on problem solution and quality of problem processing. Unpublished doctoral dissertation, University of Oregon.

Silver, E. A. (1979). Student perceptions of relatedness among mathematical verbal problems. *Journal for Research in Mathematics Education, 12,* 54–64.

Simon, H. A. (1974). How big is a chunk? *Science, 183,* 482–488.

Simon, H. A. (1975). The functional equivalence of problem solving skills. *Cognitive Psychology, 7,* 268–288.

Simon, H. A. (1989). The scientist as a problem solver. In D. Klahr and K. Kotovsky

(Eds.), *Complex information processing: The impact of Herbert Simon.* Hillsdale, NJ: Erlbaum.

Simon, H. A., & Gilmartin, K. (1973). A simulation of memory for chess positions. *Cognitive Psychology, 5,* 29–46.

Simon, H. A., & Lea, G. (1974). Problem solving and rule induction: A unified view. In L. W. Gregg (Ed.), *Knowledge and cognition.* Hillsdale, NJ: Erlbaum.

Singley, K., & Anderson, J. R. (1989). *The transfer of cognitive skill.* Cambridge, MA: Harvard University Press.

Singley, K., & Anderson, J. R. (1985). The transfer of text-editing skill. *International Journal of Man-Machine Studies, 22,* 403–423.

Skyrms, B. (1966). *Choice and chance: An introduction to inductive logic.* Belmont, CA: Dickenson.

Slamecka, N. J., & Graf, P. (1978). The generation effect: Delineation of a phenomenon. *Journal of Experimental Psychology: Human Learning and Memory, 4,* 592–604.

Sleeman, D., & Brown, J. S. (Eds.) (1982). *Intelligent tutoring systems.* New York: Academic Press.

Slovic, P., & Lichtenstein, S. (1971). Comparison of Bayesian and regression approaches to the study of information processing in judgment. *Organizational Behavior and Human Performance, 6,* 649–744.

Smith, M. (1982). Hypnotic memory enhancement of witnesses: Does it work? Paper presented at the meeting of the Psychonomic Society, Minneapolis.

Smith, S. M., Brown, H. O., Toman, J. E. P., & Goodman, L. S. (1947). The lack of cerebral effects of d-Tubercurarine. *Anesthesiology, 8,* 1–14.

Smith, S. M., Glenberg, A., & Bjork, R. A. (1978). Environmental context and human memory. *Memory & Cognition, 6,* 342–353.

Soloway, E., Bonar, J., & Ehrlich, K. (1983). Cognitive strategies and looping constructs: An empirical study. *Communications of the ACM, 26,* 853–860.

Sophian, C. (1984a). Developing search skills in infancy and early childhood. In C. Sophian (Ed.), *Origins of cognitive skills.* Hillsdale, NJ: Erlbaum.

Sophian, C. (1984b). *Origins of cognitive skills.* Hillsdale, NJ: Erlbaum.

Spearman, C. (1904). The proof and measurement of association between two things. *American Journal of Psychology, 15,* 72–101.

Sperling, G. A. (1960). The information available in brief visual presentation. *Psychological Monographs, 74,* Whole No. 498.

Sperling, G. A. (1967). Successive approximations to a model for short-term memory. *Acta Psychologica, 27,* 285–292.

Spiro, R. J. (1977). Constructing a theory of reconstructive memory: The state of the schema approach. In R. C. Anderson, R. J. Spiro, & W. E. Montague (Eds.), *Schooling and the acquisition of knowledge.* Hillsdale, NJ: Erlbaum.

Spiro, R. J., Bruce, B. C., & Brewer, W. F. (1980). *Theoretical issues in reading comprehension: Perspectives from cognitive psychology, linguistics, and education.* Hillsdale, NJ: Erlbaum.

Spoehr, K. T., & Lehmkuhle, S. W. (1982). *Visual information processing.* New York: W. H. Freeman and Company.

Squire, L. R. (1987). *Memory and brain.* New York: Oxford University Press.

Standing, L. (1973). Learning 10,000 pictures. *Quarterly Journal of Experimental Psychology, 25,* 207–222.

Starkey, P., & Cooper, R. S. (1980). Perception of numbers by human infants. *Science, 210,* 1033–1035.

Staudenmayer, H. (1975). Understanding conditional reasoning with meaningful propositions. In R. J. Falmagne (Ed.), *Reasoning: Representation and process in children and adults.* Hillsdale, NJ: Erlbaum.

Stein, B. S., & Bransford, J. D. (1979). Constraints on effective elaboration: Effects of precision and subject generation. *Journal of Verbal Learning and Verbal Behavior, 18,* 769–777.

Stein, N. L., & Trabasso, T. (1981). What's in a story? Critical issues in comprehension and instruction. In R. Glaser (Ed.), *Advances in the psychology of instruction,* Vol. 2. Hillsdale, NJ: Erlbaum.

Stelmach, G. E., & Requin, J. (Eds.) (1980). *Tutorials in motor behavior.* Amsterdam: North-Holland.

Sternberg, R. J. (1977). *Intelligence, information processing, and analogical reasoning.* Hillsdale, NJ: Erlbaum.

Sternberg, R. J. (1985a). *Human abilities.* New York: W. H. Freeman and Company.

Sternberg, R. J. (1985b). *Beyond IQ: A triarchic theory of human intelligence.* New York: Cambridge University Press.

Sternberg, R. J., & Gardner, M. K. (1983). Unities in inductive reasoning. *Journal of Experimental Psychology: General, 112,* 80–116.

Sternberg, S. (1969). Memory scanning: Mental processes revealed by reaction time experiments. *American Scientist, 57,* 421–457.

Stevens, A., & Coupe, P. (1978). Distortions in judged spatial relations. *Cognitive Psychology, 10,* 422–437.

Stillings, N. A., Feinstein, M. H., Garfield, J. L., Rissland, E. L., Rosenbaum, D. A., Weisler, S. E., & Baker-Ward, L. (1987). *Cognitive science: An introduction.* Cambridge, MA: MIT Press.

Stratton, G. M. (1922). *Developing mental power.* New York: Houghton Mifflin.

Strauss, M. S., & Curtis, L. E. (1981). Infant perception of numerosity. *Child Development, 52,* 1146–1152.

Strohner, H., & Nelson, K. E. (1974). The young child's development of sentence comprehension: Influence of event probability, nonverbal context, syntactic form, and strategies. *Child Development, 45,* 567–576.

Studdert-Kennedy, M. (1976). Speech perception. In N. J. Lass (Ed.), *Contemporary issues in experimental phonetics.* Springfield, IL: Charles C. Thomas.

Sulin, R. A., & Dooling, D. J. (1974). Intrusion of a thematic idea in retention of prose. *Journal of Experimental Psychology, 103,* 255–262.

Suppes, P. (1957). *Introduction to logic.* Princeton, NJ: Van Nostrand.

Sweller, J., Mawer, R. F., & Ward, M. R. (1983). Development of expertise in mathematical problem solving. *Journal of Experimental Psychology: General, 112,* 463–474.

Swinney, D. A. (1979). Lexical access during sentence comprehension: (Re)consideration of context effects. *Journal of Verbal Learning and Verbal Behavior, 18,* 645–659.

Taplin, J. E. (1971). Reasoning with conditional sentences. *Journal of Verbal Learning and Verbal Behavior, 10,* 218–225.

Taplin, J. E., & Staudenmayer, H. (1973). Interpretation of abstract conditional sentences in deductive reasoning. *Journal of Verbal Learning and Verbal Behavior, 12,* 530–542.

Taraban, R., & McClelland, J. L. (1988). Constituent attachment and thematic role assignment in sentence processing: Influences of content-based expectations. *Journal of Memory and Language, 27,* 597–632.

Terman, L. M., & Merrill, M. A. (1973). *Stanford-Binet intelligence scales: 1973 norms edition.* Boston: Houghton Mifflin.

Thomas, E. L., & Robinson, H. A. (1972). *Improving reading in every class: A sourcebook for teachers.* Boston: Allyn & Bacon.

Thomson, D. M. (1972). Context effects on recognition memory. *Journal of Verbal Learning and Verbal Behavior, 11,* 497–511.

Thorndike, E. L. (1906). *Principles of teaching.* New York: A. G. Seiler.

Thorndike, E. L., & Woodworth, R. S. (1901). The influence of improvement in one mental function upon the efficiency of other functions. *Psychological Review, 9,* 374–382.

Thorndyke, P. W. (1977). Cognitive structures in comprehension and memory in narrative discourse. *Cognitive Psychology, 9,* 77–110.

Thorndyke, P. W., & Stasz, C. (1980). Individual differences in procedures for knowledge acquisition from maps. *Cognitive Psychology, 12,* 137–175.

References

Thurstone, L. L. (1938). *Primary mental abilities.* Chicago: University of Chicago Press.

Tolman, E. C. (1932). *Purposive behavior in animals and men.* New York: Appleton-Century-Crofts.

Townsend, D. J., and Bever, T. G. (1982). Natural units interact during language comprehension. *Journal of Verbal Learning and Verbal Behavior, 28,* 681–703.

Trabasso, T. R., & Bower, G. H. (1968). *Attention in learning.* New York: Wiley.

Trabasso, T. R., & Riley, C. A. (1975). The construction and use of representations involving linear order. In R. L. Solso (Ed.), *Information processing and cognition,* Hillsdale, NJ: Erlbaum.

Trabasso, T., Rollins, H., & Shaughnessy, E. (1971). Storage and verification stages in processing concepts. *Cognitive Psychology, 2,* 239–289.

Trabasso, T., Secco, T., & van den Broek, P. (1984). Causal cohesion and story coherence. In H. Mandl (Ed.), *Learning and comprehension of text.* Hillsdale, NJ: Erlbaum.

Treisman, A. M., (1960). Verbal cues, language, and meaning in selective attention. *Quarterly Journal of Experimental Psychology, 12,* 242–248.

Treisman, A. M., & Gelade, G. (1980). A feature-integration theory of attention. *Cognitive Psychology, 12,* 97–136.

Tulving, E. (1983). *Elements of episodic memory.* London: Oxford University Press.

Tulving, E., Mandler, G., & Baumal, R. (1964). Interaction of two sources of information in tachistoscopic word recognition. *Canadian Journal of Psychology, 18,* 62–71.

Tulving, E., & Thomson, D. M. (1973). Encoding specificity and retrieval processes in episodic memory. *Psychological Review, 80,* 352–373.

Turing, A. M. (1950). Computing machinery and intelligence. *Mind, 59,* 433–460.

Turvey, M. T., & Shaw, R. E. (1977). Memory (or knowing) as a matter of specification not representation: Notes toward a different class of machines. Paper presented at the conference on Levels of Processing, Rockport, Massachusetts.

Tversky, A., & Kahneman, D. (1974). Judgments under uncertainty: Heuristics and biases. *Science, 185,* 1124–1131.

Tyler, R., & Marslen-Wilson, W. (1977). The on-line effects of semantic context on syntactic processing. *Journal of Verbal Learning and Verbal Behavior, 16,* 683–692.

Ultan, R. (1969). Some general characteristics of interrogative systems. *Working Papers in Language Universals (Stanford University), 1,* 41–63.

Underwood, B. J. (1983). *Attributes of memory.* Glenview, IL: Scott, Foresman.

499

Underwood, G. (1974). Moray vs. the rest: The effect of extended shadowing practice. *Quarterly Journal of Experimental Psychology, 26,* 368–372.

Vallar, G., & Baddeley, A. D. (1982). Short-term forgetting and the articulatory loop. *Quarterly Journal of Experimental Psychology, 34,* 53–60.

van Dijk, T. A. (1977). Semantic macro-structures and knowledge frames in discourse comprehension. In M. A. Just & P. A. Carpenter (Eds.), *Cognitive processes in comprehension.* Hillsdale, NJ: Erlbaum.

van Dijk, T. A., & Kintsch, W. (1976). Cognitive psychology and discourse. In W. U. Dressler (Ed.), *Trends in text linguistics.* Berlin & New York: DeGruyter.

van Dijk, T. A., & Kintsch, W. (1983). *Strategies of discourse comprehension.* New York: Academic Press.

Van Lehn, K. (1989). Problem-solving and cognitive skill acquisition. In M. Posner, (Ed.), *Foundations of cognitive science.* Cambridge, MA: MIT Press.

Van Lehn, K., & Brown, J. S. (1981). Planning nets: A representation for formalizing analogies and semantic models of procedural skills. In R. E. Snow, P. Federico, & W. E. Montague (Eds.), *Aptitude, learning, and instruction,* Vol. 2. Hillsdale, NJ: Erlbaum.

Van Melle, W. (1984). The structure of the MYCIN system. In B. G. Buchanan & E. S. Shortliffe (Eds.), *Rule-based expert systems.* Reading, MA: Addison-Wesley.

Vinacke, W. E. (1974). *The psychology of thinking.* New York: McGraw-Hill.

von Frisch, K. (1967). *The dance language and orientation of bees* (translated by C. E. Chadwick). Cambridge, MA: Belknap Press.

Vosniadou, S., & Ortony, A. (Eds.) (1989). *Similarity and analogical reasoning.* Cambridge, MA: Cambridge University Press.

Wanner, H. E. (1968). On remembering, forgetting, and understanding sentences. A study of the deep structure hypothesis. Unpublished doctoral dissertation, Harvard University.

Warren, R. M. (1970). Perceptual restorations of missing speech sounds. *Science, 167,* 392–393.

Warren, R. M., & Warren, R. P. (1970). Auditory illusions and confusions. *Scientific American, 223,* 30–36.

Wason, P. C., & Johnson-Laird, P. N. (1972). *Psychology of reasoning: Structure and content.* Cambridge, MA: Harvard University Press.

Watkins, M. J., & Tulving, E. (1975). Episodic memory: When recognition fails. *Journal of Experimental Psychology: General, 104,* 5–29.

Watson, J. (1930). *Behaviorism.* New York: Norton.

Watt, W. C. (1970). On two hypotheses concerning psycholinguistics. In J. R. Hayes (Ed.), *Cognition and the development of language.* New York: Wiley.

Weisberg, R. W. (1969). Sentence processing assessed through intrasentence word associations. *Journal of Experimental Psychology, 82,* 332–338.

Weisberg, R. W. (1986). *Creativity: Genius and other myths.* New York: W. H. Freeman and Company.

Weiser, M., & Shertz, J. (1983). Programming problem representation in novice and expert programmers. *International Journal of Man-Machine Studies, 19,* 391–398.

Wenger, E. (1987). *Artificial intelligence and tutoring systems.* Los Altos, CA: Morgan Kaufmann.

Wexler, K., & Culicover, P. (1980). *Formal principles of language acquisition.* Cambridge, MA: MIT Press.

Wheeler, D. D. (1970). Processes in word recognition. *Cognitive Psychology, 1,* 59–85.

Whorf, B. L. (1956). *Language, thought, and reality.* Cambridge, MA: MIT Press.

Wickelgren, W. A. (1967). Rehearsal grouping and hierarchical organization of serial position cues in immediate memory. *Quarterly Journal of Experimental Psychology, 19,* 97–102.

Wickelgren, W. A. (1974) *How to solve problems.* New York: W. H. Freeman and Company.

Wickelgren, W. A. (1975). Alcoholic intoxication and memory storage dynamics. *Memory & Cognition, 3,* 385–389.

Wickelgren, W. A. (1976). Memory storage dynamics. In W. K. Estes (Ed.), *Handbook of learning and cognitive processes,* Vol. 4. Hillsdale, NJ: Erlbaum.

Wickelgren, W. A. (1979). *Cognitive psychology.* Englewood Cliffs, NJ: Prentice-Hall.

Winograd, T. (1983). *Language as a cognitive process.* Reading, MA: Addison-Wesley.

Winston, P. H. (1984). *Artificial Intelligence.* Reading, MA: Addison-Wesley.

Woocher, F. D., Glass, A. L., & Holyoak, K. J. (1978). Positional discriminability in linear orderings. *Memory & Cognition, 6,* 165–175.

Woodrow, H. (1927). The effect of the type of training upon transference. *Journal of Educational Psychology, 18,* 159–172.

Woodworth, R. S., & Sells, S. B. (1935). An atmospheric effect in formal syllogistic reasoning. *Journal of Experimental Psychology, 18,* 451–460.

Yates, F. A. (1966). *The art of memory.* Chicago: University of Chicago Press.

Young, R., & O'Shea, T. (1981). Errors in children's subtraction. *Cognitive Science, 5,* 153–177.

Yuille, J. C. (1983). *Imagery, memory, and cognition: Essays in honor of Allan Paivio.* Hillsdale, NJ: Erlbaum.

Name Index

Subject Index